Hinduism in Public and Private

Hinduism in Public and Private

Reform, Hindutva, Gender, and Sampraday

edited by
Antony Copley

OXFORD
UNIVERSITY PRESS

OXFORD
UNIVERSITY PRESS

YMCA Library Building, Jai Singh Road, New Delhi 110 001

Oxford University Press is a department of the University of Oxford. It furthers the University's objective of excellence in research, scholarship, and education by publishing worldwide in

Oxford New York

Auckland Bangkok Buenos Aires Cape Town Chennai
Dar es Salaam Delhi Hong Kong Istanbul Karachi Kolkata
Kuala Lumpur Madrid Melbourne Mexico City Mumbai Nairobi
São Paulo Shanghai Taipei Tokyo Toronto

Published in India
By Oxford University Press, New Delhi

First published 2003

ISBN 0 19 566393 4

Typeset in Times Norman 10.5/12
By Jojy Philip, New Delhi 110 027
Printed by Pauls Press 110020
Published by Manzar Khan, Oxford University Press
YMCA Library Building, Jai Singh Road, New Delhi 110 001

For Martin Gilbert
Fellow Indophile

we go back a long way

Tony
September 2003

Contents

Introduction

Debating Indian Nationalism and Hindu Religious Belief

Antony Copley

The essays in this volume were first presented before a panel on Religious Reform Movements at the European Conference of Modern South Asian Studies held at Edinburgh, September 2000, and this volume is a follow-up of an earlier collection of essays, *Gurus and Their Followers: New Religious Reform Movements in Colonial India* (OUP: 2000). Rather by chance the theme of Hindutva—though with the latter being so much on the rise at the moment, this was hardly surprising—emerged as a dominant concern. So, in the aftermath of the conference, the contributors took time off to reconsider their papers and make at least some connection in their revised versions, however glancingly, with this phenomenon. It is clearly just as important to distinguish the area upon which Hindutva does not impinge from that upon which it does and it should not be overprivileged.

In my introduction, the exploration of the paradigms of public and private spheres is my own rather personal take on how the religious values promoted by the Hindu religious reform movements might relate to the religio-cultural assertions of Hindutva. And even if all contributors do attempt some connection with the phenomenon of Hindutva, the thrust of the collection, as in the previous volume, is on the religious reform movements themselves, in all their rich variety.

Indeed, at the first glance it seems strange that the concept should have become so much the dominant concern of the Indian intelligentsia.

Here are a few exploratory comments: Can a sense of Hinduness really be such an aberration? It is intriguing that the Irish Nationalist Movement, Sinn Fein, for example, translates as the seemingly collective identity of 'Ourselves'. Would we feel the same way, for example, over pursuing an identity of Englishness? But therein, of course, lies the rub. Surely the search for identity should be for an all-inclusive Indian? What would an English identity which prioritized Protestantism, at the expense of all other faiths, look like? Clearly any pursuit of an Indian identity in the narrow terms of Hinduness is a radical distortion, for it excludes Indian Muslims, Sikhs, Parsees, Jains, Buddhists, Christians, Animists, and to a degree, the Scheduled Castes and Tribals whose loyalties are, at most, but partially Hindu.

It remains something of a mystery as to why the majority Hindu community should behave as a minority and fear other religions, especially Islam in India. Could the Hindus be seriously concerned, given their own burgeoning population, about the allegedly higher birth-rate of Indian Muslims? Given a far greater influx of peasants from the villages into the city, could the inflow of refugees from Bangladesh constitute a real anxiety? Quite probably, there is some kind of an abreaction to centuries of Muslim conquest, probably far more out of a sense of injured pride than any legitimate grievance at exploitation. I have to admit, however, that wherever I have travelled as a tourist, especially in northern India, guides have repeatedly reminded me of Muslim vandalism of Hindu temples.[1] It will almost certainly make more sense to see this fear less in terms of any perceived threat or legitimate grievance and more as a kind of projection onto Muslims of all those inner fears and shame of the Hindus themselves. Is there not shame and a sense of insecurity at the way their own society has been fragmented by caste and sect? But an immediate doubt can be cast over this explanation, for, what is there to be ashamed of in such diversity, such religious pluralism, even though untouchability, a serious distortion, is not yet a thing of the past? So why do Hindus seek this new form of social integration?

One explanation has to lie in the humiliation heaped by colonialism. This shamed Hindus in ways that an indigenized Muslim rule never did. Hindus experienced a loss of manliness, an emasculation in the experience of servility before a condescending and often racist colonial state. Yet how far is this explanation valid? Governments rarely dominate people's thoughts and outlook to such a degree unless they are totalitarian, and no one seriously puts the Raj into that league.

So does the explanation lie alternatively in fear of the challenge of modernization? Can Hindus face up to its demands? Have we here an almost visceral response to the frightening challenge of change? Have we here another example of Fromm's fear of freedom, a flight from the awesome expectations and demands of independence, a retreat into blind faith? And yet the RSS and its affiliate the BJP see themselves as modernizing movements. This is no easy phenomenon to explain.

So at the outset can we risk a definition of Hindutva? Have we here a *Weltanschauung* which wraps up its understanding of India's cultural and political growth in a kind of Hindu religiosity? More sinisterly, does there lie within this cultural agenda a strongly political ambition to impose on India an authoritarian yet paradoxically modernizing ideology, and attempt under the cover of culture to fashion a less corrupt and more ascetic form of governance?

The recent celebration of the Kumbh Mela at Allahabad in January 2000, with its phenomenal turnout of some seventy million throughout the twelve-day festival, is a compelling reminder of just how alive India's great religious tradition still is. Maybe India is unique as an advanced and modern nation in still possessing a mass religious base. In the end, the questions to be confronted are, how has this religious tradition been interpreted in the recent past and what is its future to be? The role that religion has played in the history of Indian nationalism emerged as the dominant question. What was the correlation between politics and religion?

This introduces us to the first major paradigm under review, that of nationalism. Can one promote a secular nationalism in a culture so predominantly religious as that of India or must it necessarily take on the trappings of a religious nationalism? This leads us to the second dominant paradigm, that of the relationship between the private and the public spheres, for the deeper question has to be, what indeed is the role of religion in society? Is it essentially a matter of private faith, or does it ineluctably play its part in society at large?

Hannah Arendt saw an intermediary sphere, the social, and probably that is where religion has an acceptable role to play.[2]

Connecting the history of the religious reform movements to this whole debate on nationalism and Hindutva raises very troubling questions about their inherent character. This volume takes over from the earlier one, *Gurus and Their Followers*, in defining the religious reform movements less in terms of Kenneth Jones's paradigms as either transitional, that is, indigenous and unconnected to foreign rule, or as acculturative, that is, interactive with colonialism, and more in terms of the larger paradigm of modernization posing the challenge and predicament. How does the inner spiritual life adjust to the forces of necessary change? Put baldly, did any endeavour to bring about a spiritual revival lead to a collusion with Hindutva, a sharing of this particular expression of an exclusivist, integral nationalism? Were the reform movements wedded to an essentially inward religious pursuit, an inhabiting of the private sphere or did they seek to influence public life? Given that both Hindutva and the reform movements are responses to the challenge of modernization, it would be surprising if they were not, to a degree, convergent movements. Both likewise emerge from the great tradition, India's ancient Hindu culture, though this begs all kinds of questions as to its character, for it is widely recognized now that whatever the dominance of the great tradition comprising a high brahminical and sanskritized culture, there was an equally strong and immensely rich, localized folk culture.[3]

Here is another benchmark for assessing the character of these movements. How loyal were they to this tradition? But how indeed must we interpret this tradition? Should we see it as of stifling mental attitudes and frustrating social change? Or is this an orientalist's way of overemphasizing its rigidity and failing to detect its flexibility and capacity for change? Obviously critics of Hindutva believe that it is entrenched in this conservatism while defendants of the religious reform movements see them as trying to imbibe the more adaptive dimension in the past in order and to fashion a new, more socially conscious and spiritually enriching life in the present. In this sense the two phenomena are far from convergent, though critics of both will of course attack the very claims made in the name of religion. In many ways, Hindutva is a distorted image of the religious reform movements, both seeking to harness religion but for wholly divergent ends.

Two criteria could be used for measuring loyalty to the best that the great tradition had to offer. One, did Hindutva and the religious reform movements remain true to the catholicity of Hinduism, for any step towards exclusivism, and thereby towards communalism, was to taint the tradition. Two, in whatever sense they crossed over from the private into the public sphere, did they become overtly political, for again, any highly politicized programme was to compromise the tradition. The greatest temptation the devil put to Christ was to rule the world—a moral litmus test that has its parallels in the great religions.

There is no consensus on these questions. In one of the most recent and sustained accounts of Hindutva, Christophe Jaffrelot's verdict on the religious movements themselves is quite harsh: 'The origins of the movement lie in the socio-religious reforms of the nineteenth century;

the formation of Hindu nationalist identity is more easily understood as an ideological construct originating in the socio-religious reform movement of the nineteenth century.'[4] John Zavos, writing subsequently, is more charitable. Whilst readily conceding that the reform movements sought to transform the tradition, he finds no 'direct historical link between reform movements that developed in the nineteenth century—particularly the Arya Samaj—and Hindu nationalism. The search for the antecedents of Hindu nationalism has focussed too sharply on revivalism as a product of this reformist approach.'[5]

But with the rise of Hindu nationalism and the present ascendancy of the BJP, one is called upon to re-examine India's recent past. Can one any longer be certain of where in the past lay the seeds of the future? Of course analogous demands confront the historians of other countries that have recorded a sea-change in their history. All of recent Russian history has to be reviewed in the light of the collapse of the communist experiment. But one can see how disturbing it must be for India's secular historians to discover that the history of its modern religious institutions has now to take on a new resonance and that the ways in which the sadhus were/are organized and mobilized both in the past and the present are no longer part of the history of some exotic religious culture but directly relevant to the cut and thrust of political events. As India moves closer to the church–state quarrels of nineteenth-century Europe, the Indian intelligentsia necessarily takes on more and more the character of those embattled anti-clericals who challenged the power of the churches, above all Catholic, in France, Germany, and Italy. Hindutva has sought to ascribe to Hinduism some of the organizational features of the Vatican or of Mecca and Medina. But the question that was put to the European intellectuals has to be put to the Indian intellectuals: is theirs but an anti-clerical movement, an attack on the intrusion of organized religion into the public domain, or is it an attack on religion itself?[6] However, there is a variant in the Indian situation for here it is not merely a case of an embattled intelligentsia but of entire political formations, such as the Congress, caught up in this struggle.

There is of course a disturbing poignancy to this whole enquiry, for in India, once, Hinduism with its openness was a powerful example of religious tolerance—though saying this is to overlook what Wilhelm Halbfass interpreted as a repressive tolerance, and this remains a disturbing critique.[7] Now under the duress of Hindutva Hinduism runs the risk of deteriorating into but another faith with narrow and intolerant claims to the truth.

VARIETIES OF NATIONALISM

A clearer picture would emerge if it were possible to delineate the different strands in Indian nationalism, predominantly the secular strand of the Congress, and the Hindu nationalist. And despite claims of having arrived at such a delineation, an overlap and not an outright divergence of the two seems to be closer to the truth. This is, however, a multifarious story. There are other commentaries to address, often hostile to the very ideology of nationalism, and we need to see this complexity if justice is to be done to the attitudes adopted by the religious reform movements.

Jaffrelot offsets his account of the rise of Hindutva with a commentary on a secular nationalism, linked to a liberal and universalist outlook, from Rammohan Roy onwards, and which was especially adopted by the Indian National Congress. This variant of nationalism stood for territorial rather than ethnic claims, embraced all communities within that territory, belonged to a contract tradition of the formation of the state with an emphasis on individual human rights, and sought to play down the role of religion in political life. Nehru, Jaffrelot argues, saw nationality in terms of individuals, Gandhi in terms of equal human communities. There was no room here for hierarchy, let alone one dominated by the Hindus. But is it really so apparent that the Congress had a clearly defined political theory of nationality rooted in this tradition of liberal nationalism? The emphasis was always rather on its version of secularism which was a way of bridging the religious divide and offering a genuine freedom of religion.[8] A strong case has of course been recently made by Sucheta Mahajan that here was a secular nationalism, wholly opposed to communalism, which the Congress valiantly defended during the holocaust years and Nehru brought to a triumphant conclusion by the 1950s.[9]

Hindutva emerges from a different tradition, one that plays down the individual and plays up the community, one that is an organicist account of nationality, more cultural and ethnic than territorial, with an integral and exclusivist approach. If Hinduism was always at the centre of this project, it is time to examine whether the former was being appropriated rather as a form of cultural identity than out of any genuine religious belief, though the project did not hesitate to exploit religion for political purposes. Jaffrelot sees it as especially indebted to a German tradition of ethnic and cultural nationalism. The writings of the nineteenth century, J.K. Bluntschli, for example, are believed to have profoundly influenced the outlook of the RSS (Rashtriya Swayamsevak Sangh or Association of National Volunteers) leader, M.S. Golwalkar. It is of course one of the paradoxes of Hindutva that an intellectual polemic ostensibly committed to Indian renewal is so influenced by foreign models of nationality, but then that merely suggests that the idea of nationalism to begin with may be an imported one.

Let us chart the rise of Hindutva. A powerful early stimulus to the rise of Hindutva was the claim first made by Western orientalists of a so-called Golden Age of Hinduism: 'The idea of the Golden Age was to become one of the cornerstones of Hindu nationalism.'[10] And interestingly this continues to be a major source of dispute.[11] Through various agencies the ideology took root between the 1870s and 1920s. The inherent complexity of this ideology must be accepted at the outset. It is hard to isolate Hindutva from other currents of nationalism. In Zavos's account Hindu nationalism and the elite-led Indian nationalism of the Congress converge, 'occupying and struggling over the same discursive terrain, including the terrain of culture'.[12] They are both seen as expressions of an emergent Indian middle class. Furthermore, Jaffrelot in his account always detects an element of Hindu traditionalism within the Congress, expressed by the likes of Lajpat Rai and Madan Mohan Malaviya. At the same time, Zavos reminds us that V.D. Savarkar, Swami Shraddanand, and Lajpat Rai were all regarded as genuine Indian nationalists.

The role of the Arya Samaj will be assessed later but it was Lajpat Rai who played a major part in setting up the first Hindu Sabha in Lahore in October 1909, which was to become an all-India organization, the Hindu Mahasabha in 1915. All accounts stress the crucial role of a grassroots organization, the *sangathan*, seen as coming into its own in the aftermath of the Khilafat Movement and the Moplah massacres. Zavos sees as a leitmotif of Hindu nationalism the crucial need to organize, the only way to overcome the threat from within, the degeneracy of Hinduism, and the threat from without, of Islam. But this drive to organize also paid lip service to the colonial state's powerful administration, the emulation of *the others*, as Jaffrelot puts it. Swami Shraddanand held out the prospect of the temple playing a role analogous to the one of the mosque for the Muslims, in energizing the Hindus, with a map of India taking the place inside the temple of the image of a mother goddess.

The founding father of Hindutva was V.D. Savarkar and its Bible, as it were, his text *Hindutva*: *Who is a Hindu?* was published in 1923. Crucially, he drew a distinction between Hinduism as a culture and as a faith. He drew on a materialist science, the writings of Darwin, T.H. Huxley, and Herbert Spencer to fashion an ethnic nationalism. This was perhaps not a narrowly racial one, since Aryans were perceived as intermarrying with an indigenous population and Hindutva was seen as capable of embracing Christians as well as Muslims, given that they were converts from the same race. Culture counted for more than biology. One is reminded in Savarkar's opportunist adoption of Hinduism, for he was himself a non-believer, of a contemporary fellow ideologue, Charles Maurras, whose Action Française also appropriated both Catholicism and monarchism whilst he himself was a materialist-minded proto-fascist.

In Jaffrelot's account, the setting up of the RSS by K.B. Hedgewar in 1925 was the fulfilment of this early dynamic phase in the emergence of a Hindu nationalism. Zavos, to the contrary, sees it 'as a highly significant departure in the history of Hindu nationalist ideology'.[13] It is probably in the 1920s that Hindutva emerged as a distinct strand in the history of Indian nationalism. In many ways the RSS has the trappings, however superficial, of a religious reform movement and cannot be narrowly defined as a political organization. Certainly *seva,* service, plays a considerable part in its agenda. M.S. Golwalkar, who took over as leader in 1940 had, however briefly, worked under Swami Akhandananda of the Ramakrishna Mission.[14] There are many surprising features of the RSS, which make it oddly difficult to classify. Theirs is not just another version of an organicist nationalism. If analogous to a Hindu sect through its being 'a closed and dogmatic organization', it sets out, in Jaffrelot's account, to fashion an individualism: 'indeed the sect offers the only system within Hindu society where an egalitarian form of individualism can be observed.' Admittedly, the RSS ideology then turns this on its head and talks of the sacrifice of the individual: 'Here was a millenarian plan ... to extend to the whole of society the concept of a man who denies his individual personality.'[15] But in organicist accounts of society, the individual does not exist outside of a social context and normatively has no discrete existence.

Interestingly, the RSS sought influence through society; this was not a movement initially targeted at state control. Yet the objective was essentially political, 'a homogenous nation whose culture would be dominated by the great Hindu tradition'.[16] Secularists are clearly wise to be afraid of the RSS's merely cultural activity.[17] In time the RSS set up a series of front organizations, known as the Sangh Parivar (the RSS family), the noisiest of which was the VHP (Vishva Hindu Parishad—World Hindu Council), inaugurated in 1964: here was 'a network of activists capable of spreading more or less informally to the point where it could penetrate the whole of society.'[18] Yet it is almost as if the RSS saw how it overstepped the customary restraint on political activity of religious reform movements: there was always to be an uneasy relationship between the grassroots sangathan members and the front political organizations, the Jana Sangh and later the BJP. They distrusted the compromises that such political activity inevitably entailed and feared that the true purity of the movement would be betrayed.[19]

One way to examine the theme that the RSS distorts or perverts the ideals it seeks to absorb is a comparison with the true character of the *akharas*, or wrestling schools, on which its grassroots organizations, the shakhas, were modelled. Great emphasis was placed by the RSS on physical fitness. Another model was the Boy Scout movement. Joseph Alter argues that the RSS believed that this kind of physical discipline 'would unlock a sense of common purpose'. It would somehow break down those mental barriers, illusions, which prevent an awareness of a 'connectedness to a greater whole'. Ostensibly the swayamsevak or volunteer shares the same ideals as the wrestler: celibacy, a guru–disciple relationship. And here of course in this monastic character of the RSS further parallels can be drawn with other religious reform movements. Yet the wrestler is driven by different ideals, a harnessing of Shakti or energy by sexual self-control, a looking inward 'to the very core of individual character', 'a person far more protean than immutable'. Alter portrays the akhara as a balance of earth, water, and air, a space, indeed, suffused, with a Gandhian atmosphere and hence an implicit critique of Hindu chauvinism: 'militant Hindu nationalism and the somatic nationalism of the wrestler are in many ways fundamentally different despite the appearances of congruity.'[20]

It is ironic that the very terrain where current disputes between Indian secularists and Hindutva prevail, the writing of history, was the origin of the ideology. As Partha Chatterjee observes,[21] it was out of a need to discover an Indian historiography, the better to establish a counter-Indian identity to that denigration of India by foreign historians, James Mill the most notorious, that a Hindu history was born. In fatally subscribing to the orientalist myth of a Golden Age, historians drew up a picture of a classical period, followed by one of medieval decline, and whether this was prior to or because of Muslim rule, it led to an account of Muslim rule as one of medieval darkness. Out of this was to come a renaissance, the birth of a modern Hindu nationalism. Interestingly, once again, this saw Hinduism in cultural terms: 'in fact the notion of "Hinduness" in this historical concept cannot be defined by any religious criteria at all.'[22] Anything coming from within, Jainism and Buddhism for example, was acceptable, anything from without, such as Islam and Christianity, was branded as foreign.

But there were subtler and less exclusivist accounts of such a Hinduized history. It is important to recognize that there were these alternatives. Sudipta Kaviraj elucidates one such account in the writings of the late nineteenth-century Bengali historian, Bhudev Mukhopadhyay.[23] If overlooked today, Bhudev grasped the need for a sense of history, and did so in ways similar to Montesquieu, that every society imprints its distinctive collective identity on its members: 'everyday practices (this is Kaviraj's paraphrase) create the most deep-seated similarities among people—the way they build houses, their food, dress, furniture, for these reveal their way of dealing with the environment around them'.[24] In consequence, Indian Muslims can be absorbed as Indians: 'Islam in India is thus quite different from Islam elsewhere both in doctrine and in internal social practices'.[25] Bhudev had an almost providentialist theory of the growth of Indian unity; a pre-Islam cultural unity, to be succeeded by the Moghuls; they introduced significant institutional change, followed by the greater political integration of British rule: 'only colonialism could create the preconditions of nationalism.'[26] But then Bhudev seems to reverse the argument, seeing here the introduction of alien principles, and advocating that Indians, out of a need to remain true to their culture, should adopt the classical Hindu strategy of withdrawal: 'social activities and initiatives should be withdrawn from the public realm of the colonial state.'[27] And if this was regrettably concomitant with a defence of caste, at the least, Sudipta Kaviraj believes, Bhudev had the courage to be a traditionalist in a colonial setting.

And others were to reject that whole ethos of nationalism first given expression in the Swadeshi Movement. Rabindranath Tagore was appalled at its destructive consequences. Ashis Nandy, in an exploration of Tagore's political novels, tellingly analyses Tagore's critique of 'a secularized nationalism', its underlying inspiration discerned as a 'a scientized violence'.[28] The eponymous hero of *Gora* (1909) saw the concept of a national identity 'as itself exogenous' and one that 'violates the fundamental principles of Indianness and Hinduism'.[29] The issue was most clearly spelt out in *The Home and the World* (1916). Here was a battle for the soul of an orthodox Indian wife, Bhimla, caught between a fanatical supporter of the Vande Mataram movement, Sandip, and her husband, Nikhil. Sandip sought to elicit the *shakti,* the female energy in Bhimla. His was a this-worldly nationalism and one all too ready to turn against the Muslims: 'one day they shall dance like tame bears to the tune we play.'[30] In Nikhil, Tagore expressed his sense of the imminent danger of such nationalist belief: 'to worship my country as a god is to bring a curse upon it'; 'I am both afraid and ashamed to make use of hypnotic texts of patriotism'; 'to try to give our infatuation a higher place than Truth is a sign of inherent slavishness'; 'to tyrannize for the country is to tyrannize over the country'.[31] Sandip could not grasp the argument that God could not both be for one country and against another—the predicament that the belligerents of the Great War also signally failed to grasp. Nikhil was horrified at this setting up in nationalism, to use Ashis Nandy's paraphrase of the debate, of a counter-culture, a willingness 'to sacrifice Indians at the altar of a brand-new imported, progressivist history of the Indian nation-state in the making'.[32] A young acolyte of Sandip and an admirer of Bhimla, Amulya is both to murder for the cause and to be killed. Nikhil may also have been killed. Through Nikhil, Tagore acknowledged his own powerlessness in the face of this new nationalism: 'I am not a flame, only a black coal, which has gone out. I can light no lamp.'[33] Tagore, essentially a universalist and hence, however critical of the West, anxious to incorporate its insights, turned his back on an emergent Hindutva style nationalism in favour of an inclusivist one, anticipating Gandhi's 'low key, unheroic, consensual nationalism'.[34] How else could one reach out to India's multi-ethnic character? As Nandy firmly puts it: 'Any modern Indian who claims that nationalism and the principles of the nation-state are universal has to take, willy-nilly, a position against both Gandhi and Tagore.'[35]

Contemporary to Tagore's detachment from the extremist nationalism in the Congress, European writers and intellectuals such as Jean Jaurès and Romain Rolland were facing a losing battle against an equally aggressive nationalism in Europe. The ideals of internationalism and socialism upheld by the Second International could not rein in the madness that led to the Great War. Yet there was always to be in the twentieth century a strong current of thought sharing Tagore's profound disquiet at militant nationalism.[36] A Hindutva style nationalism always had its opponents. How do those two great patriotic figures in the religious reform movements, Vivekananda and Aurobindo Ghose, fit into this debate?

Is the RSS fair in seeing Vivekananda as one of their own? Or have we here another example of distortion, of misappropriation? One would like to endorse Tapan Raychaudhuri's passionate rejection of any such claim, written in a white heat of anger at the obscenity of the vandalism of the Babri Masjid structure. 'I have argued', he was to end his lecture, 'that it is difficult to imagine him as the ideological ancestor of people which incite the ignorant to destroy other people's places of worship in a revanchist spirit.'[37] He sees Vivekananda as driven by quite other ideals than those of militant Hinduism. His was an ideal of social uplift and mass literacy: 'the regeneration of the Indian people, with the masses installed in the position of primacy which they have always been denied, rather than the revival of Hindus or Hinduism was evidently his goal.'[38] Vivekananda took pride in Moghul culture and despised much of the brahminical tradition.

But there are ambiguities. Vivekananda was often intemperate, caught in the impossible position of expressing pride in his country to foreign audiences whilst being all too aware of its fallen state at home. While lecturing on Practical Vedanta he would let slip observations of this nature:

> There was only blessing and love in the religion of Christ; but as soon as crudeness crept in, it was degraded into something not much better than the religion of the prophet of Arabia.[39]

Nemai Sadhan Bose is a little more cautious in his reading of Vivekananda: 'Swamiji finds himself in the middle of a tug-of-war between the forces of Hindu fundamentalism and secularism.' He believes that for Vivekananda 'the most important thing was to be an Indian, to love India'. But his Vedantism led him to reject caste and ritual and its universalism led him to reach out to Islam: 'For our own motherland', he wrote in a letter to a friend, 'a junction of the two great systems, Hinduism and Islam—Vedanta brain and Islam body—is the only hope.'[40]

Kenneth Jones raised deeper doubts. He sees Vivekananda with his defence of orthodox Hinduism in many ways closer to the *sanatanists* of his day than to the reformers: 'It is clear that Vivekananda cannot be placed in a single category, for he was both complex and at times contradictory.'[41]

In the first of the essays in this volume, Gwilym Beckerlegge takes up the issue of the indebtedness of the RSS to Vivekananda in terms of *seva* or social service rather than his ideal of patriotism. He opens up an intriguing comparison between the relationship of Ramakrishna and Vivekananda and that of Hedgewar and Golwalkar, though here the roles were to be reversed: Hedgewar was the man of action, Golwalkar more the spiritual thinker. But again the theme of distortion creeps in; whereas Vivekananda saw spiritual impoverishment as the explanation for Indian social backwardness, Hedgewar picked on an Indian emasculation. Admittedly Hedgewar in his cult of physical fitness was influenced by Vivekananda's cult of manliness. So much hinges on whether the political agenda of the RSS divides it from a movement like the Ramakrishna Mission, one which has remained true to Vivekananda's apolitical stance. Beckerlegge speculates on whether Golwalkar's shift in political discourse from 'man' to 'our people' was both a fatal shift from individualism to a materialist nationalism and a betrayal of the renouncer ideals of the Mission, their acting instead out of a love for God?

Similar questions of indebtedness or misappropriation bedevil the linkage between Aurobindo Ghose and Hindutva. In some of the clearest interpretations we have of the interrelationship between nationalism and communalism[42] Peter Heehs has already made a case for misappropriation. Aurobindo did sit uncomfortably in the thick of the extremist movement and this certainly bothered Rabindranath Tagore. It is true Aurobindo drew on a symbolism of Krishna and Kali but again he did so as a pan-Indian; Vedantism could become the seed of a new syncretism and Aurobindo was not privileging Hinduism as its essence. And if Aurobindo in the Swadeshi Movement became embattled as a cultural nationalist against colonialism, there was little here that links him to Hindutva today: 'The similarities are superficial while the points of difference are deep.' He concludes: 'All that is central to the Hindu Right—religious syndicalism for political purpose, exclusive Hinduism, rejection of non-Hindus—was absent from the freedom movement-era religious nationalism of Bengal and elsewhere.'[43] But did Aurobindo in these claims for Vedantism manage to avoid falling into the trap of that liberal Christian theology of the turn of the century, a so-called inclusivism, which saw emergent in other faiths a kind of convergence with Christianity?[44] Heehs feels that Aurobindo was aware of this danger and in his universalism steered round it.

In the second paper in this collection Heehs pursues further this theme of misappropriation. Aurobindo's attitude to Hinduism is seen as essentially open and inclusive in its approach. But the Hindutva movement has appropriated rather the embattled nationalist Aurobindo of the Swadeshi Movement than the later and more representative universalist. The source of the ambiguity lies in Aurobindo's conflation of the idea of the religion of Vedanta with *sanatana dharma*: as Heehs puts it Aurobindo 'captured a term introduced by Hindu reactionaries for the use of neo-Vedantic progressivism'. Aurobindo's position was intrinsically a non-chauvinist account of the 'eternal religion'. Heehs is also anxious to refute those views of the post-colonialist critics who deny to Indians, on the grounds that in so doing they fall into the orientalist trap, a chance to define their own Hindu faith. Heehs is quite clear that the Hindutva movement in seeking to appropriate Aurobindo has distorted his true meaning.

If examining ideology is one way of exploring the inner connections between the reform movements and Hindutva, another is plotting just how this movement has taken root in Indian society and politics. How has Hinduism acquired a pan-Indian institutionalized structure? Here of course the paradigm of nationalism extends naturally into the paradigm of the connections between the private and public spheres.

The story in the present is a good deal easier to describe than in the past. In the recent past, the pace was set by the Vishva Hindu Parishad, initially led by Shivram Shankar Apte, an RSS *pracharak* (preacher) from Baroda and Swami Chinmayananda from Kerala, a disciple of Swami Shivananda, founder of the Divine Life Society, and himself a modern religious guru. Jaffrelot sees two forces at work: a response to an alleged threat, be it from Christian or Islamic mission, and an emulation of these so-called threatening 'others', an appropriation of their ecclesiastical structures. Hinduism had to set its own house in order. There had to be a shake up in the way Hindus were fragmented into sects, the *sampradays*, a mobilizing of its monasteries and temples, a drawing of all its sadhus into one collective organization. The 1st International Hindu Conference held at Allahabad, 22–4 January 1966, was one of many such would-be pan-Indian assemblies. Initially the VHP was more successful in attracting so-called new gurus, those most in need of establishing their credibility by association with such structures than the more traditional ones: the *shankaracharyas* of Badrinath and Sringeri significantly stayed away. A 2nd International Hindu Conference held at Allahabad in January 1979 signalled a new phase in this pressure group movement. Hindus were increasingly on the defensive with such concessions to Indian Muslims as the Shah Bano affair[45] and later the conversions of Scheduled Castes to Islam in Meenakshipuram in Tirunelveli, February 1981. Again, the VHP took the lead. So-called Hindu Solidarity Conferences were held in the south in July 1981, and replicated across India. And this time the *shankaracharyas* of Kanchi and Sringeri were to attend the one at Ramanathapuram. All this was named as the *jana jagaran*, the 'awakening of the people'. The VHP sought a further institutional gloss with the setting up of a Central Margdarshak Mandal (a group of guides who show the way) in 1982. A parliament of sadhus, a Sadhu Sansad, in 1984 was deemed a Dharma Sansad (parliament of the Hindu religion). Even so, in Jaffrelot's analysis, 'the VHP fell a long way short of having rallied enough leading personalities to give the impression of being a federation of all the Hindu sects.'[46]

But this new machinery was being harnessed to a new kind of instrumentalist politics, a rabid exploitation of communal objectives, above all, of course, of the Ayodhya issue. The 1st Dharam Sansad had unanimously demanded the 'liberation' of Ayodhya. A special militant wing, the Bajrang Dal, was set up. An even more aggressive note was struck at the 3rd Dharam Sansad in Allahabad in February 1989, coinciding with the Kumbh Mela: the VHP had this time persuaded Devrah Baba, the revered hermit of Vrindavan, to address the meeting. The sadhus were to be drawn into a satyagraha on building a new Ram temple: Ayodhya was to be seen as the most sacred site of Hinduism, its Vatican. Here was a semitized attempt to create a 'historic Hindu heartland'.[47] So, ineluctably, the forces were unleashed that led to the obscenity of 6 December 1992.

In the third essay Therese O'Toole takes up the story of cow protection, at the centre of the Hindutva story from the late nineteenth century right through to the 1950s. The cow became a symbol that could bridge the divide between the reformers and the conservatives. Here O'Toole raises very awkward questions. For what indeed was the difference here between the Congress nationalists and the Hindu communalists? In Gandhi's presentation, the protection of the cow was not to be a bargaining counter with the Muslims; Hindus, instead, were reproved for their cruelty to cows and their neglect. The Congress in 1927 asked for a kind of *quid pro quo*—Hindus were to cease playing music outside mosques while Muslims were to restrict the ritual slaughter of cows, or, at the very least, both communities were to limit their offence to one another. The protectionists and the Hindu nationalists were not impressed. But by playing on modern and secular reasons for protecting the cow the protectionists were in the end to rob themselves of their own symbol; the symbol of the cow lost its religious appeal and Hindutva had to find a new instrumentalist symbol: their choice—from which so much was to follow—was the god Ram.

Another awkward question is raised, and this time regarding the attitudes of the religious reform movements, on the nature of the relationship between the Arya Samaj and Hindutva. From its beginnings the Arya Samaj had championed cow protection. Of all the religious reform movements it is the one most convergent with the politics of Hindu nationalism. Jaffrelot hedges his bets to some degree, arguing that Dayananda's movement 'was not however a proponent of a *Hindu* nationalism' while conceding that 'it became one of the first crucibles of Hindu nationalism'. He goes along with a judgement that it was closest to Hedgewar's way of thinking.[48] Admittedly Dayananda was as embattled with the Hinduism of his day as any Protestant missionary with Catholicism: his was a Vedic fundamentalism with radical overtones. And Zavos makes a strong case that the Arya Samaj stood for a vertical transformation of Hindu society, a society, if you like, open to talents, in contrast to Hindutva's horizontal approach, integrationist and seeking to maintain the structure of castes. Zavos interprets the cow protection movement as an example of just such horizontal mobilization. Fatally, however, the Samaj was ready to compromise with Hindutva by the 1920s, the better to win over the orthodox to its programme of *shuddhi,* of reconversion to Hinduism. Is Zavos too generous in concluding that the Arya Samaj's social radicalism led it away from Hindutva and that 'the search for the antecedents of Hindu nationalism has focussed too sharply on revivalism as a product of this reformist approach'?[49]

But Harald Fischer-Tiné's essay swings the balance the other way towards the Arya Samaj as clearly endorsing Hindutva. In the historian, Acharya Ramdev, who looked on Dayananda as his guru, and in his text *History of Bharatvarsa*—the first volume appeared in 1911—there is clear evidence of a Hindutva style nationalism. Here is a conscious riposte to those orientalist and imperialist historians who insisted on India's apolitical and ineffective past. Surprisingly this was a text written for an age group of eleven to thirteen in the Gurukul Kangri, the educational experiment of the 'militant' faction of the Arya Samaj. Ramdev sought to prove, and by what he took to be contemporary standards of evidence rather than by mere nationalist rhetoric, that ancient India produced coherent stable empires and these were not, as imperial calumny would have it, oriental despotisms but democratic in character, with the separation of powers. Again, by way of a rejoinder to that colonialist myth of the effeminization of Indian people, Ramdev argued for the military prowess of ancient India, throwing in an early version of an air force for good measure. His was also propaganda for the integration of early Indian society: the Aryans, who may well have come from central Asia did so *en masse* and there was no superimposition of the twice-born castes on an indigenous *sudra* population. Women were also emancipated. Here likewise were the beginnings of a modern scientific culture. It was a curious exercise in historical revisionism, for on the one hand, he saw the Vedas as revealed texts, which could not be incorporated into any historical reconstruction, but, on the other, tried to show how a Hanuman could be interpreted as a plausible historical character, one who probably swam twenty-three miles to Sri Lanka. As Fischer-Tiné observes, these claims for an integral Indian nationalism become self-defeating through Ramdev's burdening of the Indian Muslim population with the responsibility for India's decline.

In many ways Hindutva stood for the interests of the twice-born caste elite. Only the imperatives of Indian politics were to drive the BJP into opportunist alliances with the lower castes. And the obvious point has to be made that a middle class was just as likely to respond to Hindutva for its promise of an authoritarian response to threatening radical social protest movements from below as to its nationalism. But if Hindutva is seen as expressing the conservative aspirations of an Indian middle class, just where does that leave their attitude to religion itself, and is their attitude to religion shared by the religious reform movements?

BETWEEN THE PUBLIC AND THE PRIVATE SPHERES

The critical question raised by this debate on the relationship between a political Hindu nationalism and the religious reform movements is on the role of religion in the public sphere. Is indeed religion essentially a private concern, a person's individual search for God, or has it inevitably a role to play in society at large? But that still falls well short of claiming that it has a role to play in politics.

The paradigm of the public/private sphere is, as the editors of a volume of essays on the theme confess, 'not unitary but protean'—another contributor calls it 'slippery'—but it can also be reasonably seen as 'a powerful instrument of social analysis and moral reflection if approached with due caution and conceptual self-awareness.'[49] It clearly has close connections with the paradigm of nationalism. The nation is a public arena within which a search for identity is pursued, and in observations which bear strongly on the Indian situation, Craig Calhoun suggests that if we look on 'nearly every public sphere in the contemporary world as an inescapable, if often unconscious rhetoric of identity-formation, delimitation and self-constitution', then no other solution is possible which fails to recognize 'a multiplicity of publics'.[50] This of course endorses the peculiarly Indian account of secularism, that is acceptance of a plural multi-faith society.

In many ways liberal progressive thought in the modern era has tilted the argument in favour of the private. Here was a search for privacy, for individual liberty, an escape from the tyrannies of both the state and society. Jurgen Habermas however sought to correct the balance and insisted instead on an Aristotelian standard of critical and rational discourse in the public arena, the means whereby a mature democracy can be fashioned. Richard Sennett wrote an influential text lamenting the fall of the public man.[51] But should we not now pursue more of a middle way? Alan Wolfe argues that we need both the worlds of the private and the public: 'We cannot take care of our public business without recognizing we have private selves and we cannot appreciate a private self unless we understand ourselves as public creatures.'[52]

Of course the relevance of this paradigm, worked through in the context of a modernizing Western world, to a society in many ways still as traditional as India, is in question. What is the relevance of a concept of privacy to that majority in Indian society whose lives are lived in houses without private rooms, or in large part outdoors? Only an Indian middle class has really shared in that shift from pre-modern open-plan traditional houses to those with corridors and rooms, a shift that provided the context, as Philippe Aries[53] has demonstrated, for the birth of a bourgeois sensibility. In his battle with the mores of this anglicized middle class Gandhi significantly waged a kind of war against this cult of privacy, insisting that the inmates of his ashrams shared a very exposed public community life.[54] How committedly is India moving towards a civil society in this Western sense, with its protection of privacy?

But none of this resolves the question of where the religious experience should be located. Is it essentially a private affair or should it be regulated in the public sphere? One of the consequences of the rise of the Hindutva movement is that India now finds itself facing the issue of the relationship of the church and the state. Some historians trace this to the colonial period. Robert Frykenburg sees in the exercise of control by the Raj over the religious institutions of India, demonstrated by Regulation VII of 1817 in the Presidency of Madras, the emergence of a Hindu raj: Pamela Price, in a complementary essay, points to a simultaneous emergence of a brahmin raj.[55] It was just because Nehru discerned in the Hindutva movement the threat of a theocracy that he went to such lengths to contain its challenge in the 1940s and 1950s. Does India seriously want to embark on a process which could lead to a Hindu orthodox church akin to the Russian orthodox church of Tsarist Russia?

Yet, just to demonstrate the ambiguities of this debate, it is surprising that the RSS does not see religion as tied to any public structure: 'It becomes a private concern, a matter of one's personal relationship with God.'[56] Or is this just a reminder that in the Hindutva agenda there is always a dividing line, however porous, between culture and religion?

Hannah Arendt may provide an answer to this dilemma. She felt that the private sphere has been overburdened: the family has had to take on too excessive a role of socializing and moralizing: 'We have allowed the public to be swallowed up by the private.'[57] Her corrective lay in recognizing some intermediate sphere between the public and the private, that of the social. And given that it would be merely escapist to deny the continuing hold of religion in Indian society, maybe the best prospect for India is to accept a role for religion in this social sphere. It falls short of conceding it a role in political life.

In America, by way of comparison, there is, with some exceptions, no public religion: 'But Americans also believe that a generalized "civil religion" ought to reinforce widely shared general beliefs for society as a whole and that specific religions should be responsible for the moral training and development of those who adhere to them.'[58] But once again, to emphasize the ambiguities of this debate, it could be said that shaping a new civic consciousness is exactly what the Hindutva movement seeks to do.

In all its multifariousness is it possible to point to any kind of representative, acceptable expression, of religious belief in Hinduism today? Here are two attempts to portray the act of worship itself. Chris Fuller observes:

When a camphor flame is shown in the climax of *puja* ... the divine and human participants are most fully identified in their common vision of the flame and hence in the mutual vision of each other—the perfect *darshana.*

Light, most especially the camphor flame is thus 'an extraordinarily potent condensed symbol of the quintessentially Hindu idea, implied by its polytheism, that divinity and humanity can mutually become one another.'[59]

Paul Younger strains a little harder to capture this moment:

It is a very peaceful, fulfilling experience, which might be described as something like 'rapture', the emotion which one might associate with the end of a Mozart opera, or a state in which the soul is led in Plato's Symposium.[60]

Here is a form of worship carried from the inner sanctum of temples, the shrines of private homes, out into the social sphere, endlessly given expression through festival and pilgrimage.

But there is a strong case for arguing that its intrinsic quality is fundamentally distorted when it is carried yet further into the public sphere, above all into a politicized movement such as Hindutva. Sudipta Kaviraj draws a distinction between a thick and a thin religion. A thick religion is one where a large number of criteria are employed, where an individual's religious identity is anchored in beliefs spread across a wide variety of levels—from large metaphysical beliefs about the nature of existence, to minute ritual practices in worship. Such a religion is inevitably diffuse and pluralist.

A thin religion, on the other hand, is no respecter of such particularities. 'The religion of the communalists,' he asserts 'is by contrast a comparatively thin affair and many of its effective political moves must appear ungrammatical to traditional conceptions of identity, sacrality and auspiciousness.' The portrait of Lord Rama in BJP posters as 'a restorer of moral order', 'a perpetrator of revenge' exemplifies this kind of travesty of tradition:

From the traditional point of view this wrathful Rama is wholly ungrammatical, a complete misunderstanding of the complex narrative and its iconic representation.[61]

Clearly the true character of religion is lost if it is overused in the public sphere. Did the religious reform movements remain loyal to a religion more appropriately expressed in the private sphere, or, at the least, in a merely social context?

A paper follows on the Ramakrishna Mission and the role of women. Feminists have of course turned the public/private sphere paradigm inside out. Far from seeing the private sphere as the locale for liberty, they see it instead as the site of an oppressive patriarchy and a constraining domesticity: female emancipation lies in breaking through into the public sphere, in full-time, properly and equally paid employment, in active participation, above all through electoral enfranchisement, in public affairs. This poses an enormous challenge to traditional attitudes in Indian culture, with its story of Sita, the long-suffering compliant subservient wife. Throughout those pressures for social reform in the nineteenth century and the freedom struggle of the twentieth, the status and emancipation of women was a key issue. The reformers battled with the conventions of the high castes, with those highly invidious constraints on the role of women. Perversely their means for legitimizing their high-caste status, was most notoriously demonstrated in the plight of widows.

Hiltrud Rüstau takes up the story of the delayed but eventually successful campaign to set up a monastery for women by Asha Debi Bandyopadhyaya (b. 1915). To campaign for the right for women to attain *sanyasa*, to share in the male prerogative to pursue an ascetic way of life, may seem a conservative, even a reactionary ideal, but in a traditionalist Hindu culture this was to challenge a major taboo and in fact was a radical proposal. Sister Nivedita's school for girls held out the promise of realizing Vivekananda's concern to raise the status of women as a precondition for the reform of Indian society. There was to be a similar division between the monastic and social service, replicating the parent organization, with the setting up of the Sarada Devi Math in December 1954 and the Sarada Devi Mission in 1960, but education and social service lie at the heart of the endeavour. If it falls well short of contemporary feminist ideas, the movement has at least shifted the emphasis on the role of women from wifehood to motherhood. Rather than defend gender equality it emphasizes the theme of equal but different, echoing the Proudhonian agenda, though he, it has to be said, has invariably been seen as a reactionary social moralist.[62] If this is a movement which is seen as reflecting the aspirations of an Indian middle class, it is wholly opposed, Rüstau claims, to any Hindutva style political activism, and there is a significant contrast in attitudes; whereas the VHP makes a cult of actual motherhood, the Sarada Devi celibates emphasize instead a kind of spiritual motherhood and stress the role of *shakti*, the creative energy of women. Rustau also sees a crucial distinction between the movement's commitment to Vedanta and the Hindutva's Hindu agenda. One leads to love and tolerance, the other to communal antagonism.

If the Hindutva movement in one of its accounts is seen as a bringing together of the sects into a united movement, just how do we fit the Hindu core structure of the sampraday story?

Indian pluralism defies generalizations and Indian sects are enormously varied. John Zavos differentiates between the reform movements and the sampradays: the former seeks to alter the great tradition, the latter to work within it though this is not to say that the latter does not seek to change it. He gives as an example the Satya Mahima Dharma movement in Orissa. He is ready to give mileage to Kenneth Jones's distinction between the acculturative reform movements, those that were caught up in a colonial milieu, and the transitional, those that are outside it. Yet the sampradays were both, structures within which Hinduism did manage to adapt from the nineteenth century onwards, and also a source for Hindutva. Vasudha Dalmia exemplifies this account in her portrait of the reform of the Vaishnava Pustimarg sampraday under Harischandra of Benares (1850–85) 'articulating and formulating the new amalgamation of Vaisnavata into a Hinduism of subcontinental dimension.' He answered 'a need for a religion which cohered internally in the face of immense pressures from without.' Extraordinary claims were made for Vaisnavism, for its monotheism, for the power of *bhakti*, for the worship of Krishna. It was a form of worship open to all, even to Brahmos and Arya Samajists. It could unite all the different Vaisnavite sampradays, indeed all Aryans, under its banner.[63] So where do we situate the sampradays in the story of Hindutva?

Jason Fuller provides a parallel study of Gaudiya Vaisnavite reform, in this case in Bengal, under Deputy Magistrate, Bhaktivinode Thakur. The role of the press was central, and Fuller makes an instructive comparison between the way Baptist missionaries used the press in the early nineteenth century and the way in which Bhaktivinode did. This was to fashion a new public sphere. Here was a Vaisnavite tradition that for all the contempt of the missionaries could not be suppressed. Bhaktivinode steered a clever path between the traditional and the modern, for he both wished to win over those orthodox, alienated from modernity and those *bhadralok*, who went along with the colonial system. He did so by appealing to that Victorian sense of respectability in the urban middle class; Krishna was converted into a respectable god. In this Victorianism, not just in its prudery, but in its search for a high moral purpose, we begin to identify that appeal of the Hindu Renaissance to India's emergent middle class, the social group which Zavos identifies as behind the Hindutva movement. Jaffrelot has also identified by the 1960s a close alliance between a merchant community and the religious.

Two chapters on the Mahima Dharma Sampradasay in Orissa by Lidia Guzy and Johannes Beltz focus on testing its religious integrity. Lidia Guzy looks at the movement as a whole, Johannes Beltz focuses on its blind poet, Bhima Bhoi. It is a movement founded in the early nineteenth century by Mohima Alekh. Guzy believes that as the movement has become routinized and more monastic, it has lost its original subalternist quality and become more hierarchical and authoritarian. But it remains true to its ascetic tradition and still seeks moksha—an essentially traditional Hindu ideal. Exact information on Bhima Bhoi, born in the mid-nineteenth century, is hard to find. Somewhat in the manner of an Ernest Renan Beltz who is not concerned with establishing any historical biography, but rather with exploring the ways in which a modern myth formed: there is no such thing, he claims, as a static hagiographic text. It is fascinating to see how many different constituencies try to appropriate the legends of this blind poet. But even his blindness might be a myth: only the sightless can see a formless god. Here is a charismatic figure, reaching out to dalits, tribals, women. It is scarcely surprising that there should be attempts to emasculate such radicalism and harness him instead to horizontalist programmes of brahmin ascendancy. Lydia Guzy in her fieldwork has come across some attempts by BJP politicians to annex the movement for its own Hindutva purposes but so far it has withstood such blandishments. Beltz accepts that Bhima Bhoi was used as a symbol of a Congress style nationalism, as a freedom fighter and as an opponent of communalism. But almost inevitably Hindutva has also laid claim to his legend, portraying him alternatively as a unifier of India under the banner of sanatana dharma. But the myth has too much fluidity to allow any such restricted identity. The Mahima Dharma remains an intrinsically apolitical movement.

In the final essay in the collection, Maya Warrier discusses another contemporary religious reform movement, Mata Amritanandamayi's

Mission. The emphasis is on *bhakti* and *seva*. It transcends all sectarian loyalties to Vaishnava, Saiva, or Shakta. In many ways this is a movement which most revealingly explores the attitudes of India's present-day middle class, some nine to ten million strong, almost 9 to 10 per cent of the population. We now begin to see the risks of generalizing about its religious attitudes. Several accounts identify this middle class as the backbone of the Hindutva movement. But the followers of this Mission have little interest in and nothing to do with Hindutva, seeing it as a politicized religion and quite alien to their quest for spirituality. From the Mother's embrace, from its spiritual awakening, they seek a different set of values from a materialist, consumerist, and urban culture, one that leads through social service to a higher spiritual plane, to *brahmacharya* or celibacy, to *sanyasa*, 'renouncerhood'. If its activities are in the social sphere, it is a service which renounces the fruits of action and hence remains loyal to the true ascetic ideals of Hinduism. In many ways here is a movement which answers a question I raised in *Gurus and Their Followers*: would modernity see Indians opting for the permissive freedoms of the West, or reverting to some new involvement in their own religious traditions? Here are middle-class Indians who have rejected those libertarian values, particularly sexual, in favour of some reawakened religious idealism. And it can be done without subscribing to some exclusivist, communal Hinduism.

CONCLUSION

It will be obvious that the inner links between Hindutva and the religious reform movements remain uncertain and that the very character of Hindutva itself is difficult to define. As we explored the first paradigm, the varieties of nationalism, it became clear that a specifically religious or Hindu nationalism grew out of the same intellectual climate as the secular nationalism of the freedom struggle, there was a risk of convergence, though arguably they diverged in the 1920s. Claims are made, however, for their reconvergence in the 1980s. However, a secular nationalism remains a vital preservative for India's plural society. It seems we were on safer ground in identifying a middle-class base to Hindutva but quite clearly there is no necessary affiliation between this class and this ideology and, as Maya Warrier's unusual and original essay explores, middle class attitudes can go in quite different directions. The outlook of the sampradays can likewise vary: some go along with Hindutva, others are indifferent to its claims. It may be that the religious reform movements are so diverse that they are unlikely to be subject to any generalization. But we could suggest that if they are to earn our respect they should be subject to certain constraints. If they subscribe to a chauvinist nationalism they betray the interests of religious reform. It is important to establish that such leading patriots as Swami Vivekananda and Sri Aurobindo did not endorse a Hindutva version of nationalism and have been wrongly appropriated by the movement. Possibly the Arya Samaj did cross this particular line. The religious reform movements that prove attractive are those that emphasize the more private expression of religion and limit their public activity to that of social service. As we explored the paradigm of the public and private spheres it became clear that the nature of the religious experience undergoes some fatal change the more it veers into the public sphere and is seriously compromised if it enters the political arena. Maybe it will only obscure our understanding if we oversimplify and exaggerate the divergence between Hindutva and the religious reform movements. RSS, for example, likewise sees itself as a social service organization. The theme has rather been of a distortion, even perversion of the ideal of the reform movements, a failure to reflect their commitment to religious pluralism, and their inherently apolitical stance. The great mistake of Hindutva, committed as it is to high ideals of governance, was to fail to read Gandhi's warning on the end–means debate, mistakenly understood to mean that they could come to power by exploiting communal fears without grasping that this would gravely impair their long-term objectives. However, we have to be alert to Simone Weil's warning that when force is allied to a strong idea, then its hour has come.[64]

ENDNOTES

1. It is worth adding here V.S. Naipaul's brutal judgement that it was the destructive impact of Muslim rule that turned Hindu India into a 'wounded civilisation'. He reiterates this point of view in his notorious interview in the *Literary Review*, 3 August 2001.

2. Hannah Arendt (1906–75), Heidegger's most distinguished pupil, in America became one of the most searching interpreters of the rise of anti-Semitism and totalitarianism (see her *The Burden of Our Time*, Secker and Warbure, London: 1951), and of American capitalism.

3. Still the most persuasive account along these lines is Milton Singer's *When a Great Tradition Modernizes*, London: Pall Mall Press, 1972.

4. Christophe Jaffrelot, 1993, *The Hindu Nationalist Movement and Indian Politics: 1925 to the 1990s*, London, pp. 76, 80.

5. John Zavos, 2000, *The Emergence of Hindu Nationalism in India*, New Delhi, 2000, pp. 212, 213 .

6. I explored this comparative approach in an essay entitled 'Has Religion a Future in India?', *Religion and Society*, Vol. 44, no. 2, June 1997, pp. 23–52.

7. Wilhelm Halbfass, *India and Europe: An Essay in Understanding*, New York: 1988. In summary, his argument is that tolerance is a way for a faith of avoiding any real confrontation with other faiths and traditions, a failure to admit that it may have something to learn from them, and hence is in practice a form of intolerance.

8. In most collections of Indian political theory, the emphasis tends to be on struggle against imperialism, for development, rather than on this more theoretical approach to the nature of the state and democracy. However, the leading nationalist figures, Nehru, Rajagopalachari, J.P. Narayan, were self-evidently familiar with this language. See, for example, A. Appadorai, 1973, *Documents on Political Thought in Modern India*, vols 1 and 2, Bombay: OUP, 1976.

9. Sucheta Mahajan, 2000, *Independence and Partition: The Erosion of Colonial Power in India*, New Delhi: Sage.

10. Jaffrelot, op. cit., p. 11.

11. Spokespersons of the BJP against all historical evidence claim that the Aryans were the original inhabitants of the subcontinent and dispute the very existence of a distinct Harappan civilization. This is part of an attempt to rewrite the standard historical textbooks for schools and to 'saffronize' education. See a scathing attack on this strategy in *The Hindu* (International edn), 25 August 2001.

12. Zavos, op. cit., pp. 8–9.

13. Zavos, p. 184.

14. This is the subject of an unpublished paper by Gwilym Beckerlegge, 'Iconographic Representations of Renunciation and Activism in the Ramakrishna Math and Mission and the Rashtriya Swayamsevak Sangh', submitted to the STIMW (Sanskrit Tradition in the Modern World) Seminar, University of Newcastle, June 2001.

15. Jaffrelot, pp. 44, 60.

16. Jaffrelot's summary of Golwalkar's aim, op. cit., p. 56.

17. A former colleague at the Jawaharlal Nehru University told me of the way his brother used a temple restoration committee as a point of departure for spreading the Hindutva programme.

18. Jaffrelot, p. 88.

19. Indeed the RSS and BJP are currently hardly on speaking terms.

20. J. Alter, 'Somatic Nationalism: Indian Wrestling and Militant Nationalism', *Modern Asian Studies*, 28 March 1994, pp. 557–88.

21. Partha Chatterjee, 1995, 'History and the Nationalization of Hinduism', in eds Vasudha Dalmia and H. von Stietencron, *Representing Hinduism: The Construction of Religious Traditions and National Identity*, New Delhi: Sage, pp. 103–29.

22. Ibid., p. 126.

23. Sudipta Kaviraj, 'The Reversal of Orientalism: Bhudev Mukhopadhyay

and the Project of Indigenist Social Theory' in eds Vasudha Dalmia and H. von Stietencron, op. cit., pp. 251–79.

24. Ibid., p. 257.

25. Ibid., p. 258.

26. Ibid., pp. 273–4.

27. Ibid., p. 276.

28. Ashis Nandy, 1994, *The Illegitimacy of Nationalism*, New Delhi: Oxford University Press , p. 29.

29. Ibid., p. 40.

30. Rabindranath Tagore, 1985, *The Home and the World*, London: Penguin, p. 120.

31. Ibid., pp. 29, 36, 42, 109.

32. Nandy, op. cit., p. 48.

33. Tagore, op. cit., p. 194.

34. Nandy, op. cit., p. 19.

35. Ibid., p. 4.

36. Two examples might be cited: Ernest Gellner, *Nations and Nationalism*, 1983, Oxford: Blackwell and E.J. Hobsbawn, *Nations and Nationalism since 1780*, 1990, Cambridge.

37. Tapan Raychaudhuri, 'Swami Vivekananda's Construction of Hinduism' in William Radice, ed., *Swami Vivekananda and the Modernization of Hinduism*, Delhi: OUP, 1998, p. 16. This was a lecture given at a symposium at SOAS, 26–27 November 1993. I would add on a personal note that the full enormity of that act of sacrilege only struck me during a visit to Mathura when, visiting the Krishna temple, I had to recognize that the large number of troops surrounding Aurangzeb mosque, now closed and deathly quiet, were there to prevent a similar outrage.

38. Ibid., p. 10.

39. Quoted in Wilhelm Halbfass, 'Practical Vedanta', in eds Vasudha Dalmia and H. von Stietencron, op. cit., p. 212.

40. Neman Sadhan Bose, 'Swami Vivekananda and the Challenge to Fundamentalism' in ed. William Radice, op. cit., pp. 282, 290, 298.

41. Kenneth Jones, 'Two Sanatan Dharma Leaders and Swami Vivekananda: A Comparison', in ibid., p. 243.

42. Peter Heehs, 1998, *Nationalism, Terrorism, Communalism: Essays in Modern Indian History*, Delhi: OUP.

43. See Heehs's essay, 'Bengali Religious Nationalism and Communalism', in ibid., pp. 117–18.

44. The definitive text of inclusivism was J.N. Farquhar's *The Crown of Hinduism*, London: OUP, 1913.

45. This was the disturbing case of a divorced housewife from Indore, Shah Bano, who looked as if she had asserted her right to alimony payments all the way to the Supreme Court, only for Rajiv Gandhi's government to give in to Muslim traditionalism and reassert orthodox practices through the 1986 Muslim (Protection of Rights on Divorce) Act.

46. Jaffrelot, op. cit., p. 357.

47. Jaffrelot, p. 401.

48. Jaffrelot, op. cit., pp. 17, 67.

49. Jeff Weintraub and Krishnan Kumar (eds), 1997, *Public and Private in Thought and Practice*, Chicago: University of Chicago Press, pp. xii, 38, 182.

50. Ibid., pp. 84, 91.

51. Richard Sennett, 1974, *The Fall of Public Man*, New York: Alfred Knopf.

52. Weintraub and Kumar, op. cit., p. 188.

53. Philippe Aries (1914–84), a leading member of the French Annales school of history made this point in his *Centuries of Childhood*, 1973, Penguin: Harmondsnorth, Middlesex, pp. 385–7.

54. I explore this theme in 'Is There a Gandhian Definition of Liberty? in Anthony Parel (ed.), 2000, *Gandhi, Freedom and Self-Rule*, Lanham, Maryland: Lexington Books.

55. See their essays in Keith E. Yandell and John J. Paul (eds), 2000, *Religion and Public Culture: Encounters and Identities in Modern South India*, Curzon: Richmond.

56. Zavos, op. cit., p. 194.

57. Kumar's paraphrase of Arendt's position: Weintraub and Kumar, op. cit., p. 213.

58. See Alan Wolfe, 'Public and Private in Theory and Practice: Some Implications of an Uncertain Boundary' in Weintraub and Kumar (eds), op. cit., p. 199.

59. C.J. Fuller, 1992, *The Camphor Flame: Popular Hinduism and Society in India*, Princeton: Princeton University Press, p. 73.

60. Paul Younger, 1995, *The Home of Dancing Shivan: The Traditions of the Hindu Temple in Citamparan*, New York, p. 34.

61. See Sudipta Kaviraj, 'Religion, Politics, and Modernity', in Upendra Baxi and Bhikhu Parekh (eds), 1995, *Crisis and Change in Contemporary India*, New Delhi, pp. 295–316.

62. I tried to make sense of that strange amalgam of Proudhon the radical in the public sphere but conservative in the private, in my 'Pierre-Joseph Proudhon: A Reassessment of His Role as a Moralist', *French History*, Vol. 3, no. 2, June 1989, pp. 194–221.

63. Vasudha Dalmia, 'The Only Real Religion of the Hindus: Vaisnava Self-Representation in the Late Nineteenth Century', in Vasudha Dalmia and H. von Stietencron, op. cit., pp. 176–210.

64. So Professor Antony Parel alerted me in a recent conversation. Simone Weil (1909–43), French mystic and philosopher, was born into a non-practising Jewish family and converted to Christianity in 1937. She was attracted to Catholicism, but baulked at its acceptance of the Old Testament, with its lacking universality, and refused to receive the sacraments whilst France was under the Occupation. She virtually starved herself to death.

I

VARIETIES OF NATIONALISM

Saffron and *Seva*

The Rashtriya Swayamsevak Sangh's Appropriation of Swami Vivekananda[1]

Gwilym Beckerlegge

INTRODUCTION

> From the Highest Brahma to the yonder worm,
> And to the very minutest atom,
> Everywhere is the same God ...
> Who loves all beings, without distinction,
> He indeed is worshipping best his God.

The words above taken from a website[2] have a familiar ring, especially when linked to a picture of Swami Vivekananda. In effect, the image on the website restates the essence of Vivekananda's philosophy of service to humanity, captured in the slogan 'Serve *jiva* as Shiva'.[3] The website, however, is not one maintained by the Ramakrishna Math and Mission or any other organization specifically formed to promote the tradition now associated with the names of Sri Ramakrishna and Swami Vivekananda. The website belongs to the Keshava Seva Samiti of Bhagyanagaram (Hyderabad), Andhra Pradesh. This organization describes itself as 'a unit of seva Bharati' and is an affiliate of the Rashtriya Swayamsevak Sangh (The National Volunteer Corps) or RSS, which was created by Keshav Baliram Hedgewar in 1925. According to one senior member of the RSS, the Rashtriya Swayamsevak Sangh ' ... fulfils the mission of Swami Vivekananda' (Rao, 2000).

Different meanings have been attached to Vivekananda's career. His

Western devotees, for example, tend to view him primarily as the promulgator of a universal religion, while Indian adherents to the Ramakrishna movement generally place as much emphasis on his role as an inspirer of service to humanity. But the significance of Vivekananda has not been recognized solely within the Ramakrishna movement. Vivekananda's reputed activism has caught the imagination of many other Hindus, including members of the RSS who have saluted Vivekananda as the young monk who championed the cause of Hinduism at the World Parliament of Religions in Chicago in 1893 (Bhide, 1989: 47), and as the advocate of 'man-making' education (Bharatiya Swayamsevak Sangh, 1989: 58). Hindus outside the Ramakrishna movement, however, have not necessarily subscribed in every respect to the same reading of Vivekananda's life and teaching as that transmitted within the Ramakrishna Math and Mission, whether in the West or in India. It soon becomes clear that the nature of Vivekananda's activism has been defined by some Hindus in a manner that substantially contradicts the dominant view perpetuated by the contemporary Ramakrishna movement.

Within the literature of the RSS, it is not uncommon to find Vivekananda's name linked with a succession of nineteenth-century Hindu thinkers and leaders, beginning with Dayananda Sarasvati, who fought on '... two fronts against foreign rule and the British appeasement of Muslims'. It is this same 'fight' that is currently being continued by the RSS (for example, Malkani, 1989: 116). The Ramakrishna Math and Mission, on the other hand, has remained publicly committed throughout its history to a policy of non-intervention in politics, taking its stand on Vivekananda's ruling that he and his followers should abstain from direct political activity.[4] At the same time, members of the Ramakrishna Math and Mission have been insistent that Vivekananda was a great patriot and that he provided a huge impetus to the growth of Hindu self-confidence that fed into the independence movement.[5] Consequently, it is hardly surprising that, in spite of the movement's official policy, some close to Vivekananda found it hard to walk the narrow path of raising national pride without becoming involved in direct action. His brother, Bhupendranath Datta, portrayed Vivekananda as a militant nationalist, and was himself a political activist (Datta, 1993). Vivekananda's closest Western devotee, Sister Nivedita, found that her political hopes for India made continuing membership of the Ramakrishna movement impossible. Subsequently, Vivekananda's image as an activist and a heroic defender of Hinduism and India has been a source of inspiration to several young, educated Hindus, many of whom have not chosen to identify themselves specifically with the Ramakrishna movement (see Ashby, 1974: 68). For other Hindus, as Andersen and Damle (1987: 17) note, 'Although both the Order [the Ramakrishna Math] and the Mission remained outside politics, they provided the rationale for political activity; and many revivalist activists, including the founders of the RSS, were inspired by Vivekananda's message.'

In view of the variety of ways in which Vivekananda's message has been interpreted and institutionalized within twentieth-century Hinduism, the fact that his name has been appropriated by the RSS may seem less surprising. Like the appearance of similar motifs in reports of service to humanity within both the Ramakrishna Math and Mission and the RSS, this may seem worthy of note but hardly to raise questions that merit extended consideration. Yet, the use of Vivekananda's image and teachings within the RSS is immediately intriguing, given that the RSS and the Ramakrishna Math and Mission are often placed at different ends of a spectrum of contemporary Hindu movements that range from the 'universalistic, tolerant' (Ramakrishna Math and Mission) to the 'exclusivistic, fanatical' (the RSS) (Klostermaier, 1989: 401). No less intriguing is the ready acknowledgement within the RSS that it has elaborated on Sister Nivedita's exhortation 'If only Hindus collectively pray daily for ten minutes in the morning and in the evening, they will become an invincible society.'[6] Also, as this chapter will show, Madhav Sadashiv Golwalkar, the second leader of the RSS, was profoundly affected by the teaching and example of Swami Akhandananda, one of Ramakrishna's direct disciples and Vivekananda's *gurubhai*. It would seem, therefore, that key personalities in a prominent, modern Hindu movement popularly known for its universalism and religious tolerance may have exercised a considerable influence on the formation of a second no less prominent Hindu movement but one widely regarded as nationalist and religiously intolerant.

The contrast between the respective stances of the RSS and the Ramakrishna movement that has just been outlined, however, invites qualification. For the better part of a century, Vivekananda's popular reputation as a 'universalizer' has been questioned in various critical studies that have characterized his outlook as chauvinistic, uncritical and committed to the defence and glorification of Hinduism. Farquhar's early judgement on Vivekananda as an uncritical defender of Hinduism without a 'historical conscience' (Farquhar, 1967: 204f.) has recently been endorsed by Sil (1997: 62). Vivekananda is frequently named as one of the principal proponents of 'Renaissance Hinduism', 'modern Hinduism' or 'neo-Hinduism', an expression of Hinduism that glorifies

India's past and has been strongly tinged with nationalism (see, Bharati, 1970; Hacker, 1978: 584). Klostermaier (1989: 394) observes that Vivekananda's reputed openness to other Hindu *marga*s and other religions was based, in fact, on his view of them as 'inferior' and 'spiritually underdeveloped', and Klostermaier views the inspiring of 'Hindu-India with immense pride' as one consequence of Vivekananda's vaunting of Hinduism. Whatever Vivekananda himself might have intended, in Sen's opinion, '... for successive generations of nationalistic young men, he [Vivekananda] was possibly the greatest source of inspiration' (Sen, 2000: 80).

Similarly, as we have already noted, Sister Nivedita's passionate attachment to the cause of Indian independence led her to sever her formal ties with the Ramakrishna Math and Mission. Her vigorous defence of traditional Hindu practice, for example, the worship of Kali, was probably a major cause of the split between her and other disciples of Vivekananda in London.[7] Her thesis in *Aggressive Hinduism* was that 'aggression is to be the dominant characteristic of the India that is to-day in school and classroom ...' and that passivity, weakness, and yielding defence should give way to activity, strength, and expansion (Sister Nivedita, 1992: 4). To bring about this change in attitude, Nivedita urged that Hinduism be seen, not as the preserver of past custom, but as 'the creator of Hindu character'. From thinking about protecting themselves, Nivedita calls upon Hindus to 'convert others', 'to win what we never had before', and to focus not on 'how much we kept but how much we have annexed' (Sister Nivedita, 1992: 8f.). This clarion call finds echoes in the message of the founder of the RSS.

More latterly, in the years immediately after the formation in 1964 of the Vishva Hindu Parishad (VHP), one of the major affiliates of the RSS, several senior members of the Ramakrishna Math and prominent Indian academics, who have supported the Ramakrishna movement through their writing, felt able to contribute to publications and events organized under the broad umbrella of the RSS.[8] In the decade or so after its creation, the VHP led what Hansen (1999: 101) has described as a 'relatively low-profile existence', and, he suggests, it represented a '... continuation of efforts in the 1920s to produce the "Hindu nation" through establishment of ... an all-encompassing catholic national Hinduism overriding divisions of sect and caste'. It gathered not only representatives from widely divergent religious groups and organizations within Hinduism and Sikhism but also important personalities who '... were attracted to the organization because of its role in defending Hinduism in accordance with their traditional vocation as patrons of

Hindu institutions' (Jaffrelot, 1996: 202). It would appear, at least during this phase of the VHP's development, that many found it either difficult or unnecessary to draw rigid and consistent lines between the promotion of a Hindu nationalist outlook, 'defending' Hinduism, and celebrating the cultural achievements of India and in particular the legacy of Vivekananda. This task became easier and more pressing for some as the populist agenda of the VHP and its role in pushing forward the political cause of the RSS became more evident from the end of the 1970s.

If some of the seminal personalities associated with the birth of the Ramakrishna movement have attracted ambivalent judgements, the RSS, on the other hand, has been described bluntly as 'fascist', an accusation that it acknowledges in defence of its own position.[9] Even if it were determined that such a description could legitimately be applied to the RSS, the organization's use of Vivekananda (or indeed Sister Nivedita) as a congenial point of reference clearly does not constitute grounds for categorizing Vivekananda in the same way. The use made of Vivekananda by the RSS, however, does provide a provocative starting point for reconsidering the emphases in his message and its influence. For, although Vivekananda has taken on a range of meanings for different Hindus, the repeated invocation of his name and the reference to his teachings by members of the RSS does prompt questions about the particular way in which Vivekananda's legacy has been, and continues to be, interpreted within the RSS—an organization that many hold to be antithetical to the very ideals and goals institutionalized by Vivekananda in the Ramakrishna Math and Mission. It has even been claimed that Vivekananda has become the 'perfect patron saint' of the Bharatiya Janata Party, the political party linked to the RSS (Mishra, 2002: 19).

The starting point for this particular study is not a general reference in an RSS source to Vivekananda as a heroic defender of Hinduism or great patriot but more specifically his role as a promoter of organized *seva*, service to humanity.[10] It is in this less publicized aspect of the RSS's activities that the appropriation of Vivekananda is most apparent. We shall begin by outlining briefly the place of seva within the RSS and its affiliates.

FOLLOWING VIVEKANANDA'S 'PATH OF SERVICE': *SEVA* IN THE CONTEMPORARY RSS AND ITS AFFILIATES

The RSS describes itself as a cultural organization that is committed to fostering Hindu culture and society,[11] while insisting that the term 'Hindu' here 'connotes the national entity of Bharat and not merely a religious faith' (Seshadri, 1988: Prologue, p. 6). Its thinkers make frequent reference, nevertheless, to acknowledged Hindu teachers, including Sri Aurobindo, Mahatma Gandhi, and, of course, Vivekananda, and to central Hindu concepts such as *dharma*. This, and a complete absence of reference to authorities drawn from other Indian religious traditions, indicate the extent to which the RSS is rooted in a religious world-view derived from what is conventionally known as 'Hinduism'. It would be potentially misleading, however, to describe the RSS as a 'religious movement' without qualifying the reference to its primary concern with the 'national entity' of Bharat.

Since its formation, the RSS has evolved into a *parivar*, or 'family', of affiliated *sangh*s (organizations). Recently prominent among this 'family' of organizations have been the Vishva Hindu Parishad (VHP), formed in 1964 as a religious association, and the Bharatiya Janata Party (BJP), which grew out of the earlier Jana Sangh, the political party created by RSS members in 1951. The BJP remains the political standard-bearer of these organizations. The political aspirations of the 'family', however, have long been apparent, even if not always channelled through a formally constituted political party. Accusations of complicity in the assassination of Mahatma Gandhi, of involvement in stirring up communal violence (culminating in the destruction of the Babri mosque at Ayodhya in 1992), and the prominent position occupied latterly by the BJP in Indian politics have kept the political aspirations of the sangh parivar in the forefront of the minds of its observers and critics. Many of the organizations that make up the sangh parivar, however, have also been involved in systematic but less dramatic projects devoted to the service of humanity (seva), although it would be naive to divorce these from the broader political goals of the parivar.

In 1997, according to a databank established by senior workers in the RSS to record more systematically all the seva-activities carried out within the RSS and its affiliates, there were 22,866 recorded *sevakarya*s (units of seva activity) operating across the range of sangh-inspired organizations and reaching 7 per cent of India's population (Anon., 1997: '*Sevakarya* Data'). This databank was created in 1994 and accompanied the formation of *Seva Vibhag* (Service Division), an initiative to increase the performance of service and so mark the centenary of Hedgewar's birth in 1989. Seva activities are listed in this database under the following broad headings: health care, education, social training, social development, and occasional (that is, on an *ad hoc* basis according to need).[12]

Of the fifteen 'important RSS front organizations' two bear

Vivekananda's name—the Vivekananda Medical Mission and the Vivekananda Kendra. Their combined membership is some thirty-three lakh (Mitra and Baweja, 1998: 16). The Keshava Seva Samiti, as we saw in the Introduction, describes itself as 'a unit of Seva Bharati'. Seva Bharati was set up in 1979 to co-ordinate and promote educational initiatives among Scheduled Castes. The Keshava Seva Samiti is typical of many affiliates and their constituent sections in its ready reliance upon Vivekananda's image and words. A Seva Bharati unit in Andhra Pradesh, for example, when proclaiming its defiance after a Naxalite attack on its centre, stated that '... the path of service shown by Vivekananda would be followed by them irrespective of all these threats' (Pragna Bharati Andhra Pradesh website: http://iqg.org/home2/www/index.html). In the Vivekananda Kendra, however, Vivekananda is given a prominence beyond that of the ancillary role assigned to him in the Keshava Seva Samiti. For this reason, the Kendra will now be considered in more detail.

The founder of the Vivekananda Kendra was Eknath Ranade who was transfered from the post of General Secretary of the RSS to concentrate on a project intended to promote the 'revivalist message' of Swami Vivekananda (Andersen and Damle, 1987: 113). The timing of the project coincided with the centenary of Vivekananda's birthday in 1963. In addition to publishing a volume of Vivekananda's teachings, *Swami Vivekananda's Rousing Call to the Hindu Nation*, Ranade also set out to erect a memorial stone to Vivekananda on Kanya Kumari. For local Catholic Christians, however, Kanya Kumari is associated with the mission of St Francis Xavier. Ranade's plan thus rapidly became a cause with the potential to inflame inter-communal conflict, which the Tamil Nadu government attempted to head off by refusing permission to his application to build a memorial to Vivekananda. A national campaign orchestrated by the RSS followed, which resulted in not just a memorial (erected in 1970) but a complex of buildings that would serve as a centre for a newly created lay order of young men and women dedicated to promoting Vivekananda's teaching—the Vivekananda Kendra. The first group of trainees was brought to Kanya Kumari in 1973. All were graduates, under thirty and unmarried although no vow of lifelong celibacy was required.

The Vivekananda Kendra is 'based on ideals promoted by the spiritual master Swami Vivekananda' (RSS website: http://www.rss.org/rss/www/parivar, p. 2). Its objective '... is to awaken Vivekananda's moral fibre in ordinary people' (Melwani, 1994: 2). The Kendra's efforts are channelled into welfare, nutrition, education, community welfare, and developing appropriate technology for villagers, particularly in tribal areas. It is also committed to developing research into yoga through its extensive VK Yogas programme (Vivekananda Yoga Research Anusadhana Samsthana). In addition to developing conventional applications of yoga, VK Yogas sees its yogic research as contributing to a 'knowledge base ... [that] should be the basis of National Reconstruction' (VK Yogas website, 'About Us', p. 2: http://www.vkyogas.org.in/index.html). Expanding from its original centre at Kanya Kumari, the Kendra currently has approximately 100 branches throughout India, a number very similar to the *total* number of Indian branches maintained by the Ramakrishna Math and Mission. In addition to marking the centenary of Vivekananda's birth, the Kendra declared 1993–2002 the 'Vivekananda Decade' to commemorate Vivekananda's address at the World Parliament of Religions, and initiated the 'Clean India for Cleaner Life' project during that decade.

In order to understand the connection between the extensive promotion and practice of seva within the contemporary RSS and the frequent invocation of Vivekananda's name and image, we shall now examine the different relationships between the first two leaders of the RSS, Keshav Baliram Hedgewar and Madhav Sadashiv Golwalkar, and the Ramakrishna Math and Mission.

'DOCTORJI' AND THE INSTITUTIONAL BEGINNINGS OF *SEVA*

If there is an indissoluble link between the Ramakrishna Math and Mission and the region of Bengal, the heartland of the RSS is Maharashtra and, in particular, the city of Nagpur, where Keshav Baliram Hedgewar, the founder of the RSS, was born in 1889. Although a brahmin, he showed little interest in ritual and received a modern education. Possibly fuelled by the conviction that the death of both his parents during an epidemic had been due to the 'callousness of the alien officialdom' (Deshpande and Ramaswamy, 1981: 4), Hedgewar was soon drawn to the nationalist cause under the influence of Bal Gangadhar Tilak. After the closure of local educational institutions in Nagpur following student nationalist activity, from 1910 Hedgewar pursued his higher studies in Bengal, 'the birthplace of "*Vande Mataram*"' (Deshpande and Ramaswamy, 1981: 13). One biographer has noted that Hedgewar's medical studies became a cover for the revolutionary training he received in Calcutta (cited in Deshpande and Ramaswamy, 1981: 15).

According to accounts written from within the RSS, 'public service was a consuming passion' for the young Hedgewar during his time in

Calcutta (Deshpande and Ramaswamy, 1981: 20). He formed a 'service unit' to help and care for Hindus who were victims of atrocities attributed to Muslims and his heart was 'pierced' by the apathy of Hindus facing such assaults (Deshpande and Ramaswamy, 1981: 20). In the August of 1913, he was involved as a volunteer in the relief-party organized by the Ramakrishna Mission to combat severe floods in the Burdwan (Barddhaman) district to the north-west of Calcutta. This would have been part of the Bankura and Burdwan relief-operation of 1913–14 (Swami Gambhirananda, 1983: 343). It is also reported that Hedgewar joined other volunteers during the six years he spent in Calcutta to offer service to the crowds attending the Gangasagar Mela, where he was again moved by the 'poverty, ignorance, and ill-heath [that] had utterly emasculated the villagers' (Deshpande and Ramaswamy, 1981: 22). No mention is made of the organizers of the Gangasagar Mela relief, but as the Ramakrishna Mission provided relief there in 1912 and from 1914 until 1925 (Swami Gambhirananda, 1983: 343), it is probable that this was a further occasion when Hedgewar channelled his energies through the institutional structures of the Ramakrishna Math and Mission.[13] Hedgewar returned to Nagpur early in 1916 to resume his nationalist activities without distraction. He had never intended to take up a professional post within medicine but was later to be referred to within the RSS as 'Doctorji'.

In 1920, Hedgewar was responsible for organizing young men into a volunteer unit that kept order at the annual Congress meeting in Nagpur. After Tilak's death, Hedgewar participated briefly in the non-violence campaign orchestrated by Gandhi. The suspension of this campaign in 1922 due to outbreaks of violence, and an outburst of communal violence in 1923 caused Hedgewar to rethink the causes of India's current predicament. The roots of so many of India's problems, Hedgewar came to believe, could be traced to India's past inability to defend herself from foreign aggression and occupation. He put this failure down to a lack of social cohesion and a sense of national consciousness, and the training programme of the RSS was designed to promote both these qualities. Its direct antecedent was the Nagpur Hindu Sabha, which was created in the face of British administrative and Muslim communal opposition to Hindus celebrating festivals in public processions. Hedgewar was its secretary. The Nagpur Hindu Sabba won a compromise through its demonstrations, and in the process united Hindus against two enemies—the British and the Muslims. One of Hedgewar's key assumptions by now, under the influence of V.D. Savarkar, was that Hindus were a nation (*rashtra*) and that their national identity needed to be defined, protected, and positively nurtured. The RSS would provide the training necessary for 'character building' in order to combat the 'apathy' and 'emasculation' that Hedgewar believed were undermining Hindus.

The RSS was founded in 1925 by Hedgewar, then a member of the Hindu Mahasabha, and was a practical expression of his concern about growing Muslim influence within the Indian National Congress. The RSS and its later 'family' of affiliated sanghs (organizations) all acknowledge an ideological debt through Hedgewar and Golwalkar to V.D. Savarkar (1883–1966) whose essay *Hindutva* ('Hinduness'), published in 1923, greatly shaped both the Hindu Mahasabha and later RSS thinking. The point was made earlier in this Chapter that the RSS has constantly emphasized its role as a cultural organization. In spite of the activities of the other wings of the sangh parivar, the RSS has held itself apart from direct political activity. Its critics have argued that it has been able to do this precisely *because* of the activities of the other wings of the parivar and the closeness of its relationship to these wings. The avowed apolitical stance of the RSS, however, helps to explain the uneasy relationship that developed between it and its slightly senior counterpart on the Hindu right, the Hindu Mahasabha (see, for example, Andersen and Damle, 1987: 36–40). For, in spite of Hedgewar's close association with Savarkar and an early expectation that Hedgewar's organization might form a youth wing of the Hindu Mahasabha, Hedgewar refused to support the Hindu Mahasabha's civil disobedience campaign of 1938–39. The gulf between the two organizations subsequently widened, although individuals continued to support both and move between the two. Andersen and Damle (1987: 40) suggest that this was because of the desire of the RSS leadership not to ally itself with a group that was openly in opposition to the Congress, and also Savarkar's dislike of Golwalkar. It is important, therefore, in view of the contemporary closeness between the RSS and the political wings of the sangh parivar and its historical associations with the Hindu Mahasabha, to be clear as to the kinds of activities the RSS encouraged under the leadership of Hedgewar and then Golwalkar.

The first example of an organized act of 'service' carried out by members of the RSS (the *swayamsevaks* or volunteers) under Hedgewar's leadership was reminiscent of that performed by the unit of young men formed by Hedgewar in 1920 to supervise Indian Congress meetings. In 1926, his latest band of volunteers policed a rowdy local celebration of Ram Navmi, establishing queues, providing water for devotees and protecting them from those who would batten upon the innocent. For this occasion, Hedgewar chose both the name and a uniform for the new organization. His purpose, according to Andersen and Damle (1987: 35) was '... to demonstrate the value of discipline both to the volunteers and to the general public ...'. In 1927, RSS squads were used to protect Hindu districts of Nagpur during an outbreak of communal violence, but in the next few years several senior members of the RSS left the organization in frustration over Hedgewar's insistence that the RSS restrict itself to a character-building role. By the end of the 1930s, there were about 500 branches (*shakhas*) and a women's affiliate, the Rashtra Sevika Samiti. The growth of the RSS already alarmed certain provincial governments sufficiently to ban their employees from taking part in RSS activities (see Deshpande and Ramaswamy, 1981: 137).

The style of seva fostered by Hedgewar through shakha training and rituals during the early days of the RSS appeared to owe little to movements like the Arya Samaj, which had influenced him and had a history of involvement in seva. Within the Arya Samaj, seva had typically been performed through educational activities, the care of orphans, and famine-relief, although a distinction needs to be drawn between the kinds of educational activities associated with the two wings of the Arya Samaj (Jones, 1989: 97ff.). The activities of the Ramakrishna Math and Mission fell within similar categories at that time. Yet, in spite of Hedgewar's personal involvement in the offering of seva through the Ramakrishna Math and Mission, it would seem that he did not give priority to developing comparable service initiatives within the RSS. Indeed, although Hedgewar was involved with the Ramakrishna Mission in Calcutta, it has been suggested in one critical study of the RSS that this was merely instrumental to his desire '... to enter the charmed circle of the revolutionary or political elite whose names were a source of inspiration for people ...' (Goyal, 1979: 56). It is significant, however, that Hedgewar clearly associated the conditions of poverty, ignorance, disease, and oppression that afflicted Hindus as much with an inner condition as with external structural factors relating to British rule and its response to the Hindu and Muslim dimensions of the independence movement. In this respect, Hedgewar was somewhat reminiscent of Swami Vivekananda, although the former defined this inner condition in terms of apathy or 'emasculation' rather than spiritual impoverishment.

GURUJI AND SWAMI AKHANDANANDA

After Hedgewar's death in 1940 it was announced that he had chosen Madhav Sadashiv Golwalkar (1906–73) to succeed him as *sarsangchalak* (the supreme spiritual guide of the RSS). This choice was initially regarded as surprising within the RSS on account of Golwalkar's relative youthfulness and perceived inexperience, and because Golwalkar was known for his strong spiritual inclinations rather than for the intense patriotism associated with Hedgewar.[14] Unlike Hedgewar, Golwalkar had an untroubled childhood and as a student has been described as 'remarkably apolitical' (Andersen and Damle, 1987: 41). Another resident of Nagpur, having studied biology at Banaras Hindu University, Golwalkar was given a lectureship at the same university. It was there that Golwalkar first met Hedgewar during a visit by the latter in 1931; a meeting later described by Golwalkar's publishers as 'equally epoch-making' as that between Ramakrishna and Vivekananda (Golwalkar, 1966: ix). In a similar vein, it has also been claimed that 'The traits of the personality of ... Golwalkar are somewhat similar to those of Swami Vivekananda. Social consciousness blended with spiritual aspiration was the common factor of both' (Kohli, 1993: 1). It seems that Golwalkar displayed little interest in the RSS meetings held at the university at that time, and it was Hedgewar who began to groom Golwalkar. Shortly afterwards, Golwalkar returned to Nagpur to take up the duties of a householder, to marry and to study law so that he could establish himself in that profession. It was on his return to his family home that Golwalkar '... later on came into contact with the Ram Krishan [sic] Mission in Nagpur' (Mishra, 1980: 79). In 1934, Hedgewar appointed Golwalkar as secretary to the Nagpur branch (shakha) of the RSS, and in 1935 entrusted him with the management of the RSS Officers' Training Camp.

In October 1936, however, Golwalkar abandoned his legal studies and turned his back on the RSS and left Nagpur for Bengal where he became a disciple of Swami Akhandananda, one of Ramakrishna's direct disciples and Vivekananda's gurubhai. Given that Golwalkar had shown a keen interest in religion from his late teenage years, this seemingly sudden change in direction may have represented a return to his true interests and vocation, possibly precipitated by the realization that marriage and embarking upon a career would constitute something of a point of no return. This phase in Golwalkar's life, however, was not to last because Swami Akhandananda died in February of 1937, a few months after Golwalkar's arrival.

The time that Golwalkar was able to spend with Swami Akhandananda was brief but charged with significance. Uncovering the factors that led to Golwalkar's move to Bengal, the reasons for his choice of Swami Akhandananda, and assessing the longer-term impact of this experience upon Golwalkar, however, is far from straightforward because of the patchy nature of the available evidence. In the light of Hedgewar's own passing involvement while in Bengal with relief-work organized by the Ramakrishna Mission, it is possible that Golwalkar may have heard more about that organization from his mentor. Yet, as we have already noted, Hedgewar did not dedicate the newly formed RSS to service projects and it is unlikely that he would have spoken of the Ramakrishna movement in such a way as to induce his own protégé to abandon Nagpur for Sargachhi. In lieu of evidence to the contrary, we have to assume that Golwalkar, as an educated and spiritually-inclined individual, had heard of the Ramakrishna movement independently of his connection with Hedgewar, either on his return to Nagpur or earlier. Swami Akhandananda had been President of the Ramakrishna movement since 1934 and was in any case well-known for being one of the three remaining, original disciples of Ramakrishna. It is not surprising, therefore, that Golwalkar may have turned specifically to him for spiritual guidance.

The exact nature of Golwalkar's formal relationship to the Ramakrishna movement and his status (if any) within it have been defined in different ways. Golwalkar has been described simply as a 'disciple' of Swami Akhandananda (Goyal, 1979: 78; Mishra, 1980: 79) or as travelling to Bengal 'to study yoga under Swami Akhandanand [sic]' (Andersen and Damle, 1987: 42). The fact that Golwalkar travelled to Sargachhi, the *ashram* founded by Swami Akhandananda, may suggest that Golwalkar had already formed a specific attachment to that Swami rather than to the Ramakrishna Math and Mission in more general terms. Had the latter been the case, we might have expected him to have gone first to Calcutta and possibly to Belur Math. Mishra (1980: 79), who declares himself to be an RSS member, states that Golwalkar had '... proceeded to Calcutta to take orders and then became a disciple of Swami Akhanda Nand [sic]'. This would seem to imply a more formal attachment to Swami Akhandananda's ashram than simply that of a volunteer or a devotee travelling on a personal basis to receive spiritual instruction. In another context, however, Andersen and Damle (1987: 17) explicitly state that Golwalkar was '... himself an ordained member of the Order [the Ramakrishna Math]'. This claim suggests that Mishra's account of Golwalkar 'taking orders' may imply more than merely taking direction on arrival in Calcutta.

In response to this writer's request for clarification of Golwalkar's formal relationship to the Ramakrishna movement during the 1930s, Swami Prabhananda, a senior member and historian of the Ramakrishna Math, consulted members of Belur Math who had served Swami Akhandananda in his final years. They recalled that '... Golwalkar had received spiritual initiation from Swami Akhandananda' but maintained that Golwalkar '... was never ordained as a member of the Order nor was he ever seen in *gerua* cloth'.[15] This initiation is reported as having taken place on 12 January 1937 (Kohli, 1993: 3). The preparation of any individual considering applying for acceptance into the Ramakrishna Math is lengthy, with a minimum of eight years before the individual is regarded as eligible for *sannyasa*, to which even then entry is not a matter of right. This period, moreover, is preceded by a pre-probationer year when the individual is attached to a centre. If Golwalkar's status was formalized beyond that of being a personal disciple of Swami Akhandananda, it clearly could not have been more than that of a pre-probationer at the very outset of the year that preceded formal training. On the death of Swami Akhandananda, according to 'popular belief among the swamis', Golwalkar visited Belur Math 'once or twice' and seemed intent on taking 'the path of monasticism' until persuaded back into the ranks of the RSS. Swami Prabhananda added that, once Golwalkar resumed his RSS activities, '... he became an unwelcome guest in our Math and Mission centres, particularly after the assassination of Mahatma Gandhi.' By way of a postscript, Swami Prabhananda also noted that Golwalkar had stayed briefly at the Ramakrishna Math and Ramakrishna Mission in Bombay towards the end of his life when he was ill. The head of the Bombay centre at that time was Swami Hiranmayananda who later became General Secretary of the Math and Mission.

There is no reference to Golwalkar in the fullest biography of Swami Akhandananda published by the Ramakrishna movement (Swami Annadananda, 1993), although there are constant references to admirers, disciples, and devotees being drawn to the ashram at Sargachhi during the final years of Swami Akhandananda's life when he was also President of the Ramakrishna Math and Mission. There is also an intriguing reference to Swami Akhandananda's itinerary for 1934. Having travelled to Bombay to accompany American disciples who were returning to the United States, Swami Akhandananda and his party broke their return journey to Calcutta at Nagpur at the request of the head of the Nagpur ashram. During that visit '... he initiated some specifically selected devotees. He said to some students there, who desired to be initiated, "Come to Sargachhi"' (Swami Annadananda, 1993: 282). This would have been in the latter part of November 1934, because after a three-day stay at Nagpur, Swami Akhandananda had reached Calcutta 'by the end of November' (Swami Annadananda, 1993: 282). Golwalkar had been back in residence in Nagpur studying law since 1931–2, and, during 1934 and 1935, was beginning his rise in the local RSS hierarchy under the tutelage of Hedgewar. This was also the period when, according to Mishra, Golwalkar had established some sort of contact with the Ramakrishna Mission in Nagpur. It is conceivable that an encounter with Swami Akhandananda during his visit to Nagpur in November 1934, may have precipitated a reappraisal on Golwalkar's part of the direction his life was taking. Indeed, if the 'popular belief' of the Ramakrishna Math (cited above by Swami Prabhananda) is accurate and Golwalkar was initiated by Swami Akhandananda, the Swami's visit to Nagpur may have been the beginning of the process of acceptance. Taken together, the timescale of events, and indirect and circumstantial evidence support the conclusion that Golwalkar was never admitted into the Ramakrishna Math, but, having received initiation from Swami Akhandananda, he retained a sympathy towards the movement and its teachers that lasted until his death.

There are different assessments of the impact of Akhandananda's death upon Golwalkar. According to Kohli (1993: 3), Swami Akhandananda himself foretold that Golwalkar's destiny lay with Hedgewar. Kohli appears to suggest that Golwalkar felt that '... His Spiritual dream was fulfilled ...' and that this was signalled by a death-bed blessing he received from Swami Akhandananda. Thus, according to Kohli (1993: 3), the mental conflict which had been rising in Golwalkar, subsided, and '... social consciousness became the pivot of all his activities in his life.' He thus returned to Nagpur 'with contentment' after the death of Swami Akhandananda. This account seems implausible for a number of reasons. First, it ignores the very short period that Golwalkar was able to spend with Swami Akhandananda and, in particular, that Swami Akhandananda died in the month following Golwalkar's initiation as his disciple. This, following his abandonment of his life in Nagpur, would hardly have allowed Golwalkar to benefit as fully as he had anticipated from an extended relationship with his *guru*. Second, it forms part of a reconstruction of the relationship between Golwalkar and Swami Akhandananda that includes the claim that Swami Akhandananda explicitly sanctioned Golwalkar's return to work under Hedgewar. Members of the Ramakrishna Math may have attempted to distance their organization from Golwalkar in the light of the reputation acquired by the RSS, but it is difficult to understand why Swami Akhandananda should have foreseen or encouraged Golwalkar to fulfil his destiny within the RSS. This was, after all, the life that Golwalkar had abandoned to gain acceptance as Swami Akhandananda's disciple. Again, if the 'popular belief' current within the Ramakrishna Math is well-founded, this would seem to be borne out by reports of Golwalkar's visit to Belur Math, after the death of Swami Akhandananda, and his active consideration of undertaking training for acceptance into the Ramakrishna Math. Third, the claim that this brief interlude resolved the internal conflict that Golwalkar was experiencing, presumably between the conflicting demands of social activism and renunciation, is hardly confirmed by evidence that Golwalkar did indeed immediately make social consciousness the 'pivot' of his life. As we shall see, it was sometime later and in quite specific circumstances that Golwalkar began to encourage the expansion of seva activity within the RSS.[16] More probable is the account given by Goyal (1979: 78) that Golwalkar is said to have fallen '... into a state of extreme mental depression and indecision ...' after Swami Akhandananda's death and shortly returned to Nagpur to seek Hedgewar's advice (Goyal, 1979: 78). He was persuaded by Hedgewar that he could fulfil his vocation through the RSS. He neither married nor resumed his legal studies, thus distancing himself from his family and the traditionally defined role of 'householder'.

Assuming that Golwalkar had felt spiritually drawn to Swami Akhandananda prior to his journey to Bengal in 1936, what might that suggest about Golwalkar's own religious leanings at that time? Swami Akhandananda's spiritual career after the death of Ramakrishna passed through distinct phases that to some extent found parallels in the lives of other prominent, direct disciples of Ramakrishna, including Vivekananda.[17] Of brahmin descent, Swami Akhandananda is described in the standard language of hagiographies written within the Ramakrishna movement as having been attracted to a life of austerity even as a child. He referred to himself as 'extremely orthodox in those days' (Swami Akhandananda, 1979: 2). More distinctively, even by the time he first met Ramakrishna in 1883, he had disappeared from home, having followed a holy man to Burdwan, and is said to have completed a 'pilgrimage' before being restored to his family. After the death of Ramakrishna in 1886, Swami Akhandananda undertook extensive solitary pilgrimages in northern India and Tibet but showed a desire to maintain contact with Vivekananda during a period when the latter was also pursuing a wandering, solitary lifestyle. They spent time together in Gujarat in 1892, for example. Within the standard histories of the Ramakrishna movement, however, Swami Akhandananda is best known for being the gurubhai who was most willing to support Vivekananda's promotion of organized service to humanity in the name of Ramakrishna. It was Swami Akhandananda who initiated the first service project at Khetri in 1893–4, according to sources within the Ramakrishna movement, under instructions from Vivekananda.[18] Subsequently, Swami Akhandananda initiated famine-relief in the Murshidabad district in 1897 and remained in the area to found an orphanage and ashram at Sargachhi. Such was the level of Swami Akhandananda's commitment to the practical delivery of service that he remained at Sargachhi for the rest of his life, preferring to reside there whenever he could, even when President of the Math and Mission. Vivekananda found occasion to remark that Swami Akhandananda became so absorbed in the practicalities of relief-work that 'preaching' had entirely given way to 'helping' (*CWSV*, VII: 507).

If Golwalkar's choice of Swami Akhandananda as a spiritual guide was indeed as particular and deliberate as it appears, he may well have been drawn to an individual whose spiritual career is aptly summarized in the English title given to his memoirs, *From Holy Wanderings to Service of God in Man* (Swami Akhandananda, 1979). Interpreting Swami Akhandananda's life selectively, therefore, Golwalkar could have cast this *sannyasin* in the role of the archetypal ascetic, or as an activist making Hinduism responsive to the immediate needs of ordinary people, or as one able to bring together these two expressions of the religious life into a harmonious whole. Alternatively, although this seems less likely in view of Golwalkar's ambivalent attitude to political activity during that period of his life, he may have been attracted by Swami Akhandananda's political outlook. This seems even less likely given that Swami Akhandananda had received personally from Vivekananda the injunction 'Do not mix in politics, etc., nor have any connection with them,' which in its various forms has largely shaped the policy adopted by the Ramakrishna movement since that time (*CWSV*, VI: 406). The available evidence suggests that Swami Akhandananda's socio-political outlook was entirely centred on a concern for the poor, as is evident, for example, in his criticism of the conditions of the Maharaja of Khetri's tenants and of the gulf that the Congress movement perpetuated between itself and the rural poor (Swami Akhandananda, 1979: 62, 81).

It seems reasonable, therefore, to consider whether Golwalkar adopted more marked ascetic and/or humanitarian tendencies following his relationship with Swami Akhandananda. The image of the bearded, long-haired ascetic, absorbed in religious introspection or ritual, is a common motif in depictions of Golwalkar in the RSS. It contrasts sharply with the image of Hedgewar as a national leader and activist. It is Hedgewar's image that is most frequently linked to the seva activities of the recent RSS and its affiliates.[19] If the meeting between Hedgewar and Golwalkar has been likened in the literature of the RSS to that between Ramakrishna and Vivekananda, it would seem that, in the case of the RSS, it was the master who was the activist—contrary to popular depictions of the nature of the relationship between Ramakrishna and Vivekananda.[20] It has been said that Golwalkar retained his long hair and beard in obedience to Swami Akhandananda's wishes, and his retention of this style may have signalled his continuing acceptance of Swami Akhandananda's authority (Goyal: 1979: 78). It may also have been an outward manifestation of Golwalkar's own ascetic leanings and his identification with this strand of the Hindu religious tradition, exemplified by Swami Akhandananda who in later life refused initiation to married individuals unless they were prepared to practise sexual abstinence (Swami Annadananda, 1993: 15, 282). Like many senior members of the RSS, Golwalkar neither married nor took up a career. An anecdote about the relationship between Swami Akhandananda and Golwalkar, which consciously echoes that between Ramakrishna and Vivekananda, suggests something of the powerful allure of the life of renunciation. Based on the correspondence between Golwalkar and a friend, Kohli (1993: 3) reports a judgement from Swāmi Akhandananda that, although instinctively drawn towards *samadhi*, Golwalkar's destiny lay beyond the boundaries of the ashram. Ramakrishna is said to have been recalled by the Divine Mother (Kali) from *nirvikalpa samadhi* '... for the sake of humanity', to have chided Vivekananda for being on the verge of similarly losing himself in nirvikalpa samadhi rather than acting '... like a great banyan tree giving shelter to thousands ...' (Swami Nirvedananda, 1969: 672, 685). The use of the title 'Guruji' within the RSS when speaking of Golwalkar certainly suggests that it was through his spirituality, understood along fairly traditional lines, that Golwalkar was held to have made his distinctive contribution to the development of the movement he had inherited from 'Doctorji'.

When we turn to consider evidence of a possible influence exerted by Swami Akhandananda in terms of an unequivocal commitment by Golwalkar to the promotion of service to humanity, however, we find that the RSS embraced the practice of organized seva fairly gradually. Although this humanitarian emphasis became more pronounced under Golwalkar's leadership, this did not happen immediately with Golwalkar's elevation to the role of sarsangchalak. It emerged more strongly in specific circumstances that favoured the strategic interests of the RSS, rather than appearing as a direct result of the involvement at different times with the Ramakrishna Math and Mission of either Hedgewar or, more significantly, Golwalkar (see Beckerlegge, forthcoming 2).

Golwalkar played a major part in organizing relief for Hindu refugees in the wake of Partition, in 1948 (Kohli, 1993: 5). His major contribution to the development of seva activity, however, is to be found, first, indirectly in his creation of the role of *pracharak* (full-time organizer largely responsible for the management of seva projects), and, second, in his articulation in 1954 of the concept of 'Positive Hinduism'. This new formulation enhanced the position of seva as an organizational priority of the RSS and marked the beginning of a process to construct a fuller philosophical rationale for this practice. It was central to Golwalkar's strategy of reshaping the RSS in order to recover the ground the organization lost when, together with the Hindu Mahasabha, it was banned following the assassination of Mahatma Gandhi. The growth and changing role of seva within the RSS appear to have been the outworking of a prolonged and evolving strategy to rehabilitate the RSS and its affiliates in the eyes of India's politicians and people. In the next section, we shall analyse more closely the use made of Vivekananda by major ideologues in the RSS.

THE APPROPRIATION OF VIVEKANANDA

In the years after the lifting of the ban in 1949, Golwalkar reoriented the RSS by playing down its paramilitary past while licensing a new and different kind of activism. The pracharaks, largely young graduates and all unmarried, were to be central to this strategy. In 1949, Golwalkar sent pracharaks to work under Vinoba Bhave. In 1954, Golwalkar outlined to an audience of pracharaks the tenets of 'positive Hinduism' to provide a philosophical rationale for their work. He argued that '... a person worships God through service to society and he advised his audience to carry out its work in this spirit' (Andersen and Damle, 1987: 111).

The consolidation of the RSS between 1949 and the mid-1960s placed a range of activist commitments more firmly on the agenda of the organization and its affiliates. With this, power passed to those within the RSS who favoured a greater degree of involvement in direct political action as distinct from 'character-building'. Historically there has been a tension between those in the RSS who believed that fidelity to Hedgewar entailed restricting their role to 'character-building' and those who sought to realize the vision of the RSS through organized political activity (see Beckerlegge, forthcoming 2). In practice, the 'character-building' and social projects of the sangh parivar have been subsumed to such an extent within its political and cultural vision that its critics generally imply direct, political action when referring to 'activism' within the RSS, rather than what might be termed 'social activism' expressed through philanthropy. When examining the historical growth of the RSS, however, the creation of an affiliate with the formal status of a political party marked a significant development. It is helpful, therefore, to draw a distinction, albeit necessarily a fluid one, between 'political activism' within the RSS, orchestrated formally through its explicitly political wings, and 'social activism', including seva and 'character-building', to which many affiliates commit considerable resources.

The Jana Sangh political party was established in 1951 by members of the RSS under the leadership of Shyama Prasad Mookerji, and pracharaks were permitted to serve the party. The removal of Eknath Ranade from the post of General Secretary, which he held from 1956 to 1962, to oversee the celebration of the Vivekananda centenary, was in line with this trend. Ranade, a veteran member of the RSS had served as a pracharak and had been responsible for developing the movement in Mahakoshal. During the period of Golwalkar's imprisonment when the RSS was a banned organization, Ranade was one of its most senior leaders involved in attempts to broker a compromise with the central government. In 1950, he was given the job of organizing relief for Hindu refugees from East Pakistan, much as Golwalkar had done for those leaving West Pakistan on Partition. Like Golwalkar, Ranade stood in the wing of the RSS that saw the movement's role in terms of its capacity to bring about social and so ultimately political change through moulding character, rather than by direct involvement in organized political parties. This position is comparable to that adopted by Vivekananda, although the nature and goal of the character transformation sought by Vivekananda were significantly different. The desire to mark the centenary of Vivekananda's birth within the RSS was entirely consistent with what we know about the sympathies not just of 'character builders', such as Golwalkar and Ranade, towards the Ramakrishna movement and its founders, but with the signs of the high regard in which Vivekananda has been held across both wings of the membership of the RSS (see Andersen and Damle, 1987: 138).

Ranade was replaced as General Secretary by Prabhakar Balwant Dani, who had previously held the post between 1946 and 1956 and was more sympathetic to the activist position. Balasaheb Deoras, who would be the third sarsangchalak was made Assistant General Secretary. The 'activist' tendency was increased with the formation of the Vishva Hindu Parishad (VHP) in 1964 after a meeting of the leaders of a range of Hindu groups called by Golwalkar. His aim was to create a forum to exert a unifying pressure on Hindu society and its different religious groups. The VHP was the outcome of this initiative and Shivram Shankar Apte, an RSS pracharak, was its first General Secretary. One consequence of this move was an increased level of participation in social welfare projects as a number of groups and initiatives already created by swayamsevaks were brought under the umbrella of the VHP. The Vivekananda Medical Mission was one organization that fell within this category. Thus, by the end of that decade, the RSS was involved directly or indirectly in a larger number of service projects than at any time in its previous history, and in projects of a far wider range than the 'policing' activities that had characterized the early years under the leadership of Hedgewar.

Hedgewar's reputation as the founder of the RSS has not rested on the claim that he was the movement's chief ideologue. This role has largely been assigned to Golwalkar. Hedgewar is seen rather as the instigator of a character-building training programme and as the creator of a 'totally unique' organizational concept (Mishra, 1980: 6). It was he who evolved 'the *Shakha* technique' to suit the 'supreme vision' of 'a work of national resurrection' (Deshpande and Ramaswamy, 1981: 81). Nevertheless, to this day Hedgewar's training programme is described as 'character moulding' or frequently as 'man-making' education—something that Vivekananda repeatedly insisted should be the '... ideal of all education, all training' (for example, *CWSV*, II: 15; III: 301f.). Like Vivekananda (for example, *CWSV*, V: 223), Hedgewar insisted that 'We need lakhs and lakhs of young men wholly dedicated to the uplift of the nation' in order to solve India's problems (quoted in Deshpande and Ramaswamy, 1981: 93). Again like Vivekananda, Hedgewar constantly reiterated that 'The Hindu race can save itself only through ... organization' (quoted in Deshpande and Ramaswamy, 1981: 188). Many emphases associated with Hedgewar's understanding of India's educational needs were also anticipated by Vivekananda. It must be a national education for the masses and one designed to call forth Hindus from the state of apathy into which both believed their co-religionists had fallen. Hedgewar, we noted, spoke of the 'emasculation' of the Hindus of his day. Vivekananda often referred to the 'tamasic' quality of their existence, but he too called for more vigorous physical training so that the physique of the Hindu man could match that of his meat-eating oppressor (*CWSV*, III: 242; cf. Golwalkar, 1966: 40f).

Although certain aspects of Hedgewar's ideas are reminiscent in a general sense of those of Vivekananda, Golwalkar made explicit use of both Ramakrishna and Vivekananda in his writings. His reputation as the RSS's most influential thinker was founded upon his publication in 1938 of *We or Our Nation Defined*, although its originality has been denied by critics who point to its dependence upon the writings of both V.D. Savarkar and Babarao Savarkar (see Goyal, 1979: 80), something that Golwalkar himself acknowledged (Andersen and Damle, 1987: 43). For the purpose of this study, however, we shall draw upon *Bunch of Thoughts*, an extensive volume pulled together in 1966 from Golwalkar's talks over the previous twenty-five years.

In Golwalkar's frequent references to Ramakrishna and Vivekananda there are no distinctions drawn between their respective messages, and Ramakrishna is thoroughly implicated in Vivekananda's commitment to service. In this version, it was Ramakrishna who promoted the notion of *daridra narayana* ('destitute God') (Golwalkar, 1966: 26) and who taught 'Serve man', which Vivekananda in his turn emphasized (Golwalkar, 1966: 25). Both are said to have been in tune with the teachings of 'our forefathers' who proclaimed that 'Our People is our God' (Golwalkar, 1966: 25). The shift from 'man' to 'Our People', however, is deliberate and highly significant. Golwalkar acknowledged as much when he argued that the injunction to serve 'man' (humanity) was too wide and not easily grasped, thus leading in the past to inaction, and that hence it needed to be narrowed down (cf. Golwalkar, 1966: 386f). The 'living God' in Golwalkar's system does not refer merely to the divine within the individual but more accurately to the divine within 'Our People' or the nation.[21] According to Golwalkar (1966: 25), 'This supreme vision of Godhead in society is the very core of our concept of "nation" and has permeated our thinking and given rise to various unique concepts of our cultural heritage.'

Once 'man' (the individual) has been replaced by 'Our People' (the Hindu nation), the shape of Golwalkar's argument is very reminiscent of Vivekananda's urgings to serve the poor and oppressed. Every individual (of 'our society'), Golwalkar (1966: 25f; cf. 50) maintained, is 'sacred and worthy of our service ... as a part of that Divine Whole'. It is '... God who has taken those forms of the poor, the destitute and the suffering' and 'He comes in those forms to give us an opportunity to serve Him' (Golwalkar, 1966: 26). Material possessions, consequently, become the means by which the individual can help the less fortunate. There is a strongly ascetic tinge to Golwalkar's demand that 'only a minimum should be used for our sake', and he developed this point to argue that to take more would be 'an act of theft against society', of which the individual is but a 'trustee' (Golwalkar, 1966: 26f). On a distinctive note, Golwalkar (1966: 27) concluded that 'It is only when we become true trustees that we can serve society best. Such a pure attitude of service will leave no scope for ego or self-adulation.' Like Vivekananda (for example, *CWSV*, VIII: 23), Golwalkar (1966: 27) insisted that service and duty go hand in hand, and he was critical of the constant 'clamouring' for rights.

Remembering Golwalkar's special relationship with Swami Akhandananda, it is very telling that Golwalkar (1966: 382) chose to include under the heading of 'True Service' the following verse: 'I desire neither kingdom nor heaven nor salvation. All that I desire is to remove the sorrows and miseries of all living beings.' The source and context of this verse is not identified. It is, in fact, King Rantideva speaking in the *Srimad Bhagavatam* (9.21.12). Golwalkar's use of this verse is highly significant because Swami Akhandananda took this same verse to heart as a 'motto', having heard a form of it repeatedly on the lips of Jhandu Bhat, the Gujarati philanthropist who initially inspired Swami Akhandananda to adopt a life of service (Swami Akhandananda, 1979: 58f).[22] As this verse and its particular association does not appear more widely within the literature of the Ramakrishna movement, its appearance here is strongly indicative of Swami Akhandananda's continuing influence over Golwalkar, including the latter's philanthropic ideas. This verse is now current in later literature within the RSS (see Satyanarayana, 1989: 165).

We noted earlier that, when Golwalkar was attempting to rebuild and reorient the RSS in 1954, he spoke in terms of 'positive Hinduism'. In *Bunch of Thoughts*, his editors have arranged Golwalkar's teachings on this subject around the injunction 'Live Positive Dynamic Hinduism', a formulation close to Vivekananda's 'Dynamic Religion' (*CWSV*, VIII: 407). For both, service to others was an important characteristic of 'dynamic religion', and the non-dualist basis of Golwalkar's ethic is evident. For a Hindu, the aim in life is '... the realization of his true nature—the innate Spark of Divinity, the Reality in him ...' or '... the realization of our oneness with that Ultimate Reality' (Golwalkar, 1966: 48f). The way to this goal is through the performance of '... duty in a selfless spirit' and by offering worship and service to 'man', the objective manifestation of Reality, for '... every man is a spark of the same Reality' (Golwalkar, 1966: 50). For Golwalkar (1966: 50), as for Vivekananda, 'service to humanity is verily service to God.' The former's emphasis remains on the benefit to the Hindu nation and not on the effect of practising a *sadhana* of service upon the performer, although it is evident that for others within the RSS the offering of seva is tantamount to the practice of a fully-fledged '*saadhana* [sic] of service' (Thengadi, n.d.: 2)

Just as Golwalkar attributed the message of daridra narayana to Ramakrishna without any qualification, so too he read back into Ramakrishna's 'as many views, so many ways' a hierarchical interpretation that is closer to Vivekananda's theory of an emergent universal religion. As Basu et al. (1993: 7) point out, for Ramakrishna this principle was inclusive of Christian and Muslim insights, whereas Golwalkar (1966: 103) used this notion expressly to nag-fence what he held to be 'Hinduism' (including Sikhism) in order to show how the internal variety of Hinduism has '... helped to protect and maintain the integrity of our people' against the threats posed by Islam and Christianity. Basu et al. (1993: 7) conclude that the use made of Vivekananda by contemporary advocates of *Hindutva* thus '... represents a slightly less unfair appropriation' than Golwalkar's use of Ramakrishna. They emphasize, nevertheless, how 'utterly foreign' many of the characteristics of contemporary Hindutva would have been to Vivekananda and note his capacity for self-criticism (Basu et al., 1993: 8). RSS writers ignore the positive comments that Vivekananda frequently made about Islam, and specifically about its social cohesion (for example, *CWSV*, II: 371). On the other hand, Vivekananda's claim that the followers of the Buddha misunderstood and falsified their master's teaching by creating a community distinct from Hinduism is strongly echoed by Golwalkar (1966: 66f) who referred to 'the Buddhist sect' having 'turned a traitor to the mother society and the mother religion'.[23] The evolutionist assumptions behind Golwalkar's ideas are brought out by Venkata Rao in his Introduction to *Bunch of Thoughts* where he speaks of the goal being reached at different 'paces', 'errors' being corrected on 'the climb', and the divergence of status resulting from a divergence of qualification (Golwalkar, 1966: xxx). In this respect too, one can hear echoes of Vivekananda's position. There is an important difference, however, in that Vivekananda's theory, although both hierarchical and Hindu-centric in a way in which Ramakrishna's view was not, nevertheless propounded an *inclusive* hierarchy, unlike the Hindu-centric but *exclusive* hierarchical model of Golwalkar and the later RSS.

The tendency to draw selectively upon Vivekananda's ideas and so to push to extremes emphases and refrains that are softened within the context of Vivekananda's recorded teaching as a whole is exemplified in Eknath Ranade's compilation *Swami Vivekananda's Rousing Call to the Hindu Nation*—the centenary volume referred to previously. This extensive volume is condensed from the publications of the Ramakrishna movement (Ranade, 1963: 8). The passages are given under headings, but only infrequently with precise sources, and are often brief, evidently condensed, and brought together to illustrate the editor's themes. The publisher speaks of the '... devotional attachment and singular dedication to the ideal of "Regenerated Bharat"...' that Ranade shared with Vivekananda (Ranade, 1963: 3). The purpose of the book is said to be to

'... instil the spirit of manliness, service, and sacrifice ...' in its readers and so '... inspire them to fulfil the duty they owe to their Motherland' (Ranade, 1963: 3). There is little here of Vivekananda's search for 'liberation', while striving for the 'good of the world', and of the idealism that, many critics believe, undermined the effectiveness of his attempt to transform the material and social conditions of Indian society. Ranade (1963: 5) reminds the reader that it was Vivekananda who made '... the country aware of its life-centre which was *religion* round which alone, he emphasized, could our Hindu nation be effectively and purposefully reorganized'. But, for what purpose should the nation be reorganized? For Ranade, the immediate threat was posed by Pakistan. Vivekananda is cited as one who wanted India to have 'muscles of iron and nerves of steel', and his insistence upon the need to fulfil *dharmik* responsibility is turned to the purpose of preparing the people for war with Pakistan (Ranade, 1963: 6f).[24]

The selection made from Vivekananda's teaching is tailored accordingly to Eknath Ranade's limiting definition of Vivekananda's role and concerns. A blatant misrepresentation of Vivekananda's recorded utterances is to be found in Ranade's editing of Vivekananda's lecture, 'The Great Teachers of the World' (Ranade, 1966: 131). In this lecture, Vivekananda's target is religious intolerance, but the whole nature of his indictment of '*some* [emphasis added] Mohammedans' is transformed by Ranade's substitution of 'some' by 'the', and Ranade's omission of Vivekananda's substantial recognition of the protests raised against narrowness by 'philosophic' Muslims (*CWSV*, IV: 126). In the subsequent passage that Ranade (1966: 132) extracts, Vivekananda accuses Muslims of killing 'unbelievers'. This more lurid and less measured passage is given accurately, but even its emphasis is subtly changed by being removed from its context within an extended discussion of dualism (*CWSV*, II: 352).

CONCLUSION

It has been suggested that the guide for social and individual behaviour provided by the RSS '... should be seen as a simplified version of Swami Vivekananda's "Practical Vedanta", which propagates an ethical and social application of the *advaita vedanta*' (Hellman, 1996: 241). Referring more specifically to Hedgewar, Andersen and Damle (1987: 248) have suggested that the truth offered to those who took up his challenge was '... a secularized version of advaita vedanta' because '... it took the metaphysical position' that '... all men are basically one and applied it to

Hindu society'. Both these judgements are true up to a point. The 'simplification' of Vivekananda's Practical Vedanta, to which Hellman refers, however, entailed virtually excising Vivekananda's preoccupation with the liberation of the individual. The service of the Hindu nation and its defence from internal and external enemies becomes an end in itself. Whether the change in focus from the individual to Hindu society may be accurately described as a 'secularized' version of advaita vedanta, as Andersen and Damle suggest, is questionable, given that Hindu India itself is presented as the embodiment of the divine—a view by no means unique to the RSS but hardly a secular position.

It was suggested above that many of Hedgewar's ideas were reminiscent of Vivekananda's. In fact, some within the RSS have not stopped short of affirming explicitly that Hedgewar took his '... inspiration from the ringing words of Swami Vivekananda' (Anon., 1989: 87). It may be more accurate, however, to say that there were similarities because Vivekananda and Hedgewar shared a common cause to the extent that they were both concerned to 'rouse' Hindus in the context of colonial India, albeit at significantly different points in the movement towards independence and for different purposes. Education, discipline, organization, instilling pride in culture, and calling forth a core of educated, dedicated (celibate) workers were central to both their strategies. It is evident that Hedgewar was familiar with the work of the Ramakrishna movement and thus may indeed have consciously adopted and adapted Vivekananda's message and tactics. Yet, their concerns in this respect were sufficiently similar and their missions not so far apart in time that it is equally conceivable that Hedgewar followed the course he did because it appeared to suit his ends, and not as a result of any conscious sense of picking up where Vivekananda left off. For example, it could be argued that the performance of seva was important to both because it united the served (traditionally oppressed groups) and the servers (the elite). It is important, however, to recall that Hedgewar's promotion of seva was very different in scope, nature, and purpose from Vivekananda's ideal. Moreover, although it is true that Vivekananda's desire to rekindle Hindu pride could result in inaccurate glorifications of India's past, and that his definition of Hinduism, which attempted to 'recapture' India's Buddhist and Sikh communities, has undoubtedly appealed to those within the RSS, Vivekananda would surely have been aghast at Hedgewar's casting of India's Muslims as 'the enemy within'.

The shared desire to revitalize Hindus, with the implicit recognition that the conditions of the poor and oppressed needed amelioration, may also explain common characteristics in the attitudes of Hedgewar and

Vivekananda towards the general situation of women and low-caste groups, attitudes that continue to pervade their respective movements to this day. Unlike Hedgewar, it is clear that Vivekananda's status as *kayastha,* and thus counted at least for ritual purposes as a 'clean' *shudra* within the Hindu social hierarchy in the Bengal of his day (Mukherjee, 1970: 55), caused considerable difficulties once he adopted the status of a *sannyasin,* traditionally restricted to those of brahmin birth. A preoccupation with caste status is much in evidence in Vivekananda's letters even prior to his first visit to the West. Once committed to the promotion of seva, however, Vivekananda envisaged what he termed a 'Shudra Revolution' and rejoiced at the sight of brahmins offering seva to those of shudra status. Yet, Vivekananda stopped short of advocating the outright abolition of the caste system even while heaping fiery criticism upon the heads of privileged groups for exploiting the poor. Similarly, he was open in his admiration for the independent women he encountered in the West but laboured over the question of what role women were to have in the delivery of seva in India. Although he offered *sannyasa* to one of his Western women followers, he took a far more conservative line about the maintenance of women's traditional roles as mothers and wives in India.

For Hedgewar, as we have seen, the building of a Hindu nation could only follow from healing social divisions and, although this essay has suggested that Hedgewar's own involvement in seva activity was far more limited than popularly presented by the RSS, the organization he created has from its earliest days encouraged members from all castes. As the range of seva activities increased with the expansion of the sangh parivar, so too did the level of involvement with tribal peoples (see Beckerlegge, forthcoming 2). A popular view within the contemporary movement appears to be that the significance and practical importance of caste identity will diminish as individuals take on a more inclusive identity within the Hindu rashtra (for example, Hansen, 1999: 121f). This aspiration stands as an ideal, akin to Vivekananda's 'Shudra revolution', rather than constituting an engagement with structural factors. In much the same way, the RSS has done little to challenge traditional Hindu assumptions about women's roles, although its affiliates include those like the Rashtra Sevika Samiti, created specially for women, and some of the activities of the sangh parivar have encouraged the mass participation of women, allowing a few women to achieve prominence during populist campaigns. As in the Ramakrishna movement, male celibacy and asceticism have been closely associated with the leadership of the RSS, and to this day women continue to accept the authority of this elite, with some finding the fullest outlet for the expression of their own commitment to the ends of these movements within separate organizations ultimately under the umbrella of these male hierarchies. Both the Ramakrishna movement and the RSS have intervened to improve the conditions and status of low-caste groups and women, and many of their projects can be shown to have brought immediate benefits to specific target groups. Yet, both retain signs of being influenced by their formation in a period of Indian history when their respective founders sought to bring about certain social and cultural changes while retaining the support of higher social groups, and without pressing for reform in areas, such as the opportunities open to women, which would undoubtedly have proved divisive. As in the case of seva, we have no reason to conclude that Vivekananda's influence was a major factor in shaping Hedgewar's thinking about the place of low castes or women in the community he was attempting to build. Both were drawn to address the needs of these groups to some extent in the process of realizing their overarching goals in which seva offered to oppressed groups played a key role.

Much of the theoretical underpinning provided by Golwalkar to support the increasing commitment within the RSS to organized seva has been woven explicitly from strands running through Vivekananda's teaching. Yet, as we noted, the move to increase the offering of seva within the RSS does not appear to have been a direct cause of Golwalkar's personal attraction to either Vivekananda or the Ramakrishna movement. Instead, it stemmed from the need of the post-Independence RSS to rehabilitate itself and to consolidate its position, and from its attempts to shed or soften its image as a communal, paramilitary police-cum-defence force. Once committed to this strategy, however, Golwalkar's personal sympathy towards the Ramakrishna movement enabled him to construct a philosophy of service to suit the needs of the RSS from his reading of Ramakrishna and Vivekananda. As we noted at the start, Vivekananda's popular reputation as a dynamic defender of Hinduism, in any case, had recommended him to many within the rank and file of the RSS, and to major figures such as Eknath Ranade. Golwalkar's notion of 'Positive Hinduism' thus rested easily and naturally upon generalized acknowledgements of Vivekananda's role as 'heroic monk' and originator of a style of Hinduism marked by activism and service to others.

Just as the nature and scope of seva encouraged by Vivekananda differ from that practised within the RSS so too do notions about the key workers in the Ramakrishna movement and the RSS, although both movements evoke the ideal of the *karmayogin*. Vivekananda's use of the sannyasin as a deliverer of organized service to humanity has frequently been acknowledged as an astute retention of a powerful Hindu symbol. The ideal swayamsevak and pracharak of the RSS also hark back to this Hindu role model in their dedication, asceticism, and celibacy and, like Vivekananda's 'young lions' have tended to be well-educated. Hedgewar declared, however, that the swayamsevak, although initiated '... is not like an ochre-robed monk'. Hedgewar explained that the swayamsevak '... does not proclaim, "I make no distinction between gold and mud." He knows the difference quite well, but is not enamoured of the glitter of gold. He willingly says, "The gold is for society. I shall be content with mud" .... It is only such a worker who can render true service and also inspire the spirit of sacrifice in the people' (quoted in Deshpande and Ramaswamy, 1981: 211). It could be argued that such discrimination must underlie any consistent policy of social activism and that Hedgewar's view is actually more internally coherent at this point than Vivekananda's insistence that disinterested sannyasins provide the ideal role-models for action in the world. Hedgewar's imagery, however, is far removed from the stand that the Ramakrishna Math and Mission has taken upon Ramakrishna's repugnance at the prospect of valuing 'gold' or indeed discriminating between it and 'mud'. Hedgewar insisted that swayamsevaks offer their loyalty to the organization and not to the person of sarsangchalak, although Bhatt and Mukta (2000: 415f.) have observed that in practice 'The leaders of the RSS, especially Hedgewar and Golwalkar, are virtually deified within the RSS and its offshoot organizations, both in India and the diaspora.' Golwalkar continues to be referred to as 'Guruji' within the RSS, but the title 'guru' has not been accorded to other holders of the office of sarsangchalak. Andersen and Damle (1987: 37) nevertheless maintain that the '... guru model of authority governs the leadership principle of the RSS'. Thus, in the Ramakrishna Math, the sannyasin offers service to an organization that is the 'earthly symbol' of an enlightened teacher (Swami Tapasyananda, n.d.: 36), while, at the annual festival of Guru Dakshina, swayamsevaks offer money to their 'guru'—the *bhagva dhwaja* (the banner of Shivaji) (Andersen and Damle, 1987: 93).

The difference between the swayamsevak of the RSS and the *sevaka* of the Ramakrishna Math and Mission is brought out in the following statements from the two movements. Hedgewar declared 'A Swayamsevak is not a coolie engaged in volunteer service, but a hero sacrificing his all for the nation' (quoted in Bharatiya Swayamsevak Sangh, 1989: 19). In a history of the Sri Ramakrishna Math and Mission in Madras, the role of the sevaka is explained in these terms: 'Members of the Math ...

are not mere attendants or employees, but volunteers imbued with the spirit of Siva Seva. Not the superior air of condescendingly throwing a bit of help to a sufferer, but the regard and reverence due to a Deva ... is what animates them' (Anon., n.d.: 28).[25]

In their respective responses to the challenges facing Hindus over approximately the last hundred years, both Vivekananda and the leaders of the RSS have selectively reformulated aspects of their Hindu inheritance. The appeal by both movements to the principles of advaita vedanta for a consistent ethical framework that would foster an activist outlook is but one example of this process. Vivekananda's redefinition of the role and responsibilities of a sannyasin is another. Although commentators have rightly noted a certain tension in Vivekananda's thought between his glorification of India's Hindu tradition and his quest for a universal religion, this tension has been entirely lacking in the preoccupation of the RSS with the 'Hindu nation'—'Our People'. Thus, as we observed at the outset of this essay, while in some respects Vivekananda's contribution to the complexities of recent Hinduism resists easy categorization along the spectrum from 'universalistic/tolerant' to 'exclusivistic/fanatical', the ideologues of the RSS have ensured that the RSS is free of such tensions and inconsistencies. As a consequence, their distinctive reformulation of seva and the ideal of sevaka gave licence to the *kar sevak*s of Ayodhya. The general appeal made to Vivekananda as the 'heroic monk' within the RSS when encouraging its members to redouble their humanitarian efforts does not represent a falsification of Vivekananda's legacy, which has never been confined in India merely within the structures of the Ramakrishna Math and Mission. It is evident that more specific aspects of Vivekananda's teaching have also been absorbed into the philosophy of the RSS. It is the carefully tailored selectivity of the RSS's borrowing from Vivekananda and the narrowness of its conception of whom the swayamsevak should serve, however, that leads us to conclude that its appropriation of Vivekananda's advocacy of seva was ultimately no more legitimate than Golwalkar's use of Ramakrishna to exclude Muslims and Christians from the Hindu rashtra.

ENDNOTES

1. This chapter is a version of two closely related papers presented respectively at The International Association for the History of Religions, 18th Quinquennial Congress, University of Durban-Westville, in August 2000, and at the 16th European Conference on Modern South Asian Studies, University of Edinburgh, in September 2000. The author's attendance at the former was made

possible through a grant from the Arts Faculty Research Committee, The Open University, and at the latter through the generosity of the Spalding Trust.

2. http://hindunet.org.RSS.//www/service/.

3. This verse is very close in substance to Vivekananda's poem 'The Living God' (Vivekananda, 1989, *The Complete Works of Swami Vivekananda*, III: 169—henceforth CWSV). Even if it is a reworking or compression of that poem, it remains totally in accord with the ideas that Vivekananda expressed in 'The Living God'.

4. See, for example, CWSV, V: 46, 218; VI: 406; Swami Gambhirananda, 1983: 161ff.

5. See Beckerlegge (2000b, Ch. 2), for a discussion of treatments of Vivekananda's relationship to the blossoming independence campaign by those close to the Ramakrishna movement and by historians.

6. Golwalkar (1966: 368) freely acknowledged that the RSS had elaborated on Sister Nivedita's exhortation 'If only Hindus collectively pray daily for ten minutes in the morning and in the evening, they will become an invincible society.'

7. Sister Nivedita's relationships with other prominent followers of Vivekananda in London, in particular Henrietta Muller and Mrs Ashton Jonson, are discussed in Beckerlegge (2000b: 8).

8. For example, Swamis Gambhirananda and Ranganathananda, together with the historian, R.C. Majumadar, contributed to the volume produced by the Vivekananda Kendra to mark the inauguration of the Vivekananda Rock Memorial in 1970. See Anon. (1970), *India's Contribution to World Thought and Culture,* Madras: Vivekananda Rock Memorial Committee (Eknath Ranade, Organizing Secretary). Swami Nirvedananda and the historian, Nemai Sadhan Bose, contributed to the special issue of *Vivekananda Kendra Patrika* (Vol. 7, 1978), which was devoted to the Indian Renaissance.

Dr Lakshmi Kumari, President of the Vivekananda Kendra, played a prominent role in the All-India Devotees' Convention organized by the Ramakrishna movement as part of the centenary celebrations of the Ramakrishna Mission in 1998 (Swami Sunirmalananda, 1998: 154). The convention drew delegates from private centres that make up the Ramakrishna-Vivekananda Bhava Prachar Parishad (an association for the dissemination of the ideas of Ramakrishna and Vivekananda). These centres run by admirers of Ramakrishna and Vivekananda, although not formally affiliated to the Ramakrishna Mission, subscribe to a broad code devised by the Mission. They accordingly receive recognition as constituents of the 'Third Order' (a lay order) of the Ramakrishna movment, complementing the Ramakrishna Math and Mission, and the Sarada Math and Mission.

9. See Rashtriya Swayamsevak Sangh website under 'Library', for 'Is Parivar Fascist?', and under 'Admirers and Critics' (http://www/hindunet.org.RSS).

10. The designation 'organized seva' is explained in Beckerlegge, 1995: 396f.

11. See, for example, 'RSS: The Mission' and the statement of mission attributed to Keshav Baliram Hedgewar, the founder of RSS, in the website (http://www.RSS./org/RSS./www/mission.htm as of 17 February, 1999. This statement is repeated in other RSS publications.

12. For an account of forms of seva performed in another contemporary Hindu movement, see Warrier's discussion of the Mata Armitanandamayi Mission in this volume. Warrier notes the extent to which forms of seva frequently overlap in contemporary Hindu movements, although the concerns of the these movements and the justifications they offer for the practice of seva may differ significantly.

13. For a topical account of the Ramakrishna movement's level of involvement in service at this time, see Anon., (1912).

14. Andersen and Damle (1987: 63f., n. 85) note that some believe that Hedgewar's nomination of Golwalkar may have been fabricated by those who attended to Hedgewar just prior to his death, including Golwalkar himself.

15. The information concerning Golwalkar was provided by Swami Prabhananda in an e-mail of 20 April 1999, which has been quoted directly in this paragraph.

16. For a fuller account of the development of seva activities within the RSS, see Beckerlegge (forthcoming, 2).

17. For a full account of the life of Swami Akhandananda, see Swami Annadananda, 1993. For a critical evaluation of Swami Akhandananda's contribution to the development of service to humanity in the Ramakrishna movement, see Beckerlegge (2000a).

18. This popular understanding of the respective roles of Akhandananda and Vivekananda is challenged in Beckerlegge (2000a).

19. Iconographic representations of Ramakrishna, Vivekananda, Hedgewar, and Golwalkar are examined in Beckerlegge (forthcoming, 1).

20. Recent critical studies of the origins of the Ramakrishna Math and Mission have challenged the extent to which Ramakrishna can accurately be described as an 'activist' in terms of involvement in service to others. For a historiographical review, see Beckerlegge (2000b, Ch. 3). The extent of Vivekananda's activism and commitment to service to humanity has been reconsidered in Beckerlegge (1995).

21. On the 'Nation God', see Golwalkar (1966, Chs 7 and 8).

22. This link is explored in detail in Beckerlegge (2000a).

23. Vivekananda's definition of 'Hinduism' and in particular his judgements on Buddhism are dealt with at length in Beckerlegge (2000b, Ch. 3).

24. Warrier makes a similar point in her discussion of the Mata Amritanandamayi Mission (this volume) about the difference between movements that focus on 'external enemies' and those that focus on 'internal enemies' that impede the individual's spiritual progress.

25. See also Warrier's account (this volume) of the ideal of seva in the Mata Amritanandamayi Mission.

REFERENCES

(Swami) Akhandananda. 1979. *From Holy Wanderings to Service of God in Man* (2nd edn), Madras: Sri Ramakrishna Math.

Andersen, W.K. and S.D. Damle. 1987. *The Brotherhood in Saffron: The Rashtriya Swayamsevak Sangh and Hindu Revivalism*, Boulder and London: Westview Press.

(Swami) Annadananda. 1993. *Swami Akhandananda* (trans. from Bengali by N.C. Bhattacharya), Calcutta: Advaita Ashrama.

Anon. 1912. 'The Ramakrishna Mission', in *The Hindoo Patriot*, 14 October, pp. 2–9.

Anon. 1987. *Gram Seva 1987*, Narendrapur: Ramakrishna Mission Ashram.

Anon. 1989. 'Successful 42 Years of Sangh Work in Kenya', in Bharatiya Swayamsevak Sangh, *Amar Bharati Souvenir 1989*, Nairobi: Bharatiya Swayamsevak Sangh, East Africa.

Anon. 1997. *Seva Disha: Building an Integrated and Self-Reliant Society* [online]. Available from http://hindunet.org/hssworld/seva/sevadisha [Accessed 27 April, 1999].

Anon. (n.d.) *Sri Ramakrishna Math and Mission: A Bird's-Eye View*, Madras: Sri Ramakrishna Math.

Ashby, P. 1974. *Modern Trends in Hinduism*, New York and London: Columbia University Press.

Basu, T. et al. 1993. *Khaki Shorts and Saffron Flags: A Critique of the Hindu Right*, New Delhi: Orient Longman.

Beckerlegge, G. 1995. *A Study of Continuity within the Ramakrishna Math and Mission with Reference to the Practice of* Seva, *Service to Humanity*, unpublished Ph.D thesis, University of Lancaster.

——. 1998. 'Swami Vivekananda and *Seva*: Taking "Social Service" Seriously' in W. Radice (ed.), *Swami Vivekananda and the Modernization of Hinduism*, Delhi: Oxford University Press.

——. 2000a. 'Swami Akhandananda's *Sevavrata* (Vow of Service) and the Earliest Expression of Service to Humanity in the Ramakrishna Math and Mission', in A. Copley (ed.), *Gurus and their Followers*, Delhi: Oxford University Press.

——. 2000b. *The Ramakrishna Mission: The Making of a Modern Hindu Movement*, Delhi: Oxford University Press.

——. Forthcoming 1. 'Iconographic Representations of Renunciation and Activism in the Ramakrishna Math and Mission and the Rashtriya Swayamsevak Sangh', in *Journal of Contemporary Religion*.

——. Forthcoming 2. 'The Rashtriya Swayamsevak Sangh's "Tradition of Selfless Service"' in J. Zavos, A. Wyatt, and V. Hewitt (eds), *Deconstructing the Nation: Politics and Cultural Mobilisation in India*, New Delhi: Oxford University Press.

Bharati, A. 1970. 'The Hindu Renaissance and its Apologetic Patterns', in *Journal of Asian Studies*, Vol. 29, no. 2, pp. 267–87.

Bharatiya Swayamsevak Sangh. 1989. *Amar Bharati Souvenir 1989*, Nairobi: Bharatiya Swayamsevak Sangh, East Africa.

Bhatt, C. and P. Mukta. 2000. 'Introduction: Hindutva in the West: Mapping the Antinomies of Nationalism', *Ethnic and Racial Studies*, Vol. 23, no. 3, pp. 407–41.

Bhide, L.S. 1989. 'Working for a Better Tomorrow', in Bharatiya Swayamsevak Sangh (1989), *Amar Bharati Souvenir 1989*, Nairobi: Bharatiya Swayamsevak Sangh, East Africa, pp. 43–7.

Deshpande, B.V. and S.R. Ramaswamy. 1981. *Dr. Hedgewar, the Epoch-Maker: A Biography*, Bangalore: Sahitya Sindhu.

Datta, B.N. 1993. *Swami Vivekananda: Patriot-Prophet* (2nd rev. edn), Calcutta: Navabharat Publishers.

(Swami) Gambhirananda. 1983. *History of the Ramakrishna Math and Mission*, (3rd rev. edn), Calcutta: Advaita Ashrama.

Golwalkar, M.S. 1966. *Bunch of Thoughts* (2nd imp.), Bangalore: Vikrama Prakashan.

Goyal, D.R. 1979. *Rashtriya Swayamsevak Sangh*, New Delhi: Radha Krishna Prakashan.

Hacker, P. 1978. 'Aspects of Neo-Hinduism as Contrasted with Surviving Traditional Hinduism', in P. Hacker, *Kleine Schriften*, Wiesbaden: Franz Steiner Verlag GMBH.

Hansen, T.B. 1999. *The Saffron Wave: Democracy and Hindu Nationalism in Modern India*, Princeton: Princeton University Press.

Hellman, E. 1996. 'Dynamic Hinduism', in D. Westerlund (ed.), *Questioning the Secular State*, London: Hurst and Company.

'His Eastern and Western Disciples'. 1979. *The Life of Swami Vivekananda*, Calcutta: Advaita Ashrama.

Jaffrelot, C. 1996. *The Hindu Nationalist Movement and Indian Politics, 1925 to the 1990s*, London: Hurst and Company.

Keshava Seva Samiti (n.d.) *RSS: Service*, [on line]. Available from http://www.hindunet.org.RSS./www/service/ [Accessed 21 January, 1999].

Klostermaier, K. 1989. *A Survey of Hinduism*, Albany: State University of New York.

Malkani, K.R. 1989. 'Vasudaiva Kutumbakam: A Socio-Historical Perspective', in Bharatiya Swayamsevak Sangh. 1989. *Amar Bharati Souvenir 1989*, Nairobi: Bharatiya Swayamsevak Sangh, East Africa, pp. 109–17.

Melwani, L. 1994. 'Vivekananda Kendra' *Hinduism Today*, June, pp. 1–3, [on line]. Available from http://www.spiritweb.org/HinduismToday/94–06–Vivekananda Kendra.html [Accessed 23 April, 1999].

Mishra, P. 2002. 'How the British Invented Hinduism', in *New Statesman*, 26 August, pp. 19–21.

Mitra, S. and H. Baweja. 1998. 'RSS on ... the Rampage', *India Today International*, 28 September , pp. 12–17.

Mukherjee, S.N. 1970. 'Class, Caste, and Politics in Calcutta, 1815–38', in

E. Leach and S.N. Mukherjee (eds), *Elites in South Asia*, Cambridge: Cambridge University Press.

(Swami) Nirvedananda. 1969. 'Sri Ramakrishna and Spiritual Renaissance', in H. Bhattacharya (ed.), *The Cultural History of India*, Vol. 4, *The Religions*, Calcutta: The Ramakrishna Mission Institute of Culcutta.

(Sister) Nivedita. 1992. *Aggressive Hinduism* (6th edn), Calcutta: Udbodhan Office.

Ranade, E. 1963. *Swami Vivekananda's Rousing Call to the Hindu Nation*, Calcutta: Swastik Prakashan.

Suryanarayan, Rao, K. 2000. 'Rashtriya Swayamsevak Sangh Fulfils the Mission of Swami Vivekananda' [online]. Available from http://hindunet.org/vivekananda/gv_2000_talks/sr_rss_fulfils_viveka [Accessed 8 January 2001].

(Swami) Saradananda. 1979. *Sri Ramakrishna, The Great Master* (Swami Jagadananda trans.) (5th rev. edn), Madras: Sri Ramakrishna Math.

Satyanarayan, M.C. 1989. 'Hindu Thoughts on Service', in *Virat Hindu Sammelan Souvenir*, London: Vishva Hindu Parishad.

Seshadri, H.V. 1988. *RSS: A Vision in Action* (December reprint) [online]. Available from http//:hindunet.org/rss/www/library/books/Vision [Accessed 17 February 1999].

Sil, N.P. 1997. *Swami Vivekananda: A Reassessment*, Selinsgrove: Susaquehanna University Press and London: Associated University Press.

Sirsikar, V.M. 1988. 'My Years in the RSS', in E. Zelliot and M. Berntsen (eds), *The Experience of Hinduism*, Albany: State University of New York.

Swami Sunirmalananda 1998. 'All-India Devotees' Convention: A Report', *The Vedanta Kesari*, Vol. 85, April, pp. 149–55.

(Swami) Tapasyananda. n.d. 'For Enquirers about the Monastic Order of Sri Ramakrishna', in Anon., *Sri Ramakrishna Math and Mission: A Bird's-Eye View*, Madras: Sri Ramakrishna Math.

Thengadi, D.B. n.d. 'What Sustains Sangh?', Available from http://hindubook.org/dbthengadi/ [Accessed 17 May 1999].

(Swami) Vivekananda. 1989. *The Complete Works of Swami Vivekananda*, Calcutta: Advaita Ashrama.

'The Centre of the Religious Life of the World'*

Spiritual Universalism and Cultural Nationalism in the Work of Sri Aurobindo

Peter Heehs

Two constant themes in the thought of Sri Aurobindo are the universality of the spiritual reality or Brahman, and the special importance of one particular country, India. To say that the Brahman is 'universal' is to understate its importance in Aurobindo's system. Brahman is all that is, the source of the universe and of everything in it, but at the same time transcendent of the universe and all its forms. It would nevertheless not be incorrect to say that to Aurobindo, Brahman is 'universal' in the usual sense of the term: common to (or, the true essence of) all humans as well as all non-human nature. Given the centrality of this universal principle in Aurobindo's thought, it comes as something of a surprise to find him constantly stressing the unique value and importance of one particular geographical and cultural unit among the hundreds that exist. 'India', as he wrote in a typical passage, 'is the centre of the religious life of the world and its destined saviour through the Sanatana Dharma.'[1]

Against the charge that Aurobindo's spiritual universalism and cultural nationalism are inconsistent, it might be argued that the two belong

* The author, a member of the Sri Aurobindo Ashram Archives and Research Library, accepts full responsibility for all observations and judgements in this essay. They should not be taken as representing the views of the trustees or other members of the Sri Aurobindo Ashram.

to different and unrelated spheres. Aurobindo rarely mentioned India in his philosophical writing and referred infrequently to Brahman in his political journalism and speeches. It is possible to appreciate his philosophy without being aware of his politics, or to admire his political work without being interested in his philosophy or yoga. This line of argument fails for several reasons, however. First, Aurobindo was a systematic thinker. Although he concentrated on a single subject in each of his various works—metaphysics in *The Life Divine,* literary criticism in *The Future Poetry,* sociology in *The Human Cycle,* nationalist politics in the articles published in *Karmayogin* and *Bande Mataram*—he did not consider his treatments of these subjects to be separate from one another, but rather to form a consistent system, each part of which reinforced the rest. This is demonstrated by the fact that his references to spiritual topics in his political writings and speeches are not incidental but integral parts of his argument. His references to India in his metaphysical works are less central but by no means fortuitous.

Even if Aurobindo's thought were more compartmentalized than it actually is, it is unlikely that his political ideas would escape the scrutiny of students of philosophy. The reputations of the greatest German and Japanese philosophers of the twentieth century—Martin Heiddegger and Kitaro Nishida—suffered greatly after scholars showed that their fascist inclinations before and during World War II were consistent with the chauvinistic nationalism present in their pre-war thought. Aurobindo's position before, during and after the war was always resolutely anti-fascist, but the recent adoption and promotion of him by organizations like the Rashtriya Swayamsevak Sangh (RSS) and Vishwa Hindu Parishad (VHP), which are often characterized as fascist and communalist, have caused some critics to regard him as a perhaps unwitting progenitor of Indian fascism and communalism.[2]

In a previous essay I have shown that Aurobindo's political utterances cannot rightly be taken as encouraging or supporting communalism.[3] At worst they might be said (retrospectively) to show insufficient awareness of the gravity of the Hindu–Muslim problem and the need of finding an early solution that would satisfy both groups. During his political career (roughly 1902–10), Aurobindo believed that all Indians had to concentrate on the single goal of independence, leaving social and economic problems to be worked out after the country was free. This was a reasonable approach given the general unwillingness to accept even the possibility of independence when he began work. Whether a more energetic engagement by Indian nationalists with the Hindu–Muslim problem between 1905 and 1935 could have prevented the partition of the country in 1947 is one of those questions that historians will debate, without issue, for decades to come. In the present essay I intend to show that Aurobindo's statements about the unique importance of India, which might now appear to be chauvinistic or worse, were also products of the historical moment in which they were uttered. That they were not meant to be statements of universal truths can be seen by comparing them with the more liberal, internationalist statements he made during and after his career in politics. There remains some unresolved tension between his philosophical universalism and political particularism. This is especially apparent when writings of different periods, written for different purposes, are read side by side. Nevertheless, Aurobindo's politics do not discredit his philosophy any more than his philosophy invalidates his politics.

I take as my starting point in this investigation the sentence quoted at the end of the first paragraph above. It occurs in a statement of Aurobindo's long-term plans in a letter of 1912. His work, he explained, would have four parts, of which the first was 'to explain the Sanatana Dharma to the human intellect in all its parts, from a new standpoint'. More specifically, he said that he had to 're-explain the whole Veda and Vedanta in such a way that it will be seen how all religion rises out of it and is one everywhere. In this way it will be proved that India is the centre of the religious life of the world and its destined saviour through the Sanatana Dharma'.[4] Personal and rhetorical, these sentences were not meant for logical analysis, but it is necessary to analyse them if we want to seize Aurobindo's full meaning. The principal terms are (1) *Veda and Vedanta,* which Aurobindo had to re-explain in order to show how it (note the singular) was (2) *the source of all religions.* It thus would be established that (3) *India* (the home of Veda–Vedanta) was the centre of the world's religious life, and thus in a position to become (4) *the saviour of the world* through Veda–Vedanta, which Aurobindo identified with the *sanatana dharma* (the 'eternal religion', a term that will be dealt with at length below). Unpacking the statement further with the help of other ideas of Aurobindo's that are not explicit in the passage, we arrive at this basic paraphrase: Veda–Vedanta was the source of all 'religion', by which Aurobindo meant not 'belief-system' but 'law of being' (*dharma*). This sanatana dharma was 'one everywhere' but had a special affinity with Veda–Vedanta. India, the home of Veda–Vedanta, was thus the centre of the world's religious life and the 'destined saviour' of a world increasingly dominated by European materialism.

I propose three readings of this passage: one in which it is viewed in its biographical and historical context; a second in which it is taken to be as a statement of invariable truths; and a third in which its elements of lasting value are extracted from its early twentieth-century context.

A DISCOVERY OF INDIA

Like Jawaharlal Nehru several decades later, Aurobindo Ghose 'discovered' India as a young adult after receiving a completely European upbringing. Educated in England between the ages of seven and twenty, he knew little about the country of his birth when he returned to it in 1893. A prize-winner in Greek and Latin, he had studied Sanskrit and Bengali for only two years and was far from mastering them. When he wanted to read the Upanishads, he had to rely on the translations of Max Muller in the *Sacred Books of the East* series. This was his introduction to the Vedantic idea of *atman,* which made a great impression on him. He decided that the atman was something to be realized in life, but it was a number of years before he made a deliberate effort to arrive at this realization or even to study the Upanishads in depth.

Atman and other Vedantic concepts had been known to certain classes in the Indian subcontinent for at least 2500 years when they were 'discovered' by European orientalists at the end of the eighteenth century. The story of this discovery has often been told and I will not repeat it here.[5] I will however recall three points that are relevant to the present discussion. First, early Indologists, European and Indian, were more interested in texts (the Vedas, the Upanishads, the *Bhagavad Gita,* Manu) than in the practices of the religion they named Hinduism. From these texts they created the image of 'spiritual India' that became an important topos in the intellectual history of both continents. Finally, this image was put to both positive and negative use in the construction of Europe's idea of India. On the one hand, India was put forward as the homeland of a great spiritual philosophy that had something important to teach Europe; on the other hand, it was presented as a country whose people were too absorbed in spirituality to take any interest in the active life. The positive view led to an enthusiasm for things Indian during the early part of the nineteenth century, as well as a more lasting interest that continues to this day. The negative view resulted in a stereotyping of Indians as unworldly and incapable of self-government, and therefore in need of foreign rulers.

The texts that colonial Indologists were interested in were almost entirely those of what is now called the great tradition of Hinduism: the Vedas, the Upanishads, the Gita, etc. These texts, and their commentaries, were not generally read in India at that time. 'Concealed within the dark curtain of the Sungscrit language, and the Brahmins permitting themselves alone to interpret, or even to touch any book of the kind, the *Vedant,* although perpetually quoted, is little known to the public: and the practice of few Hindoos indeed bears the least accordance with its precepts', noted Rammohan Roy in 1816.[6] This assessment is supported by other contemporary accounts. Even the *Gita* was little read.[7] Broadly speaking, the brahmins studied logic and the *smriti*s while the literate public read the Mahabharata and the Ramayana mostly in vernacular translation.[8] It was the much-maligned orientalists, Indian as well as European, who made the Upanishads a subject of general scholarly attention. These texts formed the basis of the teachings of Rammohan Roy's Brahmo Samaj, just as, in western India, the Vedas became the basis of the teachings of Dayananda Saraswati. Although novel in their formation, these and other nineteenth-century reform cults claimed to be going back to the original sense of the early texts of 'Hinduism'.

In reaction against Rammohan's neo-Vedantic Hinduism and the neo-Vedic form of Dayananda, some orthodox Hindus formed organizations to promote traditional beliefs and practices. Some of these groups, disdaining the European word 'Hinduism', referred to themselves as *sanatana dharma sabha*s. The phrase 'sanatana dharma' means, briefly, 'invariable law' or 'eternal religion'. Although it is now popularly believed that this term was used in ancient scriptures as the indigenous name of the religion we now call Hinduism, this usage is neither ancient nor scriptural. 'Sanatana dharma' does not occur at all in true scripture *(sruti),* that is, the Vedas and the Upanishads. In the *Gita* the nearest match comes in the first *adhyaya.* Presenting his moral quandary to Krishna before the great battle, Arjuna remarks: 'With the destruction of the family the eternal family laws (*kuladharmah sanatanah*) are lost.' Elsewhere in the Mahabharata, 'sanatana dharma' occurs fairly frequently, notably in the line-ending phrase '*esha dharmah sanatanah*'. This generally must be translated as 'this is the immemorial custom', as when Savitri tells Death that she must follow her dead husband because such is the immemorial custom of the wife.[9] The same phrase occurs occasionally in the *Manusmriti* and other *dharmashastra*s. After the famous injunction that one should 'tell the truth and speak with kindness' but not 'tell the truth unkindly nor tell a lie out of kindness', Manu adds: 'This is a constant duty: "esha dharmah sanatanah".'[10] In later literature also the phrase follows statements of customary duty, as in the fifth act of Bhavabhuti's *Uttararamacharita.*[11] In none of these texts, however, does sanatana dharma signify the religious system prevailing in India taken as a whole. The term was in fact not applied to the Vedic or brahmanic or Hindu religion before the third quarter of the nineteenth century, when it was taken up by orthodox groups who felt threatened by attempts by reformers like Rammohan and Dayananda to purge Hinduism of such practices as image worship and the rite of *sati*.[12] And it was not until the beginning of the twentieth century that the term began to be applied to the modern or neo-Vedantic form of Hinduism, which presented itself as a 'universal religion'. I will demonstrate that Aurobindo's speeches and writings did much to bring about this change of significance.

After his return to India in 1893, Aurobindo found himself drawn to the culture of his native country—at a time when 'foreign-returned' Indians tended to cultivate the tastes and habits they had picked up abroad. At the same time he began to give expression to his anti-colonial political ideas, which he had arrived at during his stay in England. His first published writings in India were a critique of the rhetoric of the Indian National Congress. When he was asked by his editor to tone these articles down, he turned to the less controversial field of literature. Between 1894 and 1902 he read, translated, and wrote critical pieces about old Bengali lyric poetry, the Sanskrit epics, and the poetry and plays of Kalidasa. In some of his essays he began to develop a social and cultural criticism that had as its main components a dismissal of European 'materialism' and an endorsement of traditional Indian values.

Aurobindo's political and social ideas were strongly influenced by poets of the English Romantic movement, notably Shelley and Wordsworth, by later English critics such as Carlyle, Ruskin, and Arnold, by European political theorists such as Mazzini, and by accounts of the French, Italian, and American revolutions. In these works he encountered the idea of cultural and national freedom and of the necessity of revolution to attain it. From some of the same sources he absorbed the Romantic critique of European 'mechanism', not only in the form of physical machinery but in social and government action. He gave expression to this and other Romantic themes in his writings of this period and later.[13]

Around 1902 Aurobindo turned his attention to the Gita and Upanishads, and at the same time began reading the sayings of Sri Ramakrishna (1836–86) and the works of Swami Vivekananda (1863–1902). So many of Vivekananda's ideas recur in Aurobindo's writings and speeches that it seems likely that Aurobindo borrowed some of them directly, though the parallels may also be due to indirect influence, separate descent from a common origin, or independent origination.[14] Among ideas held in common by the two, the most relevant to the present discussion are the following: (1) Vedanta as the essence of

Hinduism; (2) the superiority of Vedantic Hinduism to other religions; (3) the essentially spiritual nature of Indian society; and (4) the capacity of Indian spirituality to transform the world.[15] These points correspond roughly to the four terms in Aurobindo's letter of 1912 cited above. All four ideas were in fact in general circulation from the beginning of the nineteenth century, and Aurobindo certainly encountered them in his reading of Indian religious innovators and Western Indologists, as well as certain European Romantic writers. But he gave the expression of each point an individual turn, most tellingly in his use of the term sanatana dharma in his expression of point (4). In the letter of 1912 and in other pre-1910 writings,[16] he made sanatana dharma the equivalent of Vedic–Vedantic Hinduism. This is dramatically different from its normal usage in the late nineteenth century, when it was understood to mean customary orthodox Hinduism *in opposition to* the Vedantic or Vedic reform cults. It would seem that it was only after Aurobindo popularized the term sanatana dharma in this sense in a speech of 1909, that it came to mean 'the religion of Vedanta'.[17] Aurobindo had in effect captured and redefined a term introduced by Hindu reactionaries half a century earlier. His redefinition of Hinduism as sanatana dharma was open and inclusive. As he wrote in an article published in 1909: 'This sanatana dharma has many scriptures, Veda, Vedanta, Gita, Upanishad, Darshana, Purana, Tantra, nor could it reject the Bible or the Koran; but its real, most authoritative scripture is in the heart in which the eternal has its dwelling.'[18] This is a far cry from the earlier use of sanatana dharma as a label for exclusive orthodox Hinduism.

Taking all these factors into consideration, one arrives at a reading of the passage from the letter of 1912 as it might have been intended by Aurobindo as a recently-retired leader of the Indian independence movement, who considered the preservation and promotion of India's spiritual culture more important than the simple replacement of a foreign administration by an indigenous one. This reading might be expressed as follows: 'It is necessary to show that the central teaching of Veda–Vedanta, that is, the universality of the Divine Principle both in and beyond the world, is the source of all religions. Since India is the repository of the eternal religion (sanatana dharma) represented by Veda–Vedanta, it is the centre of the religious life of the world as well as its destined saviour from (European) materialism and mechanism.' This set of ideas was an elaboration of lines of thought put forward and developed by earlier Indian and Western thinkers, but Aurobindo gave them a distinctive form through his own reading of the texts and (a point he often emphasized) his own spiritual experiences.[19] His privileging of

Veda–Vedanta was made possible by the rediscovery, redaction, and translation of the texts by eighteenth- and nineteenth-century orientalists of India and Europe. His idea that India was the centre of world religion was anticipated by the eighteenth- and nineteenth-century notion of 'spiritual India', and given special force by his rejection of the materialistic and mechanistic civilization of Europe and his condemnation of British colonialism. His conviction that spiritual India would be the saviour of the world followed naturally from his belief in the primacy of India and its religion, the sanatana dharma, which, in his transformation of the nineteenth-century meaning of this term, meant a non-sectarian but recognizably Indian 'eternal religion', which had the power to counteract the bad results of European materialism and colonialism. That European civilization was moving towards a self-destructive cataclysm was a persistent theme in his writings right up to the outbreak of World War I, which he took as a fulfilment of his prophecies.

'THIS GREAT AND ANCIENT NATION'

In recent years the term 'sanatana dharma' has again shifted its meaning, away from Aurobindo's inclusive Veda–Vedanta towards a more reactionary creed that defines itself chiefly in terms of opposition to 'foreign' religions like Islam and Christianity. This redefinition of sanatana dharma is part of the politicization of Hinduism that helped transform the Indian political scene during the 1990s. Aurobindo, Vivekananda, and other neo-Vedantic innovators are often invoked to give their posthumous blessings to this endeavour. The 1998 election manifesto of the Bharatiya Janata Party (BJP) begins with the following quotation from an editorial published by Aurobindo in the political journal *Bande Mataram* in 1907: 'This great and ancient nation was once the fountain of human light, the apex of human civilisation, the exemplar of human courage, the perfection of good government and settled society ...'[20] On the first page of the manifesto, the publicist explains: 'This ageless nation is the embodiment of the eternal values enshrined in the concept of "Sanatana Dharma", which, according to Maharishi Aurobindo, is synonymous with Indian nationalism.'[21]

There is no special reason why the BJP should not cite the writings of Aurobindo or other political or spiritual leaders in the presentation of its policies. Aurobindo himself conceded in 1920, after politicians began citing old statements of his in support of their views, that 'the recorded opinions of a public man are public property'; he did however ask that his statements not be distorted or applied out of context to questions they were not intended to cover.[22] The passage cited by the BJP above, as well as passages cited by other Hindutva groups referred to below, cannot be said to be distorted. They are not fully contextualized, but citations rarely are. What is worrisome about them is the possibility that they might be taken to imply Aurobindo's endorsement not of Indian cultural nationalism and anti-colonialism in general, but of the recent Hindutva programme, including the destruction of the Babri Masjid, the violent 'cultural policing' of the Bajrang Dal, the persecution of Indian Muslims and Christians, etc.

I have shown elsewhere that the wholesale appropriation of Aurobindo, Vivekananda, and other neo-Vedantins by the Hindu Right is unwarranted.[23] A group of Indian and Western historians have done the same in regard to Vivekananda.[24] It must be conceded, however, that certain things said by Aurobindo and Vivekananda lend themselves to use by Hindutva proponents because of their superficial resemblance to pronouncements by Hindutva leaders like V.D. Savarkar and M.S. Golwalkar. The passage under discussion from Aurobindo's letter of 1912 would not be immune from this treatment. A Hindutva enthusiast could read it as follows: 'Properly understood, the Vedas and Vedanta are the source of all religions. It follows that all other cultures are inferior to India's, since it alone has preserved the essential truth of the religion of the Vedas. As the homeland of Hindu culture, India is the centre of the religious and cultural life of the world. It is prevented from manifesting its pre-eminence by Pakistan and other foreign enemies, and internal enemies in league with them, all of whom conspire to prevent India from playing its destined role in the world, which is to show other nations the truth of which it alone is the guardian. When other nations have accepted this truth, along with the cultural pre-eminence of India, there will be peace everywhere.' This reading is exaggerated and would perhaps not be endorsed by responsible spokespersons of the BJP. But statements similar to those I have invented can be found in public pronouncements by extreme Hindu Right politicians (justifying indiscriminate attacks on Christians, for example), or in internet postings by non-resident Indians (glorying in India's possession of nuclear weapons), or in tea-stalls in every part of the country (calling for the use of these weapons). In this reading, the sanatana dharma or eternal religion is simply the Hindu religious tradition as contained in its scriptures and as transmitted orally by religious professionals, family members, et al. Its universality is due to the fact that all other religions are derived from it historically. As the home of all religions, India is the guru of the nations, and ought to be granted the priority to which its position entitles it.

Such a chauvinistic reading has little in common with Aurobindo's understanding of sanatana dharma and its relation to Indian nationalism so far as these can be recovered by historical and biographical criticism. To him the universality of the sanatana dharma stemmed from the universality of the spiritual experiences which were the source of the knowledge of the authors of the Vedas and Upanishads. People who practised other religions or no religion at all could have the same experiences and arrive at the same knowledge independently. The 'Hindu religion' was so called only

> because in this peninsula it grew up in the seclusion of the sea and the Himalayas, because in this sacred and ancient land it was given as a charge to the Aryan race to preserve through the ages. But it is not circumscribed by the confines of a single country, it does not belong peculiarly and for ever to a bounded part of the world. That which we call the Hindu religion is really the eternal religion, because it is the universal religion which embraces all others. If a religion is not universal, it cannot be eternal. A narrow religion, a sectarian religion, an exclusive religion can live only for a limited time and a limited purpose.[25]

It would be easy to put parts of this passage to chauvinistic use; indeed, most of it has been placed by the Vishwa Hindu Parishad on its official website.[26] But Aurobindo's meaning is clearly not chauvinistic. The 'eternal religion' was not the property of any particular country; if it was it would not be eternal. If the Hindu religion was called the 'eternal religion' (sanatana dharma) it was because it was based on the truths of the 'universal religion' that is one everywhere, and therefore not the specific property of India. Aurobindo's expression of this idea was rather roundabout, but he was after all addressing a political rally and not a philosophical convention.

'NOT AN ANGLICIZED ORIENTAL PEOPLE'

All of Aurobindo's statements on the primacy of Hinduism and India were made in a specific historical context: that of a struggle for political and cultural independence, of which he was a leader. This context is omitted when passages from Aurobindo's writings are cited by groups associated with the Hindu Right. On the first page of the website of the Bharatvani Institute, a group linked with a publisher of Hindutva tracts, occurs this sentence from a chapter of Aurobindo's *Defence of Indian Culture,* written in 1920: 'India of the ages is not dead nor has she spoken her last creative word; she lives and has still something to do for herself and the human peoples.'[27] Even as it stands, this affirmation could hardly be objected to, but it takes on a wider meaning when it is read with what follows in Aurobindo's article: 'And that which we must seek now to awake is not an anglicized oriental people, docile pupil of the West and doomed to repeat the cycle of the occident's success and failure, but still the ancient immemorial Shakti recovering her deepest self, lifting her head higher towards the supreme source of light and strength and turning to discover the complete meaning and a vaster form of her Dharma.' The second part of this sentence, however florid, shows that India's dharma as Aurobindo conceived it was not fixed in the immemorial past, but was rather in a constant process of development. The first part of the sentence is of more current interest, for it anticipates one of the central concerns of contemporary post-colonial criticism.

Over the last twenty years, scholars influenced by Foucault, Said, and others have applied themselves to the decipherment of the discourses of knowledge/power in the colonial world. Applied to India, post-colonial criticism has given its attention to the administrative, legal, geographical, and educational discourses of the British government. This has brought into historical focus something that was experienced on a day-to-day basis by Indians living under British rule: the systematic promotion of British ways of thought and action at the expense of their Indian equivalents. Aurobindo's opposition to British rule was based in part on his conviction that it was throttling forms of cultural expression that were superior to what was offered in exchange. His promotion of Indian spirituality, literature, art, polity, etc. in works like *The Defence of Indian Culture* was an attempt to counterbalance this British cultural imperialism, which was sufficiently aggressive to raise real fears that it might destroy many old and valuable cultural patterns. This aggressiveness necessitated an aggressive defence, which gives many of Aurobindo's cultural writings a rather polemical tone. It is this aggressive promotion of indigenous culture in Aurobindo's political and polemical works, rather than the more balanced assessments that occur in his later works, that is seized on by nativist spokespersons.

Nativist exaggerations of Indian cultural achievements have invited attacks by post-colonial critics, who assert that 'Hinduism', 'Indian spirituality', 'Indian painting', and so forth are 'nothing but' constructs of universalizing post-Enlightenment European and Europeanized Indian thought. There is something to be said for these analyses. The eighteenth- and nineteenth-century self-definition of Hinduism, to the degree it can be pinned down, certainly does bear the impress of the discovery of Vedic and Vedantic texts by European orientalists and the subsequent reconstruction and reformation of indigenous religion by Rammohan, Dayananda, and others. On the other hand, to assert or imply that

Hinduism itself, that is, the systems of practice and belief to which the name was applied in the early nineteenth century, is itself a modern construct is absurd. These systems have been defining and redefining themselves for the last 3500 years. To say that one moment of redefinition between 1770 and 1870 'created' Hinduism is simply false. Worse, the assertion that colonial orientalists single-handedly defined Hinduism prolongs the very sin post-colonial orientalists condemn in their predecessors: it denies to Indians the right to define their own culture and its products.

In the light of these considerations, I will reconsider the four points raised by Aurobindo in his letter of 1912. My aim will be to arrive at a reading of the passage under discussion that goes beyond its immediate historical context and avoids the misunderstandings and misapplications of Hindutva spokespersons on the one hand, and post-colonial critics on the other.

The Veda and Vedanta that Aurobindo felt commissioned to 're-explain' were, in his view, a single system of spiritual knowledge and practice aiming at active union with the Absolute. Aurobindo's 'psychological' interpretation of the Veda is controversial, and he was himself dissatisfied with his presentation of it. On the other hand, his belief that the principal teaching of the Upanishads was the knowledge of the Brahman and the way to achieve it, was far from novel. Many passages in the Upanishads put forward this aim; later it was made the central tenet of Vedanta as systematized in the Brahmasutras. Subsequent commentators, beginning with Shankara, brought out this aim in different ways. From them and their followers the idea was transmitted to nineteenth-century orientalists like Rammohan Roy and Paul Deussen. Vivekananda, Aurobindo, and other neo-Vedantists took this aim for granted, and found it confirmed experientially by their own practice of yoga. Their writings helped to establish the Vedantic reading of Hinduism that is still predominant in certain circles. This reading is summed up in the following passage from a lecture by S. Radhakrishnan: 'All sects of Hinduism attempt to interpret the Vedanta texts in accordance with their own religious views. The Vedanta is not a religion, but religion itself in its most universal and deepest significance.'[28]

This Vedantic reading of Hinduism is open to criticism. There is much in the Upanishads that has no direct relationship with Brahman-knowledge, and much in Hinduism that has no direct relationship with Vedanta. Other readings of Hinduism abound, for example those laying stress on theism, devotionalism, etc. Predominant in popular practice, these readings are increasingly apparent even in popular English-language catechisms. The only way one could demonstrate the exclusive correctness of the Vedantic interpretation of Hinduism would be to assume a timeless Vedantic essence of Hinduism—but this would be to assume what is being demonstrated. Aurobindo based his assumption of the Vedantic essence of Hinduism on his own spiritual experiences. These are, as William James might say, beyond intellectual scrutiny.[29] At the same time they cannot legitimately be used by people who have not had the same experiences as the basis of their own understanding of Hinduism. As Aurobindo himself affirmed, one can only know the truth of Brahman through individual experience. This is why, after writing the passage under discussion in the letter of 1912, he spoke of the need of establishing a system of yogic practice that would enable others to experience the Brahman on their own.

So viewed, Aurobindo's statement that his interpretation of Veda–Vedanta demonstrates that 'all religion arises out of it and is one everywhere', should be taken as meaning that his interpretation could possibly open the way to others to obtain the experience of the truths of the Upanishads. Short of that, all he could hope for would be to create a climate of understanding where Vedanta would be granted as much respect as other philosophical systems, so that those so inclined might use it to discover the truth of the Divine and the world. The religion that was 'one everywhere' could obviously not be any particular religion, based on a particular set of texts and incorporating a particular set of practices. It would have to be something that was at the core of all religions, Indian and other. This, the true sanatana dharma, could not be something exclusively Indian. The only priority that India might claim would be to have been the homeland of four religions that have living traditions of spiritual thought and practice. These traditions could make India the saviour of the world if they encouraged people to turn away from the destructive practices of nineteenth- and twentieth-century mechanism, which has brought the world to the brink of self-destruction.

When Aurobindo wrote his letter of 1912, the India whose priority he asserted was a part of the British empire. Its culture was regarded by most of the governing class as inferior in every respect to the British. In such circumstances, Aurobindo's seemingly chauvinistic linking of Truth and India was understandable. But even at this time he did not believe that India held a patent on Truth. In an essay written in 1912 or thereabouts in which he criticized the appropriation of Indian thought by the (European–American) Theosophical Society, he stated:

There is no law of Nature by which spiritual knowledge is confined to the East or must bear the stamp of an Indian manufacture before it can receive the imprimatur of the All-Wise. He has made man in his own image everywhere, in the image of the Satyam Jnanam Anantam, the divine Truth-Knowledge-Infinity, and from wheresoever true knowledge comes, it must be welcomed.[30]

Such liberal, internationalist sentiments become frequent in works like *The Ideal of Human Unity* (written 1915–18), though for many years the aggressive promotion of India and things Indian remained central to Aurobindo's writing, notably in *The Defence of Indian Culture* (1919–21). After the country had achieved independence, he had no further need of this stance. In a message of 11 August 1949, he gave a quite different turn to the thoughts expressed in his letter of 1912:

It has been customary to dwell on the division between the two sections of the human family [the East and the West] and even oppose them to one another; but, for myself I would rather be disposed to dwell on oneness and unity rather than on division and difference. East and West have the same nature, a common human destiny, the same aspiration after a greater perfection, the same seeking after something higher than itself, something towards which inwardly and even outwardly we move. There has been a tendency in some minds to dwell on the spirituality and the mysticism of the East and the materialism of the West; but the West has had no less than the East its spiritual seekings and, though not in such profusion, its saints and sages and mystics, the East has had its materialistic tendencies, its material splendours, its similar or identical dealings with life and Matter and the world in which we live.[31]

If before the end of his life Aurobindo ceased to promote exclusive cultural nationalism, there is no justification for advocates of political Hinduism to make misleading use of exclusivist statements he made while India was under colonial rule.

ENDNOTES

1. Sri Aurobindo, letter of August 1912, published in the *Supplement* to the Sri Aurobindo Birth Centenary Library, 1973, Pondicherry: Sri Aurobindo Ashram, p. 434.

2. A number of essays containing criticisms of this sort may be found on the internet. Two rather poorly argued examples are Ramasamy Muniappan, 'Aurobindo's Frauds Exposed' <http://free.freespeech.org/delhi/teling/a-h/auro_fe.html> and Shyam Rao, 'Sanskrit Literature and its Drawbacks', <http://www.dalitistan.org/books/a_sans/a_sans5.html>. More temperately and intelligently, the Marxist scholar Aijaz Ahmad wrote, in an article first published in *Frontline* (30 January–12 February 1999), that 'some of the most influential figures in the literary and cultural fields', such as Aurobindo, B.G. Tilak, and B.C. Chatterjee, 'were deeply attracted by a cultural nationalism that was distinctly revivalist in character and religiously exclusivist by implication'. He went on, however, to note: 'This is not to say that either Tilak or Aurobindo would be quite approving of what the Hindutva of our own day is and does'. The

philosopher Ken Wilbur was sufficiently disturbed by the 'unfortunate slander that has been circulating' that some of Aurobindo's writings 'have a racist overtone'; to defend him against such allegations in his foreword to A.S. Dalal's compilation and study of Aurobindo's psychological writings, *A Greater Psychology: An Introduction to Sri Aurobindo's Psychological Thought*, 2001, New York: Tarcher.

3. Peter Heehs, 1998, 'Bengali Religious Nationalism and Communalism', in *Nationalism, Terrorism, Communalism*, Delhi: Oxford University Press, pp. 96–123.

4. Sri Aurobindo, in *Supplement* to the Sri Aurobindo Birth Centenary Library, 1973, Pondicherry: Sri Aurobindo Ashram, pp. 433–4. It may be objected that a rhetorical passage in a personal letter cannot be taken as a balanced presentation of Aurobindo's project. But the letter is in fact (I speak as a biographer conversant with all his works) the best single statement of his project among his writings.

5. Good accounts of this history of the European discovery of Indian thought and religion may be found in: Richard King, 1999, *Orientalism and Religion*, London: Routledge; Ronald Inden, 1990, *Imagining India*, Oxford: Basil Blackwell; and Joscelyn Godwin, 1994, *The Theosophical Enlightenment*, Albany, NY: SUNY Press.

6. Rammohan Roy, *Translation of an Abridgement of the Vedant* (Calcutta: 1816), reproduced in Bruce C. Robertson (ed.), 1999, *The Essential Writings of Rammohan Roy*, Delhi: Oxford University Press, pp. 2–3.

7. Charles Wilkins, trans., 1785, *The Bhagavat Geeta or Dialogues of Kreeshna and Arjoon*, London: C. Nourse, p. 23; Sivanath Sastri, 1972, *A History of the Renaissance in Bengal*, Calcutta: reprint: Editions Indian, p. 42. Cf. *Sri Gitarahasyam* (n.p., 1928), which says that even in the middle of the nineteenth century, the Gita remained 'silently embedded in Vyasa's far-famed epic, or else formed the subject of grave study and Solomon reflection' by priests and pandits. Even in 1933 a columnist could write in the *Statesman* (Calcutta): 'Educated India is indeed more familiar with Arnold's translation than with the original Sanskrit, and Mr. Gandhi ... records in his autobiography that he did not know the poem at all till he read [Edwin Arnold's translation entitled] *The Song Celestial* ('A Lost World', *Statesman*, 16 August 1933).'

8. Debendranath Tagore, cited in Amiya P. Sen, 1993, *Hindu Revivalism in Bengal 1872–1905: Some Essays in Interpretation*, Delhi: Oxford University Press, p. 31; R.C. Majumdar, 1960, *Glimpses of Bengal in the Nineteenth Century*, Calcutta: Firma KLM Private Ltd., p. 11; Nemai Sadhan Bose, 1976, *Indian Awakening and Bengal*, Calcutta: Firma KLM Private Ltd., pp. 92–3.

9. *Mahabharata,* Vanaparva 297, 21, Gita Press edition, Gorakhpur. It is interesting to note that the same phrase, translated into Prakrit, occurs in the Buddhist *Dhammapada* (6), and the Jain *Acaranga Sutra* 1.4.1.

10. *Manavadharmashashtra* 4.138, translated by Wendy Doniger and Brian K. Smith, 1991, in *The Laws of Manu*, New Delhi: Penguin, p. 87.

11. Bhavabhuti [fl. 700 CE], *Uttararamacharita* 5.22. It would appear that the phrase is used here as a tag, after the manner of the Mahabharata, Manu and other smritis.

12. According to J.N. Farquhar, 1967, *Modern Religious Revival Movements in India*, Delhi: Munshiram Manoharlal, reprint, p. 187, a Sanatana Dharma Rakshini Sabha was founded in Calcutta in 1873 'to counteract modern tendencies'. See also Nemai Sadhan Bose (1976), p. 169. According to Amiya P. Sen (1993), p. 28, however, the Sanatan Dharma Rakshini Samaj was founded in Calcutta in the 1860s; thirty years earlier anti-Brahmo Dharma Sabhas had been founded in the same city. According to Bruce C. Robertson (*Raja Rammohan Roy*, 1995, Delhi: Oxford University Press, p. 165), the pandits who banded together against Rammohan Roy and his ideas, did so in the name of the sanatana dharma, 'of which they deemed themselves the guardians'. In northern India, Din Dayalu Sharma began to organize Sanatana Dharma Sabhas around 1887 (Kenneth W. Jones, 1994, *Socio-Religious Reform Movements in British India*, Cambridge: Cambridge University Press, p. 78). Farquhar (p. 316) gives the date 1895 for Din Dayalu's founding of Sanatana Dharma Sabhas in Hardwar and Delhi. For a general discussion of the changing meanings of the term 'dharma' in Indian thought, see Wilhelm Halbfass, 1988, *India and Europe*, Albany, NY: SUNY Press, Chs. 17 and 18.

13. Aurobindo would have encountered the theme of anti-mechanism in Blake, Wordsworth, and Carlyle. See Carlyle's 'Signs of the Times' for a classic presentation of anti-mechanical ideas (Thomas Carlyle, 1955, *Selected Works, Reminiscences and Letters,* ed. J. Symons, London: Hart-Davis, pp. 19–44). The theme of anti-mechanism occurs throughout Aurobindo's writings. It may be added that he believed that Gandhi's practical application of Carlylean anti-mechanism, the *charkha*, was not to be taken seriously, and was resigned to India's Industrialization.

14. Numerous references in Aurobindo's works give support to the idea that he was influenced by Vivekananda. Not only did he mention Vivekananda frequently in various writings, but on at least one occasion cited a long passage from one of his letters, an unusual practice for him. Aurobindo also acknowledged receiving spiritual help from Vivekananda, or rather from Vivekananda's spirit, at a particular point in his practice of yoga. As for indirect influence, Vivekananda came into the public eye in 1897 and remained in it till his death five years later. By the time Aurobindo began reading him, his ideas were circulating around India in many forms. In regard to common descent, the seeds of many of Vivekananda's ideas may be traced to sources anterior to him—Ramakrishna, Rammohan Roy, Bankim Chandra Chatterjee, et al. Aurobindo came under the influence of these same thinkers. But independent origination of the same idea cannot be ruled out, since both Vivekananda and Aurobindo were original thinkers.

15. I give here representative statements from the works of Vivekananda and Aurobindo dealing with these four points. The passages from Vivekananda are

from speeches he delivered just after his return from the West in 1897; those from Aurobindo from an article of 1908 and a speech of 1909.

Point I. VIVEKANANDA: 'Whatever his philosophy or sect, everyone in India has to find his authority in the Upanishads. ...Therefore, perhaps the one name in modern times which would designate every Hindu throughout the land would be "Vedantist" or "Vaidika", as you may put it; and in that sense I always use the terms "Vedantism" and "Vedanta"' (Swami Vivekananda, *Collected Works of Swami Vivekananda* [hereafter *CWSV*] [Calcutta: Advaita Ashrama, n.d.], 3: 229).

AUROBINDO: 'Something drew me to the truth of the Vedas, the truth of the Gita. the truth of the Hindu religion. I felt there must be a mighty truth ... in this religion based on Vedanta' (Sri Aurobindo, 'Uttarpara Speech' [May 1909], reprinted in *Karmayogin*, 1972, Pondicherry: Sri Aurobindo Ashram, p. 7).

Point 2. VIVEKANANDA: Ours is the true religion because it teaches that God alone is true, that this world is false and fleeting. ... Through renunciation is the way to the goal and not through enjoyment. Therefore ours is the only true religion' (Vivekananda, *CWSV* 3: 180).

AUROBINDO: 'That which we call Hinduism is really the eternal religion, because it is the universal religion which embraces all others' (Sri Aurobindo, 'Uttarpara Speech', p. 9).

Point 3. VIVEKANANDA: 'In India, religious life forms the centre, the keynote of the whole music of national life' (Vivekananda, *CWSV* 3: 220–21).

AUROBINDO: 'We are Hindus and naturally spiritual in our temperament, because the work we have to do for humanity is a work which no other nation can accomplish, the spiritualization of the race' (Sri Aurobindo, 'Spirituality and Nationalism' [28 March 1908], reprinted in *Bande Mataram*, 1972, Pondicherry: Sri Aurobindo Ashram, p. 799).

Point 4. VIVEKANANDA: 'Those that tell you that Indian thought never went outside India ... do not know the history of their own race. ... Whenever the world has required it, this perennial flood of spirituality has overflowed and deluged the world' (Vivekananda, *CWSV* 3: 222).

AUROBINDO: 'When you go forth, speak to your nation always this word, that it is for the Sanatana Dharma that they arise; it is for the world and not for themselves that they arise. ... [God] is giving them freedom for the service of the world' (Sri Aurobindo, 'Uttarpara Speech', p. 8).

16. See for example the passage cited in point 4 of the previous note.

17. The speech is question is the 'Uttarpara Speech' referred to and cited in note 15. The only use of the term 'sanatana dharma' in Vivekananda's works that approximates to Aurobindo's equation of it with Vedanta occurs in a passage where he refers to the 'one Eternal religion of the Vedas (Sanatana Dharma)' which was embodied by Sri Ramakrishna (*CWSV* 3: 183–4). (The index to Volume 4 lists another occurrence, but it is not on the page cited.) I would have to go through the literature of all the well-known and not so well-known figures of the new religious movements of colonial India to see if Aurobindo was the first one to use the term in this sense, but his Uttarpara speech, sometimes

published under the title 'Sanatana Dharma', seems to be the first well-known source.

18. Sri Aurobindo, 'The Ideal of the Karmayogin', in *Karmayogin*, 1972, p. 19.

19. Sri Aurobindo, 'Sri Aurobindo on Himself', in *Sri Aurobindo Archives and Research* 7 (1983), pp. 163–5. A critical scholar is not of course obliged to accept this claim at face value; on the other hand there is no special reason to doubt that Aurobindo had such experiences, or that they provided him with a confirmation of his interpretation of the Vedanta.

20. *BJP election manifesto '98* (on-line edition) <http://www.bjp.org/manifes/manifes.htm>; Sri Aurobindo, 'The Vanity of Reaction' (*Bande Mataram,* 7 October 1907), reproduced in the volume *Bande Mataram* (Pondicherry: 1972), p. 560.

21. *BJP election manifesto '98.*

22. Sri Aurobindo, *Supplement,* p. 498.

23. Peter Heehs, 1998, 'Bengali Religion, Nationalism, and Communalism', in *Nationalism, Terrorism, Communalism*, Delhi, pp. 68–95.

24. William Radice (ed.), 1998, *Swami Vivekananda and the Modernization of Hinduism*, Delhi.

25. Sri Aurobindo, 'Uttarpara Speech', p. 91.

26. 'Sanatana Dharma: The Hindu Dharma: Quotes' http://www.vhp.org/englishsite/a-origin_growth/sanatanadharma.htm.

27. *Bharatvani Institute* <http://www.voi.org>. In a disclaimer, the Institute explains that it takes its inspiration from authors published by the Voice of India (who provide the content of the site), although it has no formal connection with that 'New Delhi-based commercial concern'. The Voice of India is the publisher of a series of books and tracts promoting Hindutva interests.

28. S. Radhakrishnan, *The Hindu View of Life,* London: G. Allen and Unwin Ltd., 1957 (1927), p. 23.

29. I mean this in the spirit of a statement in one of James's late essays: 'One cannot criticize the vision of a mystic—one can but pass it by, or else accept it as having some amount of evidential value' (from 'A Pluralist Mystic', in *Memories and Studies* [New York: Longmans, Green, 1911]).

30. Sri Aurobindo, *Essays Divine and Human* (1997), Pondicherry: Sri Aurobindo Ashram, pp. 67–8.

31. Sri Aurobindo, *On Himself* (1972), Pondicherry: Sri Aurobindo Ashram, pp. 413–4.

Secularizing the Sacred Cow

The Relationship between Religious Reform and Hindu Nationalism

Therese O'Toole

INTRODUCTION

Many writers have drawn attention to the relationship between movements for religious reform and religious nationalism in India in the late nineteenth century.[1] Several have argued that organizations engaged in Hindu religious reform, such as the Brahmo Samaj, the Arya Samaj, and the Ramakrishna Mission facilitated the development of Hindu nationalism. Stated briefly, it is argued that such organizations made possible the imagining of a Hindu nation in a variety of ways: through the semitization of Hinduism (that is, through the creation of a conceptually unified Hindu community with common doctrinal beliefs), the reform of 'corrupting' social practices (such as child marriage or caste discrimination), and the positing of a past Hindu Golden Age with a vision of Hindu resurgence.

In this essay I want to consider how the activities and concerns of religious reformers translated into Hindu nationalist ideology. I argue that some issues and symbols were used as bridges between Hindu reformism and nationalism and that one such issue—that of cow protection—is illustrative of some of the processes involved in the linking of religious reform with Hindu nationalism. The cow protection movement was, as Peter van der Veer argues, neither a religious reform movement nor a nationalist movement. It was rather a campaign that functioned as an interface between them, and furthermore 'set a model for the communication of Hindu nationalism'.[2] It reflected the concerns of both reformers and nationalists and provided political ground for ideological formation. Both reformers and nationalists drew on the issue of cow protection to unify and mobilize Hindu society. Section two considers the place of cow protection within debates about religious reform and how these linked to the development of Hindu nationalism.

The issue of cow protection rose to prominence from the 1890s onwards and became a feature of a broader Hindu nationalist agenda throughout the 1920s and 1930s. A disturbing feature of the campaign to protect the cow was the violence directed against Muslims, such as the riots that broke out in 1893 and 1917 over cattle sacrifice for the Muslim festival of Baqr-Id. The campaign to protect the cow came to be seen as part of the general communal malaise infecting Indian politics during the struggle for independence. Nevertheless, common perceptions about communalism do not necessarily fit the cow protection movement. Section three considers the debates about communalism in this period and in subsequent scholarly work, and how these relate to the activities of the cow protection movement.

Section four examines the impact of the discourse on communalism and related debates about secularism on cow protectionists' objectives and strategies. It is argued that these shaped the ideological development of political Hinduism. Protectionists attempted to legitimize cow protection by cloaking the issue in pseudo-scientific terms—to posit the cow as an economic issue first and a religious issue second. In this respect, cow protectionists attempted to secularize the symbol of the sacred cow. The adoption of this strategy, however, served to undermine the objectives of the movement (to secure general, constitutional, and legal recognition of Hindu mores). The cow protection movement was a political failure in the sense that it failed to gather support across India (its support base was largely confined to the north); it was associated with violence; the Congress refused to incorporate cow protection within its nationalist programme; recognition of cow protection was secured within the Constitution but only in rather ambivalent terms; and, while cow slaughter is generally prohibited in India today, cow protectionists failed to secure an all-India ban on slaughter.

The essay concludes that the cow protection movement illustrates some of the problems inherent within the political impulses of Hindu religious reform during the period prior to independence.

BETWEEN RELIGIOUS REFORM AND HINDU NATIONALISM: THE IDEOLOGICAL DEVELOPMENT OF THE SACRED COW

The origins of an organized political movement to protect the cow date back as far, at least, as the 1860s with the growth of the Sikh *Kuka* movement (or *Namdhari* sect) in the Punjab.[3] The Kukas were a Sikh religious reform movement concerned with asserting the unity of the Sikh community, its separateness from the Hindus, and with resisting Hindu incursions into Sikh practice. As such, cow protection was included in a programme that highlighted the moral and religious uplift of Sikhs, and was concerned with stemming the degeneracy of Sikhism, arising in part from its assimilation with Hinduism. Throughout the 1860s the Kuka movement became increasingly violent and their activities were heavily curtailed by the colonial government. The movement itself became widely discredited by the 1870s.[4]

The issue of cow protection began to assume an organized form again in the 1880s under the auspices of the Arya Samaj, founded in 1875 by Dayananda Saraswati, and this time became associated with a programme concerned with Hindu social and religious reform. The Arya Samaj's programme was directed at revitalizing and unifying the Hindu community and in this the Arya Samaj had its antecedents with the Brahmo Samaj. Like the Brahmo Samaj, the Arya Samaj was engaged in a critique of Hindu social and religious custom, attacking practices such as child-marriage, widow-burning *(sati),* the bar on widow remarriage, caste-discrimination, and image worship. Its reforming impulse was also closely linked with the objective of unifying the Hindu community. Dayananda, for instance, argued that the disparities in belief and worship among Hindus, the corruption of priests, the development of degenerate social practices, and post-Vedic accretions had resulted in the fragmentation of Hindu society, with attendant political repercussions. He suggested:

> The causes of foreign rule in India are: mutual feud, child-marriage, marriage in which the contracting parties have no will in the selection of their life-partners, indulgence in carnal gratification, untruthfulness and other evil habits, the neglect of the study of the Veda, and other malpractices. It is only when brothers fight among themselves that an outsider poses as an arbiter.[5]

Hence Dayananda, and other religious reformers, perceived a need to unify Hinduism and Hindu society in order to resist attacks by Muslim and British invaders. Dayananda expounded many of his main ideas on religious reform in *Satyarth Prakash* (The Light of Truth), which was published in 1875. In Satyarth Prakash, and in a later pamphlet *Gokarunanidhi* (Ocean of Mercy for the Cow), written in 1881, Dayananda linked the protection of cows with his critique of Hindu society and attacks on foreign government, as well as with the utility of the cow. For example, in *Gokarunanidhi*, he asserted:

The slaughter of cow [sic] and other animals leads to the ruin of the rulers and the ruled ... for, it was during the last seven hundred years that flesh-eating foreign races who started slaughter of cow [sic] and other animals came in considerable number and inhabited India.[6]

And in *Satyarth Prakash*, he observed:

During the rule of the Aryas, no slaughter was allowed of cows or other serviceable animals. Then men and other creatures lived happily in the Aryavartta and other countries of the world. Milk, butter, oxen, and other animals were in abundance and supply of food articles was up to the mark. From the time the flesh-eating foreigners have come to India and begun slaughtering cows, etc., and the rule has passed to wine-drinking officials. the miseries of the Aryas are gradually increasing.[7]

Although Dayananda's arguments about cow protection, and his critique of Hindu practice, had an implicit political content, the Arya Samaj and Dayananda himself remained ostensibly apolitical. The vision of politics enunciated in *Satyarth Prakash* reflected a moderate, limited, paternalistic, monarchical system staffed by virtuous persons with a knowledge of the Vedas, who ruled in the interests of the common weal: but *Satyarth Prakash* did not contain a programme for political action. According to Heimsath, Dayananda had instructed his followers to avoid political involvement and had prohibited the Samaj from taking any active political role. Although Dayananda was in favour of indigenous rule, arguing that 'Foreign government cannot be perfectly beneficial even when it is free from religious bias, race-prejudice, and embued [sic] with parental justice and mercy',[8] he did not explicitly attack British rule because, Heimsath suggests, 'he recognized that an open attack on the British was not feasible, or even right, while Indians were disunited and weakened from degenerate customs.'[9] This linking of cow protection with the moral quality of government was later drawn on by the cow protection societies (*Gaurakshini Sabha*s) used as a basis for attacking both Muslim and British rule.

A main concern of Dayananda in *Satyarth Prakash* and *Gokarunanidhi* was to stress the superiority of Vedic knowledge and Aryan civilization in relation to Muslims and the British. His arguments often rested on comparing ancient Aryan achievements with those of foreign rulers. His criteria furthermore often absorbed the features or rationale of Mughal and British rule (such as in the assertion that ancient Aryans had, like the

British, cannon, guns, and science).[10] The dominance of colonialist epistemology is evident in the claims made by Dayananda and later Arya Samajists that Vedic knowledge had been based on scientific principles, as well as in the utilitarian tone of Dayananda's teachings on the cow.[11] In *Gokarunanidhi*, for example, he overlaid arguments based on Hindu religious or cultural tradition with a highly functional rationale for cow protection, urging the reader to take a pragmatic approach to the issue of cow slaughter. He argued that cow protection was a practical imperative, elaborating that the milk of one cow and her six female progeny over the course of their lives would provide sufficient food for a meal each for, at the rate of 25,740 persons per cow, a total of 1,54,440 [sic] persons.[12] Whilst other animals were also useful, and a ban on all animal slaughter was an ethical ideal, the cow's abundance and the special qualities of her milk made her particularly valuable, thus a ban on cow-slaughter was of greater significance:

> Though a she-buffalo yields more milk than a cow but her milk is not so helpful for the happiness of mankind as that of a cow, for, cow's milk is congenial to intellectual life and healthy constitution of men.[13]

A ban on slaughter furthermore, he argued, would increase the milk supply and encourage the poor away from dependence on food grains, thus keeping the prices low and decreasing the 'amount of refuse voided by the human system'; whilst the prevalence of slaughter since the arrival of the foreigners had led to a decline in agriculture and other profitable occupations, as well as an increase in the prices of cattle, milk, and milk products. The functional, economic aspects of Dayananda's defence of the cow were further developed by cow protectionists in their attempts to persuade the Congress to adopt the issue within its own nationalist agenda.

Gokarunanidhi ended with a detailed prescription for the establishment of cow protection societies (*Gokrishyadi Rakshini Sahha*s) including rules for aims, membership, meetings, subscriptions, expenditures, elections, and duties of officials. The societies were charged with bestowing 'manifold comforts on the people of the whole world and never [injuring] anybody', preaching Vedic science, providing mutual assistance among members, and purchasing, maintaining, and preserving cattle. Their constitution thus posited them as something akin to Pinjrapole societies, rather than political campaigning organizations.

During the 1880s, Dayananda toured the country lecturing on Hindu reform and establishing cow protection societies. He established his first *gaushila* (cattle sanctuary) in Rewari in 1879,[14] a cow protection society was established in Agra by 1881,[15] and another in Calcutta in 1882.[16]

Although, the Arya Samaj and the cow protection societies were officially separate, and The Ten Principles constituting the Arya Samaj made no mention of cow protection, there was significant overlapping of membership. Indeed, these movements came to be seen as virtually synonymous by contemporary observers. Commenting on religious rioting in Rohtak, Punjab, for example, the *Punjabi Akhbar* of 14 September 1889, commented:

Kine-slaughter has been practised in India ever since the Muhammadan conquest, and ... the present agitation in favour of the preservation of kine is due to the preachings of the Aryas, who go about exciting the feelings of the Hindus.[17]

The Arya Samaj's association with cow protection helped it to overcome some of the objections from traditional Hindus to its reforming agenda. The activities of Arya Samajists in the latter half of the nineteenth century had created conflict between them and orthodox Hindus, who had become increasingly hostile to the growing critique of Hinduism by the British and the Arya Samajists, and they responded by rallying around a defence of traditional Hinduism. For example, Dayananda's success in establishing the Arya Samaj in the Punjab led to the founding by orthodox Hindus of the Sanathan Dharma Rakshini Sabha (Society for the Protection of the Eternal Religion) under the leadership of Pandit Shraddha Ram, which set itself in constant opposition to the Arya Samaj.[18] In the United Provinces, the fund-raising activities of the Arya Samaj among the bathing pilgrims along the Ganges prompted Pandit Din Dayalu Sharma to found a counter-organization, the Gau Varnashrama Hitaishini Ganga Dharma Sabha (the Religious Association for the Benefit of the Cow, Social [caste] Order, and the Ganges).[19] He called for the need to protect *varnashramadharma* against the anti-casteism of the Arya Samaj, for further religious preaching and establishment of *Sanatan Dharma Sabha*s, 'and for the defence of Hinduism from critics both within the community and outside of it'.[20]

The conservatism of the Hindu orthodoxy was directed then at any innovations in Hindu practice. Indeed even within the Arya Samaj there were those who apparently pulled back from radical reform, viewing it as 'a rejection of community custom' and regarding radical reformers as 'denationalized'.[21]

Whilst many reformers also attacked legislative moves by the British to interfere in Hindu practices, preferring reform from within, they gave reform a crucial role in the unification of Hinduism. Their advocacy of the cause of cow protection helped to bridge the differences between them and orthodox Hindus. This was also true of the Hindu Mahasabha in the 1920s as it attempted to smooth over its internal differences by focusing on the issue of the cow. Freitag argues that the:

unparalleled success [of the cow protection movement] in north India can be attributed to at least two important characteristics: first its platform appealed alike to orthodox, traditionalistic, and reformist Hindus; and second, its organizational structure united urban centres and their rural surroundings.[22]

Under the auspices of the Arya Samaj, the cow became a bridging symbol in the unification of a Hindu community; it also helped to popularize the Arya Samaj's message, which was otherwise limited by its insistence on textual purity.

The issues brought to the fore by reformers contributed to a growing Hindu consciousness, and in 1908 a Hindu provincial conference was convened in the Punjab which drew on concerns of reformers and fused these with themes of Hindu unity. These themes included: 'questions of language—Sanskrit, Hindi, and Panjabi—the popularization of Hindu scriptures and literature, the celebration of Hindu festivals, the creation of a "true" Hindu history, cow protection, and the encouragement of traditional Hindu medicine.'[23]

From the 1890s, cow protection societies came to assume a more extensive organizational, and communal, form. There appears to be little comprehensive documentation of their spread, numbers, and composition. The focus of cow protection activity, as well as the violence of 1893 and 1917, seems to have been largely concentrated in the North-West Frontier Province, United Provinces and the Punjab, although sabhas were established throughout the country, and the riots of 1893 spread to Maharashtra and Bengal. The south, however, appears to have been generally untouched by the violence associated with the campaign against cow slaughter. Van der Veer attributes the success of cow protection campaigns in northern India to the predominance of brahminical theology in this region, with its particular emphasis on the cow. The eventual linking up of cow protection with the championing of Hindi and the Devanagari script (through connections with various northern provincial Hindu sabhas and later the all-India Hindu Mahasabha) is also a possible reason for the preponderance of cow protection activity in the north. Thus in these areas, cow protection cut across a variety of organizational structures, which perhaps may have associated the cow more particularly in the eyes of the south with north Indian concerns.

The campaigns of the Gaurakshini Sabhas in the 1890s to 1917 have been well documented by Pandey and Freitag.[24] Pandey, for instance, has shown the ways in which the sabhas effectively campaigned in the villages, drawing attention to, and castigating, the neglect of aged and hence economically redundant cattle. The Gaurakshini Sabhas called upon Hindus to donate funds to, or to establish, gaushilas for cattle which had reached the end of their economic life. Uneconomical cows were often abandoned and, whilst they were not actually slaughtered, Raj argues that the practice of starving redundant or surplus cows had been common among peasants.[25] Hindus were enjoined to protect the cow and to take action against the ritual and everyday slaughter of cattle by Muslims. In this way, the Gaurakshini Sabhas were involved in substantial innovation of 'good' Hindu practice and the marking out of the Hindu community from others.

In terms of social status, the composition of the Sabhas was quite diffuse, comprising Hindu princes, *zamindar*s, merchants, and middle castes. Local landowners or zamindars were also cited by official records of the late nineteenth century as patrons of the movement, as well as organizers of the disturbances, and it is suggested that they used their influence to bring their tenants and other subject castes to the cause.[26] As wealthy landowners and men of influence were held responsible for the establishment and organization of cow protection societies, priests were cited as the main disseminators of gaurakshini propaganda, and they were accused of using their pilgrimage networks to co-ordinate anti-Muslim violence.[27] Wandering *sadhu*s, or *fakir*s were frequently held responsible by official records for spreading the movement and inciting riots.[28] Freitag suggests that following official censure, leadership of the Gaurakshini Sabhas passed down from zamindars to rural-based notables to lower subordinate officials.[29] Pandey also cites the involvement of non-elite, non-land-owning groupings in the cow protection riots, and he suggests this was related to 'struggles between (and within) castes and classes that [were] divided over many different issues'.[30]

The Gaurakshini Sabhas' campaigns increasingly involved attacks on Muslims, particularly during the Muslim festival of Baqr-Id, which often involved the sacrificing of cattle. Significant rioting in the north of India was reported in 1893, with regular rioting occurring annually throughout the 1890s, 1900s and 1910s,[31] and in 1917, when serious disturbances were again recorded, particularly in Shahabad, over Muslims' right to slaughter cows versus organized Hindu cow protection campaigns. Such violence increasingly marked cow protection as a strongly anti-Muslim and often anti-British issue, as the conflict targeted the beef-eating Christians and Muslims.

There were three recurring themes associated with the cow, which helped to communicate a model of Hindu nationalism. The first of these themes was the metaphor of the sacred cow as synonymous with Hindu society and the Indian nation. Such metaphors conveyed the attempt by both reformers and nationalists to standardize and homogenize Hindu society. Thus the symbol of the cow under threat was used to portray the Hindu community under threat. Its protection was portrayed as an essential aspect of a legitimate state. Such metaphors acquired a popular resonance. Even Gandhi, who vigorously denounced the anti-Muslim and anti-British tendencies of cow protectionists,[32] spoke of the cow and India as synonymous. In a letter to one of his followers in which he commiserated on the loss of his wife and daughter, for instance, he remarked:

India is all you have, call her daughter or mother, what you will. You can get much from her and give her much. You will receive a hundred times more than you give. She is a *Kamadhuk* [sacred cow, which according to fable yielded all that one desired), but how can she yield milk if we don't so much as feed her with hay?[33]

A second theme of cow protection was resistance to the accretion of non-Hindu beliefs and practices and attacks on non-Hindus. As noted above, Dayananda had linked cow slaughter with the coming of the foreigners and the decline of the Hindus. Cow protection was also incorporated later on in anti-Muslim agitations by Arya Samajists. For example, in the Punjab, an Arya Samajist, Pandit Lekh Ram, spoke against cow-slaughter, conversion of Hindus, and Islam. In *A Treatise on Waging War, or the Foundation of Muhammedan Religion* (published in 1892), he argued: 'All educated people started looking down upon the forcible conversions and even started objecting to their very basis. Since then some naturalist Mohammedis [Muslims of Persian origin] are trying, rather than opposing falsehood and accepting truth, to prove unnecessarily and wrongly that Islam never indulged in Jihad and the people were never converted to Islam forcibly. Neither any temples were demolished nor were ever cows slaughtered in the temples.'[34] The increasingly sectarian tone of the Arya Samaj in this regard was perhaps partly motivated by the internecine struggle over the direction of the Arya Samaj which broke out after Dayananda's death in 1883.[35] The Mother Cow was also evoked in anti-Muharram slogans which accompanied Tilak's publicization of the Ganapati festival from 1893,[36] and during the Shivaji festivals of 1896 and 1897 innovated also by Tilak.[37] Anti-Muslim sentiments were particularly evident in the village campaigns of the Gaurakshini Sabhas. For example, in the run up to the 1917 riots, Gaurakshini Sabhas distributed *patia*s (snowball or chain letters) throughout the villages urging Hindus to take direct action against Muslim defilers of the mother cow, and these letters included dire warnings against those Hindus who refused to act, which often culminated in physical attacks on Muslims and their property.[38] Forms of social and physical coercion were deployed not only against Muslim cattle owners, but also against Hindus who sold cattle to Muslims. In some areas the sabhas even established their own 'courts' to try those who sold cattle to Muslims, and levied fines or meted out religious penalties to those found guilty.[39]

The cow was also incorporated into resistance to colonial interventions into Hindu practices. The colonial state, by initiating legislative reforms of Hindu practice, had prompted a backlash among orthodox and reformist Hindus. Thus, in 1892, the defence of Hinduism against British interference and the protection of the cow were made synonymous when a committee of cow protectionists and Bharat Dharma Mahamandala members met at the Hardwar Kumbha Mela. At this meeting, it was 'decided to attack with increased vigour the Muhammedan practice of kine-killing as a mark of the displeasure at the new [Consent] Act and also to prevent further interference in Hindu religious matters'.[40]

A third theme was the association of the sacred cow with Hindu patriarchy and conceptions of the female body.[41] Peter van der Veer argues that the role and understanding of gender decisively shaped perceptions of the cow, particularly in the recurring image of the cow as Gau Mata:

> Mother cow is ... only one image in a repertoire of images concerning the female body and the interplay of femininity and masculinity. However, it is a crucial image, since as a mother the cow signifies the family and the community at large. She depends on the authority and protection of the male of the family. While mother cow refers to family and nation alike, her protection refers to patriarchal authority and to the Hindu state, the rightful kingdom of Rama *(ramrajya).* It is within the logic of religious discourse that the protection of the cow becomes the foremost symbol of the Hindu nation–state. Sacrifice of the cow signified simultaneously the illegitimacy of British rule and an insult to Hindu patriarchy.[42]

Van der Veer argues that the degree to which the sanctity of the cow was affirmed was at once a judgement of the moral quality of the state, as well as a gauge of the order and stability of Hindu society. Indeed, Gandhi—ever adept at weaving symbols with popular resonance into the nationalist agenda—made precisely such kinds of figurative evocations of the mother cow:

> If we will have swaraj through self-purification, we must not make women a prey to our lust. The law of the protection of the weak applies here with peculiar force. To me the meaning of cow protection includes the protection of the chastity of our women.[43]

Nevertheless, I would disagree with van der Veer's claim that there was an *a priori* link between the sanctity of the cow and political statements about the moral character of the state. These were a function of the self-conscious linking of the sanctity of the cow with political issues. It was in these circumstances that protectionists moved from viewing cow-slaughter as an 'insult to Hindu patriarchy' to proposing it as a bargaining issue. For example, in the 1920s, protectionists offered Muslims a limited right to slaughter cows in return for a general ban on slaughter, building on a *quid pro quo* reached with the Muslim League during the Khilafat campaign.

In ideological terms, it is important to realize that the symbolic importance of the cow became increasingly complex, and should not be interpreted as merely the flag under which Hindu nationalists mobilized for their cause. The cause of the cow was in fact propagated by those who were not, ideologically speaking, Hindu nationalists (Gandhi for example). Among those who were, not all were adherents to the cause. Veer Savarkar (President of the All-India Hindu Mahasabha), for instance, dismissed as folly the campaign to protect the cow. Swami Vivekananda argued that the salvation of the Hindus lay in three Bs: 'beef, biceps, and Bhagvad-Gita'.[44]

COW PROTECTION AND COMMUNALISM

The development of Hindu political consciousness has been problematic, particularly because it has frequently been associated with violence. The political expression of Hindu identity, van der Veer notes, is generally termed 'communalism' rather than 'religious nationalism'. The term 'communalism' is not merely a neutral term meaning 'ethno-religious identification'. It connotes, as Pandey argues, something quite specific in the Indian context, such as 'sectarian strife', where it is assumed that the boundaries of the community are ready-made, rather than constructed.[45] Nevertheless, the political movement to protect the cow did not simply draw on innate support for the cow—protectionists transformed the symbol of the cow considerably to make it politically operational.[46] Once the cow had been politicized, moreover, the symbol and the demands of the movement did not assume some sort of stasis. The symbolic significance of the cow and the strategy of cow protectionists shifted over time as this section shows.

'Communal' is also often used to connote 'non-national' in two ways. Firstly, as Peter van der Veer notes, in the way that modernization theorists have counterposed 'communalism' to 'nationalism', where 'communalism' is viewed as the way traditional societies manifest 'nationalism'—based on the understanding of 'nationalism' as modern and secular. The evidence of European and anti-colonial nationalisms, however, does not generally support such a dichotomy. Secondly, as Pandey notes, 'communalism' has often been regarded as in opposition to the true nationalists—specifically the Congress. He argues that there is a recurring tendency among nationalist historiographers and commentators to characterize communalism as 'nationalism gone awry'.[47] Hence, the use of the term is very much an issue of ideological contestation. Yet, protectionists sought to redefine the nature of the symbol of the cow from a common Hindu belief to one that effectively implied a national 'invented tradition'. In other words, both 'nationalists' and 'communalists' were engaged in defining the community and the character of the state that reflected the cultural composition of that community. The following section four discusses the ways in which cow protectionists sought to overcome this marginalization by appropriating the secular terms of Congress' language of politics. Thus, to some extent, the character of the cow protection movement was shaped and informed by this discourse on communalism.

Communal politics is also frequently regarded as zero-sum game politics. The rise of tensions over the issue of cow slaughter has led many to view the Hindu campaign for cow protection and Muslim rights to cow slaughter as mutually exclusive. This however was not necessarily the case since a number of *quid pro quos* were struck or mooted even at the height of the so-called communal period. These efforts at political bargaining will be discussed in this section with regard to two issues of importance in the 1920s and 1930s: the Khilafat movement and the issue of music before mosque. Protectionists operated politically, appealing and adapting to a variety of interests. Even they did not see the taboo against cow slaughter as immutable, and were willing to accept limited slaughter to achieve certain goals.

The Khilafat movement was established in 1919 with the aim of securing international support for the defence of the residual powers of the Khalifa of Turkey, following the defeat of the Ottoman Empire by the Western allies. Support in India took the form of an all-India Khilafat Movement which aimed to exert pressure on the government by securing mass support for a campaign of non-cooperation. The Congress adopted the Khilafat cause, and under Gandhi's authority pegged it to a nationalist programme of non-cooperation. In return for Hindu support for Khilafat, Hindu leaders demanded pledges from Muslims that they would desist from cow slaughter. The Congress, however, would not openly endorse this demand, or propose that Hindu support would be contingent on such an agreement on the part of Muslims.

Calls by protectionists for an end to Muslim slaughter of cows in return for Hindu support for Khilafat were loudly condemned by Gandhi. The response by Muslims to Hindu 'concerns' about the slaughter of cows, he insisted, should be one informed by goodwill; just as Hindu support for Khilafat should be an open-hearted gesture towards their Muslim brethren. During the process of cementing Hindu support for Khilafat towards the end of 1919 he argued:

> If we are one people, if we regard one another as brothers, then Hindus, Parsis, Christians, and Jews born in India have the clear duty of helping the Muslims, their fellow country men in their suffering. That help which demands a return is mercenary and can never be a symbol of brotherhood. ... The noble traditions of the Hindus require that they help their Muslim brethren. If the Muslims feel themselves bound in honour to spare the feelings of Hindus, then, whether we help in the matter of the Khilafat or not, they may stop the slaughter of cows. I do not wish to make my help in the cause of the Khilafat conditional on anything. On the contrary, I feel that there is greater protection for cows in help given unconditionally. Only if we serve one another without laying down conditions can affection and fraternal love grow among us and the path to cow protection be cleared. I, therefore, hope that all Hindus will make the Khilafat cause their own without insisting on any conditions.[48]

However, the notion of a Khilafat–cow protection compromise appears to have emanated as much from Gandhi's negotiations with Muslim leaders as from protectionists. A letter from Gandhi to the *Bombay Chronicle* of September 1919 recounts a conversation with the Maulana Abdul Bari Saheb.[49] In it, the discussion of the terms for Hindu support for a Khilafat agitation suggests that Muslim leaders, in communication with the Congress, were preparing to offer precisely this compromise:

> 'If we do not help you and do justice to you, Hindus, I [Abdul Bari] for one cannot claim nor even take for my fellow-religionists your active help.' I [Gandhi] said, 'Surely, you do not for one moment consider that I have spoken in any spirit of bargaining. The question that is behind the thought you have now just expressed, viz., that of cow-killing, can be decided on its own merits and can await solution, for the ripening of true friendship between us and for an impartial discussion.' He immediately intervened as soon as I had finished the sentence and said, 'Please excuse me. I know you want to help, because our cause is just and because we are children of the same soil, and not because you want any *quid pro quo*. But do we not owe a duty to ourselves? Islam will fall to pieces if it ever takes and never gives. It must be faithful above all. The nobility of our creed ... requires us to be strictly just to our neighbours. Here it is a question of taking service. The Hindus will judge our faith, and rightly by our conduct towards them. That is why I say: if we take from

you, we must give to you ... .' The Maulana has been true to his word. I know ever since this conversation, he has been preaching among his followers and friends the necessity of abstention from cow-killing and today of all days, one of the most sacred of Islam, he has thought of the Hindus and sent me the following telegram:

In celebration of Hindu-Muslim unity no cow sacrifices in Firangi Mahal this Bakrid-Abdul Bari.

To which I have sent the following reply.

Delighted with your great act of renunciation. Pray accept Id Mubarak.[50]

Following this, Gandhi denounced all notions of a *quid pro quo,* and sought to prevent the airing of Khilafat and cow protection from the same platform.[51] Notes by Gandhi on the speech to Delhi Khilafat Conference of November 1919 reveal that he went to considerable exertions to prevent cow protection being discussed in tandem with Khilafat.[52] However, although Gandhi repeatedly condemned the idea of any *quid pro quo*, he continued to speak in the language of reciprocity, asserting that a gesture of goodwill on the part of Hindus over Khilafat was destined to procure a reciprocal response on the part of Muslims:

I do not know of a single instance in history of a great sacrifice by the Hindus having gone unrewarded. What was done before now was a kind of bargaining. There is no place whatever for bargaining in our dealings today.[53]

Bargaining aside, Gandhi's appeal to orthodox Hindu support for Khilafat was framed in terms of its potential benefit to the cow protection cause, and he even posited the campaigns as synonymous:

The Hindus' participation in the Khilafat is the greatest and the best movement for cow-protection. I have therefore called Khilafat our *Kamadhuk*.[54]

And again:

As soon as the Muslims realize that for their sake the Hindus are ready to lay down their lives, they will desist from cow-slaughter ... . I am associating with the Muslims only with this faith and I tell all the sadhus that, if they sacrifice their all for the sake of Khilafat, they will have done a great thing for Hinduism.[55]

Despite Gandhi's stated unwillingness to tie cow protection with the Khilafat issue, the Muslim League passed a resolution of intent that Muslims would endeavour to curtail slaughter, at its conference, held in Amritsar from 27 December 1919 to 1 January 1920 (held concurrently with the 34th AICC session). This announcement was greeted with relief by the Congress, and it was hailed as a success for the Conference:

Moslem League Conference also held at Amritsar simultaneously with the Congress passed similar resolutions on general Indian questions setting seal upon Hindu-Moslem unity by recommending Muslims to abolish cow-killing at Bakrid festival. In short Amritsar National Week witnessed complete success of Indian Nationalist principles unparalleled upheaval of public spirit among masses, and burial of religious feud.[56]

The spirit of reconciliation initiated by the League resolution, however, was limited in two ways. Firstly, although leading Muslims had signified their intent to defer to Hindu opinion, they could not guarantee that this gesture would be observed by all Muslims throughout the country. Following the resolution, a leading League member warned Gandhi about false hopes being raised regarding the prospect of complete cessation of slaughter. In reply, Gandhi admitted the limits to the step, but argued for the imperative of preventing slaughter since 'when two great communities live side by side, the religious sense of one demands a scrupulous regard for the practices of the other'. Within this logic, he went on to argue, cow slaughter was 'indefensible on moral grounds'—although slaughter for the Europeans, naturally, remained the most pressing problem.[57] Moreover, the *Englishman* of Calcutta allegedly reported in November 1922, that 'Shaukat Ali might shout at the top of his voice for the protection of the cow, but Municipalities generally could not prohibit slaughter owing to Mahomedan opposition.'[58]

Secondly, despite the League's ratification, the Congress itself did not call for prohibition on slaughter. The 1919 Amritsar Congress passed resolutions denouncing the export of milch cattle and breeding bullocks, and thanking the Muslim League for recommending the discontinuation of cow slaughter at the Baqr-Id.[59] Although protectionists welcomed the resolution from the League platform, they did not view it as a victory for prohibition on slaughter, since the Congress itself had failed to ratify the resolution.

Cow protection societies continued to lobby the Congress to pass resolutions from its own platform supporting a ban on cow slaughter. The language of protectionists was conciliatory. and stressed the economic necessity of protection, as well as the potential for the cow issue to set the seal on Hindu–Muslim unity. For example, the Cow Preservation League of Calcutta forwarded a resolution to the 37th AICC session to be held in Gaya, urging the Congress to adopt cow protection in view of the steps taken by the Khilafat and Muslim League:

While welcoming the growing unity between the Hindus and the Muslims regarding the protection of cows and while feeling thankful for the practical steps which are being taken out of deference to the Hindu sentiment by Khilafat and Mohommedan Conference in the matter of the prevention of cow-slaughter, this Congress is of opinion that in order to further cement the growing solidarity between the Hindus and Mahommedans in this behalf and in order to further the economic interests of this country, greater efforts should be made to invite the attention of the country to the unanimity of feeling entertained in this matter by the leaders of both the communities and in particular to the keenness of the religious sentiments of the Hindus.[60]

As the General Secretary of the Cow Preservation League stressed, Muslims would be conceded the freedom to perform *qurbani* at the *Baqr-Id*, so long as they accepted a general moratorium on slaughter:

We were not unaware of the likely opposition ... by our Mahommedan fellow countrymen ... . In view of the economic situation arising out of the wretched condition of cattle it may be taken for the interest of the country it may be proposed as a matter of compromise that the Moslems would have an absolutely free hand in killing cattle on the Bakr-Id day, the day of their religion but for other days they would also try and prevent slaughter as much as possible.[61]

Protectionist societies continued throughout the early 1920s, to demand the Congress acknowledgement of the issue, lobbying individual figures and demanding representation from the Congress platform.[62] These representations were largely framed within economic terms. However, political events following the collapse of the Khilafat non-cooperation campaign in 1922 began to be superseded by obliquely communal appeals, and greater intransigence on the part of Hindu and Muslim groupings.

In this period, there was considerable conflict over long-standing Muslim grievances over Hindus conducting noisy processions outside mosques, and continued Hindu demands that Muslims desist from cow slaughter.[63] So much so that in 1924 Gandhi went on a fast to allay communal violence, denouncing the killing of humans in order to save the cow. Sarkar suggests that much of this conflict was whipped up by politicians, who encouraged Hindu intransigence on certain issues for electoral purposes. For example, in Allahabad in May 1926, repeated calls by Muslims for a compromise on the music before mosque issue (requesting a mere 5–10 minute break during evening prayers) were rejected. He argues then that it was noteworthy that Hindus, neither then nor later on, offered the 'obvious' *quid pro quo* of abandoning music before mosque 'even though the latter was hardly an indispensable part of Hinduism while Baqr-Id was a central religious function'.[64] There are however a number of objections to this. Firstly, presumably as far as some sections of Hindu opinion were concerned, a *quid pro quo* had already been reached during the Khilafat non-cooperation campaign. Particularly, since in order to preserve that alliance, the Congress had been forced to gloss over the growing pan-Islamicist connotations of Khilafat as radical mullahs became increasingly politically visible. Secondly, some cow protectionists may have believed that a dispensation for slaughter at the Id exclusively was a concession far enough. Thirdly, during the Khilafat movement, some Muslim leaders, such as Wahed Hussain, Moulana Abdul Haque of Amritsar, and Hakim Ajmal Khan, proffered the commitment to abandon cow *qurbani* on the basis that cow slaughter was *not* an essential component of the Baqr-Id festival. Some theologians had apparently suggested previously that the practice of slaughtering cows at the Baqr-Id rested on a misinterpretation of '*Baqr*', which was taken to stipulate cow *(baqrat),* but in fact denoted *bakri*—goat.[65] Thus there were leading Muslims who were willing to argue that cow slaughter was not enjoined by Islam. Finally, this *quid pro quo* was in fact suggested by cow protectionists. For example, the Cow Preservation League of Calcutta proposed a resolution to the Congress in 1922 making precisely this offer:

> Kindly pass resolution that Hindus will stop music before masjids and Mohammadans will stop cow killing and will not object to legislative movements abolishing cow slaughter in municipal cantonments ... and public slaughter houses.[66]

The Congress, however, did not adopt this resolution, and did not pass any resolution on the question until 1927, under circumstances which seriously alienated communal leaders. In 1927, the Congress decided to call a Hindu–Muslim Unity Conference in Calcutta, in which the communal issue would be discussed, building upon previous attempts to forge a compromise on communal issues (such as the Unity Conference held in Delhi in 1924). However, the Conference failed to resolve issues of increasing sectarian strife, or to achieve agreement on the 'cow protection versus music before mosque' question. The Congress did pass a resolution framing a proposal that both sides would seek not to antagonize the other, without curtailing the rights of either to continue slaughter or processions:

> Whereas no community in India should impose or seek to impose its religious obligations or religious views upon any other community, but free profession and practice of religion should, subject to public order and morality be guaranteed to every community and every person, Hindus are at liberty to take processions and play music before mosques at any time for religious and social purposes, but there should be no stoppage nor special demonstration in front of the mosque nor shall songs or music played in front of such mosques be such as is calculated to cause annoyance, special disturbance, or offence to worshippers in the mosques. Mussalmans shall be at liberty to sacrifice or slaughter cows in exercise of their rights in any town or village in any place not being a thoroughfare nor one in the vicinity of a temple nor one exposed to the gaze of Hindus. Cows should not be led in procession or in demonstration for sacrifice or slaughter.[67]

The response to this resolution on the part of protectionist groups was round condemnation, and following this a barrage of telegrams was sent to the Congress Committee vilifying the resolution. Protectionists claimed the resolution jeopardized Hindu–Muslim unity and disregarded Hindu sentiment. For example (the telegrams tended to be identically worded):

RESOLUTION PASSED BY CALCUTTA CONGRESS WORKING COMMITTEE REGARDING COW KORBANI HAS CAUSED WIDESPREAD ALARM AND PAIN AMONG HINDUS SUCH RESOLUTIONS ON RELIGIOUS QUESTIONS HURTING FEELINGS OF GENERAL HINDU PUBLIC WILL PROMOTE DISUNITY AND ALIENATE LARGE SECTIONS OF PEOPLE FROM CONGRESS IN NATIONAL INTEREST EARNESTLY REQUEST YOU TO EXERT YOURSELF AND SEE THAT IT IS EITHER NOT TAKEN UP BY CONGRESS OR RESCINDED.[68]

The Congress conceded that the impact of the Unity Conference was likely to be limited at first, that further negotiations were required, and that the compromise resolution had received adverse criticism in some quarters. With regard to the question of representation at the conference, it was observed that 'some of the leaders were obliged to be absent from the Conference and from the All India Congress Committee.'[69] The All-India Hindu Mahasabha complained bitterly, however, that the Congress had manoeuvred Hindu opinion out of the Conference by calling it at 'unreasonably short notice and without consulting the Hindu leaders of the other provinces'.[70]

Unsurprisingly, the Congress' ambiguity on the matter neither appeased protectionists, nor did it reassure Muslims of Congress' secular intentions—indeed suspicions of a clandestine pact were raised in some quarters. Attempts during the 1930s to win over Muslim opinion (through calls for the League to immerse itself in the Congress and for the Congress to launch a 'Muslim mass contact campaign'—or 'Muslim massacre campaign' as some sections of the Muslim press renamed it) were beleaguered by such non-committal stances.[71] These attempts were also compromised by the activities of some Congress men at the local level in campaigning for Hindu issues (membership of the Mahasabha was only ruled as a disqualification for Congress membership in December 1938). Cow protectionists continued to campaign to have a ban on slaughter underpinned by legislation. In the deliberations leading up to the framing of the constitution there was continuing pressure by protectionists to enshrine the sanctity of the cow in the founding document of the new republic. This was met with resistance by the Congress leadership, which put it at odds with some of its own membership.

COW PROTECTION AND SECULARISM

In the process of nationalizing the sacred cow, the symbolic value of the cow underwent a shift. Both colonialist and nationalist discourses exerted a secularizing pressure on cow protectionists, and they increasingly cast their arguments within secular terms. The formulations of the cow by protectionists shifted as the movement struggled to gain recognition of the issue at a national level, through the organs of the Indian National Congress, and within the Constitution. As part of these efforts, there were ongoing attempts to emphasize the role of the cow in terms of its importance to the Indian nation, rather than merely as an expression of Hindu sentiment. These formulations tended to weave around three themes. The first centred on the long-standing assertion of the economic utility of the cow and the decisive role that the standard of India's cattle played for the general prosperity of the country (as enunciated by Dayananda Saraswati). The second theme related these economic concerns to the question of Indian national pride. The third theme drew out the potential of the issue of the cow for cementing harmonious relations between Hindus and Muslims. Common to all of these was the stress laid upon the cow as a nationalist issue *complementing* the secular agenda of the Congress.

Firstly, in economic terms, the asserted deterioration in the numbers and quality of India's cattle was posited as a root cause of a variety of social and economic ills, from the 'abnormal alarming increase in infant mortality' to tubercular diseases.[72] The insufficient numbers of cattle were also linked to declining agricultural output, as cattle were either too few or too weak for ploughing purposes and produced insufficient quantities of dung for fertilization. The indiscriminate slaughter of working cattle and lactating cows, the export of cattle,[73] milk, butter, *ghee* and meat, protectionists argued, meant that India's cattle wealth continued to atrophy. Such arguments were similar to the conclusions drawn by government advisors and cattle husbandry specialists. Colonial governmental reports on the state of India's cattle continually stressed low output and poor quality but suggested decreasing the numbers of cattle as a solution to these problems (usually without explicitly mentioning culling or slaughter).[74]

Secondly, it was alleged that the wasting away of India's cattle wealth and decline in the availability of cattle products seriously detracted from Indian national pride. As one protectionist claimed—in terms very similar to those elaborated by Dayananda in *Satyarth Prakash*:

> Everybody is familiar with the ancient glory of the Indians, their great thinking power which enabled them to enunciate with great accuracy high scientific and astronomical truths which, in the present day, are established only with the aid of numerous physical and chemical instruments. It must be admitted that the marvellous brain power of ancient people was in a large part due to the abundant quantity of

milk, which, by itself is a food that supplies all wants of the human system. It would be an evil day for the nation if such a food has to be withdrawn from the dietary [sic] of the people. Yet it is precisely this danger with which we are confronted today.[75]

Thus in order to restore India to its former status, and make it a nation in the 'true sense' of the word nation, immediate steps were needed to curtail slaughter and export.[76]

Thirdly, and often related to this, was the argument that the cow potentially embodied a unity issue, in that the recognition by Muslims of the economic and national importance of the cow would contribute to the sealing of harmonious relations between India's two great communities. Much of the lobbying attempts by Cow Protection Societies stressed this, perhaps assuming the argument made by Gandhi (and hence the moral authority) that India's great cultural heritage rested on the ability of Indian culture to embrace diversity. Thus Muslim acceptance of a taboo against cow slaughter would represent an exemplar of a peculiarly Indian approach to resolving internal differences.[77]

Protectionists sustained these arguments, and pressure on the Congress, during the Constituent Assembly debates, when they argued for the inclusion of cow protection within the Constitution. This proposal met with resistance from key Congress figures, including Nehru and Ambedkar, but they were unable to jettison it completely. A watered-down version of the principle eventually became Article 48 of the Directive Principles of State Policy, entitled 'Organization of agriculture and animal husbandry':

The State shall endeavour to organize agriculture and animal husbandry on modern and scientific lines and shall, in particular, take steps for preserving and improving the breeds, and prohibiting the slaughter of cows and calves and other milch and draught cattle.[78]

This was a highly ambivalent clause, and left the principle of cow protection open to compromise and conflicting interpretations. For example, the article specified, as a statement of intent, the preservation of useful cattle (young, milch, and draught) rather than a blanket ban, and did so by emphasizing the role of cattle in terms of animal husbandry. Its inclusion within the Directive Principles meant that a ban on slaughter was a non-justiciable objective. Consequently, it deferred the decision to criminalize cow slaughter to the States rather than the Union government.[79] This resulted in certain legal difficulties following its acceptance in the Constitution, since in some cases Article 48 was interpreted by the courts as insufficient to empower municipal governments to close slaughter houses, but was permitted in others.[80] It also clashed with other constitutional principles such as the right to pursue one's livelihood.[81]

Thus State bans on cow slaughter tended to be patchy,[82] contested, and unclear.

CONCLUSION

The symbol of the sacred cow, it has been argued here, underwent considerable reformulation at the hands of protectionists. In the period from the late nineteenth century to Independence, cow protection was associated with movements for Hindu reform, and the symbol of the cow came to be used emblematically in the assertion of Hindu nationalism. Such formulations often clashed with the ideals of the Congress' brand of secular, liberal nationalism, yet they also sometimes merged as the symbol of the cow was championed—or appropriated—in varying idioms, both sacred and secular. These complex formulations, however, were subject to a mass of inner tensions and contradictions. Perhaps nothing testifies more to the complexity of the cow as a Hindu nationalist symbol than the ambivalent status accorded to it in the Constitution of 1950.

Although the cow recurs as a symbol of Hindu identity, it is not a prominent feature of Hindu political consciousness. It is problematic for several reasons. Firstly, its association with north India (particularly the links between cow protection and the campaign for Hindi and Devanagari) undermined its potential as a pan-Indian national symbol post-Independence. Secondly, the tendency of protectionists to posit the cow as an economic issue first and cultural issue second (although always a religious issue), robbed it of its symbolic power, The tendency of cow protectionists to frame arguments against cow slaughter in economic terms meant that the religious, cultural, and symbolic value of the cow was severely downgraded. The sacred cow symbol became awkwardly embedded into a developmentalist debate, which tended to lean towards cow slaughter rather than protection. Thirdly, the partial constitutional concession to protectionists (with the inclusion of Article 48) placed the struggle to protect the cow on a regional rather than union level. Thus the campaigns became *ad hoc* and regional in character, undermining their nationalist significance. The Nehruvian state was therefore successful to a large extent in marginalizing the cow as a Hindu symbol, if less so in promoting a coherent secularism. Finally, the advocacy of the symbol of Lord Ram as a nationalist symbol, and exemplar of state tradition (through the evocation of Ram Rajya) superseded the rural bias, and the economically ambivalent nature of the cow as a Hindu nationalist symbol.

ENDNOTES

1. See Peter van der Veer. 1994. *Religious Nationalism: Hindus and Muslims in India*, Berkeley: University of California Press; Kenneth Jones, 1976, *Arya Dharma: Hindu Consciousness in 19th Century Punjab*, Berkeley: University of California Press.

2. Van der Veer, ibid., p. 66.

3. Kenneth W. Jones, 1989, Socio-*Religious Reform Movements in British India*, Cambridge: Cambridge University Press, pp. 90–4; and John R. McLane. 1977. *Indian Nationalism and the Early Congress*, Princeton, New Jersey: Princeton University Press, p. 281.

4. For a detailed and interesting study of cow symbolism in Kuka politics see Harjot Oberoi, 1992, 'Brotherhood of the Pure: The Poetics and Politics of Cultural Transgression', in *Modern Asian Studies*, 26, 1, pp. 157–97.

5. Charles Heimsath, 1964, *Indian Nationalism and Hindu Social Reform*, Princeton, New Jersey: Princeton University Press, cited p. 128.

6. *Gokarunanidhi: Ocean of Mercy for the Cow*, translated by Rai Bahadur Ratan Lal, 1996, published by Sarvadeshik Arya Pratinidhi Sabha, Delhi: p. 19. I am grateful to Harald Fischer-Tiné for his comments on an earlier draft of this essay and for making the pamphlet *Gokarunanidhi* available to me.

7. *Satyartha Prakasha: The Light of Truth*, translated by Ganga Prasad Upadhyaya, 1960, Allahabad: Kala Press, Chapter 10, part 18, pp. 377–8.

8. *Satyartha Prakasha*, op. cit., p. 318.

9. Heimsath, op. cit., p. 128.

10. *Satyartha Prakasha*, op. cit., p. 389.

11. The influence of colonialist epistemology on nineteenth and twentieth century Indian political thought has been thoroughly discussed by Partha Chatterjee, 1986, *Nationalist Thought and the Colonial World: A Derivative Discourse?*, London: Zed Books; Gyan Pandey, 1992, *The Construction of Communalism in Colonial North India*, Delhi: Oxford University Press; and Van der Veer, op. cit.

12. *Gokarunanidhi*, op. cit., p. 13.

13. Ibid., p. 12. The suggestion that cow's milk had particular benefits for intellectual capacity was later drawn on by a cow protectionist, petitioning the Congress in 1922, see endnote 76.

14. K.C. Yadav (ed.), 1978, *Autobiography of Dayanand Saraswati*, Delhi: Manohar, p. 104. Anthony Parel also states that there was an Arya Cow Protection Society in Delhi in 1879, 'The Political Symbolism of the Cow in India', *Journal of Commonwealth Political Studies*, 1969, Vol. 7, fn. 13.

15. *Autobiography*, op. cit., page 69, from extract of letter from Dayananda to Mulraj, Agra, 12 January 1881.

16. Peter Robb, 'The Challenge of Gau Mata: British Policy and Religious Change in India, 1880–1916', *Modern Asian Studies*, 1986, Vol. 20, no. 2, p. 293.

17. Cited by Kenneth W. Jones, 1976, op. cit., pp. 152–3.

18. Ibid., Chapter 2 passim.

19. Kenneth W. Jones, op. cit., 1989, p. 78.

20. Ibid., p. 79.

21. Jones, op. cit., 1976, p. 271.

22. Sandria B. Freitag, 'Sacred Symbol as Mobilizing Ideology: The North Indiana Search for a "Hindu" Community', in *Comparative Studies in Society and History,* 1980, 22, 4, p. 606.

23. Jones, op. cit., 1976, p. 289.

24. Gyan Pandey, 'Rallying Round the Cow: Sectarian Strife in the Bhojpuri Region, c. 1888–1917', *Subaltern Studies II*, 1913 Ranajit Guha (ed.), Delhi: Oxford University Press, Freitag, op. cit.

25. K.N. Raj, 'India's Sacred Cattle: Theories and Empirical Findings', in *Economic and Political Weekly*, March 27, 1971. pp. 717–22.

26. Pandey. 1983, op. cit., pp. 100–1.

27. McLane, op. cit., p. 300.

28. Ibid., p. 301.

29. Freitag, op. cit., pp. 619–20.

30. Pandey. 1983, op. cit., pp. 64–5.

31. See Public and Judicial Department Records, Annual Files, L/PJ/7/132. 'Information about communal riots during last 10–15 years', Oriental and India Office Library.

32. *The Collected Works of M.K. Gandhi*, Ministry of information and Broadcasting, Publications Division, Delhi (henceforth *CW*), Vol. 14. 1917–18, 'Speech on Cow Protection, Bettiah', pp. 2–4, in which he argued: 'These days cow protection has come to mean only two things: first, to save cows from the hands of our Muslim brethren on occasions like the Baq-r-Id and, secondly, to put up gaushalas for decrepit cows. We do not go the right way to work for protecting the cows against our Muslim brethren. ... Those who want to stop others from sinning must be free from sin themselves. Hindu society has been inflicting terrible cruelty on the cow and her progeny. The present condition of our cows is a direct proof of this. My heart bleeds when I see thousands of bullocks with no blood and flesh on them, ... I shudder when I see all this and ask myself how we can say anything to our Muslim friends so long as we do not refrain from such terrible violence?'

33. Ibid., p. 1.

34. Cited in Jones, op. cit., 1976, p. 150.

35. For a fuller discussion of the increasing communal tendencies of the Arya Samaj, see Harald Fischcr-Tiné, 'Kindly Elders of the Hindu Biradiri: The Arya Samaj's Struggle for Influence and its Effect on Hindu-Muslim Relations, 1880–1925', in Antony Copley (ed.) 2000, *Gurus and their Followers: New Religious Reform Movements in Colonial India*, Delhi: Oxford University Press.

36. The condemnation by Hindu revivalists of Muharram represented simultaneous efforts to promote the Ganapati festival while denouncing Hindu participation in the Muslim festival of Muharram, which included sentiments expressed

in song, such as 'What boon has Allah conferred upon you/That you have become Mussalmans today? Do not be friendly to a religion which is alien .... The cow is our mother, do not forget her,' cited in Sumit Sarkar, 1989, *Modern India 1885–1947*, Hampshire: Macmillan, p. 60; and also in G.R. Thursby, 1975, *Hindu–Muslim Relations in British India: A Study of Controversy, Conflict, and Communal Movements in North India 1923–8*, Leiden: E.J. Brill, p. 89.

37. See Parel, op. cit., endnote 36, for the text of a song evoking the symbol of the cow during the Shivaji festival.

38. A selection of these patia letters has been translated by Pandey, op. cit. (1992). One of these declares: 'This patia comes from the world of the cow. It brings an entreaty to brother Hindus. The religion of the cow is being destroyed. What crime has she committed that she should be killed by non-believers ...', p. 262.

39. McLane, op. cit., p. 313; Freitag, op. cit.

40. McLane, op. cit., p. 299. The Age of Consent Bill was passed in 1891, setting the legal age of marriage at twelve in an effort to stamp out child marriage, which was common amongst Hindus.

41. Charu Gupta argues that such female imagery was evident in the formation of other national icons, see 'The Icon of Mother in Late Colonial North India: "Bharat Mata", "Matri Bhasha" and "Gau Mata"', in *Economic and Political Weekly* (24 November 2001).

42. Van der Veer, op. cit., p. 90.

43. *CW*, Vol. 19, 1920–1, pp. 574–5.

44. Cited in Ashis Nandy, 1983, *The Intimate Enemy: Loss and Recovery of Self under Colonialism*, Delhi: Oxford University Press, p. 47. For an interesting discussion of the links between physical prowess and Hindu nationalism (as well as the relationship between akharas and gaushilas), see Joseph S. Alter, 'Somatic Nationalism: Indian Wrestling and Militant Hinduism', in *Modern Asian Studies*, (1994), 28, 3, pp. 557–88.

45. Pandey, op. cit., 1992, ch. 1.

46. See Pandey, op. cit., 1983.

47. Pandey, op. cit., 1992, p. 14.

48. *CW*, Vol. 16, 1919–20, pp. 319–20, from 'Punjab Letter', about 1 December 1919.

49. Abdul Bari, a leading Muslim theologian of the Firangi Mahal ulama group in Lucknow, had developed close ties with Gandhi during the campaigns of 1919, coming out in favour of the anti-Rowlatt *satyagraha* after meeting with Gandhi in mid-March of that year.

50. *CW*, Vol. 16, pp. 90–1, from 'Letter to the Press', 16 September 1919.

51. *CW*, Vol. 16, 'Punjab Letter', 1919–20, pp. 319–20.

52. Gandhi commented, 'My ideas on both [the Punjab Wrong and cow protection] had already been formed. If I allowed the issue of cow protection to be discussed, the cause would be harmed'. *CW*, Vol. 16, op. cit., p. 319.

53. *CW*, Vol. 19, pp. 304–5.

54. *CW*, Vol. 20, p. 192.

55. *CW*, Vol. 19, p. 254, from 'Speech at Public Meeting, Vadtal', 6 December 1921.

56. Incas-Rand Communication, London to Congress Reception Committee, Amritsar, 2 January 1920, *All-India Congress Committee Files* (Jawaharlal Nehru Memorial Museum and Library) (henceforth *AICC*), 1/1919, part I, p. 265.

57. *CW*, Vol. 16, pp. 508–9, from 'Letter to Asaf Ali', dated 25 January 1920.

58. *AICC*, 12/1922, p. 21, letter from Cow Preservation League to Hakim Ajmal Khan.

59. B. Pattabhi Sitaramayya. 1969, *History of the Indian National Congress: Volume 1 (1885–1935)*, Delhi: S. Chand & Co., p. 181.

60. *AICC*, 12/1922, p. 39, letter to Hakim Ajmal Khan from Cow Preservation League, Calcutta, dated 20 December 1922.

61. Ibid., pp. 35–41.

62. *AICC*, 12/1922, pp. 29–31.

63. Sarkar, op. cit., p. 233. For an account of the riots which occurred in Delhi over cow slaughter in 1924, see Thursby, op. cit., pp. 82–8.

64. Sarkar, op. cit., p. 196.

65. See McLane, op. cit., p. 279, footnote. Moreover, many have argued that the choice of cow for slaughter at the Id festival had been driven primarily by economic considerations, given that the cost of a cow relative to that of a camel, buffalo, goat or sheep was considerably lower. See, for example, Thursby, op. cit., p. 76.

66. *AICC*, 12/1922, p. 67, from telegraph of 27 December 1922 to Motilal Nehru from Cow Preservation League.

67. See *India in 1927–8*, 1928, J. Coatman (Director of Public Information, Government of India), Calcutta: Central Publication Branch, pp. 20–1.

68. Telegram to Chairman, Congress Reception Committee from All India Marwari Agarwala Panchayet [sic], 22 December 1927: *AICC*. G64/1926, p. 101 Other organizations sending similar protests by telegram included: the Cow Protection Society, the Sanatan Dharma Mandal, the Cow Preservation League, the Pinjrapole Society, the Arya Samaj, the All-India Hindu Mahasabha and local Hindu sabhas from Salkea, Aurangabad, Saharanpur, Patna, Najibabad, Bombay Presidency, Kushtia, Pabna, Gorakhpur, Nowgong (Assam), Darjeeling, Chittagong, Rajshahi district, Dacca, Kheri, Kanth, and Mokameh; the Marwari Chamber of Commerce, Marwari Association, Calcutta; Sanatan Dharma Sabhas from Agarwal, Monghyr (and Gaurakshini Sabha), and the Chuva Sevasamiti.

69. AICC Secretaries' Report of the work done during the year 1927: *AICC*, G60/G63/1927, p. 63.

70. See copy of the Resolution no. IV passed by All-India Hindu Mahasabha Committee: *AICC*, G64/1926, pp. 37–9.

71. *AICC*, B9/1938, p. 133.

72. Professor Shibban Lal Saxena, *Constituent Assembly Debates*, 7/12: Wednesday, 24 November 1948. *AICC*, 12/1922, pp. 35–41.

73. *AICC*, 1/1919 pt. II, p. 519, Resolution proposed to the Congress by Govindji Sheth and seconded by Neki Ram Sharma (no. xviii) on *Exportation of Milch Cows*: 'This Congress is of the opinion that, in view of the serious economic danger to the country caused by the exportation to foreign country [sic] of milch cows and breeding bullocks, the government should take immediate steps to prohibit such exportation.'

74. For example, *Animal Husbandry and Dairying*, February 1948, National Planning Committee Series, Bombay: Vora & Co. Publishers Ltd., pp. 17–23; *Report of the Royal Commission on Agriculture in India*, June 1928, HMSO, India, pp. 20–4.

75. *AICC*, 12/1922, pp. 5–11, letter from General Secretary, Cow Preservation League to Motilal Nehru, dated 19 November 1922.

76. *AICC*, 1/1999, part II, pp. 431–2.

77. Or as Ainslie Embree and Van der Veer (op. cit.) might argue, subsuming difference within a dominant Hindu world-view. See Embree, 1989, *Imagining India: Essays on Indian History*, Mark Juergensmeyer (ed.), Delhi: Oxford University Press.

78. A.R. Malhotra, 1951, *The Constitution of India*, Delhi: Indian University Publishers, pp. 162–3.

79. This was reinforced by Article 246, List II, 7th Schedule, provisions 15 and 16, which made the 'preservation, protection, and improvement of stock' and cattle pounds the responsibility of State governments; ibid., p. 560.

80. For example, in the case of *Mangru Meya v. Budge Budge Municipality* (1950) in West Bengal, the courts ruled that authority to ban slaughter had to come from state or national legislation, but in the case of *Buddhu v. Allahabad Municipality*, the court ruled the municipal government did have the authority to ban slaughter of cows within its jurisdiction, and this was in keeping with Articles 47 and 48. See Simoons. 1980, 'The Sacred Cow and the Constitution of India', in *Food, Ecology, and Culture: Readings in the Anthropology of Dietary Practices*, J.R.K. Robson (ed.), New York: Gordon & Breach, p. 123.

81. As in the case of Buddhu above (who was a butcher), ibid.

82 Bruce Graham notes that by 1966 'a total ban on cow slaughter, as interpreted by the Supreme Court had been imposed by this date in all the northern states and in Gujarat, the Vidharba region of Maharashtra, Bihar, Orissa and parts of Mysore, and a partial ban, on the slaughter of young and useful cows only, had been imposed in several other states and regions, including Assam, West Bengal, and Madras. Only Kerala and the coastal regions of Andhra Pradesh had not imposed any ban,' 1993, *Hindu Nationalism and Indian Politics*, Delhi: Cambridge University Press, p. 149.

Inventing a National Past
The Case of Ramdev's *Bhāratvarṣ kā itihās* (1910–14)[1]

Harald Fischer-Tiné

> National History is that golden chain which links the past with the present and the future. It keeps alive in a people the spirit of unity, inspires them with common ideals, infuses in them common interests and common sentiments [...] hence all civilized nations look upon the preservation of their history as their paramount duty.[2]

I

The relevance of history-writing as a powerful weapon in both the colonial exercise of creating a cultural hegemony and the anti-colonial critique of this hegemony has been stressed by a number of scholars of South Asian History in the past decades.[3] Most recently Daud Ali has analysed the relationship of these two epistemic projects pointing to the inherent contradictions of an anti-colonial or 'nationalist' representation of the past which 'presupposed and contested the structures of colonialist historiography'.[4] It is this contradictoriness and the implications evolving from it that will be the focus of the present essay. The object of analysis is the History of Bhāratvarṣa (*Bhāratvarṣ kā itihās*) written in Hindi and published in two volumes 1910–14[5] by Acharya Ramdev, one of the leading figures of the so-called 'radical wing' of the Hindu reform movement Arya Samaj. Ramdev's book is of interest for several reasons: it represents not only one of the earliest attempts at writing an overtly 'national' history outside of Bengal but it was also a pioneering endeavour in the sense that it was the first noteworthy historical narrative with a clearly nationalistic outlook in what was to become the national language—Hindi. Thus it combined two of the most crucial points on the agenda not only of early Hindu nationalism but also of today's political forces of Hindutva. In spite of its obvious relevance, *Bhāratvarṣ kā itihās* has hitherto been completely overlooked by students of early Indian nationalism.[6] Before going into details of our case study, however, let us first set the frame of our analysis by briefly recalling some of the basic features of the above-mentioned competing and yet so closely interrelated appropriations of the past.

The use of history in the colonial project had two dimensions: First the past of the subjected culture was constructed in a manner that allowed the legitimization of colonial rule. The colonized had to be represented as inert, inferior, and incompetent, particularly in the fields of politics, administration, and warfare. This becomes strikingly evident in the portrayal of 'the Hindus' in the early products of British historical scholarship on India.[7] Secondly and even more importantly the existence or lack of a tradition of historiography itself became an indicator of a society's 'rationality' and its degree of civilization. By claiming that the Indians did not have a historiography worth the name, the English could justify their 'benevolent despotism'[8] not only with the 'findings' of their historical research but also with the methods with which they had attained them. Their supposed cultural superiority thus would make them the tool of Providence in educating their backward subjects, sunk in timeless stagnation. Since conceptions of time and history differing from those prevalent in nineteenth-century Europe were equated with 'unconsciousness' or childishness,[9] the transmission of Western historiography became an integral part of their colonial *mission civilisatrice*.

This double-edged strategy of 'appropriation of past by conquest'[10] proved to be paradigmatic for most of the nationalist historians who tried to construct a 'counter-history' starting from the 1880s.[11] Instead of political shortcomings, defeats, and internecine quarrels they tended to paint the picture of a glorious past determined by military prowess and 'national' solidarity.[12] All the virtues denied to Indians (or more specifically Hindus) by imperialist history writers like Mill, Lyall, and Wheeler had already been reclaimed in a fiery rhetoric by the first generation of Bengali pioneer-historians like Bankimcandra Chatterjee or Bhudev Mukhopadhyay. Towards the end of the century, nationalist writers of history aimed more and more at demonstrating their rational and 'scientific' approach towards their subject, and historiography at large, thus attempting to falsify the colonial stereotype of the 'irrational' and childish Indian. For the early nationalists, this 'submission under the law of the enemy'[13] seemed to be the most promising method to make themselves heard and to underline their political claims. This, however, is where the dilemma starts. The 'invention of tradition' or rather the translation of carefully selected elements of their own cultural repertoire into alien categories ended up in confirming the hegemonic claims of these categories. As we shall see now, it was out of this basic paradox that a number of inconsistencies and contradictions emerged that eventually proved fatal for emancipatory aims.

II

THE AUTHOR AND THE BOOK

Ramdev was born in 1881 in a small village in Hoshiarpur district (Punjab). Ramdev's father—a private teacher in a village—had already been a follower of Swami Dayananda. In the early 1890s he sent his son to the D.A.V. High School in Lahore, where he soon got into trouble because of his sympathies for the more radical programme of social reform advocated by the rival Gurukul faction of the Samaj.[14] After his expulsion from the college, he worked for a while as editor of the *Arya Patrika* and joined a number of Arya Samaj sub-organizations among which the youth wing Ārya Kumār Sabhā[15] and the Ārya Bhrātrī Sabhā,[16] the latter a body devoted to caste reform, were the most important. In 1904[17] he finally passed his B.A. examination and worked for a while as headmaster of a school in Jalandhar. He then received a scholarship to study at the Teacher's Training College, Lahore. Once he had finished his training there in 1906 he was offered a well-paid job as school inspector and everything seemed set to pursue the typical career of an English-educated babu. Ramdev, however, turned down the tempting offer and joined the Gurukul Kangri[18] as a professor of Indian History and English Literature in the newly opened college section of the institution. He lived and worked in Kangri, with only minor interruptions, until 1932.

The Gurukul Kangri was an experimental educational institution run by the 'militant' faction of the Arya Samaj. Ramdev's *Bhāratvars kā itihās* was conceived as a textbook for the institution and it can hardly be understood without looking at the general aims of the school. The Gurukul was founded in 1902, near the holy city of Hardwar. It was one of the numerous attempts at providing an alternative and indigenous educational institution, deeply rooted in the 'national' culture. But in contrast to many other such endeavours undertaken in India during the first two decades of the twentieth century, its ambitions went much further than that. It was supposed to play the role of a blueprint for a whole network of branches that would be founded all over India and finally replace the existing system of education completely. In the meantime, the Gurukul *snātaka*s (graduates) and Brahmacharis were expected to promote 'national regeneration' not only through their work but also through the example of their life. The school itself was perceived as a laboratory (*prayogśālā*) in which the values and the modes of living together for the nation they wanted to build could be given a trial. On the agenda articulated by the Gurukul founders, the revival of Sanskrit, the spread of *ārya bhāṣā* (Hindi) as the national language and the rewriting of ancient Indian history figured most prominently. Ramdev's contribution to the latter goal was undoubtedly the most significant achievement made by a Gurukul teacher and its influence transcended the narrow circle of the Arya Samaj adherents.[19]

Apart from teaching, writing books,[20] and fulfilling his administrative duties as headmaster, Ramdev also edited the Gurukul's English monthly *Vedic Magazine and Gurukula Samachar* and wrote countless articles for it during his years in Kangri. In 1925 he travelled through South Africa to raise money from the local Indian community for a Girl's Gurukul in Dehra Dun which he founded a year later. This institution played a central part in the final years of his life. Nevertheless, he found the time to get actively involved in politics in the early 1930s. In the course of Gandhi's Civil Disobedience campaign he was arrested for taking part in a *satyāgrah* and spent almost a year in the jails of Rawalpindi and Multan. In 1935 and 1936 he was elected president of the Arya Pratinidhi Sabha, Punjab, the central body of the radical Arya Samajists. Suffering from bad health since his imprisonment, he finally died in Dehra Dun in 1939.

The immediate background for the composition of his *Bhāratvarṣ kā itihās* [henceforth *BVKI*] was his appointment as a professor of history in Kangri in 1906. The notes which he made for his lectures right from the beginning formed the basis for his history of ancient India, the actual writing of which started in early 1909. One and a half years later the first volume, covering the period from the beginnings of Vedic civilization to the Mahābhārata-epoch, was published by the Gurukul press. The book met with remarkable success—the 2000 copies of the first edition were sold out after two months and a second edition had to follow as early as

1911.[21] Three years later in 1914 the second volume came out. It continued the historical narrative until the pre-Buddhist period. A slightly revised edition of volumes I and II came out in 1924. This version was reprinted without any alteration in 1996.[22] A third and final volume was co-authored by Satyaketu Vidyalankar and dealt with the Buddhist period. It was published as late as 1933.

Immediately after the publication of the first volume, the book was integrated into the curriculum of the Gurukul. It became compulsory reading for the classes 6–8.[23] It is difficult to understand why the Gurukul authorities decided to introduce the textbook in the high school and not in the college section of the institution, From the reminiscences of the Hindi novelist Yashpal—trained in the Gurukul Kangri ca. 1911–18—we know for certain that Ramdev's complicated historical narrative remained rather enigmatical for pupils in the age-group of eleven to thirteen.[24] Tongue in cheek, one would like to add that it is not too difficult to share this assessment even for an adult reader today. Nonetheless the *BVKI* remained in use as the standard textbook for ancient Indian history in the Gurukul Kangri and the schools affiliated with it until the 1970s.[25]

That the first volume caused quite a stir can be seen not only from the fact that it sold fairly well, it is also evident from the reviews in various newspapers and journals. One of Ramdev's biographers mentions that V.D. Savarkar, who was later to become the leader of the Hindu Mahasabha was one of the admirers of Ramdev's work. He read the book while in prison in the Andamans and mentioned it later several times as evidence for the fact that magnificent 'scientific' works could be written in Hindi.[26] From the same source we know that the famous Hindi poet Maithili Sharan Gupta was inspired by Ramdev's magnum opus to write his patriotic poem *Bhārat Bhārati*.[27]

The British colonial authorities also showed keen interest in Ramdev's historical account, though they were far less enthusiastic about it. Shortly after its publication, the C. I. D. handed over a copy of *BVKI* to an expert in order to find out whether it was seditious and should hence be banned. The final report recommended abstention from a ban but was highly critical of the book:

> The writer [Ramdev, H.F.T.] begins by saying, with the arrogance that is peculiar to the leaders of the Arya Samaj, that no fair and reliable history of India exists, as European writers are generally biased. [...] As history the book is beneath contempt. The writer says that his object in writing Indian History is 'to impart lessons to Indians for the amelioration of their condition' and accordingly [...] the book is calculated, and obviously intended, rather to provoke discontent with the present than to give a faithful picture of the past.[28]

It ought to be mentioned that the reproach of a lack of scientific objectivity is shared by writers who were not *eo ipso* in opposition to the political project of the Arya Samaj. In his account of the development of historiography in Hindi, the Indian historian H.L. Singh arrives at the conclusion that '[Ramdev's book] but for its nationalist outlook would merit little attention.'[29] The author, however, claimed to have produced a scholarly study which was meant to be taken seriously even in the light of Western standards. He provided the book with a bibliography and an index[30] and most of the 780 pages of the first two volumes contain footnotes with references to or excerpts from the original sources in Sanskrit. In the Preface of the first edition of Volume I, the author states:

In this book no assumption will be brought forward that cannot be proved [with a reference]. Some of the reasons why I differ with the views of other historians are given the proper place and especially in the appendices.[31]

In the context of the historical work of Bankimchandra Chatterjee, Sudipta Kaviraj has suggested the distinction between 'imaginary history' and 'academic history'.[32] The case of Ramdev's book shows, however, that this is a doubtful categorization. From an outsider's point of view, Ramdev's *BVKI* would clearly count as one of the products of an 'imaginary history'. But there can also be no doubt over the author's conviction about having produced a sound 'academic history'. This is quite evident from the way he discusses the sources and literature he used to write his account of ancient Aryan greatness. He claims to have read 'almost every single book in English on ancient Indian History that was available'.[33] Among the Western historians, philosophers, and Indologists, he refers to the names of James Tod, Mountstuart Elphinstone, Vincent A. Smith, Roper Lethbridge, Friedrich Max Müller, Abel Remusat, John Stuart Mill, Johann Kaspar Bluntschli, and Albrecht Weber. Of course he was also familiar with the writings of 'sympathizers' like Annie Besant, B.G. Tilak, and particularly the influential Bengali economist and sociologist, Benoy Kumar Sarkar.[34]

Having delineated the impact from outside and the secondary literature used by Ramdev, we can now turn to the inner structure of the two volumes under scrutiny and the sources underlying his 'research'. The first volume (*khaṇḍ*) is divided into five parts (*bhāg*), and the second volume into four parts. Each part is again subdivided in several chapters (*paricched* or *adhyāy*). The basis for the division is a scheme of periodization based on his main sources. Only the introductory part of Volume I (*BVKI*, I.1)[35] and the concluding part of Volume II (*BVKI*, II.4)[36] differ from this scheme. *BVKI*, I.1 grapples with the more general question of whether there has been an indigenous historiographical tradition in India and discusses the sources. Under the heading 'The expansion of the Indian civilization in foreign countries,[37] Ramdev tries to prove in the nine chapters of *BVKI*, II.4 that the Vedic civilization had a fundamental impact on, and thus was mainly responsible for the development of all the major 'high-cultures' of the world.[38] He cites (sometimes rather implausibly) philological and archaeological evidences to prove that not only China, Persia, Afghanistan, Greece, and Rome but also Egypt, America, Black Africa, and the Celtic civilizations drew heavily on the achievements of the Aryas. This is quite obviously a reversal of the well-known imperialist argument, that the Indians owed all their (humble) cultural achievements to their contact with Babylonians, Greeks and Romans.[39]

All the other *bhāg*s (that is *BVKI*, I.2–*BVKI*, II.3) are structured on the basis of the (literary) sources used. Thus, we get the following picture of the overall structure of the book:

STRUCTURE OF RAMDEV'S *BVKI*

Part	*Title/Content*	*Pages*
I. 1	The good of history • Did the Aryas have an historiography? • Sources for the History of ancient India • Transhistorical character of the Veda	1–50
I.2	History of the *Brāhmaṇa* period	51–189
I. 3	History of the *Manusmrti* period	190–278
I. 4	History of the *Rāmāyaṇa* period	279–351
I. 5	History of the *Mahābhārata* period	352–80
II.1	Civilization in *Mahābhārata* period	1–69
II.2	Political History from the *Mahābhārata* period to the pre-Buddhist epoch	71–110
II.3	The *Śukranītisāra*[40] period	111–254
1I.4	The expansion of Indian civilization	255–362
Index		363–84

With the exception of *BVKI*, I.1 and *BVKI*, II.4, the composition of the several parts is more or less homogeneous. Each part starts with a discussion of the principal source text and the problem of its exact dating. Subsequently, a number of chapters or sub-sections deal with issues like statecraft, social organization, jurisprudence, and education in the respective period. The text consists mainly of a series of translated quotations from the sources, which are only interrupted by longish interpolations with the author's comments or refutations of the interpretation of the sources by Western scholars. Narratives of actual historical 'events' are very rare. If such passages appear at all, they do so mostly in the context of a historicizing, account of incidents mentioned in the epics Rāmāyaṇa and Mahābhārata.[41]

As far as the language is concerned, the book is written in a heavily sanskritized style of Hindi—or *ārya bhāṣā*, as the Arya Samajists used to call it—that can hardly be called elegant. The excessive quotations in (Vedic) Sanskrit make it almost inaccessible for a readership without the background of a Hindu education.

RAMDEV'S INSTRUMENTALIST CONCEPT OF HISTORY

Ramdev's view of history and his concept of indigenous 'Indian' historiography was deeply influenced by the thoughts of his nationalist contemporaries and especially by the writings of Arya Samaj ideologues like Swami Dayananda,[42] the founder of the Gurukul, Mahatma Munshiram, and Lala Rallaram.[43] History had to play a clearly defined role in the process of 'national awakening': it was a medium to promote the pride and self-esteem of the members of the nation-to-be. A truly national historiography for India—for Ramdev and most of the other members of the Arya Samaj Hindu-historiography—had to act as a corrective for the distorted views of Indian history expressed by Western orientalists and historians. In a longish article published in the *Vedic Magazine* of August 1907, the fatal consequences of an exposure to these misrepresentations of history in government schools were recounted:

> National History which plays a most prominent part in the formation of manly character, is not only distorted, but, on occasions, even grossly misrepresented. Most of the books on Indian History taught in our schools do not practically contain any account of what is called the Hindu period, notwithstanding the fact that, in order to imbue the hearts of our youths with a sense of their national greatness, it is necessary to impart into them an extensive knowledge of the pristine glory and greatness. [...] the courses [...] tend to drive home to [our boys'] minds the notions that Indians are, by nature, fitted for nothing except grovelling in dust and passing their lives in low servility. The character of Indian great men is very often depicted in the darkest hue. The result is, that our boys grow up thoroughly degraded and devoid of any faith in their own strength and capabilities.[44]

'To imbue the hearts of the Indian youth with a sense of their greatness' was exactly what Ramdev's opus was written for. In the tradition of the understanding of history current in late nineteenth-century Europe, he regarded the past as a freely available resource for the production of a sense of national identity. This becomes clear when he provides a definition of what Indian history ought to be:

Indian History [*bhāratīya itihās*] is the account of the rise and fall of the Aryan people, of their efforts and mistakes, of their suffering caused by their stupidity and egoism and of the happiness caused by the wisdom of their leaders. There can be no doubt, that the inhabitants of Bharat will become inspired, that our national pride [*jātīya abhimān*] will be aroused, if we study the history of India and become aware of the glorious deeds of our ancestors. It is equally certain that the awareness of the faults of some of our ancestors will make us proceed firmly on the road of progress (*unnati*).[45]

Given the biased character of the existing works by Western authors and the effects so drastically described in the above quotation from Alakh Dhari, the 're-discovery'[46] of India's past becomes a patriotic act and Ramdev perceives an 'urgent necessity that the history of the civilization of the ancient Aryan nation[47] be written from a truly historical and national [*svadeśiya*] point of view'.[48] Just how strongly this national perspective is dependent on the orientalist writings as a negative reference-point becomes evident in the subsequent part of the introductory chapter, when the author refutes the orientalist argument that historiography and thinking in historical terms had been unknown in ancient India. As we have already seen, this was a crucial point on the agenda of nationalist historians since 'a-historicism' was seen by the colonizers as proof of irrationality and backwardness. Ramdev does not call into question this *a priori* assumption and willingly concedes: 'Indeed, if this reproach was true, we had to suppose that our ancestors had been only half-civilized'.[49] Consequently he tries to establish (citing a number of evidences from the *Candogya upaniṣad*, from the Atharvaveda and the famous Kashmiri chronicle *Rājataraṅgiṇi*) that in Vedic India not only history-writing but also 'historical science' [*aitihāsik vijñān*] was widespread[50] and 'that the same methods of history writing used by modern scholars were well known by the Aryan historians'.[51] Anticipating possible objections by Western scholars he further declares:

Now the following question arises: If the ancient Aryas were indeed familiar with the advantages of history [writing], then why do we not have a chronological History of India giving a detailed account of all the events with the exact dates? How could it exist? Does the world still not know about the religious bigotry [*sampradāyik pakṣpāt*] of the Muslim invaders? How could Indian books that attacked the [teachings of the] Quran possibly have survived a time in which the attempt to forcibly convert the unyielding offspring of Bharata to Islam was undertaken, a time in which thousands of wives were robbed from their husbands and thousands of sisters from their brothers [...]?

This is another important *leitmotiv* of almost all the historical accounts produced by Arya Samajists or members of other Hindu revivalist outfits. If the so-called 'Islamic period' is mentioned at all, it is mostly in order to explain the shortcomings and deficiencies of contemporary Hindu society.[52] In the same way that the supposed 'bigotry' of the Muslim invaders and the atrocities they committed are held responsible by other authors for phenomena as diverse as the decline of 'traditional' Indian mathematics and medicine,[53] the introduction of *purdah*,[54] or the practice of child-marriage,[55] they are used here by Ramdev to explain the loss of the fruits of Aryan historical research. Since all the chronicles and historical accounts fell prey to the Muslim rulers' appetite for destruction, one has to rely on the sources alone to get a picture of the past.[56] Ramdev is convinced that the religious texts that have been saved contain sufficient historical information for a detailed reconstruction of past events. The accounts of foreign travellers (Megasthenes, Al Biruni, Fa Hsien) and archaeological findings could be used to gather further evidence.[57]

It is in keeping with the character of the Arya Samaj that the Veda[58] is *not* included in the list of historical sources. The founder of the Arya Samaj, Swami Dayananda had firmly established the view that the Veda was universal 'divine knowledge' revealed directly to man and therefore was in a sense 'prehistoric'.[59] Ramdev shares this view and moreover tries to show that the Veda in this respect differs completely from the holy books of all other religions because these were written by men and therefore subject to history.[60]

In the vein of Dayananda's works, Ramdev also goes to great lengths to prove that the dating given by orientalist scholars for the composition of important Hindu religious texts is completely wrong. With the help of the astronomical calculations employed by Bal Gangadhar Tilak in his book *Orion*, Ramdev arrives at the conclusion that the first Brahmana-texts (that is, the first religious texts containing information of historical relevance) must have been composed around 12,000 BC.[61] The Mahābhārata war is thought to have taken place around 5000 BC whereas the epoch of the *Śukranītisāra* is situated between the Great War and the birth of the Buddha,[62] that is, around 2000 BC. Accordingly, the two volumes under scrutiny cover a period of roughly 10,000 years, from 12,000 BC to 2000 BC. The considerable gap between the dates given by Ramdev and those accepted among Western orientalists is explained with the latter's philological incompetence. Ramdev holds that they did not have the necessary proficiency in Vedic Sanskrit and arrived at the wrong conclusions because they ignored the fact that many words had a completely different meaning in 'pre-classical' Vedic times as compared to the 'classical' Sanskrit they were familiar with.[63] Moreover, Western scholars were ideologically biased. They either were Christians (like M. Monier Williams) who had no interest in letting the world know that the sacred texts of the Hindus were much older than the Bible or they were adherents of the evolution theory whose world-view was at stake if they admitted the existence of textual sources so ancient and yet perfect in every respect.[64] To further expose the orientalists' limited command of Vedic Sanskrit, the author adds an appendix with selected errors of translation.[65]

III

DISCOVERING INDIA'S FUTURE IN THE PAST

We have already seen that for early Hindu nationalists like Ramdev, the basic criteria for the usefulness of historiography were determined by the verdicts and prejudices of the very imperialist historians whose authority they wanted to contest. While the mainstream of British colonial historiography tried to deny contemporary Indians all the qualities considered necessary for self-government and political autonomy, many Indian nationalists were eager to prove that they had indeed always possessed these qualities, even long before the Europeans. The French political scientist Christophe Jaffrelot has described this phenomenon in the context of the extremist faction of the Indian National Congress:

> Les extrémistes prétendent en effet s'inspirer des traditions indigènes, ce qui, pour eux, veut surtout dire hindoues. [...] Dans leur effort pour revaloriser une culture hindoue soumise au joug colonial ils n'ont de cesse de la comparer à celle de l' Occident. Aux Britanniques qui vantent les mérites de leur système politique ils retorquent, que l'Inde antique, loin d'avoir été le cadre d'un despotisme oriental, fut le berceau de la démocratie.[66]

Here again it is important to note that the glorification of the Aryan past is not completely 'invented' by Hindu nationalism. It reflects the important late nineteenth-century European discourse on 'Aryanism'.[67] Whereas contemporary India was regarded as 'degenerated' and despotic, many Indologists (including Max Müller) had drawn a very positive picture of the ancient Aryas, describing them as dynamic, well-organized, and combative.[68] Most of the second generation leaders of the Arya Samaj were familiar with the work of Max Müller and his English epigones and even Dayananda had been aware of their writings. Therefore to find 'signs for political achievements' formed a first important goal of nationalist historiography. Apart from the democratic traditions mentioned by Jaffrelot, the potential for state formation and successful governance were also important issues in this category. Closely related is a second thematic complex that can be circumscribed as 'martial traditions'. This was a reaction to the powerful colonial stereotype that portrayed the Hindus as weak, cowardly, and effeminate and hence ill-equipped for military achievements. A further assessment to be refuted concerned the colonial perception of Hindu society as totally fragmented and torn by internal frictions and antagonisms. Here the 'legacy of solidarity' had to be constructed. The tradition of unity and social integration had to include particularly two groups which were perceived as marginalized in contemporary Hindu society: Untouchables and women. One final point may be of particular importance for the legitimacy of the aspirations of the Gurukul project. To enhance the weight and credibility of their educational agenda, the Hindu reformers pointed to 'traditions of rationality and learning' in the earliest Aryan history. We shall now analyse some significant examples of these four themes as represented in *BVKI* in more detail.

'Signs for political achievements' are searched for and found by Ramdev in all periods of the 10,000 years of Aryan history he covers in his book. One of the most influential and indestructible orientalist myths he wants to attack is the alleged inability of the Hindus to build empires of some territorial significance and to keep them together over a notable period of time. He is confident of having the necessary evidence to prove the existence of a huge kingdom in Bhāratvarṣ during the *Mahābhārata* period—long before great empires were established in Europe. In his introduction to the political history of that period he notes:

> It is obvious, that Bhārat had attained a high degree of political development at the time of the Mahābhārata. At that time the whole of Bhāratvarṣ was united under one government. Hastinapur was the capital of the entire empire. The ruler of Hastinapur was the Emperor of Bhāratvarṣ and the surrounding countries.[69]

More details about the exact boundaries of this Arya kingdom follow a few pages later:

> Some archaeologists and historians adhere to the highly incorrect and misleading opinion that the whole of India had never been united under one central rule before the establishment of the British Raj. However, Maharaja Yudhiṣṭhir was the only and uncontested ruler (*cakravarti*) of the entire Bhāratvarṣ. His colossal empire extended from the Hindukush mountains to Cape Kumari. Moreover there were a number of tributary states.[70]

To prove that the ancient Aryas possessed the capability to administer an enormous empire was only part of the self-designated task. In order to make the glorious Aryan empire of old into a blueprint for a future independent India, he needed to show that the quality of government and administration, the whole 'political culture', lived up to modern expectations and was even superior to the one prevalent in contemporary England, the self-proclaimed 'motherland of democracy'. If it was possible to prove the superiority of the Aryan political institutions even in such a diachronic comparison, then there could be no doubt that the early European empires would have looked like barbarous autocracies if contrasted directly with their equivalents in India. Keeping these considerations in mind, Ramdev's partiality to the method of diachronic comparison on his search for the 'roots of democracy' in Vedic India becomes quite understandable.

As early as in the times of the *Brāhmaṇas* (ca. 10,000 BC as we will recall) Ramdev finds the necessary evidence to invalidate the widespread orientalist cliché of the so-called 'oriental despotism'.[71] He wants to establish that the rulers in ancient India, far from being despots, were always especially qualified for their job by a combination of outstanding learning and moral integrity. According to his hypothesis, only 'a serious Vedic scholar'[72] [*vedom kā gambhīr jñāni*] was accepted as a ruler:

> Generally it is stated, that the king in ancient times was a despot [*nispratibandh*] and that nobody else could restrict his powers, that he could do whatever he pleased and that he could kill or incarcerate people who had aroused his anger. But this view is absolutely unfounded. From what we have said above it becomes absolutely clear that only a person who was both religious [*dhārmik*] and a great scholar especially in the field of politics could become king. People who were lacking these qualifications could never become rulers.[73]

Even more impressive is his exposition of the same argument in the context of the so-called *Manusmṛti* period.

> The people who claim that the kings in ancient Āryavarta had indulged in sensuous pleasures and spent most of their time stupefied by narcotics are completely wrong. From the account of the king's daily duties given in the *Manusmṛti* it is understood that the king was a hardworking man entirely devoted to the good of his people. He never wasted any of his time and was constantly busy in thoughts and deeds to augment the prosperity of his people and to protect them [from enemies].[74]

Given the egalitarian bias of Arya Samaj ideology, it is not surprising that Ramdev constantly underlines that the personal merits of the ruler were in no way connected with his caste[75] origin.[76] In this regard the ancient Aryas had even been more egalitarian—and hence more democratic—than the English in early twentieth century. In England, Ramdev argues, the son of a Lord was entitled by birth to decide over the passing of laws and amendments in the House of Lords 'no matter how stupid, uneducated, and depraved he might be'.[77]

In Bhāratvarṣa, by contrast, the ability of any aspirant for the throne had been guaranteed by both careful selection according to qualification and a rigid training for the responsibilities of ruling.[78] King Rama and his father Daśaratha are portrayed at length as outstanding examples of an ideal ruler possessing all the necessary qualities.[79] Just how important a virtue is moral integrity can also be seen in Ramdev's theory of degeneration. According to him, the gradual decline of 'character' among the *rājā*s, and their ever-growing affinity towards 'drinking, gambling, and women'[80] that had set in around 5000 BC was an important factor for the political decline that eventually led to the end of the golden epoch in Aryan history.

However, brilliant monarchs who defined themselves as 'first servants of the people',[81] did not by themselves ensure a democratic mode of government. For this purpose institutions that confine and control royal power are needed, as well as fora for the articulation of public opinion. Here again, the pioneer of Arya Samaj-historiography has no problems in finding overwhelming evidence for the existence of such institutions in the sacred texts. Already in the Brāhmaṇas he sees clear proto-democratic tendencies. The king had always been subject to the rules and regulations prescribed in the Veda which, thus, almost becomes a constitution. Moreover, there had been a kind of 'parliamentary control' of which even the most powerful and most perfect ruler had not been free:

> It is written in *Āpastambasūtra* [...] that the king ought to erect a house of parliament,[82] in the south of the capital that has several doors on the north and on the southside, so that everybody could see what happened inside and outside.[83]

In this parliament the king had to discuss new laws with representatives of all groups of the people [*prajā ke pratinidhi*] who were affected by it. In case of disagreement, the *brahman sabhā* had the authority to decide. In spite of its name, this board did not consist of members that were Brahmans by birth but rather of persons of high moral standards who had acquired great scholarly learning, because 'Brahman did not denote a [member of] a particular caste but brahmin and "virtuous" scholar were synonym terms.'[84] Taken together, these merits of this ancient Aryan democracy lead Ramdev to an enthusiastic assessment:

> Oh what an ideal system of government! The legislative function was in the hands of representatives of the ordinary people, but to provide a balance to their limited intellectual capabilities, and in order to guarantee objectivity, the right to oppose their decisions and to improve them was with the council of the greatest and most virtuous scholars of the country.[85]

The achievements of Vedic democracy also included a strict separation of legislative, executive, and judiciary functions. Furthermore the practices of jurisdiction including punishment for criminal offenders had been most advanced. While the debate whether capital punishment was appropriate for a civilized society was a fairly recent one[86] in England, the ancient Aryas had replaced this cruel practice by more humane methods:

The ancient Aryas believed that the betterment of the offender was the sole aim of punishment and not the application of counter-violence [*prati-hiṃsa*]. Therefore, they tried to work on a control of the delinquent's lower self through ascetic practices. The objective was to remove the basic instincts which were at the root of the crime, thereby turning the former criminal again into a useful member of the society and the nation.[87]

Thus, Ramdev identifies quasi-democratic patterns of government and administration even in the earliest period of the Aryan empire around 10,000 BC. This system had been further elaborated in the subsequent millennia[88] and reached such a perfection in the pre-Buddhist era of the *Śukranītisāra* that Bhāratvarṣa of that time could justly be called a 'crowned republic'.[89] By now, the monarch was assisted by a council of ministers with ten members, which had to be consulted every time an important decision was taken.[90] Moreover there was a legislative assembly [*vyavasthāpikā sabhā*][91] whose members consisted of the ministers, some delegates appointed by the king and, again, representatives [*pratinidhi*] of all the four *varṇa*s. On the basis of these 'findings', Ramdev concludes that the system of government in ancient India cannot but be called a constitutional monarchy [*niyamit rajtantra*], a definition he tries to verify using the criteria established by J.K. Bluntschli,[92] an influential nineteenth-century Swiss scholar of constitutional history.

The quest for martial traditions was also partly determined by the parameters of Western scholars but here, the views of colonial administrators and military experts were equally important. Ronald Inden and several other scholars have dealt with the dissemination of the prejudice that Hindus possessed no military virtues whatsoever held by James Mill and his later epigones. However, the direct impact of the army in the transmission of this myth should also not be underestimated. By 1880, the recruitment of native soldiers was completely based on the famous martial race theory, according to which only very few of the numerous ethnic groups of the Indian subcontinent were 'fit for service'.[93] It was clearly evident from the recruiting handbooks, that Sikhs and Muslims were generally credited with greater 'martial qualities' than the 'effeminate' Hindus. These stereotypes were soon internalized by some of the classes that were in close contact with the British and a certain masculinizing tendency became a characteristic feature of many different strands of early Hindu nationalism. This was particularly important for the Gurukul-wing of the Arya Samaj.[94] As Indira Chowdhury has already reminded us, a reinterpretation of the past was an ideal means of legitimizing such measures on an ideological level.[95] The aim of these historiographical attempts was to prove that the weakness and 'effeminacy' of the Hindus were in no way inherent to their 'character'. It was seen as an outcome of a long process of degeneration, a relatively recent phenomenon which could be stopped. In particular, the ancient and medieval history was used to highlight the 'manly virtues' and military prowess of earlier generations and to celebrate their heroic deeds on the battlefield. Many (Hindu-) nationalist historians found their material in the so-called Islamic period of Indian history, portraying the Marathas and the Rajputs as 'manly' protagonists of a heroic fight put up against the 'foreign domination' of the Muslim dynasties.[96] Ramdev's starting point was somewhat different, because he grappled with ancient history only. As there were no threatening invaders, he does not dwell much on heroic military achievements against external aggressors. Instead he concentrates on the brilliant military talents of the Aryas and the sophistication of their weapons and strategies. He tries to prove that the Aryas entertained a permanent army of professional soldiers as early as 5000 BC[97] and claims that these impressive forces could even be extended by the recruitment of volunteers in times of need:

> When they saw that the country was in danger, the young men joined the army as volunteers. Intoxicated by the love for their country, countless youths served in the army on a voluntary basis without receiving any remuneration.[98]

This way, nineteenth-century ideals of patriotism and civil responsibility are projected into a distant past. Similarly he tries to demonstrate the high civilizational standard of the Aryas by claiming that wars in ancient times had not been mere bloody massacres but that any form of military conflict was regulated by an elaborate code of behaviour and that the decision regarding the declaration of war or peace was actually taken by the brahmans whose outstanding moral qualifications have already been touched upon.[99]

The most striking feature of Ramdev's account of the military achievements in Vedic India is his lengthy description of the modern arsenal of weapons that had been in use. Like his ideological guru Swami Dayananda, he has not the slightest doubt that sound evidence for the existence of firearms, guns, and shells can be found in the sacred texts.[100] He vigorously refutes the view expressed by Western historians that these technical innovations were unknown in the Indian subcontinent before the establishment of Muslim sultanates in north and central India:

Some historians believe that the use of gunpowder has begun in Bhāratvarṣ only after the Musalmans have come to this land. These people ascribe the credit for having invented gunpowder to the Arabs. They claim that the inhabitants of India had come into contact with gunpowder for the first time during their wars against the Muslims. But this theory is incorrect and diametrically opposed to the facts. In the first volume of our history, we have already proved the existence of firearms with references from the Mahābhārata. In the *Śukranītisāra* one can definitely find formula [for the production of] gunpowder. In the same book there are several references to cannons, guns and shells.[101]

From the chapter on the Manusmṛti period we further learn that the technical know-how for the construction of fortresses was similarly advanced and that elaborate preventive measures for the protection of civilians were undertaken in those days.[102]

Being well-informed about the latest military innovations and strategies of his own time, Ramdev seeks to convince his readers that there was enough evidence in the sacred texts of the threefold division of the military forces in ancient Bhāratvarṣ. He argues that the soldiers had moved on the ground, on sea, and in the air. To prevent any critique by people who could possibly doubt the existence of an Aryan air force, he cites a verse from Manu's law-book in which, according to him, there were clear references to the existence of pilots. He then concludes:

If this *śloka* leaves no doubt that there were people during the time of the *Manusmṛti* who steered airships, how then could one be led to believe that the people in the war ministry had not undertaken efforts to make use of such vessels? Does not the German ministry of war constantly try to use the imperfect airships of Count Zeppelin [for its purposes]?[103]

Western corroboration for this argument was most welcome. Ramdev heavily draws on the publications of Gustav Oppert,[104] a German Indologist, to support his revisionist view of Indian military history. In another case, the plausibility of the victory of Ram over thousands of demons is established by means of a comparison with the conquest of Mexico by a handful of Spanish conquistadors as described by the American historian Prescott.[105]

The legacy of solidarity postulated by Ramdev certainly is not as central an issue of *BVKI* as the ones analysed so far, but one can still cite a number of examples of his attempts at getting this important nationalist message across to the reader. The definition of a brahman and the author's insistence, that caste background did not have the slightest influence on the selection of a monarch indicate a new evaluation of the caste system. The rigid social organization is regarded as a later corruption of the earlier practice. In Ramdev's imagined national past, there is no room for any kind of divisive forces that could jeopardize the unity of the 'nation in the making'. Such phenomena, therefore, have to either be omitted or reinterpreted in such away as to strengthen the act of homogenization which is the ultimate goal of Ramdev's history-writing. This can be exemplified with reference to Ramdev's position towards the popular Arya-theory. He vigorously refutes the hypothesis put forward by many Western scholars, that the shudras were the descendants of the Dravidian aborigines of India, while the members of the three twice-born castes descended from the Aryan invaders.

Some European historians hold that the twice-born (Aryas) had come from Central Asia and the shudras had been the aborigines [*ebarijniīz*] or *ādivāsi*s of this country. [...] This contention cannot be backed by a single proof. From the accounts of the Aryan immigration that can be found in the oldest Sanskrit literature, we learn that the Aryas have come from the land of Trivishtapa (you can also call it greater Central Asia if you will) to this country and have called it Aryavarta. If there had lived some other race here before their immigration it would definitely have been mentioned in the scriptures in one form or another.[106]

This way he could produce the evidence that all Hindus had common ancestors and formed a racially homogenous entity. This, in turn, was regarded, from the middle of the nineteenth century onwards, as a crucial criterion for the legitimacy of any claim for 'national' autonomy and played an important role in the various strands of Hindu nationalism.[107] The only point of becoming a shudra, according to Ramdev, was not racial segregation but a lack of aptitude for higher education.[108] The assertion of Western Indologists, that there was adequate evidence in the *Manusmṛti* to indicate that shudras were treated like slaves in ancient India is repudiated. With a number of alternative translations, the Acharya tries to establish that quite the reverse was true.[109] He underlines that the same laws had been valid for members of every *varṇa* and emphasizes that there had been but 'one common dharma for all the four castes'.[110] At the same time, he fails to find 'even the slightest hint' for the complex regulations on commensuality or the evil of untouchability in the ancient sciptures.[111]

Predictably enough, a similar bias can be noticed when Ramdev tackles the issue of the treatment of women in the heyday of Bhāratvarṣa. Next to the integration of low castes and 'Untouchables', women's uplift was one of the core issues on the agenda of the Gurukul-faction of the Arya Samaj and this is reflected in his rereading of the sacred texts. He tries to furnish proof of the fact that in ancient times women had also been initiated with the sacred thread (*yajñopavīta*) and thus were accepted as equal members of the community. Consequently, they also had unrestricted access to institutions of higher education.[112] Evils (*kūrīti*) like purdah, which excluded women from public life, had had their origins much later, in the pre-Buddhist period.[113] The first signs of a beginning of curtailment of women's rights in this epoch are interpreted as a significant indicator of the beginning of the decline of Bhāratvarṣa. Talking about the *Śukranītisāra* period he states:

> The situation of women in those days gave much cause for concern. They had lost their rights and were regarded as mere servants of their husbands. In a way, their autonomous existence had already been destroyed. In this respect the epoch was already so degenerated that there were not even a few independent scholars and law-experts that would have protested against such negative developments in society.[114]

It has already been suggested, that the 'quest for traditions of rationality and learning' evident in many chapters of *BVKI* was brought about to some extent by the specific situation of the Gurukul Kangri for which the book was written. It would, however, be simplistic to see the chapters on indigenous traditions of 'scientific' scholarship and learning as mere propaganda for the novel type of education advocated by the Gurukul-founders. David Arnold has recently shown how important the invention of these traditions had been in nationalist circles outside the Arya Samaj.[115] It is evident that it was much easier to reclaim the capacity for rational thinking denied by the colonial masters if it could be shown that, first, the authoritative scriptures of the Hindus (or 'Aryas')[116] were not in contradiction with the principles of rationality and, secondly, a genuine tradition of 'scientific' research and teaching had been in existence in India for thousands of years before the arrival of the British. In an age marked by a blind faith in science of those classes from which most of the colonial rulers were recruited, such a line of argument possessed a strength that can hardly be overestimated. The seminal contribution of Ramdev to this project which distinguishes him from earlier Arya Samaj scholarship, must be seen in the framework he provides for the claim of rationality. It is now completely separated from the religious context (in which it had been situated in Dayananda's *Satyārth Prakāś* and *Ṛgvedādibhāṣyabhūmikā*) and presented instead as the result of a critical analysis of historical sources and thus of truly scientific' research. We shall now analyse a few typical examples from the wealth of material in illustrating this point offered by *BVKI*.

The most impressive passages in which the tendency to demythologize the 'puranic mode of story-telling'[117] is clearly evident can be found in the chapter on the Rāmāyaṇa period. Ramdev interpolates a long section in his narrative to prove his contention that 'Hanuman and his followers were human beings and not monkeys with tails.'[118] He argues that the word 'monkey' was just a metaphor, a literary device used by Valmiki to evoke an idea of the swiftness and dexterity of Hanuman and his friends. Similarly the use of the verb 'to fly' for Hanuman's movement from one place to another had to be understood as a metaphor for his quickness, 'for such a means of locomotion is not compatible with the laws of creation'.[119] The problem of Hanuman's crossing the sea to Sri Lanka is also explained with a theory which is eminently compatible with the laws of nature:

Today the distance between Lanka and India is 58 miles. In the middle between Lanka and India there are two Islands called Manar and Rameshwar, therefore the distance on the sea is only 23 miles (see *International Geography*, p. 504), and the water is not very deep also. The channel between England and France is 21 miles wide; if some athletes can cross the channel, how could it then be regarded as impossible that a swimmer like the youthful hero and Brahmachari Hanuman covered the distance of 23 miles swimming?[120]

This is a demonstration of the historical reliability of religious epics which is quite typical of Ramdev's line of reasoning.

Let us now move on to the second aspect involved in this issue: the construction of a genealogy of science and 'rational' education in ancient Bhāratvarṣa. It hardly needs to be reiterated that here, again, the author's findings are largely determined by his intention to discredit orientalist stereotypes:

Almost all Western scholars and their epigones in our country are not getting tired of claiming that there had been no organized system of education in ancient Aryavarta. [...] The Aryas had not had the slightest idea of the advantages of the modern university-system [*yunivarsiti praṇāli*]. But this contention is absolutely unfounded. A thorough study of the Brāhmaṇas shows that the educational system at that time was highly developed.

To give a solid basis to his argument, Ramdev ascribes a completely different meaning to the *pariṣads*[121] mentioned in the *Upaniṣads*. He argues that it was evident from a number of references that the word '*pariṣad*' in the old text had exactly the same meaning as the modern word 'university'.[122] According to his reading, a pariṣad was a university 'in which 21 *upādhyāyas* (*profesar*)' were employed.[123] Apart from these university-like institutions, there were also *gurukul*s situated in areas far from worldly influences, in which *brahmacāri*s (celibatarian students) used to be instructed by *vānaprasthas*.

As regards the curricula and the educational aims of these institutions, Ramdav is eager to place emphasis on the fact that the students did not waste their time in 'spiritual daydreaming' as Western Indologists would have people believe.[124] Instead pariṣads and gurukuls had been places of 'serious scholarship'.[125] He is even able to give a detailed list of the several disciplines which had been in full bloom as early as 10,000 BC. These include among others:[126]

- history [*itihās*]
- grammar and philology [*vyākaraṇ and nirukt*]
- anthropology [*pitrayan*]
- mathematics [*gaṇit vidyā*]
- physical geography [*fizikal jiāgrafī*]
- mineralogy [*khānoṁ kī vidyā*]
- logic [*tark śāstra*]
- zoology [*prāṇiyoṁ kī vidyā*]
- astronomy [*jyotiṣi*]
- military science and statecraft [*dhanuvidyā* and *rājśāsan vidyā*]

IV

The present essay has attempted to illustrate a fundamental problem of 'national' historiography in colonial India by analysing Ramdev's *Bhāratvarṣ kā itihās*, an important and yet hitherto neglected early fruit of historical research with a clearly (Hindu-) nationalist bias. We have noted that, on the one hand, the propagation of a revisionist view of history seemed to be an effective way of contesting colonial authority, but on the other hand, most of the proponents of such a view remained trapped in the values and categories of specifically European discourses of rationality and historicity thus reinforcing colonial claims of civilizational superiority. As we have subsequently demonstrated, Ramdev's book is heavily marked by this paradox.

The analysis of the contents of the first two volumes of his monumental book has shown how vehemently the author tries to discredit the British colonial view of Indian history. He is anxious to evoke an idea of the greatness and glory of the Aryan 'nation' and provide ample evidence of its civilizational achievements. However, the evaluation of just when a nation deserves to be called civilized and which achievements are desirable at all, is based exclusively on contemporary 'Western' criteria. Accordingly, the armies of ancient Aryavarta are depicted as armed forces, organized in a rational manner, and equipped with highly sophisticated weaponry. Equally, Ramdev finds evidence for the existence of a highly developed system of government informed by democratic principles, and constructs a long tradition of supposedly 'modern' phenomena like rationality, scientific research, and mass popular education.

Of special import is the historical craft itself. Ramdev is at pains to demonstrate that the Hindus are not an ahistorical people and that even the ancient Aryas had possessed not only a historical consciousness but also a long tradition of sophisticated academic history-writing. Both the hundreds of references to the fabrications and 'distorting' accounts of Western historians and Indologists as well as the sheer choice of his main topic demonstrate who Ramdev's true addressees are. There is no evidence, however, that the Western scholars under attack reacted to Ramdev's criticism. Instead, there are a few hints that his bold and rather unusual line of argument was not taken seriously in academic circles. A brief glance at the history of the reception of *BVKI* has confirmed that the book was read in the first place by Indian nationalists with a clear Hindu bias. Furthermore, it obviously had a considerable impact on later historical research within the Arya Samaj. It would be an important topic in its own right to explore as to what extent Ramdev's book has influenced Savarkar and other Hindutva ideologues of the 1920s and 1930s. At present it can only be stated that there are not only quite a few indications that *BVKI* was widely read and vividly discussed in the Hindu nationalist circles of the time, there are also striking similarities in the arguments used by both.[127] However, there are also hints that it would be equally worthwhile to compare the book with the products of the 'secular' brand of nationalistic history-writing of the Nehruvian type to arrive at a just assessment of Ramdev's contribution to Indian historiography.

In order to act as a homogenizing agency and promote unity and solidarity within the intended nation, Ramdev—and here he definitely is in line with later Hindu nationalist interpreters of the past—employs simplistic dichotomies. *Dasyu*s, *mleccha*s or Muslims provide the contrast against which the virtues of the Aryas can be played up beyond proportion. Even if the so-called Islamic period is not dealt with directly, there is ample evidence in some of his interpolations that he believed the Muslims to be largely responsible for India's decline. It is certainly no exaggeration, therefore, to say that, in a sense, the contents of *BVKI* are as exclusionist as the heavily sanskritized language in which it is written. One could thus conclude that Ramdev's ambitious historiographical project turned out to be a failure on two different levels: as contestation of a colonial interpretation of the past it was not able to break free from the premises of the colonizers, and as a 'national' history it provoked disharmony and fissiparous tendencies rather than integration.

ENDNOTES

1. I am grateful to Dr. Indra Sengupta (Heidelberg), Dr. Evelin Hust (New Delhi), Dr. Margrit Pernau (New Delhi), Dr. Ravi Ahuja (Berlin), and Dr. Therese O'Toole (Birmingham) for reading earlier drafts of this essay and making valuable suggestions for its improvement.

2. 'National History', in *Vedic Magazine & Gurukula Samachar* [henceforth *VM & GS*], IV(6), 1910, pp. 30–3, p. 30.

3. The lion's share of research has been devoted to the influence of colonial 'texts of power'. For some examples see Guha, R., 'Dominance without Hegemony and its Historiography', in idem. (ed.), 1989, *Subaltern Studies VI. Writings on Indian History and Society*, Delhi: Oxford University Press, pp. 210–309; Inden, R., 'Orientalist Constructions of India', *MAS*, 20 (3), 1986, pp. 401–46, pp. 424–6; Ludden, D., 'Orientalist Empiricism: The Transformations of Colonial Knowledge', in Breckenridge, C. and Van der Veer, P. (eds), 1995, *Orientalism and the Postcolonial Predicament: Perspectives from South Asia*, Philadelphia: University of Pennsylvania Press, pp. 250–78, pp. 263–5; Metcalfe, T.R, 1996, *Ideologies of the Raj*, (Repr.) Delhi: Cambridge University Press (=NCHI, III.4), pp. 85–92. The issue of indigenous 'national' histories has been touched upon by Guha, R., 1988. *An Indian Historiography of India: A Nineteenth-Century Agenda and its Implications* (*Sakharam Ganesh Deuskar Lecture on Indian History 1987*), Calcutta: Bagchi Chatterjee, P., 1993, *The Nation and its Fragments: Colonial and Postcolonial Histories,* Princeton: Princeton University Press and idem: 'History and the Nationalization of Hinduism', in Dalmia, V. and H.V. Stietencron (eds), 1995, *Representing Hinduism: The Construction of Religious Traditions and National Identity*, New Delhi–Thousand Oaks–London: Sage, 1995, pp. 103–28; see also Kaviraj, S., 'The Imaginary Institution of India', in Chatterjee, P., G. Pandey (eds), 1993 *Subaltern Studies VII*, (Repr.) Delhi, pp. 1–40.

4. Ali, D., 1999, 'Introduction', in idem (ed.), *Invoking the Past: The Uses of History in South Asia,* New Delhi: Oxford University Press, pp. 1–12, p. 2.

5. A third volume was written by Ramdev together with Satyaketu Vidyalankar and published as late as 1933. Since it has not been available for me, my study deals with the first two volumes exclusively.

6. The only reference to the work I could find at all are a couple of sentences in Singh, H.L., 'Modern Historical Writing in Hindi', in Philips, C.H. (ed.), 1961, *Historians of India, Pakistan and Ceylon*, London: Oxford University Press, pp. 461–72, p. 463.

7. Most prominent in this regard is James Mill's famous *History of British India*, first published in 1817. But countless other examples can be found with a similar bias throughout the nineteenth century. See e.g., Hugh Murray's *History of British India* (1859) J.T. Wheeler's *History of India from the Earliest Times* (5 Vols, 1867–76), Roper Lethbridge's *A Short Manual of the History of India. With an Account on India as it is* (1881). A somewhat more moderate view was presented in Mountstuart Elphinstone's *The History of India,* 1841; John C.

Marshman's *The History of India from the Earliest Period to the Close of Lord Dalhousie's Administration* (3 Vols, 1869); Alfred Lyall's *Rise and Expansion of the British Dominion in India* (1894); and W.W. Hunter's *History of British India* (2 Vols, 1899–1900). Further details can be found in Stokes, E.T., 'Administrators and Historical Writing in India', in Philips, *Historians of India,* pp. 385–403.

8. The term 'benevolent despotism' is used Smith, V.A., 1908, *The Early History of India*, Oxford: Clarendon Press, p.331. His book became the standard history of ancient India in the beginning of the twentieth century.

9. Chowdhury, I., 1998, *The Frail Hero and Virile History: Gender and the Politics of Culture in Colonial Bengal*, Delhi: Oxford University Press, p. 42. For a more general perspective on this phenomenon see also Gyan Prakash: 'After Colonialism', in idem (ed.), 1995. *After Colonialism: Imperial Histories and Postcolonial Displacements*, Princeton: Princeton University Press, pp. 3–17, p.4.

10. Guha, 'Dominance without Hegemony', loc. cit., p. 212.

11. For details see Guha, *An Indian Historiography of India,* passim.

12. It has to be mentioned that this type of straightforward nationalistic glorification of the past was not the only way to write a 'national' history. The tradition of writing highly sophisticated economic history—the best-known examples being R.C. Dutt's *Economic History of British India,* published in 1902 and Dadabhai Naoroji's *Poverty and Un-British Rule in India*—has its roots in exactly the same period. A discussion of this important strand in Indian historiography, however, is beyond the scope of this essay.

13. Rothermund, D.: 'Der Traditionalismus als Forschungsgegenstand für Historiker und Orientalisten', in *Saeculum,* 40(2), 1989, pp. 142–8.

14. Rāmgopāl Vidyālaṁkār, 'Ācārya Rāmdev', in Dharmpal (ed.), 1991 *Ācārya Rāmdev-jī ādarṣvād ke jyotistambh. vyaktitva evaṃ kṛtitva,* Naī Dillī: Vaidik Prakāśan, pp. 9–32, p. 9.

15. The Ārya Kumār Sabhā was modelled after the YMCA. For details cf. Rama Deva, 1908, *Vedic Dharma and Young India*, Lahore: Arya Kumar Sabha, passim.

16. For Ramdevs role in the sabhā, see Nardev Śāstrī, 'Ācārya Rāmdev-jī ke saṃsmaraṇ', ibid., pp. 84–6, p. 84. A detailed account on the work and aims of the organization can be found in Graham, J.R., 1943, 'Arya Samaj as a Reformation of Hinduism with Special Reference to Caste', unpublished Ph.D. thesis, Duke University, pp. 477–87.

17. There are differing views regarding the date of his graduation. The year 1904 is given by Saxena, G.S., 1990, *Arya Samaj Movement in India* (*1875–1947*), New Delhi: Commonwealth Publishers, p. 80. Bhāratīya, B., 1991, *Ārya lekhak koś* (*Ārya Samāj tathā ṛṣi Dayānand viṣayak lekhan se juṛe sahastrādhik lekhakoṁ ke jīvan evaṃ kāryvṛtt kā vistṛat vivaraṇ*), Jodhpur: Dayānand Adhyayan Saṃsthān, p. 234.

18. For a more detailed account of the Gurukul Kangri, cf. Fischer-Tiné, H., 'The Only Hope for Fallen India: The Gurukul Kangri as an Experiment in

National Education, in G. Berkemer et al. (eds), 2001, *Explorations in the History of South Asia: A Volume in Honour of Dietmar Rothermund*, New Delhi: Manohar, pp. 277–99.

19. The direct influence within the historiographical tradition of the Arya Samaj is evident. Dharmdatt Vidyālaṃkār, probably a student of Ramdev's, wrote a book entitled *Prācīn Bhārat meṃ svarājya*, which was published in 1920. Countless articles published mainly in the *Vedic Magazine* upheld similar views. For a typical example, see 'The Ancient Glory of a Conquered Race', *The Vedic Magazine and Gurukula Samachar* 10(9), 1917, pp. 679–85.

20. The most important are: *Vedic Dharma and Young India* (1908); *The Arya Samaj and its Detractors* (1910); the collected essays in *Ārya aur dasyu* (1918); and *Purāṇmat paryālocan* (1919; together with Jaydev Vidyalankar).

21. Cf. Rāmdev, 'Dvitiyāvṛtti kī bhūmikā', in *BVKI*, I, p. 11 [roman page-numbers] and *VM & GS*, IV (7/8),1911, p. 1.

22. Rāmdev, 1996, *Bhāratvarṣ kā itihās*, 2 Vols, Haridvār: Svāmi Śraddhānand Anusandhān Prakāśan Kendra.

23. Gurukula Kangri (ed.), 1913, *Prospectus and Rules Relating to Examinations, Admission, etc.*, Kangri: Gurukula Printing Press, pp. 37–42.

24. Yaśpāl, 1994 [1941], *Sinhāvalokan*, 3 Vols, Illāhābad: Lokbhārati Prakāśan, Vol. I, p.40.

25. Personal communication from Dr. Dharmvir Arya, graduate of the Gurukul Kangri and president of the Ārya Paropkāriṇi Sabhā, Ajmer, 10-12-1996.

26. Cf. Śaṇkar Dev Vidyālaṁkār, 'Jñānyogī Ācārya Rāmdev jī', in Dharmpal (ed.), 1991, *Ācārya Rāmdev jī ādarṣvad ke jyotistambh,* New Delhi, pp. 51–60, p. 55.

27. Ibid.

28. NAI, Home Deptt. Poll., -B, Proceedings, March 1911, 'WRDCI for February 1911', pp. 14f.

29. Singh, 'Modern Historical Writing in Hindi', p. 463.

30. *BVKI*, II, pp. 363-84.

31. Rāmdev, 'Prathamāvṛtti kī bhūmikā', in *BVKI*, I, pp. 9f., p. 9 [roman page numbers; this and all the following translations from Hindi are the present author's].

32. Kaviraj, S., 'The Imaginary Institution of India', p. 19.

33. Ramdev, 'Prathamāvṛtti kī bhūmikā', in *BVKI*, I, pp. 9f.

34. Ramdev referred especially to Sarkar's book *The Political Institutions and Theories of the Hindus*, published in Leipzig in 1922. Biographical details about Sarkar can be found in Frykenberg, R.E., 'Benoy Kumar Sarkar, 1887–1949: A Political Rishi of Twentieth Century Bengal', in Berkemer, G. et al. (eds), *Explorations in South Asian History,* New Delhi: Manohar, pp. 197–217. The impact of Sarkar's work on Ramdev is particularly evident in the preface of the third edition brought out in 1924.

35. *BVKI*, I.1, pp. 1–50.

36. *BVKI*, II.4, pp. 256–363.

37. *Bhāratīya sabhyatā kā videśī meṁ prasār*.

38. This fundamental hypothesis is already brought forward in the first chapter of this part, where Ramdev postulates that 'The material standard of Bhāratvarṣa was already so high in those days that its civilization began to expand to other countries. In those times Bharatvarsa was indeed the civilizational teacher of the world', *BVKI*, II. 4, p. 267.

39. This widespread hypothesis is attacked in a number of other Arya Samaj publications. Cf. 'The Ancient Glories of a Conquered Race', in *VM & GS*, IX (9), 1917, pp. 679–85 or Sarḍa, H.B., 1906, *Hindu Superiority: An Attempt to Determine the Position of the Hindu Race in the Scale of Nations,* Ajmer: Rajputana Printing Works.

40. The *Śukranītisāra* is an early medieval text on society and policy in the vein of the famous *Arthaśāstra*. It includes contributions of various authors but is ascribed to the mythical sage Śukra. It probably was made available to Ramdev through a critical edition by G. Oppert, which was published in Madras in 1882. I am grateful to Pandit K.P. Aithal for this reference. Quite interestingly, Jawaharlal Nehru uses the same source in his *The Discovery of India,* to construct a legacy of democratic village governments. Cf. Nehru, J., 1992 [1946], *The Discovery of India,* (Repr.) Delhi: Jawaharlal Nehru Memorial Fund, pp. 248–50.

41. Cf. e.g. *BVKI*, 1.4, pp. 279-351 and *BVKI*, 1.5, pp. 352–80.

42. Cf. Jordens, J. T. F, 1978, *Swāmī Dayānanda: His Life and Ideas,* New Delhi: Oxford University Press, pp. 111–13, 124f.; Jones, K.W., 'Swami Dayananda Saraswati's Vision of the past, Present and Future', in Garg, G. R. (ed.), 1984, *World Perspectives on Swami Dayanand,* New Delhi: Concept Publishers, pp. 276–84; Jordens, J.T.F, 'Dayananda Saraswati's Concept of the Vedic Golden Age', in idem (ed.), *Dayananda Saraswati, Essays*, pp. 64–76; Llewellyn, *Arya Samaj as a Fundamentalist Movement*, pp. 160f. The influence of Dayanand's ideas on Ramdev is discussed in Rākeś, V., 'Prastāvnā', in *BVKI,* pp. 3–8, especially pp. 3–5.

43. Lala Ralla Ram wrote an extensive introduction to the first prospectus of the Gurukul Kangri in which the urgent necessity for independent historical research on the history of ancient India from a 'strictly national point of view' was declared to be one of the *raison d'être* of this new type of educational institution. Cf. Arya Pratinidhi Sabha, Punjab (ed.), 1902, *The Rules and the Scheme of Studies of the Gurukula sanctioned by the Arya Pratinidhi Sabha, Punjab, together with an Introduction by Lala Ralla Ram,* Lahore: Punjab Printing Works, pp. 13–15.

44. Alakh Dhari, 'The Essential Elements of Sound Education', *VM & GS*, 1(2), 1907, pp. 21–6, dort pp. 24f.

45. *BVKI*, I.1, pp. 3f.

46. The rhetoric of a (re-)discovery of the true India as something forgotten was very popular with Indian nationalists of diverse backgrounds (see e.g., Nehru's *The Discovery of India*). It was certainly influenced by orientalist paradigms. For an insightful analysis of this problem, see Parekh, B., 1999, *Colonialism, Tradition, and Reform: An Analysis of Gandhi's Political Dis-*

course, New Delhi–Thousand Oaks–London: Sage, pp. 52f.

47. *Jāti*, the Hindi word used here by Ramdev, could also have the meaning 'people'.

48. 'Prathamāvṛtti kī bhūmikā', *BVKI*, I, p. 9.

49. *BVKI*, I, p. 6.

50. *BVKI*, I.1, pp. 7f., 11.

51. *BVKI*, I.l, p. 14.

52. More details about this interesting phenomenon can be found in Chatterjee, *The Nation and its Fragments*, pp. 112–14 and Chowdhury, *The Frail Hero and Virile History*, pp. 52–4. Chowdhury reminds us of the fact that this verdict was shared by orientalists like Max Müller.

53. Cf. Arnold, D., 'A Time for Science: Past and Present in the Reconstruction of Hindu Science, 1860–1920', in Ali (ed.), *Invoking the Past*, pp. 157–77, especially pp. 158–60.

54. Cf. For example Mathur, J.S., 'A Rationalistic View of the Arya Samaj', in *VM & GS*, III(10), 1910, pp. 34–41, especially pp. 37f.

55. Cf. Shraddhanand, S., 1926, *Hindu Sangathan. Saviour of the Dying Race*, Delhi: Akhil Bharat Hindu Mahasabha, pp. 351f. and Śraddhānand, 'Rāmāyaṇ kī rahasya kathā', in Bhāratīya, Bh. (ed.), 1987, *Svāmī Śraddhānand Granthāvalī*, XI Vols, Dillī: Govindrām Hasānand, Vol. VI, pp. 184–93, pp. 186f. See also Har Dayal, 'Some Aspects of Hindu Civilization under Muhamadan Rule', in *VM & GS*, II (3), 1908, pp. 11–17. Ramdev, however, is of the opinion that the evil of child-marriage had its origin already in the Mahābhārata-period; cf. *BVKI*, II.1, p. 41.

56. For Ramdev's discussion of the source material available, see *BVKI*, I.1, pp. 15–25.

57. His work, however, is based almost exclusively on the religious texts mentioned above.

58. Veda here is understood in the narrower sense as the Vedic *saṁhita*s only.

59. Cf. Jordens, J.T.F, 'Pilgrimage to the Sources: Dayananda Sarasvati and the Vedas', in idem (ed.), 1998, *Dayananda Sarasvati: Essays on his Life and Ideas*, New Delhi: Oxford University Press, pp. 13–24, especially pp. 19–21. See also Llewellyn, J., 1993, *The Arya Samaj as a Fundamentalist Movement: A Study in Comparative Fundamentalism*, New Delhi: Manohar, p. 160.

60. *BVKI*, I 1, pp. 29f.

61. *BVKI*, I 1, p. 34.

62. About 500 BC. Interestingly, in this case, the dating of Western Indologists is accepted.

63. The way Ramdev articulates his argument bears testimony to his 'Western' educational background: 'To want to understand the Vedas on the basis of the language of the Purāṇas is as ridiculous an undertaking as [...] if you wanted to understand Chaucer with a dictionary of today's English'. *BVKI*, I.1, p. 34.

64. Ibid., p. 35.

65. Ibid., pp. 44–9.

66. Jaffrelot, C., 1998, *La Démocratie en Inde. Religion, Caste, Politique*,

Paris: Fayard, p. 65. The extremists pretend to be inspired by indigenous traditions, which, for them, basically means Hindu traditions. [...] In their effort to strengthen a Hindu culture which has been deformed under the colonial yoke, they constantly compare it to the cultural achievements of the West. To the British, who praise the merits of their political system, they reply that Indian—far from being the homeland of Oriental despotism—was the true cradle of democracy.

67. Cf. Bhatt, Chetan, 2001, *Hindu Nationalism, Origins, Ideologies and Modern Myths*, Oxford–New York: Berg, pp. 12–21.

68. Cf. ibid., and Thapar, Romila, 'The Theory of Aryan Race and India: History and Politics', in Idem, 2000 *Cultural Pasts: Essays in Early Indian History*, Delhi: Oxford University Press, pp. 1108–40, p. 1111.

69. *BVKI*, II.4, p. 4.

70. Ibid., p. 29.

71. Cf. Inden, 1990, *Imagining India*, Oxford: Basil Blackwell.

72. *BVKI*, I.2, p. 85.

73. *BVKI*, 1.2, p. 87. For examples from later periods, see also *BVKI*, II.1, pp. 25f., and *BVKI*, II.3, pp. 125–30.

74. *BVKI*, I.3, pp. 261f.

75. 'Caste' must here be understood in the sense of *varṇa*.

76. In his chapter on the *Manusmṛti* period Ramdev goes so far as to assert that the *rājā* had been elected by a conference of delegates from all the four castes [*caturvarṇoı kī sabhā*]. Cf. *BVKI*, 1.3, p. 258.

77. *BVKl*, 1.2, p. 95.

78. Details about the special type of education granted to the princes can be found in the chapter on the *Śukranītisāra* period. Cf. *BVKI*, II.3, pp. 128–30.

79. *BVKI*, 1.4, pp. 294–9.

80. *BVKI*, II.1, p. 46. Ramdev devotes a whole sub-chapter entitled 'The Corruption of the Kings' [*rājāoṃ kī vilasitā*] to this problem. See also *BVKI*, II.3, pp. 254f., where Ramdev describes the degenerating effects of the establishment of wine-shops licensed by the government.

81. Cf. *BVKI*, II .1, p. 19. See also *BVKI*, II.3, pp. 139f. and 146.

82. The Hindi expression used by Ramdev is *sabhā bhavan*. It is explained in brackets with the transliteration of the English words [*hāusāf pārlimenṭ*].

83. *BVKI*, 1.2, p. 93.

84. *BVKI*, 1.2, p. 95.

85. *BVKI*, 1.2., p. 96.

86. *BVKI*,1.2, p. 101.

87. *BVKI*, 1.2, p. 106.

88. See e.g., *BVKI*, 1.3, pp. 259–66 and *BVKI*, 1.4, pp. 299f.

89. *BVKI*, II.3., pp. 125,145.

90. *BVKI*, II.3, p. 133.

91. *BVKI*, II.3, pp. 148f.

92. Johann Caspar Bluntschli (1808–81), was born in Zürich and later was appointed Professor for International Law in Munich and Heidelberg. He was

renowned as one of mid-nineteenth century leading theoreticians of the state. The English translation of his *Lehre vom modernen Staat* went into seven editions in Britain and was widely read in India as well.

93. See Metcalf, *Ideologies of the Raj*, pp. 125–8. For a more detailed treatment also see Omissi, D., 1998, *The Sepoy and the Raj: The Indian Army, 1860–1940,* (repr.) Basingstoke: Macmillan.

94. For an excellent treatment of the beginnings of these endeavours, see Rosselli, J., 1980, 'The Self-image of Effeteness: Physical Education and Nationalism in Nineteenth-Century Bengal', in *Past and Present*, pp. 121–48. For an exhaustive discussion of the Gurukul Kangri's contribution to this 'man-making mission', see Fischer-Tiné, H., 'Character Building and Manly Games—Viktorianische Männlichkeitsideale und ihre Aneignung im frühen Hindu-Nationalismus', in *Historische Anthropologie,* 9 (3) 2001, pp. 432–56.

95. Chowdhury, *The Frail Hero and Virile History*, pp. 40–65.

96. Ibid., pp. 54–9.

97. *BVKI*, II.1, p.5.

98. *BVKI*, II.1, p. 6.

99. *BVKI*, II.1, pp. 10–12.

100. Ibid., pp. 7f. and *BVKI*, II.3, pp. 186–91.

101. *BVKI*, II.3, p. 186.

102. *BVKI*, I.3, p. 268.

103. Ibid.

104. Gustav Oppert (1836–1908) was born in Hamburg. He lived in Madras from 1872 to 1893 and worked as a guardian in the Oriental Manuscript Library of the Presidency College. Among his publications, *On the Weapons, Army Organization and Political Maxims of Ancient Hindus,* 1880, and *Original Inhabitants of Bharatvarsha or India*, 1893, are the most prominent. I am grateful to Dr. Indra Sengupta, Heidelberg, for providing me with biographical information on Oppert.

105. William Hickling Prescott (1791–1859) had brought out the tremendously successful *History of the Conquest of Mexico* in 1843. Ramdev quotes extensively from this book.

106. *BVKI*, I.3, pp. 235f.

107. The most influential attempt to prove that the 'Hindu nation' was an ethnically homogenous group in spite of their different geographical and caste-origin was undertaken in V.D. Savarkar's well-known book on Hindutva about a decade later. Cf. Savarkar, V.D., 1989 [1924], *Hindutva: Who is a Hindu,* Bombay: Veer Savarkar Prakashan, pp. 84–91.

108. 'Those who are not able to pursue advanced studies [*vidyādhyayan*] because of their limited intellect are called shudras no matter if they are the sons of brahmans, kṣatriyas, vaiśyas or śūdras. When the son of a shudra was intelligent and attained learning through his education, he also was the object of great veneration.' *BVKI*, I.2, p. 146.

109. *BVKI*, I.3, pp. 237–40.

110. *BVKI*, I.3, p. 240.
111. *BVKI*, I.2, p. 148.
112. *BVKI*, I.2, pp. 128f.
113. *BVKI*, I.2, pp. 140f. and *BVKI*, II.3, pp. 250–4.
114. *BVKI*, II.3, p. 250.
115. Arnold, 'A Time for Science', passim.
116. In the Arya Samaj tradition Ramdev refers only to the Vedic *saṃhita*s and the so-called *ārṣ granth* as authoritative. According to Swami Dayananda, later texts like the *purāṇā*s were corrupted by interpolations and represented but a fuzzy idea of the original divine knowledge. For details of this classification scheme see, Llewellyn, *Arya Samaj as a Fundamentalist Movement*, pp. 192–4.
117. Chatterjee, 'History and the Nationalization of Hinduism', pp. 104–10.
118. *BVKI*, I.4, pp. 331f.
119. *BVKI*, I.4, p. 338.
120. *BVKI*, I.4, p. 339.
121. *Pariṣad* (Sanskrit/Hindi): literally: council, conference.
122. *BVKI*, I.2, p. 71.
123. *BVKI*, I.2, p. 72.
124. *BVKI*, I.2, p. 72.
125. *BVKI*, I.2, p. 72. For a similar argument, see also 'The Ancient Glories of a Conquered Race', *VM & GS*, IX (9), 1917, pp. 679–85.
126. The following is based on *BVKI*, I.2, pp. 53f.
127. See the discussion of Savarkar's concept of history in Bhatt, *Hindu Nationalism*, Oxford.

II

PUBLIC AND PRIVATE SPHERES

'The Hindu Woman's Right to *Saṁnyāsa*'

Religious Movements and the Gender Question: The Sri Sarada Math and the Ramakrishna Sarada Mission

Hiltrud Rüstau

Sannyāse hindunarīr adhikār (The Hindu woman's right to *saṁnyāsa*)[1] was the title of an essay published in the Bengali journal *Udbodhan* of the Ramakrishna Mission in September 1946. Reading this title today, some questions may come to the mind: Can the realization of the right to saṁnyāsa contribute to further progress on the equality of gender? And anyway, does there exist nowadays any doubt about this right of women to saṁnyāsa? At the Maha Kumbh Mela in Allahabad in 2001 we observed female *saṁnyāsins* standing on the carriages of the Mahanirvani Akhara, and there was even one carriage with a woman sitting on the throne. Gita Bharati (born in 1944) is well-known for being the first *saṁnyāsinī* who has been elected as a Mahamandaleshwari of the Nirvani Akhara. That means she has been appointed as a spiritual leader of the Akhara, having the right to give saṁnyāsa to the male members of the order. Uma Bharati (born 1959), also belonging to this order, is a saṁnyāsinī, a member of the Bharatiya Janata Party (BJP) and a minister of the central government as well.[2] She was one of the leading personalities of the Akhil Bharatiya Sadhvi Sammelan, a meeting of women *sādhus* at the Kumbh Mela in Hardwar in 1998, organized by a group of female ascetics, which was affiliated to the Vishva Hindu

Parishad (VHP). Also Sadhvi Ritambara is closely connected to the *saṅgh parivār*, the Hindu nationalist 'family'. She is one of the most fiery orators of the BJP and known for training women in the use of weapons. There is a group within the BJP called the Sadhvi Shakti Parishad. Its aim is to build up a network of *sādhvīs*. This organization might have some hundred members by now.[3] Though the number of female ascetics is still much smaller than that of males, there is no scarcity of *saṁnyāsinīs* in today's India.

That shows, generally speaking, that in Hindu society, tremendous changes have taken place since the article mentioned above was published.

G.S. Ghurye stated in his book *Indian Sadhus* some years ago: 'Indian Sadhuism is ... seen to be a process of long evolution. It has shown great vitality and readiness to adapt itself to changing circumstances without foregoing its fundamental principles.'[4]

One of the most striking characteristics of our time is the growing gender consciousness in India as elsewhere. Social changes have dramatically changed the living conditions of women as well. Out of this results the need to redefine our understanding of femininity.

In order to understand how far Hindu sādhuism has adapted itself to this demand, we will focus our attention on the Sri Sarada Math. This ascetic organization is unique as it is the very first monastic order up to now run only by women, completely independent of men. It is the only ascetic women's order existing so far, where women take all the decisions regarding their order completely independent of male priests or monks, and this includes their religious life in its entirety.

In reading Asha's article we are reminded of Bal Gangadhar Tilak's famous statement: '*Swarāj* is my birthright ...' which gave the national liberation movement a new orientation. Similar to Tilak, Asha stressed the fundamental right of the Hindu women to saṁnyāsa in general. She did not ask for any exceptions to be made for a few spiritually advanced female devotees. And we are also reminded of Swami Vivekananda's speech in Chicago in 1893 where he stressed that human beings in general are divine, so this divinity is our birthright.

The method Asha used to back for her demand is similar to that of Rammohan Roy and Vidyasagar in their struggle against *satī*, for the education of women and the remarriage of widows: she gave examples from the ancient scriptures and quoted extensively from Sanskrit texts, thus legitimizing her demand.

She started her arguments by saying that the aim of human life in general is the realization of God, *brahmacarya* and *saṁnyāsa* being the way to reach this aim. Therefore men and women had an equal right to renunciation. In order to prove that women were as capable of developing their spirituality as men, she pointed out the names of important female *ṛṣi*s mentioned in the *Ṛgveda* and in the *Upanīṣads*. She showed that in Vedic times women performed sacrifices independent of men, they underwent the *upanayana* ritual and had knowledge of Vedic mantras. Simultaneously she pointed out Buddhist and Jain ascetic traditions in which the institution of female asceticism was were well-established.

But in order to justify her demand she first referred to the *guruvacana*, that is to Swami Vivekananda's revolutionary intention to establish a women's Math, already clearly pronounced in the Belur Math rules of 1899 just after its foundation. According to rule no. 1: 'This Math is established to work out one's own liberation, and to train oneself to do good to the world in every way, along the lines laid down by Bhagavan Sri Ramakrishna. For the women too there will be started a similar Math.' Also in rules no. 2–4, the women's Math is mentioned.[5]

Furthermore Asha quoted 'From the Diary of a Disciple' of the year 1898,[6] where Vivekananda stressed the urgent need for establishing a women's Math, and also from his letter to his brother and disciple written already in 1894: '... we must first build a Math for Mother. First Mother and Mother's daughters, then Father and Father's sons ...'.[7]

She quoted Sarat Chandra Chakravarty's report of a dialogue with Vivekananda in Belur Math in 1901 on this topic extensively: 'It is very difficult to understand why in this country so much difference is made between men and women, whereas the Vedanta declares that one and the same conscious Self is present in all beings .... If a man can be a knower of Brahman, why cannot a woman attain to the same knowledge?'[8] Asha quoted the sketch Vivekananda drew of a future women's Math as well: Unmarried girls or *brahmacārinīs* and widows should live there. Devoted married women should also be allowed to stay there now and then. Men should not be involved in the internal concerns of the Math at all. Elderly *sādhus* of the Belur Math should manage the affairs of this Math only from a distance. A girls' school should be attached to the Math. Those students who are able to renounce everything should live in the Math per-manently, taking the vow of celibacy with the permission of their guardians. These celibate nuns should become the teachers and preachers of the Math later on. Other students should be allowed to study there as 'day- scholars'. The guardians of these girls could marry them off later on.[9]

But nearly fifty years passed and there were still no signs of a women's Math. That was the reason why Asha wrote her article.

She did not demand the right to lead an ascetic life for Hindu women in general. This right had always been in existence, especially when we take into consideration the many different kinds of temporary asceticism practised in the life of a housewife, or the ascetic way of life prescribed for widows. There were many different ways of leading a life of renunciation and dedication to the service of others—living in an *āśram* serving the *guru* and the devotees, taking up a teaching profession in any of the educational institutions of the Ramakrishna Mission, or working as a nurse in one of the hospitals run by the Mission. But that was not what Asha was striving for: 'We don't want to be hospital nurses or school teachers only. We want direct realization'.[10]

There were ascetic orders in Hinduism which accepted women, mainly of the Vaishnava and especially of the Shakta denomination.[11] In general there was no ban on women discipleship in any Vaishnava sect. The brahmin orders of the Shaivas however are much more strict in this respect. Nearly all the major and near-major Shaiva sects did not admit women as ascetic disciples, as it was observed by Tripathi at the end of his field studies twenty-five years back.[12] But there are sufficient examples to prove that in Vaishnava orders, the right of women to saṁnyāsa was denied, and any contact of the male ascetics with women had to be strictly avoided. On the other hand, there are also examples of female ascetics in brahmin Shaiva orders. But the attaining of *brahmacarya* or saṁnyāsa exceptionally in individual cases was also not what Asha wanted.

SAṀNYĀSA WITHIN HINDU ASCETICISM

In order to understand Asha's demand completely, let us go over a few facts about Hindu asceticism in general. There are many ascetic orders in India, and an innumerable number of sadhus. The term 'sādhu' is used for a person who leads an ascetic life and has got *dikṣa* or initiation, so that he or she belongs to a line of gurus. Asceticism in Hinduism is a complex of widely varying practices, beliefs, and motives. The multifaceted variety of this phenomenon can only be explained by its historical development. Asceticism in Hinduism came into being with a complicated merging process of pre-Aryan or pre-Vedic, Vedic, and post-Vedic roots. These existed side by side and influenced each other from time to time in the course of history but they were never systematized. Roughly speaking there were always two streams of asceticism in Hinduism.[13] Firstly there is the popular asceticism, which has to be seen in close connection to the *śramaṇa* tradition. It is mainly connected with shaktism and tantrism and as well with the Bhakti movement. And secondly there is the ascetic tradition of the brahmin elite, based on the world-view of the *Upaniṣads*. In the *Dharma Sūtras* this asceticism was looked upon by the brahmins with some suspicion, because of its denial of Vedic ritual. Later on, in the *Dharma Śāstras*, it was, incorporated into mainstream brahmin ideology, where the four *āśramas* were to be interpreted as the four stages of life one has to pass through one after the other.[14] According to this ideology, a saṁnyāsin is a person who at the end of his life would have left everything to his sons, renounced everything, that means he would have no property, no housing, and no connection whatsoever with his past. Manu, considered as the father of the Indian legal system, gave the highest importance to the *gṛhasthāśrama*: because everybody subsists by receiving support from the householder, he called this stage of life the most excellent order.[15]

In contrast to this it was also common practice to choose the way of saṁnyāsa directly after the completion of the stage of *brahmacārin*, skipping the stages of householder and forest-dweller.

The ritual for saṁnyāsa is described in the so-called minor or *Saṁnyāsa Upaniṣads*, and it is mainly characterized by the fact that the renouncer sacrifices himself to Brahman and fulfils all the death rituals for his forefathers, his parents and for himself according to the Vedic ritual. In this way he fulfils all his duties. After that he becomes socially and legally dead.

A first reformation of Hindu asceticism was connected to the name of Shankara (788–820). By organizing the *daśnāmī* orders he is said to have given the current form to the brahmin Shaiva ascetic practice, which had a strong influence on the Vaishnava orders developed later. Ascetics of the *daśnāmī* orders are called *saṁnyāsins*, whereas the followers of the Vaishnava *sampradāyas* go, at least at the Kumbh processions, by the term '*Bairagi*'. The ten orders of Vedic Shaiva ascetics organized by Shankara exist by and large to date.[16] Shankara developed certain rules for the life in a Math, including structures, initiation rituals as well as rules for the renaming of the ascetics after they had got saṁnyāsa.

Thus the term 'saṁnyāsa' in its proper sense means, first, the *āśrama* of the last stage of one's life and, second, a certain ascetic vow and ritual, connected with the ten orders supposed to be founded by Shankara.

When Asha demanded the right of saṁnyāsa for the Hindu women, she asked for the women's right of having their own Math within this structure of daśnāmīs, a demand which from the point of common brahmin understanding was something unheard of. Whereas we can find some names of learned women notwithstanding the common rejection of education for women, it was very rare that women were initiated into saṁnyāsa.[17] Certain reasons were given in the orthodox brahmin literature on why women were not able to lead a life of renunciation. It was said that women as such were weak, fickle, seductive, and only interested in sex, so that they never lived a life independent of men. Women were said to be always ritually impure due to menstruation and delivery. Since women were not given the holy thread they were not allowed to acquire Vedic knowledge which was the condition *sine qua non* for saṁnyāsa. Though it was claimed that women were initiated into the community of the three upper *varṇa*s by the marriage ritual and the *mantra*s connected with it, in reality women were thought of as incapable of rising above the status of *śūdra*s.[18] And śūdras, of course, were not to be given saṁnyāsa. But what mattered most was that in general the role of women was totally reduced to family life: the only aim in the life of a girl was to marry, and being married, her only god was to be her husband.[19] The only way for her to attain salvation and a better rebirth was to serve her husband and the family. Therefore the idea that a woman be allowed to give up her family in order to lead a life as an independently living ascetic was completely rejected by orthodox brahmins.[20]

According to this understanding of women shared by Shankara and his followers, women had only very little chance of being admitted as ascetic disciples by the *swāmi*s in one of the daśnāmī orders, with just a few exceptions in the past.[21]

Notwithstanding the fact that it was already difficult for a woman to leave the family and to be accepted by a guru for ascetic discipleship, nowhere is it mentioned in the past that women were allowed to give saṁnyāsa.[22]

But when Asha demanded a Math for women, it implied the right to give saṁnyāsa as well. She based her revolutionary demand on that of Swami Vivekananda, though he did not mention this in particular. He spoke mainly just about brahmacarya.[23]

SWAMI VIVEKANANDA'S REFORM OF HINDU ASCETICISM

The names of Swami Vivekananda and the Ramakrishna Math and Mission founded by him are synonymous with a second comprehensive reformation of brahmin Shaiva asceticism after Shankara's organization of the daśnāmī orders.

Primarily there are mainly two main new concepts connected with the Ramakrishna order. According to the traditional understanding saṁnyāsins should avoid work, which means that they should not be forced to engage in any social activity. Furthermore only brahmins or at least *dvija*s were thought to be fit to become ascetic disciples in the daśnāmī orders. Though there are sufficient examples that in pre-modern time śūdras also were admitted into the different monastic orders, it can be stated that in general only male members of the dvijas were accepted as ascetic disciples into the orders of the daśnāmīs because only males, having passed the stage of brahmacarya, were thought as being fit to get saṁnyāsa. The precondition for brahmacarya was the upanayana ritual accompanied by the *gāyatrī mantra*, and the bestowal of the *yajñopavīta*, the holy thread given only to the so-called twice-born. Moreover, the opinion that was handed down was that only brahmins could become saṁnyāsins.[24] Nevertheless there are also examples of saṁnyāsins of śūdra origin.[25] Yet not only as an exception but as a rule the Ramakrishna Math accepts everybody independent of his social or even religious background.[26] And its understanding of leading a life of renunciation and spirituality is characterized by the famous saying of Ramakrishna: 'Shiva is *jīva*': to serve men is the service of God. The Ramakrishna order aims at preaching 'those truths which Sri Ramakrishna has, for the good of humanity, preached and demonstrated by practical application in his own life, and to help others to put these truths into practice in their lives for their temporal, mental and, spiritual advancement.' The Mission should work for 'the establishment of fellowship among followers of different religions, knowing them all to be so many forms only of one undying Eternal Religion.' The methods of action were: 'To train men so as to make them competent to teach such knowledge or sciences as are conducive to the material and spiritual welfare of the masses, ... to provide and encourage arts and industries; and ... to introduce and spread among the people in general Vedantic and other religious ideas in the way which they were elucidated in the life of Sri Ramakrishna'.[27]

The first activity of the newly founded organization in 1897 was famine relief. Similarly the rules for the monks living together in the Math, lay stress on philanthropic work. There are two clearly pronounced aims: 'to work out one's own liberation, and to train oneself to do good to the world in every way ("*ātmano mokṣārtham jagaddhitaya*", as Vivekananda put it).'[28] The aims of the order are learning, preaching, teaching, and social work in their broadest sense, besides the individual aim of leading a spiritual life, unattached to the world of phenomena.[29]

The Maths in India had also been centres of education, medical service to the pilgrims, studies, and scholarly discussions in the past.

Besides this, they served as shelters and centres for the organization of the orders. They owned land and got different kinds of gifts from their devotees. So administrative tasks were not unknown to these Maths. Therefore Swami Vivekananda could use a well-known traditional structure which he, following his observations in the USA and Europe on the role of an organization in general, improved upon to better suit his aims.[30]

This way a very modern organization came into being which was at the same time firmly rooted in the ancient tradition. With regard to the rituals for worship, for the consecration of brahmacarins, saṁnyāsins, etc., Vivekananda took up traditions which were at least more than two thousand years old. In addition to this he developed a detailed liturgical concept combining new elements of the worship of Ramakrishna with traditional rites and texts.

The Ramakrishna Math is commonly classified within the daśnāmīs as belonging to the group of the Puris, because Ramakrishna was initiated into saṁnyāsa by the saṁnyāsin Totapuri. There are some doubts with regard to the *paramparā*—the uninterrupted *guru*–disciple–succession for saṁnyāsa in its strict sense.[31] But since then the saṁnyāsa ritual is strictly followed according to the rules of the daśnāmīs.

Thus, even though the Ramakrishna Math is very traditional, it has changed the concept of saṁnyāsa tremendously by admitting ascetic disciples from all levels of the society, which implies also giving the opportunity for studying the holy scriptures to everybody, and including active social service in the agenda of a renouncer.

The concept of organizing a women's Math was something even more revolutionary than that.

There were two main reasons for Vivekananda's interest in establishing a Math for women. The first reason was to find a place where Sarada Devi, Ramakrishna's widow, could live together with some other women who belonged to the household of Ramakrishna, all of them widows who led a pious and ascetic life. But the most decisive reason was that Vivekananda was of the opinion that without female education India would not be able to regain its national vigour. Women should be enabled to improve their life conditions themselves. And for this he needed dedicated female workers who were not bound to their own family circle but could devote themselves to social service, to education, and to preaching Vedanta philosophy among women: 'These dedicated nuns will in time be teachers and preachers of the Math. In villages and towns they will open centres and strive for the spread of female education.'[32]

The starting point for this project was the arrival of Sister Nivedita in India, and the girls' school founded by her. The importance of this school for female education and in the long run even for the foundation of a women's Math can hardly be overvalued. But though Swami Vivekananda most probably had talked to Sister Nivedita about his idea of a women's Math, this idea was obviously not taken up by her. It seems, that she was not much concerned with organizing a women's Math. This holds true for Sister Christine as well.[33]

THE LONG WAY TO THE FOUNDATION OF THE SARADA MATH

Nearly fifty years after the foundation of the Ramakrishna Math, a women's Math was yet to be established. That is when Asha wrote her article.

What was the reason for this delay? Asha pointed out the early death of Swami Vivekananda, which of course might have been an important cause. Wendy Sinclair-Brull is of the opinion that Vivekananda after his return from the West had changed his mind; he had thought of the Math mainly as a home for Sarada Devi who in the meantime was completely absorbed in her care for her relatives. What she needed was 'not a Math in Calcutta, but a home where she could live with her relatives, and at the same time receive visitors.'[34] But this is not very convincing since the Math was not meant only for Sarada Devi but was part of Vivekananda's whole concept for the improvement of India's future by educating the women of the country.

The lethal accident of Sudhira Bose (1889–1920) without any doubt is one of the reasons why the Math did not come into being earlier. She was one of the very first Indian teachers at the girls' school, and came from a typical Bengali *bhadralok* family that was close to the Brahmo Samaj. Her family did not force her to marry when she expressed her intention to live an unmarried life. Her brother[35] was closely connected with the national movement. He met Sister Nivedita, and through her, Sudhira got the job as a teacher. Sudhira was very dedicated, intelligent, and brave; she would have spared no energy in realizing Vivekananda's project.[36] But it is doubtful whether she would have been able to overcome what was called by the Ramakrishna Mission 'unfavourable' 'adverse social conditions'. More precisely: 'His (Vivekananda's) idea ... could not take shape at that time because of lack of education among women and the prevailing social conditions.'[37]

One reason for the delay was the fact that the leading Swamis of the

Ramakrishna Math were obviously not very interested in a women's Math. So the late Vice-President of the Sri Sarada Math, Pravrajika Dayaprana (died in 2000), remembered that in the year 1937 she had asked the then president of the Ramakrishna Mission whether something could be done with regard to a women's Math and the answer was: 'Why, we have our Nivedita School.'[38]

Against this backdrop, Asha was discontent with being fed hopes of becoming either a nurse or a teacher.

But when she wrote her article in 1946, times had changed. Women were drawn into the national upheaval, especially by the Gandhian movement. The self-confidence of women belonging to the urban middle classes had grown, and mothers as well as daughters took an active interest in the political activities of the male members of their families. They consciously started to make the cultural tradition of their country their own, and together with, a common interest in education for girls of the middle and upper strata of society. Eventually these preconditions would contribute to the realization of Vivekananda's project of a women's Math. Of course, the international situation after the end of World War II, was one of general enthusiasm for ideals such as liberty, democracy, and equality.

Asha Debi's (Bandyopadhyaya) life typically illustrates these tendencies. Born in Calcutta in 1915 she got a good education. Her father was close to the national movement and also to the Ramakrishna Mission. He participated in Gandhi's salt *satyāgraha* and was imprisoned by the British more than once. In 1940 Asha got the *dikṣa mantra* from the president of the Ramakrishna Mission and shifted to an āśram founded by young women, of which her father had become the male guardian.[39] She passed her M.A. examination at the Calcutta University, and the teacher's examination as well. She had read Vivekananda's writings and was fascinated by the idea of having a women's Math. In Calcutta she founded the Sarada Mahila Ashram, where spiritually committed female students lived together in a community. She was in close contact with her *mantra-guru,* the president of the Ramakrishna Mission. Probably it was due to his conversations with her that at the annual monks' conference of the Mission in 1946 this president made the following statement:

> The problem of women workers has not received our due attention so long. They have not been given any appreciable scope for leading a monastic life in the Sangha yet. There are hundreds who are ready to renounce the world and consecrate their lives to the cause. Their demand is growing more and more ... it is high time that the case of women who earnestly desire to dedicate their lives to the Sangha should receive your careful and sympathetic consideration.[40]

Encouraged by this statement, Asha wrote the above-mentioned article. But for some time nothing happened.

In the year 1949, first personal contacts were established between the teachers of the Nivedita School in Calcutta and teachers of the Sarada Mandiram in Thrissur, Kerala, also belonging to the Ramakrishna Mission.[41] In 1950 Asha and her friends of the āśram got the status of Dedicated Women Workers of the Rarnakrishna Mission, that is they got recognition as lay devotees committed to a celibate life. This status was already given to inmates of the Matri Mandir, an āśram attached to the Nivedita School, and to inmates of the Sarada Mandiram in Thrissur.

In 1951 the Ramakrishna Mission acquired a plot of land just opposite the Belur Math on the other side of the Hooghly. At the monks' conference in 1952 it was recommended by the Trustees of the Math and Mission to take decisive steps towards the foundation of a women's Math. Some participants of the conference were reluctant to agree to this plan. They pointed at Buddha who is supposed to have said that in case women were to be admitted into the *saṇgha,* it would be condemned to perish in five hundred years, and this, they said, was exactly what happened to Buddhism in India. Besides this, public opinion would not accept saṁnyāsinīs, because women were considered to be unfit for the ascetic way of life. The foundation of a women's Math would lead the Ramakrishna Mission into trouble.[42]

THE WOMEN'S MATH COMES INTO BEING

Notwithstanding these objections, the decisive steps to establish a women's Math were taken, when, on the occasion of the hundredth anniversary of Sarada Devi's birthday, the first batch of seven Dedicated Women Workers was given brahmacarya. A year later, on 12 December 1954 the Sri Sarada Math was founded as a branch of the Ramakrishna Mission. Four years later, at the end of 1958, these brahmacārinīs got initiated into saṁnyāsa by the president of the Ramakrishna Mission. The secretary general officiated as *ācārya* of the ceremony, and recited the mantras according to the rules.

The saṁnyāsinīs also got new names. Since there were no examples to go by for the female form of the common ascetic title (*swāmi*), and the annex of the name (*ānanda*), the president fixed the annex of *prāṇa* (breath of life, principle of life). Although grammatically of masculine gender, because of its closeness to the energy of life, it is associated with *śakti*. So instead of *swāmi*, female ascetics were addressed as *pravrājikā*.[43]

In August 1959 the Trustees of Belur Math gave the full responsibility of the Math to the newly initiated *saṁnyāsinīs*. Asha Devi became the general secretary, that is the administrative head of the Math. At the end of the year 1959 the president of the Sarada Math gave *dikṣa mantra*, brahmacarya, and saṁnyāsa initiation for the first time in the presence of the other saṁnyāsinīs of the order. A new chapter in the history of Hindu female asceticism had been written.

In 1960 the Ramakrishna Sarada Mission was founded with the aim to spread education among women and children and to do social work among them.

Pravrajika Bharatiprana was to become the first president. Her original name was Sarala. She was born in 1894. Like Asha she also came from a brahmin family of Calcutta. Already married at a very early age she attended the Nivedita School, and, when forced by her family to move in with her in-laws, she left her home and took shelter in the school. Sudhira and her brother helped her to hide. Neither Sister Nivedita nor Sister Christine approved of this step. Sister Nivedita even asked: 'Will leaving home be considered good in the land of Sita and Savitri?'[44]

Later, on Sudhira's recommendation, Sarala was trained as a nurse in a Christian hospital, which again generated much controversy because in those days to work as a nurse was unthinkable for a girl from a brahmin family. Sarada Devi, Ramakrishna's widow, supported this step strongly by pointing at the possible demand for future nursing service within brahmin circles. Sarala got the dikṣa mantra from her. Already in 1923 she was initiated into saṁnyāsa by one of the leading Swamis of the Ramakrishna Mission according the śakta-ritual. Between 1927 and 1954 she lived a secluded life in Varanasi. She died in 1973.

Pravrajika Bharatiprana was a person very much suited to become the first president of the newly founded Math, in so far as through her a direct connection with the roots of the movement was established; as a child she had met Swami Vivekananda personally, and she had been very close to Sarada Devi whom she nursed until her death in 1920.

The first institution founded by the Math was a college for girls. Since the Ramakrishna Mission handled over a number of institutions focusing on work among women,[45] the activities and responsibilities of the Math grew very fast.

After Bharatiprana's death Pravrajika Mokshaprana (Renu Basu) became president. Born in 1915, she came from a Calcutta *kāyastha* family. After mantra initiation by the president of the Ramakrishna Mission she passed her M.A. in Ancient Indian History and Culture at the Calcutta University, and the teachers' examination as well. She could convince her family not to force her to marry, and in 1946 became the headmistress of the Nivedita School.

Muktiprana, the first secretary-general, died in 1994. Pravrajika Shraddhaprana became her successor. She came also from the first group of saṁnyāsinīs, who had been connected with the Sister Nivedita Girls' School.[46] Meanwhile Shraddhaprana has become the president after Mokshaprana's death in 1999. The General Secretary's position is now occupied by Pravrajika Amalaprana who belongs to a younger generation.[47]

STRUCTURE, RITUAL, RULES AND REGULATIONS

The whole structure of the Math and Mission, the rules and rituals have been taken over from the Ramakrishna Math and Mission.[48] Even the logo is the same, though slightly changed. The Sri Sarada Math and the Ramakrishna Sarada Mission lay stress on the fact that 'though legally separate' they are 'basically one with the Ramakrishna Math and the Ramakrishna Mission'.[49] Already Swami Vivekananda when talking about the co-operation of men and women and the necessity to impart education to women had spoken about the bird being able to fly only when it could use its two wings. Only by using these two wings could India hope for a happier future, he said.

The Sarada Math considers itself as the necessary completion of the Ramakrishna Mission: 'Sri Sarada Math is actually the women's wing of the Ramakrishna Order. Thus the ideal behind the two Maths is the same. But legally the two Maths are separate. Thus the Sri Sarada Math is totally independent so far as its administration is concerned. But there is mutual respect and cordial relationship without any interference.'[50]

Sri Sarada Math and Ramakrishna Sarada Mission are two different organizations. The Math is a network of 'monasteries' for the female ascetics, the saṁnyāsinīs, whereas the Mission was founded 'with the object of carrying on cultural, charitable, and similar activities among women and children',[51] its members are saṁnyāsinīs and female lay devotees as well. The main social workers of the Mission are the saṁnyāsinīs of the Math. Stress is laid by the Mission on educational work by running different kinds of schools, training centres, libraries, etc., on medical service by running hospitals, charitable dispensaries, etc., on relief work in case of catastrophes, epidemics, etc., and on rural uplift. Though there does not exist any decisive difference with regard to the work of both the institutions, the Math emphasizes religion and preaching, whereas the Mission lays stress on social service in general.

The headquarters of both the organizations are in Dakshineswar. The Math is a trusteeship, whereas the Mission is a non-profitable association. Both own separate funds and maintain separate accounts: the Math fund consists of donations only whereas the Mission fund consists of donations, fees, subscriptions, and grants from public bodies as well as from the central and local governments. Donations to both the institutions are exempted from income tax. Both organizations are closely linked to each other in so far as the Trustees of the Math form the Governing Body of the Mission simultaneously.

A board of trustees[52] take decisions that concern the Math as a whole as there are issues related to budgetary allocation, new spheres of activity, overall policy decisions, and so on. The office-bearers within the Board of Trustees are the President, the Vice-President(s), the General Secretary, the Assistant Secretary, and the Treasurer.[53] The president is the spiritual head: only she gives dikṣa and initiates into brahmacarya and saṁnyāsa once a year on Sarada Devi's birthday.

The trustees appoint the presidents of the different branch centres. The Math and Mission centres are financially independent of the Headquarters, each centre being responsible for its own funding. New activities as the foundation of a new centre, are proposed and prepared by members of the local Sarada Sanghams—associations of lay devotees of the Holy Mother. Before the opening of a new centre can be agreed to by the Board of Trustees, the material basis for its future development must be indicated.

The branch centres submit regular reports to the headquarters in Dakshineswar, and periodically the General Secretary publishes a detailed report of the activities and the financial affairs of the Sarada Math and the Ramakrishna Sarada Mission.

The Managing Committee of the Mission consists of the lay president, the monastic secretary and some other lay members. There are monthly committee meetings, and reports are published annually.[54]

There is a continuous development of the Math and the Mission. In 1997[55] seven centres of the Math were established in different states of India and one in Australia. In 2000 three more centres had been established. The number of the Mission centres in 2000 was fourteen, that is one more centre was set up after 1997.[56] The centres of the Math and the Mission are in West Bengal, Delhi, Tamil Nadu, Kerala, Madhya Pradesh, Arunachal Pradesh, Gujarat, Maharashtra, Karnataka, Orissa, Uttar Pradesh, and Uttranchal. In 2001 a combined centre of Math and Mission was established in Andhra Pradesh.[57]

Since 1980 the semi-annual magazine *Saṁvit* (Spiritual wisdom)[58] has been published in English, followed in 1987 by the quarterly magazine *Nibodhata* (Aspire for supreme knowledge) in Bengali.

By laying stress on active social service instead of aiming only at one's own salvation, the Sarada Math follows consequently the new orientation given by Swami Vivekananda. Sarada Devi, the wife of Ramakrishna, too had understood her husband always in this sense. There was never any doubt about her understanding of *sādhana*—religious endeavour—as being characterized by two objects: the liberation of the self and the welfare of the world which according to her included the study of the *śāstra*s and the training in practical abilities as well.[59]

In spring 2000,189 saṁnyāsinīs and forty-six brahmacārinīs belonged to the Math,[60] whereas the Mission had 184 members in all, of whom 106 were monastics.[61]

The age limit for entering the Math is fixed between eighteen and twenty-five. Graduation is the minimum qualification required for joining the order. The applicants have mostly completed secondary school education, B.A. or even M.A. Some have finished their Ph.D. or got a vocational diploma. In general the applicants come from educated middle-class families from different parts of India. Often the families are already connected with the Ramakrishna Mission or the Sarada Math having got initiation from there, or the example of a saṁnyāsinī working in one of the branch centres might have impressed the young applicant. With regard to the caste background, it can be supposed that the girls come mainly from the upper castes with the exception of Kerala where besides Nayars, Irava girls especially join the order though there is no caste barrier. Nevertheless girls from brahmin background are preferred for tasks like pūjā and cooking. In general, the girls join the order only with the agreement of their parents.

There is nothing like a recruiting campaign. The president gives dikṣa mantra when she is travelling through the country. This can be taken as a first step in the career of becoming a saṁnyāsinī. If the girl wants to join the order she has to pass a health examination first. After that her time as a pre-probationer starts which lasts for two years. She lives in one of the branch centres and works with the different projects there. This period is followed by four years of probation, of which two years have to be spent at the headquarters in Dakshineswar. The schedule there is fixed. Besides other duties, the girls have to attend classes in many subjects, get trained in Sanskrit and read the scriptures—the *Bhagavadgītā*, the *Devīmāhātmya* (*Caṇḍī*), and the main Upaniṣads. They learn Bengali (in case they are from other parts of India) and English too, and discuss extensively the writings of Swami Vivekananda, the biographies of Ramakrishna, Sarada Devi, etc. The girls also learn to do pūjā according to the prescribed ritual. They have to participate in the chores and support the saṁnyāsinīs and brahmacārinīs in their social work.

After these four years as probationer, the Trustees decide whether brahmacarya can be given. The girl has to pass a health examination again before she gets initiated into brahmacarya. In general five years as a brahmacārinī will follow, and following the decision of the Trustees saṁnyāsa will be given by the president. Both the ceremonies will take place only in Dakshineswar.

At the brahmacharya ceremony, the vows are made to live a celibate life, to meditate, to pray, and to do work as service to God. According to the ancient ritual, all previous deeds, all ignorance is sacrificed to brahman in the *homa* fire, by saying: 'We offer ourselves and all we have at the feet of Sri Ramakrishna.'[62] In contrast to the male renouncers at the Belur Math whose heads are shaved clean except for a tuft left at the crown (*śikhā*), the heads of the girls are not shaved, nor do they get the holy thread. But they get the gāyatrī mantra as a symbol of their now having got the status of brahmins. Unlike their brothers in Belur Math, they do not get a new name.[63]

The saṁnyāsa ritual starts a manner similar to the ritual for *brahmacarya*. In preparation for the ceremony, mantras have to be learned, cloth has to be dyed with *gerua*. This time a barber has come to shave the head of the brahmacārinī except for the tuft at the crown. Another male is needed for the ceremony: one day before the actual ritual a brahmin specialized in the death ritual is called to carry out the *śrāddha* ritual, that is the candidate performs the obsequies of her father and mother and of herself and does the *tarpaṇa* for her forefathers.[64] Here the question that arises is how far these funeral ceremonies are really suited for women, because they are traditionally understood as to be carried out only by male members of the family.

The ritual of *ātma śrāddha*—sacrificing the Self—signifies her death to the world. The ceremony starts with the *virāja homa*, by which the body, mind, and senses are purified. The virāja homa includes the sacrifice of one's own former personality in the fire, as well as that of all ignorance and delusion, so that one can recognize herself as *brahman*. The tuft is now cut off by the guru. This is followed by a bath in the Ganga. After that the new gerua clothes are worn. Finally the girls get their new ascetic name, chosen by the guru.

Though it is difficult to say something more definite on the brahmacarya and saṁnyāsa ceremony because of its secrecy, we have to rely more or less on John Yale's (that is, Swami Vityatmananda's) description, approved by the Ramakrishna Math.[65] We can say that these ceremonies follow the centuries-old rituals, with a few new elements added to them.[66]

The same holds true for the rituals in the temple. In the temple in Dakshineswar, Sarada Devi is the focus of worship. Her picture is in the centre, flanked by the pictures of Ramakrishna and Vivekananda. The pūjā follows the ritual of the Kali temple in Dakshineswar. It is a mixture of different forms of tantric rituals, mainly of the Śrīvidyā and the Kālīkula cult. The liturgy of *ārati* and *mangalārati* was developed by Swami Vivekananda who was also the composer of some of the hymns. The *Devīmāhātmya* plays a decisive role everywhere.

All the rituals in the temple are, of course, performed by saṁnyāsinīs, who act as *pūjārinī*s.

The pravrājikās of the Sarada Math understand themselves as belonging to the Vedic dharma tradition founded by Shankara:[67] 'Sri Sarada Math is recognised as belonging to the Daśnāmī Puri saṃpradāya just as the Ramakrishna Math. Sri Ramakrishna was initiated by Totapuri, (daśnāmī), and hence all his saṁnyāsin disciples were of the Puri saṃpradāya. The first batch of saṁnyāsinīs of Sri Sarada Math received saṁnyās from Swami Sankarananda (Puri), the seventh President of the Ramakrishna Order. Hence all the saṁnyāsinīs of Sri Sarada Math belong to Puri saṃpradāya.'[68]

Whereas it is taken for granted that the Sarada Math belongs to the daśnāmīs, and in spite of the fact that during the saṁnyāsa ceremony the ascetics get secret mantras by which they are able to recognize other ascetics, there is no contact with ascetics of other orders: 'Sri Sarada Math being a Math exclusively for women, we avoid any distinct relationship with other monastic orders as they are all for men. For the same reason we are not keen to participate in Kumbh Mela, though there is no written rule against it.'[69]

HOW FEMININITY IS UNDERSTOOD

The members of the Sarada Math are entirely conscious of the novelty of their institution as a female ascetic order. So they are very strict about respecting the rules and regulations of a saṁnyāsin order and are always keen to avoid everything which can bring them discredit. Thus, for example, compared with Vivekananda's concept of a more open women's Math there is a rigorous and detailed training programme for the probationers to which no outsider can have access.

The pravrajikas are fully aware of their femininity and do not try to hide it by imitating masculine traditions. Though due to their saṁnyāsa vow the pravrajikas see themselves as being beyond the gender differences, they consciously lay stress on their femininity by concentrating on their work with women, and discussing questions of equal rights for women in their lectures and contributions to the journal. Time and again they publish reports and essays through which the intellectual and spiritual capability of women around the world and in the course of history are demonstrated.

The life conditions of women have dramatically changed in India during the last decades. Especially women from the urban middle strata have got a lot of new educational and professional opportunities. They participate actively in many different spheres of public life and play a considerable role in politics too. The joint family system is being replaced more and more by small families. All this leads to the redefining of the concept of femininity without surrendering the traditional understanding of female identity. Thoughts on women in the journals of the Sarada Math have to be understood within this context.

We find many articles published in *Saṃvit* in which the role of women in society is analysed. The following are some of the dominating features.

To begin with: Womanhood is not exclusively or predominantly defined by wifehood, as was implied in the ancient ideal of *pativratā*—the wife who took the vow of dedicating her life solely to the well-being of her husband. This pativratā-ideal was the pivot of *strīdharma*, the special duties of the wife, as was described in the different scriptures and illustrated by numerous myths.[70] Already during the struggle for independence, the ideal of motherhood had been brought to the fore.[71] And motherhood is closely associated with womanhood in the Sarada Math: femininity means motherhood. But this implies that, to explain womanhood, mainly the biological gender differences are taken into account without analysing the social relations and their influences which lead to the degradation of women and the inequality in gender relations. That makes it difficult to prove the necessity for a change in gender relations based on equal rights. When it is said that women in general are more inclined to tolerance and peace due to their motherhood than men are, differences in social background and behaviour are overlooked.

Women are said to be generally responsible 'for the preservation of the race', for the transmission of the culture to the next generation.[72] This had already been an important aspect of Swami Vivekananda's demand for overcoming the miserable life conditions of women: Mothers should be made fit to properly educate the future generations. So education of women was first of all seen as a means to an end and not so much as an end in itself—women's right to self-realization. But essays published in *Saṃvit* showed very convincingly that defining women as mothers did not necessarily imply biological motherhood. In the past the rejection of an ascetic life for women was a result of the common understanding which limited the role of women to their responsibilities as wives and mothers—their strīdharma. This contradiction was now resolved by Vivekananda's new interpretation of asceticism. By connecting the endeavour of individual salvation with social service, female asceticism, too, got a new dimension—the motherly taking care of the needy. Female ascetics are giving up biological motherhood, to replace it with spiritual motherhood. Thus they are symbolic mothers who do not have to give up the vow of celibacy.

Another important aspect of femininity is the stress laid on the theological concept of shaktism. This concept, which got prominence in the philosophical and theological discourses of the Middle Ages, was also taken up in the ideology of the national struggle for independence. According to this concept, the supreme reality represents the unity of Shiva and Parvati, male and female, brahman and *śakti*, or absolute spirit and its energy. As this unity is without differences, it can be interpreted as being feminine and masculine at the same time. The world we live in is the manifestation of śakti; she is the loving mother, the energy by which the world is created, maintained, and destroyed. Śakti is the divine strength, and women in general are her worldly manifestation. Therefore they are always characterized by strength and energy. The main scripture for this is the *Devīmāhātmya*, which can be symbolically interpreted as the description of male power (the demons) suppressing women until the feminine power is finally victorious. The *Devīmāhātmya* is described as a sacred book on 'primal feminine power which manifests Herself whenever you pray to her'.[73]

Yet, another aspect is the demand for equal rights for men and women. Both men and women are part of one unit, both are equally valuable but different. Here elements of Advaitic philosophy can also be seen such as the mythical unity of *Ardhanārīśvara* (half-man half-woman: Shiva and his wife are one within one form). Male and female belong together and complement one another. The feminist emancipation movement is criticized for aiming at making women the same as men. It is widely recognized that today there is an economic necessity for women to earn their own money. From this it follows that women have to simultaneously look after their career and their household. However, it is not clear how this can be achieved, although women are admonished not to neglect their children. But it is also clearly recognized that within this process, the masculine role needs to change: men, too, have to become equal partners, in the family as well as in household work.

Furthermore it is said that women should play an important role as spiritual teachers. As a result of the difficulties and problems that confront mankind today: 'The new cycle must see the masses living Vedanta, and this will have to come through women.'[74] Female asceticism is therefore justified because there must be people who give up all worldly attachment and dedicate their life to the teaching of spirituality. Pravrajika Vivekaprana, one of the leading theoreticians of the order and former Secretary of the Ramakrishna Sarada Mission, New Delhi, calls women to be more active in the field of intellectuality. Women are not less intelligent than men, she says, but they have forgotten how to think for themselves, leaving thinking only to men. But women should think about the problems of the world and how they could be solved in order to renew society. Men were mainly warriors and discoverers. While their inventions have made life easier for everyone, there is necessity for more.

As the first example for this new understanding of femininity, Sarada Devi is mentioned. With her a new, feminine or motherly dominated age had started.

The essays in the English magazine *Saṃvit* reflect the life conditions of the women of the middle and upper strata of the society. The problems of women in the villages and in the slums are not touched on in these articles although they are well-known to the saṁnyāsinīs. Vivekaprana, for example, is working actively in a Delhi slum area teaching children and women.

SARADA MATH AND HINDUTVA

The foundation of the Sarada Math as an ascetic order exclusively for women was not only the result of changed social conditions but it also prompted the further development of female asceticism. Since some of the outstanding sādhvīs of the BJP circles also belong to the daśnāmī saṁnyāsins, it is fair to ask whether there is a connection between them and the Sarada Math. This seems to be of relevance as the saṇgh parivār uses Swami Vivekananda as an integrating figure of national identity in its propaganda, among others. Without going into much detail it can be stated that Vivekananda never demanded an organized 'Hindutva' in the sense of a monolithic Hindu state. The term he mainly used was 'Vedanta'. He stressed the unity of India with its many different religions, and he always spoke with much respect of Islam or Buddhism and their importance in the Indian culture. He understood real religion as combining love and tolerance devoid of any tendency of exclusion and division.

But before establishing a comparison we should remind ourselves that the pravrajikas from the Sarada Math take great pains to stress that they are unconnected to politics. For example, in general they do not participate in elections. And they are not part of any other religious or political organization. This of course does not exclude the local level, at which some co-operation with other religious or even political groups or movements is possible.

When we compare the understanding of womanhood as found in the journals of the Sarada Math with the concept of femininity of female BJP activists, though there are some common features, there are mainly a lot of differences.[75]

Both react to the same type of social problems and both mainly attract women from the urban middle classes and the upper castes. However, whereas the influence of the BJP among women is especially strong in the north, north-west and central India (most of all the Hindi-speaking area), the Sarada Math has its strongholds mainly in the eastern and southern parts of the country (West Bengal, Tamil Nadu and Kerala).

Both try to respond to social changes by defining a new female identity. Both understand womanhood mainly as motherhood. But there is a decisive difference. When the women wings of the Vishva Hindu Parishad appeal to the motherly feeling of women, they very often use the picture of real motherhood. The picture of the infant Ram (*Rām lalla*) is an appeal to the mother in every woman. The women are called upon to take an active part in liberating this baby from imprisonment. This idea is closely connected to the concept of śakti as the religious ideal of womanhood. Only, in this context, it is usually not understood as a symbol of cosmic energy in general, of a moving force and part of the divine absolute. Here śakti is understood to be a real force to be used in the fight for Hindutva: 'In the Hindutva movement much stress is laid upon the awakening of maternal power ("*mātṛśakti ka abhyuthan*").[76] *Śakti* is understood as militancy, as it can be seen, for instance, in military training programmes for women. So the Sadhvi Ritambara imparts training with weapons (sword and *lathi*) to women.

In both cases the biological determination of womanhood is stressed: because women are life-giving mothers they are always strong, tolerant, and able to suffer. But this is overemphasized by Uma Bharati, when she says: 'Women are inherently superior as a created species. Men are not such noble beings that women should fight for equality. Instead they should fight to be treated with respect ... . If women combine the *mādhuryā* (sweetness), their femininity, with self-pride and political awareness, they can teach the whole world the path of liberation.'[77] Vivekaprana also stresses that women can teach a lot, not because they are women but because of their spiritual endeavour. In *Saṃvit* there are many examples of women who in the course of history, in different countries, in different religious communities, and in different spheres of life, contributed immensely to cultural development, thus proving the importance of the development of female intellectual and spiritual capabilities. Not only should women be educated to be good mothers but the full development of their potential is also inevitable for further progress. So, when some of the essays published in *Saṃvit* stress that nowadays women have to take up a job in order to contribute to the income of the family, it is also acknowledged that women have the right to self-realization, and to develop their abilities.

Neither the pravrajikas from the Sarada Math nor the BJP-connected saṁnyāsinīs confine women to their family and home, but allow them to take on a public role. But in the case of the BJP activists, this is always understood from a political angle, for instance, the woman *per se* is idealized as the mother of the nation; women are declared to be mothers of Bharat's children. The nation itself is understood as the goddess, Bharat Mata, Shakti, the divine manifestation of the Hindu nation. This Mother India has to be defended with all means including physical power.

But the most striking difference between these two groups can be seen in their different world-views, although both claim to be founded on the same Vedic heritage. In the publications of the Sarada Math, the term 'Vedanta' dominates. It is the philosophy of the Advaita Vedanta in its 'practical' interpretation that Swami Vivekananda provides. This means, the *mahāvākya* '*tat tvam asi*', the unity of everything existing, is the command for seeing God in one another, independently of caste, religion, sex, language or country, so that there is no real otherness. So when we enter one of the centres of the Sarada Math or the Ramakrishna Sarada Mission, we are impressed by the general atmosphere of love, understanding, and peace. Although the number of the saṁnyāsinīs is still small, the social work they are doing in the field of education and health service, and at times of disasters, is well recognized everywhere.

In contrast to this, in the groups close to the BJP, the term 'Hindu' prevails: 'The Hindu is the beginning and the end ("*Hindu hi ādi ant hai*").'[78] This is combined with anti-Muslim tirades and defamation of Christians. Violence against Muslims or Christians is not only justified but often whipped up, for instance, by speeches of Sadhvi Ritambara.

Peace is only to be given a chance within the Hindu community. All others are excluded.

So the final difference between these two groups of female ascetics is the active participation in politics of the BJP. Social work done by VHP workers including sādhvīs, is dominated by political aims. Using the traditional public respect for ascetics, they represent religious fundamentalism with all its consequences. How real asceticism can be combined with being a professional politician, is difficult to explain if one understands the real meaning of saṁnyāsa.

CONCLUSION

Summarizing we arrive at the conclusion that with the Sarada Math, something has been created that although being very conservative, is very far from any form of fundamentalism. The idea is revolutionary: a Math run only by female ascetics who give saṁnyāsa to other women according to the orthodox brahmin tradition and are interpreting the traditional values of the dharma for women in a new way—this is something altogether new. Although the motherly aspect is also stressed by female ascetics of other organizations, the concept of social service is much more comprehensively, efficiently, and systematically worked out in the Sarada Math.

The Sarada Math is very modern but also very traditional from many points of view. But let us go back to the demand raised by Asha. The demand for the right of women to live an ascetic life has to be seen as a protest against patriarchal structures, but only within a limited sphere, nevertheless a sphere which is important for people who are craving to lead a spiritual life. Unfortunately Asha did not take into consideration the question of shudras or outcastes—did she think that these people also had the right to saṁnyāsa? Today everybody is admitted into the Ramakrishna Sarada Order, provided that the applicant has a certain educational standard—which necessarily implies exclusiveness.

Nevertheless, something else has to be mentioned to show the real importance of the Sarada Math: Asha's demand implied the desire of women to organize their religious activities themselves, without any interference from a male priest, monk or even the pope. They can protect and guide themselves. No elderly saṁnyāsinī of the Sarada Math is forced to get up when a young Swami of the Belur Math appears—it would be the case within Buddhism or Jainism.[79] The saṁnyāsinīs from the Sarada Math make decisions themselves. The ordination is done by them alone, without any male interference.

Without any doubt, the Sri Sarada Math and the Ramakrishna Sarada

Mission are the result of a growing female self-confidence. They came into being through the efforts of the women themselves who put pressure on the Swamis of the Ramakrishna Math. And simultaneously they have contributed to a further strengthening of the self-confidence of Indian women, at least among the urban middle classes in West Bengal. However, their influence remains very limited, not only because of their small number but also because they fight shy of publicity.

The Sarada Math is an example of how institutionalized religious structures are changing along with society. The movement is a very special 'symbol of women's rise to strength'[80] and symbolizes a soft revolution against male hegemony, while simultaneously remaining traditional.

ENDNOTES

1. Āśā Debī, '*Sannyāse hindunarīr adhikār*', *Udbodhan*, Calcutta 1353/1946, vol. 48, p. 430–8. I am deeply indebted to Keshab Chandra, Kolkata, who helped me to read the article.

2. Uma Bharati was already four times elected as a member of the Lok Sabha.

3. Cf. Katharina Poggendorf-Kakar, Gottin, Gattin, Mutter. Hinduistische Frauen der urbanen Mittelschichten im sozio-religiosen Kontext, Ph.D thesis, Berlin, 2001, p. 242. See also *Hindu Frauen Zwischen Tradition und Moderne*, Stuttgart: Metzter, 2002.

4. G.S. Ghurye, 1964, *Indian Sadhus*, Bombay: Popular Prakashan, p. 228.

5. Swami Gambhirananda, 1983, *History of the Ramakrishna Math and Ramakrishna Mission*, Calcutta, p. 108.

6. Swami Vivekánanda, 1990, *Complete Works, Vol. VII*, Calcutta: Advaita Ashrama, p. 107 seq.

7. *Letters of Swami Vivekananda*, 1960, Calcutta: Advaita Ashrama, p. 216.

8. Swami Vivekananda, op. cit., Vol. VII, pp. 214, 219.

9. Ibid., p. 217.

10. Āśā Debī, 'Sannyāse hindunarīr adhikār', op. cit., p. 438.

11. The followers of Nimbarkas (since the twelfth century) or the Madhvagauriyas (the followers of Caitanya, since the sixteenth century) accept women. The Kabirpanthis (since the fifteenth/sixteenth century) have established the Mai Shakhas in Chhattisgar (Jharkhand), the mother branch, in which only female ascetics are organized, in contrast to the Bapa Shakhas, the father branch. (Cf. G.S. Ghurye, *Indian Sadhus*, op. cit. p. 191) In the movement of the Siddha Yoga today, many female ascetics play a leading role. We can mention also Anand Mayee Ma, who was venerated by her devotees as a divine incarnation. Especially within the Shakta asceticism, women as *Yoginīs* were of great importance. Here we can point out the Bhairavi Brahmani, who taught Ramakrishna tantrism, and, what matters most, took care of his public image as an incarnation of God. At present Mata Amritananadamayi Ma of Kerala attracts

many people. She was to be one of the representatives of Hinduism at the World Peace Summit of Religions in New York in August 2000. Though her disciples are called *brahmacārins* and *brahmacārinīs* (she gives *saṁnyāsa* too) she does not belong to the *daśnāmīs*; she had no *guru* and no knowledge of Sanskrit and follows the *bhakti marg*.

12. B.D. Tripathi, 1978, *Sadhus of India*, Bombay: Popular Prakashan, p. 131.

13. Besides ascetics who got saṁnyāsa from a *guru*, there is also 'what is called the "*svatantrasādhu*": one dons the ochre robe, takes a monastic name and sets out as a monk or settle somewhere.' Swami Agehananda Bharati (1980), *The Ochre Robe*, Santa Barbara: Ross-Erikson, p. 146.

14. Among the Indian law-givers there existed three different schools of thought with regard to the *āśramas*: 1) there is really only one āśrama, that is the *gṛhasthāśrama*, 2) a person should pass through the āśramas one after the other in order without omitting anyone of them, and 3) after completing the *brahmacarya* āśrama a man has the option of becoming either a householder or a saṁnyāsin immediately after completing his studies. Cf. R.M. Das (1962). *Women in Manu and his Seven Commentators*, Varanasi: Kanchana Publication, p. 100.

15. Manu III, 77–9, quoted in R.M. Das, op. cit., p. 101.

16. Shankara is said to have founded four Maths at the four corners of India. These Maths are the headquarters of the ten orders also founded by him. Whether these orders and these Maths were organized in reality by Shankara or by anyone else a few centuries later, is of no importance. What we know for certain is that at least since the thirteenth century, these four Maths have been in existence. Later on the *ākhāṛās*, ascetic regiments (or a special type of Math), came into being. The different daśnāmī orders are connected with the Shaiva *daśnāmī ākhāṛās*. With regard to the Kumbh Mela, these daśnāmī orders are in a certain sense under the control of the ākhāṛās as, for instance, the Puris join the Nirvani ākhāṛā in the procession. Some of the *jagadgurus* (heads of the Maths founded by Shankara) do not accept this control of the ākhāṛās. So they do not attend the Kumbh Mela. (Information given by Swami Gautamananda, President, Ramakrishna Math Chennai, 7 July 2001 during a talk in Bindweide, Germany.)

17. Panini provides evidences of the existence of educated women, for instance, when he mentions the term *ācāryanī*, the female form of *ācārya*, religious teacher. In Kāmasūtra IV,1.9, we have a reference to the existence of female ascetics belonging to the brahmanical orders, when Vatsyayana warns the *nagaraka*'s wife against female ascetics.

18. Cf. I. Julia Leslie, 1989, *The Perfect Wife, The Orthodox Hindu Woman according to the Strīdharmapaddhati of Tryambakayajvan*, Bombay, Calcutta, Madras: Oxford University Press.

19. According to Manu women were not allowed to recite sacred mantras. Cf. II,66 'The nuptial ceremony is stated to be the Vedic sacrament for women; serving the husband equal to the residence in the house of the teacher and the household-work the same as the daily worship of the sacred fire.' II,67 (quotation from R.M. Das, op. cit., p. 71).

20. For more information see Meena Khandelwal, 'Ungendered Ātma, Masculine Virility and Feminine Compassion: Ambiguities in Renunciant Discourses on Gender', *Contributions to Indian Sociology* 31,1,1997, p. 79.

21. Till today many *sādhvīs*, ranking themselves with the daśnāmīs are not fully initiated. Cf. C. Ojha, 'Feminine Ascetism in Hinduism: Its Tradition and Present Condition', *Man in India*, Vol. 61(3), 1981, p. 266.

22. For further discussion on the present situation with regard to this topic see Catherine Ojha, 'Feminine Ascetism in Hinduism: Its Tradition and Present Condition', op. cit., p. 254. Unfortunately Ojha does not give any source for her claim that saṁnyāsinīs within the daśnāmīs had acquired high status such as heads of feminine monastic institutions, which according to her implied that they could give saṁnyāsa to other women. It would have been very interesting indeed to know from where Ojha got this information. In any case it is a very new development that women have reached a position which allows them to give saṁnyāsa according to the daśnāmī tradition.

23. Cf., e.g., Swami Vivekananda, op. cit., Vol. VII, p. 218.

24. Even today only boys from brahmin families are admitted to the Sanskrit school of the Sringeri Math as the present author was told by one of the leading Swamis during her visit in 1993.

25. See, e.g., Haripada Chakroborti, 1973, *Asceticism in Ancient India*, Calcutta: Punthi Pustak, p. 90 seq.; Yugal Kishore Mishra, 1987, *Asceticism in Ancient India*, Vaishali: Prakrit Jain Institute Research Publication Series 29, p. 98. For statistical data on the attitude of sādhus towards śūdras and outcastes, see B.D. Tripathi, op. cit., p. 195 seq.

26. It is difficult to get statistical material about the social background of saṁnyāsins—those who gave up everything including every memory of their past. But there are some data to prove that the Ramakrishna Math, and the Sarada Math as well, really opened up for people from non-brahmin background. So, e.g., when a new branch of Belur Math was opened in Kerala on (Puranattukara), of the six new saṁnyāsins none was a brahmin, three were Nayars, and two came from a low caste, and one from a so-called outcaste family. See Wendy Sinclair-Brull (1997), *Female Ascetics: Hierarchy and Purity in an Indian Religious Movement*, Richmond: Curzon Press, p. 55. Also at present many of the inmates of the Sarada Math come from backward communities, e.g., from the Iravas in Kerala. Ibid., p. 157.

27. Swami Gambhirananda, op. cit., p. 95.

28. Ibid., p. 108.

29. These aims which had been a revolutionary innovation of Hindu asceticism one hundred years back are nowadays, to a certain extent, generally accepted.

30. 'The term organization means division of labour. Each does his own part, and all the parts taken together express an ideal of harmony ...'. Swami Vivekananda, 1990, *Complete Works,* Vol. VI, Calcutta: p. 295. See also Hans-Peter Müller, 1986, *Die Rāmakrishna-Bewegung: Studien zu ihrer Entstehung, Verbreitung und Gestalt*, Gütersloh: Gütersloher Verlagshaus Mohn, p. 86 seq.

31. Before Ramakrishna died he had given the *gerua* cloth to the first batch of his disciples and had sent them also for the ritual of begging for alms, which is part of the ceremony. But the initiation was not complete. Later on, the disciples initiated themselves according to the prescribed ritual in all its details, which they came to know from a saṁnyāsin of the Purī order; but no initiated saṁnyāsin was present at the ceremony, as per the rule.

32. Swami Vivekananda, op. cit., Vol. VII, p. 218.

33. Though Nivedita did not directly contribute to the foundation of a women's Math, Swami Ranganathananda is nevertheless right when he says that the school founded by her was 'the nucleus of such an Order', because the decisive and final impetus for its foundation was given by women closely linked with this school and strongly influenced by it. Swami Ranganathananda, 1971, *Eternal Values for a Changing Society*, Bombay: Bharatiya Vidya Bhavan, p. 809. In contrast to this, see H.P. Müller, op. cit., p. 147.

34. Wendy Sinclair-Brull, op. cit., p. 65.

35. Debabrata Bose, editor of the revolutionary Dawn Society's magazine, later on Swami Prajnananda. He joined the Ramakrishna Order in 1909.

36. At the age of sixteen Sudhira went on a pilgrimage. To protect herself, she, dressed up as a saṁnyāsinī. It is said that in the following years, the desire to live the life of a saṁnyāsinī took hold of her mind. Cf. 'Sudhira Devi—A Biographical Sketch', *Pravrajika Bharatiprana*, 1992, Calcutta: Sri Sarada Math, p. 162.

37. The General Report of Sri Sarada Math and the Ramakrishna Sarada Mission, Calcutta, 1997, p. 4.

38. *Nivedita School. Centenary Souvenir 1898–1998*, 1998, Calcutta: Ramakrishna Sarada Mission, p. 136.

39. This followed exactly the traditional understanding. According to Manu, women always desire and need protection: 'A woman must never be independent'. Proper protection should always be guaranteed—by the father, the husband or the son. Cf. R. M. Das, op. cit., p. 247.

40. Quoted in *Pravrajika Muktiprana*, 1994, Calcutta: Sri Sarada Math, p. 13.

41. In 1927 the Ramakrishna Mission near Thrissur, Kerala founded a school with an attached hostel for *harijans*. Since the necessity arose of taking care of some orphaned girls, a hostel for girls was opened in 1935. Here lady teachers who were in charge of the hostel stayed. In 1948 the Sri Sarada Mandiram was built for them and for a group of dedicated women workers. Since then the Sri Sarada Math in Puranattukara near Thrissur is the second most important centre of the Sri Sarada Math and the Ramakrishna Sarada Mission besides Dakshineswar.

42. Wendy Sinclair-Brull, op. cit., p. 72. It has to be mentioned here that in the USA already in 1909 Laura Glenn (Devamata) got initiated by Swami Paramananda. In the course of time, two women's convents came into being. In 1947 another one, the Sri Sarada Math in Santa Barbara, California, was started by followers of the Vedanta Society of Southern California. Here female devotees

also got initiated into brahmacarya, a fact which, of course, influenced further development in India as well. See H.P. Müller, op. cit., p. 148 seq.

43. This is the female form of one of the oldest Sanskrit terms for renunciation. A *pravrajaka* was a mendicant, some one who had no house, no property.

44. *Pravrajika Bharatiprana*, 1992, Calcutta: p. XIII. Nivedita and Christine feared bad consequences for their school by supporting such a case which was a criminal one in the eyes of the police. Also Sarada Devi had at first some objections and asked Sudhira: 'You have taken such a great responsibility upon yourself', Sudhira just answered: 'Mother, I have already done it, so what can I do?' Ibid.

45. E.g., the Nivedita Girls' School and the Matri Bhavan in Calcutta.

46. Shraddhaprana was at first lecturer at the Annie Besant College in Varanasi and between 1948 and 1968 she was Headmistress of the Sister Nivedita's Girls' School. Since 1959 she is one of the trustees of the Math.

47. She was born in 1931 and joined the Math in 1957. In 1965 she was given saṁnyāsa. Amalaprana was professor of history at a college in Bangalore before she became the head of the Vivekananda Vidyabhavan, a college for women in Calcutta. In 1994 she was appointed as Assistant Secretary.

48. The saṁnyāsinīs could make use of the experiences gained by the *swāmi*s in the course of time. That includes, e.g., the regulation of the relationship between the Math and the Mission: the Math, inaugurated in 1898, is an autonomous religious body, managed by a Board of Trustees. The Ramakrishna Mission Association, which though founded already in 1897, was officially registered according to the laws in 1909. Its structure is a democratic one. The Trustees of the Math are ex officio members of the Governing Body of the Mission. The number of non-monastic members of the Mission is limited. The development of rules and regulations of the Ramakrishna Math and the Ramakrishna Mission Association was a long process, starting with the first rules given by Swami Vivekananda up to the Rules and Regulations of the Ramakrishna Order from 1935 and 1937, revised in 1958. In the rules adopted in 1935, the schedule for training of the novices was fixed among other things.

49. General Report of the Sri Sarada Math, op. cit., p. 5.

50. Pravrajika Jnanadaprana, Assistant Secretary, in a talk on 22 March 2000 in Dakshineswar.

51. Sri Sarada Math and Ramakrishna Sarada Mission, Calcutta, 1996, p. 8.

52. The General Report April 1995–March 1997 gives the names of sixteen members of the Governing Body of the Mission, i.e., of the Trustees of the Math.

53. Being a monastic institution, details of the Math's internal structure, etc. are, of course, secret. Since a few more details are known with regard to the Ramakrishna Math, we can conclude that likewise the office-bearers of the Sarada Math are elected by the Trustees and that periodically meetings of the senior nuns including the presidents of all the branch centres take place. At these meetings, topics of general interest might be discussed and recommendations be given to the Board of Trustees. The seniority of nuns supposedly depends on how long they belong to the Math.

54. The Ramakrishna Sarada Mission follows in general the same rules as described for the Ramakrishna Mission. See *The Ramakrishna Mission: Memorandum of Association and Rules and Regulations*, 1963, Rev. Ed., Howrah.

55. The General Report April 1995–March 1997, op. cit., p. 6.

56. Ramakrishna Sarada Mission. Report of the Governing Body on the Working of the Association in 1999–2000, p. 2.

57. See for further details: www.srisaradamath.org/activities.htm

58. *Saṁvid*, wisdom, is a term first used in the *Yogasūtras* of Patañjali, understood as knowledge leading to enlightenment. In the *Viṣṇupurāṇa*, this term is used synonymously with *cit*, understood as *śakti*, the energy of God. In this sense the term is also mentioned in the *Devī Bhāgavata Purāṇa* as an attribute of the Goddess, cf., e.g. VII, 32: 'My real self is known by the names *cit*, *saṁvit*, *para brahman* and others,' *Śrī Mad Devī Bhāgavatam*, 1921, *Sacred Books of the Hindus*, Vol. XXVI, Allahabad: p. 707.

59. Cf. Pravrajika Bharatiprana, op. cit., p. XIV. l

60. According to Pravrajika Jnanadaprana, talk on 22 March 2000 in Dakshineswar. For the year 1987 the numbers of eighty-seven saṁnyāsinīs and seventy-three brahmacārinīs were given. Wendy Sinclair-Brull, op. cit., p. 85.

61. Ramakrishna Sarada Mission. Report of the Governing Body on the working of the Association in 1999–2000, p. 4. In 1981 the Mission had 121 members in total, sixty-seven of whom were monastics. See W. Sinclair-Brull, op. cit., p. 85.

62. John Yale (1961), *A Yankee and the Swamis*, London: George Allen and Unwin Ltd, p. 202.

63. The brahmacārinīs in Belur Math get a new name combined with '*caitanya*' and are usually addressed as 'Maharaj'.

64. Wendy Sinclair-Brull, op. cit., p. 173.

65. John Yale, op. cit.

66 Cf. also Swami Agehananda Bharati, op. cit., p. 151. According to him the *Virāja homa* comes first, then the *śikhā* is cut off, then follows the symbolical burning of the brahmacarin's 'corpse' with the *śrāddha* ritual, and finally the ascetic takes his bath in the Ganga, clad only in the 'four directions'.

67. Sri Sarada Math is 'a monastic organization of saṁnyāsinīs of the Ramakrishna Order'. It 'is the outcome of the spiritual awakening affected by the dynamic teachings of Sri Ramakrishna, Sri Sarada Devi and Swami Vivekananda. It is a symbol of women's rise to strength—strength that is born through faith ...' and 'it is in the tradition of the Vedic Dharma.' Editorial, *Saṁvit* 1, 1980, p. 2.

68. Talk with Pravrajika Jnanadaprana, see note 50.

69. Ibid.

70. Cf. Julia Leslie, op. cit. She demonstrates that in the *Strīdharmapaddhati*, e.g., nothing is said about the behaviour of a mother whereas the rules and regulations of the wife's behaviour are dealt with in detail.

71. In this connection the famous saying of Manu is often only partly quoted:

'To be mothers were women created' omitting the second part of the sentence: 'and to be fathers, men', Manu IX, 96.

72. Rakhi Sarkar, 'Indian Women at the Threshold of the Twenty-first Century', in *Saṁvit*, 1996, 34, p. 28.

73. Pravrajika Vivekaprana, 'The Life of Sarada Devi and Its Validity for Us Today', in *Saṁvit*, 1999, 39, p. 26.

74. 'Women and People'. Editorial, in *Saṁvit,* 1988, 18, p. 2.

75. This comparison is partly based on Katharina Poggendorf-Kakar, Göttin, Gattin, Mutter, op. cit., part 3, p. 211.

76. Tanika Sarkar, 'Women's Agency within Authoritarian Communalism: The Rashtrasevika Samiti and Ramjanmabhoomi', in Gyanendra Pandey (ed.), *Hindus and Others*, 1993, Delhi, p. 24.

77 K. Young, 'Women in Hinduism', in A. Sharma (ed.), 1994, *Today's Women in World Religions*, Albany: State University of New York, p. 98.

78. The 'would-be sannasin' Vijay Dube, quoted in Tanika Sarkar, op. cit., p. 26.

79. In the Buddhist *Vinayapiṭaka, Cullavagga* 10.3, it is said, e.g., that any nun, no matter how long she had been in the order, must behave towards any monk, even the rudest novice, as if he were her senior. Monks must be present in the ordination of nuns, etc. See Nancy Aur Falk, 'The Case of the Vanishing Nuns: The Fruit of the Ambivalence in Ancient Indian Buddhism', in N.A. Falk and R. Gross (eds), 1980, *Unspoken Worlds: Women Religious Lives in Non-Western Cultures*, San Francisco: Harker and Row, p. 215.

80. Editorial, *Saṁvit*, 1, 1980, p. 2.

Re-membering the Tradition

Bhaktivinoda Ṭhākura's '*Sajjanaṭosanī*' and the Construction of a Middle-Class Vaisnava Sampradāya in Nineteenth-Century Bengal

Jason D. Fuller

> Another reign has commenced in the East; and amidst the numerous blessings which have flowed from it, one of the most important is, the introduction of that mighty engine of improvement to which it is itself so highly indebted—the press—which bids the slumbering powers of the human mind sleep no more, which arouses every energy into increased vigor, and which, in its mighty progress, subdues the inveterate prejudices of ages, annihilates error, and not only elicits truth, but disposes the mind to welcome it in all its brightness.[1]

So did a British missionary describe the enlightening and modernizing potential of the printing press for colonial Bengal in the widely circulated *Friend of India* in 1821. The author's metaphorical choices are telling. They are, of course, reflective of the context of colonial domination in which they arose. The passage describes the proto-imperial acknowledgement of a new 'reign' in the East from which 'blessings' flow forth while the existing or indigenous order is characterized by its intellectual 'slumbering', lack of arousal, 'inveterate prejudice', and 'error'. Though there is nothing particularly surprising about a colonial missionary referring derogatorily to the intellectual capacities of the so-called natives of Bengal in the first half of the nineteenth century what *is* remarkable about the sentiment expressed in the passage is the metaphorical recognition, in 1821, of the recently introduced vernacular press as a powerful tool of colonial domination as such.[2]

The press is acknowledged to be a means of manipulating consciousness. It is employed to 'subdue' and 'annihilate' the proclivities of the natives while it is designed to 'elicit', and 'dispose' them to higher (colonial) forms of knowledge and self-understanding. The aggressive verb forms are by no means accidental or arbitrary. In 1825 the same journal would proclaim about the press: 'Under an enlightened and wise government, this mighty engine of civilization will in a few years compensate for the injustice of ages. So strong indeed are the fetters of ignorance in which the system of the Vedas has bound the people, that no *power* but that exercised by the press, appears sufficient to burst them. The press will ... dispel the clouds of ignorance, as the sun scatters the mists which the night assembles.'[3]

What is striking in this regard is not the somewhat obvious detail that British missionaries had a negative perception of Hinduism or the 'system of the Vedas', but rather that they self-consciously endeavoured to deploy the 'press'[4] (liberally conceived) as a primary tool of colonial cultural domination. The press was understood from the earliest decades of its installation in Bengal to be a means of exercising power and asserting dominance.

This, I think, has often been overlooked with respect to the so-called reformation and revitalization of Hindu religious traditions in colonial Bengal. Although scholars have occasionally drawn attention to the use of tracts, pamphlets, and other propagandistic literature by Hindu reformers what has never fully been problematized is the unequal power relationship expressed therein.[5] By introducing the press as the primary medium through which colonial 'subjects'[6] would be influenced and controlled, the missionaries helped to set off a chain reaction of events which would eventually bring about the undoing of their very project. The rise of the press in Bengal instigated a corresponding reconfiguration of power relationships among Christian propagandists, *bhadraloka*[7] reformers, and indigenous religious practitioners (either subaltern or traditional elite) such that new strategies of accommodation and contestation were enabled and very specific groups were uniquely positioned to take advantage of them.

It may be that to conceptualize the religious field of cultural activity as a bilateral debate, carried out largely in print, between 'Hindus' (whether 'reform-minded' or 'traditionalist') and Christians does as much to obscure our understanding of religious developments during the period as it does to clarify it. Namely, what is concealed by a reliance upon simple Christian-impact/Hindu-response models is the set of intra-Hindu power struggles carried out among competing social formations (within what Partha Chatterjee has called the 'inner' domain of cultural activity)[8] which sought the right and privilege to define which types of Hindu traditions and communities would 'respond' to the Christian challenge.

The nineteenth century was not just a period when Hindus felt compelled to defend themselves against Christian attacks in print, it was also a period when the questions of Hindu self-definition and self-representation were brought to the fore and opened for debate and intra-communal contestation. Although it is not indefensible to speak of 'Hindu' patterns of indigenous response to colonial-missionary instigation, nevertheless it must be acknowledged that the very notion of 'Hindu' and what it meant to be some variety of Hindu (Vaiṣṇava, Śaiva, Śākta) were notions hotly debated and contested among competing social groups during the period. Confronted by colonial-missionary critiques of native beliefs and practices, indigenous reformers scrambled furiously to define and delimit (imaginatively) coherent communities which could compete with scripture-based protestant formations.

What is too seldom considered in scholarship relating to religious reform movements in colonial Bengal is the fact that in the process of defending so-called indigenous 'communities' (whether Śākta, Śaiva, Vaiṣṇava or more generally 'Hindu') through the medium of print, these communities were themselves, in many important respects, being constructed—or at least, radically restructured. Through the medium of print, the middle class, especially in the last three decades of the nineteenth century, began to turn to religion and to *imagine*[9] discrete and idiosyncratically conceived religious communities in their zeal to assert a national identity and to fend off the anomie generated by colonial bureaucratic fatigue.[10] Fancying that existing religious communities had been corrupted and were in a state of disarray, bhadraloka reformers sought to recover and reclaim them through a process of retrieval and remembrance in print.

By remembering (literally re-membering) forgotten and neglected religious communities, the bhadraloka subjected these very communities (imagined in the new mode) to the same pressures that were visible in other areas where they endeavoured to assert their dominance and aspirations to hegemony. The communities that were imagined by middle-class reformers after 1857 were communities that could withstand the pressures of missionary and secular critique while at the same time remaining defiantly indigenous and thoroughly modern. These communities were imagined in print, and they were largely created and sustained by print. They had very definite boundaries and as often as not were defined precisely in opposition to elements (members) that had been jettisoned in the act of reforming and purifying.

By this, I do not wish to suggest that Hindu communities were invented *ex nihilo* in the nineteenth century. Nor do I wish to recapitulate an oft-argued point that the idea of 'Hindu' or 'Hinduism' was a nationalist imposition which sought to unify various competing communities under a common rubric.[11] That is not the discussion in which I wish to intervene. Scholars examining the changing social landscape of nineteenth-century India have tended to reduce questions of identity to the binary opposition of the nation and communalism. Although I recognize the utility of the concept of Hindutva for understanding twentieth-century socio-political developments (particularly after the term became popular in the 1920s), it is my contention that the idea of a unity of all Hindus and of the equation of Indian nationalism with Hindu nationalism should not be uncritically assumed to be the ultimate *telos* of all reform and revivalist efforts in the colonial period. Although it is tempting to read back the concept of Hindutva into all reform and revivalist movements, one must not lose sight of the fact that not all religious reformers had the word Hindu as part of their active vocabularies. Rather, some of them were concerned with issues other than Hindu-ness and, in fact, were explicitly anti-Hindu (at least certain varieties of pan-Indian Hinduism) in their thought and activities. One such reformer was Bhaktivinoda Ṭhākura.

Bhaktivinoda was, what some would call, a neo-Vaiṣṇava reformer in the late nineteenth century. The movement that he founded (the Gauḍīya Maṭha) became one of the most powerful religious institutions in Bengal and today the movement, along with its affiliate—the International Society for Krishna Consciousness—counts millions amongst its followers with branches all over the world. But one would be hard pressed to discern a generically Hindu message in Bhaktivinoda's writings. In fact, Bhaktivinoda often remarked that he had more in common with Christians and Muslims than he did with so-called Hindus (that is, of the monistic variety). Rather, Bhaktivinoda considered himself a Vaiṣṇava—nothing more, nothing less. His goal was to define and delimit a 'pure' Vaiṣṇava *sampradāya*. He did not define the world in terms of Hindu and non-Hindu. Rather he defined it in terms of Vaiṣṇava and non-Vaiṣṇava.

I would suggest that in order to more accurately understand the universalizing movements of Vivekananda, Aurobindo, and others, one needs to peer beneath the umbrella of 'Hinduism' in order to see the ways in which non-universalizing traditions and communities were themselves defined and constructed in the colonial period. What I would like to suggest is the somewhat modest proposition that in the nineteenth century certain loosely amalgamated constellations of Vaiṣṇava belief and practice, which had hitherto been characterized by amorphousness and porous boundaries, became consolidated, structured, delimited, and in a word, institutionalized, through the auspices of the press and the agency of Bhaktivinoda Ṭhākura. In doing so I would like to make a few connections—between a Vaiṣṇava periodical, the middle class, and discourses of power—that are not often made when discussing modernization and religious reform.

To conceptualize the state of affairs in colonial Bengal as a situation wherein competing, well-formed religious communities vied for power on an equal footing—as Christian impact/Hindu response models are wont to do—is to obscure the many levels of complexity inherent in the processes of 'hybridization' indicative of the period.[12] I will not here attempt to offer solutions to the vexing problems of interpretation so much as I would like to further muddy the waters by problematizing one-dimensional understandings of Hindu–Christian encounters. To do this I would like to trace the ways in which a normative Gauḍīya Vaiṣṇavism was delimited and imagined through the intervention of the middle-class reformer Bhaktivinoda Ṭhākura in the nineteenth century.

If we may be permitted, for our purposes, to follow the subaltern studies' model and divide Bengali society in the nineteenth century into three internally differentiated yet coherent classes, comprising British rulers, middle-class intermediaries and subaltern masses respectively, then we are able to discern a variety of power relationships which are important for any consideration of cultural encounter and religious reformation in Bengal. It is my contention that the press, as an instrument of *power*, worked in several directions and that it was not only a tool of domination by the colonizing British but also an instrument of resistance.

If we conceive of the press as a locus for the negotiation of power relationships in colonial Bengal then we can discern, at least, three important struggles. Print technology was, on the one hand—especially in the first half of the nineteenth century—intended to be used to structure the consciousness of the emerging middle class. And, though modestly successful in this regard, the press (in this case almost exclusively in the vernacular) was nevertheless used in the last three decades by the same middle class to contest the unidirectional flow of power from the British establishment to the cultural intermediaries. So too this contestation had its own consequences as middle-class reformers began to intervene in traditional spheres of indigenous religious activity by restructuring and reconfiguring communities and traditions in their attempts to fend off criticism. In short, I would agree with Chatterjee who argues that in the post-rebellion period, the middle class asserted their social agency through the inauguration of a process of 'self-disciplining'[13] which, I believe, in turn served to reconfigure the religious landscape in the modern era.

The two main points in the following are: first, that the use of the press by Bhaktivinoda Ṭhākura was a means of resistance to colonial structures of domination in as much as it dealt with the very themes which had been proscribed by the modernizing establishment; and second, that these acts of adaptive resistance (whether epiphenomenally or intentionally) served to define, delimit, and all but create the very Vaiṣṇava 'community' that he purported to defend.

Those who have come to conceptualize the idea solely in terms of the nation and communalism might object to my use of the term 'community' in the context of Bhaktivinoda's reform efforts. After all, how does one prove that the audience of a particular item of print culture conceives of itself as a coherent unity? Such reservations would be misguided. If the continued existence of the Gauḍīya Maṭha for over 120 years were not enough to prove it, we know that Bhaktivinoda and his followers established various *maṭha*s and *mandira*s throughout Bengal. They established voluntary organizations, lobbied local officials for property rights, and raised funds for numerous community building projects. Readers of Bhaktivinoda's periodical, *Sajjanaṭosanī* wrote articles, contributed money, went on pilgrimages together, and subscribed year after year to the official journal of their movement. There can be no doubt that Bhaktivinoda was addressing himself to a community of like-minded Vaiṣṇavas when he wrote. The real questions are these: How did he define this community and what were the consequences?

THE MIGHTY ENGINE OF IMPROVEMENT

The etiology of the peculiar optimism of the Baptist missionaries of Śrīrāmapura apropos of the press in the first half of the nineteenth century is not difficult to trace.[14] For the missionaries believed, as did the vast majority of quasi-secularist colonial reformers also promoting 'development' in the colony, that there was a structural affinity between pre-Enlightenment Europe and nineteenth-century India. The analogy, founded upon an evolutionary or developmental understanding of history and civilizational maturation, presupposed two things: first, that the printing press, once introduced into a primarily oral society, would apodictically generate more rational and democratic forms of religion; and second, that, with the development of the rational capacities of the indigenes would come a corresponding admiration for and eventual acceptance of protestant Christianity. For the vast majority of protestant missionaries and colonial reformers, Westernization, modernization, and Christianization were coterminous.[15] In order to further their goals of development, the missionaries conspired with the less obviously partisan bureaucratic advocates of reform throughout the early nineteenth century to encourage the habits of reading and writing among the indigenous population.[16] But the missionaries were not insistent that Bengalis be brought to literacy through reading only Christian works. Prosyletization, if we can call it such, was for them a much more subtle enterprise which entailed more than the simple distribution of copies of the Bible in the vernacular. Rather any socially progressive works were to be encouraged in all fields: mathematics, science, history, philosophy. Yet, what was *not* to be read or published was anything relating to Hinduism. Reading in and of itself was conceived to be a wholly good enterprise with only one exception. Under no circumstances were texts dealing with 'superstition' to be tolerated: 'The press should not be suffered, even for a limited period, to become the auxiliary of superstition. ... Most disastrous would it be, if the greatest engine of improvement yet discovered by man, should, through our supineness, serve to augment the evils we are so anxious to remove. Most disastrous would it be, if the schemes of education now on foot should serve only to create readers for idolatrous publications ... .'[17] In order to encourage the habit of reading in general and good reading habits in particular, the missionaries helped with the extension of the colonial educational system and the expansion of a print market in both the vernacular and English.

To achieve their goals of modernization and Christianization, the missionaries sought the assistance of the emerging colonial middle class which would comprise the Bengali literati acting in the capacity of cultural intermediaries between the British and the subaltern masses. They were to be the producers of culture who would lead a print revolution with the assistance of the British educational system. By increasing literacy rates through education and the circulation of printed material, the religious monopoly of indigenous brahmins would be destroyed. '...[E]very year, by enlarging the circle of readers, [we] will increase the demand for new works, which it will be advantageous for the literati to supply. Thus [will be] one of the strong holds of priestcraft demolished, never again to rise.'[18] The hope of the proponents of the press in pre-rebellion Bengal was that it would destabilize traditional Bengali beliefs and practices; leading superstitious Hindus to 'modernize' and, we might reiterate, eventually accept some variety of protestant Christianity as the highest form of religion.

However, as we now know, this was not to be the case. Rather, by the 1870s and 1880s Christianity had made little headway in Bengal and the publication of so-called 'superstitious' Hindu texts, which had been dismissed as anachronistic vestiges of a former time at the turn of the nineteenth century, was now the rule rather than the exception. After achieving a high degree of literacy, and after having been subjected to the likes of Kant, Hegel, and John Stuart Mill in British schools, many among the educated colonial middle class from the 1850s onward not only refused to become Christians but rather used their accumulation of cultural capital and skills in writing and printing to begin seeking out, recovering, reclaiming, defending, and in the process creating or creatively structuring indigenous traditions and communities which they perceived to have been overlooked, unfairly criticized, lost, and neglected by the colonial establishment. Chief among the traditions that were being reclaimed in late nineteenth-century Bengal was Gauḍīya Vaiṣṇavism.

BENGALI VAIṢṆAVISM BEFORE THE RISE OF PRINT IN THE NINETEENTH CENTURY

By the middle of the nineteenth century, the *idea* of 'Gauḍīya Vaiṣṇavism'[19] had come to attain an ambivalent status in the Bengali imagination. Although more than one-fifth of the region's population professed to be followers of Caitanya[20] throughout the nineteenth century, including a large number of wealthy and prominent *comprador* elites residing in the colonial capital, nevertheless, in the view of an increasingly influential *class* of reform-minded, urbane culture-producers, Vaiṣṇavism was considered to be a degenerate and debased form of religion—the concern of libertines, prostitutes, Untouchables, and beggars. Though the social integrity of Gauḍīya Vaiṣṇava beliefs and practices in rural Bengal was assured, to the urban bhadraloka in the first half of the nineteenth century they were embarrassments to be ignored or, if engaged at all, to be mercilessly ridiculed and chastized. The religion of Caitanya was perceived by many to be a regressive impediment to necessary and inevitable modernizing projects enabled by the colonial milieu.

At the turn of the nineteenth century there were, generally speaking, two categories of religious specialists that were considered to be Gauḍīya Vaiṣṇavas in Bengal. These were the lineal descendants of the followers of Caitanya who were known as *gosvāmī*s or *gosain*s, principally centered in Santipura (Advaita *vaṃśa*) as well as Navadvīpa, Baghnapāḍā, and Kharda (Nityānanda vaṃśa). They were preceptors to house holding (*gṛhastha*) Vaiṣṇavas. The second group consisted of the *vairāgī*s or mendicants who were either itinerant wanderers or quasi-coenobitical monastics who lived in, or were attached to, *ākhḍā*s.[21] H.H. Wilson summed up the general impression of Vaiṣṇava organization when he wrote that: 'The Chaitanya sectaries consist of every tribe and order, and are governed by the descendants of their Gosains. They include some *Udasina*s or Vairagis, men who retire from the world and live unconnected with society in a state of celibacy and mendicancy: the religious teachers are, however, married men and their dwellings, with a temple attached, are tenanted by their family and dependants.'[22]

If there could be said to have been any organizational coherence to Gauḍīya Vaiṣṇavism in the early nineteenth century, it would have been centered on the gosvāmīs. The gosvāmīs were often men of relatively 'large fortunes' who commanded the ritualized respect of vairāgīs and householders who patronized them and their ākhḍās. The gosvāmīs conducted wedding ceremonies and claimed revenue upon the initiation of disciples. But by far their largest source of income came through the overseeing of funerary rites and the inheritance of wealth from disciples. William Ward wrote: '... the Gosaees [gosvāmīs] obtain the largest sums at the deaths of such of their disciples as die intestate. At Calcutta nearly all the women of ill-fame profess the religion of Choitunya before their death, that they may be entitled to some sort of funeral rites: as almost all these persons die intestate, and have no relations who will own them, the Gosaees obtain their effects.'[23]

Though the gosvāmīs lent a bit of structure to Gauḍīya Vaiṣṇavism through their common lineage ties, patronage networks, organization of *melā*s, and ritualized functions, there cannot be said to have been any Vaiṣṇava community or coherent organizational establishment as such in the nineteenth century. As Ramakanta Chakravarty notes about pre-colonial developments: 'Gauḍīya Vaiṣṇavism still had no central organization. For a long time some sort of control over the Gauḍīya Vaiṣṇavas was exercised by the leading *Akhdas* of Navadvipa and Kalna. [Yet] heresy often raised its head. The *Spastadayaka*s for instance respected the tenets of the Caitanya cult but repudiated the authority of the gurus.'[24] Power was dispersed and the tendency was toward inclusion rather than exclusion.

At the end of the eighteenth century and into the early nineteenth, the gosvāmīs began to cultivate ties to the wealthy landholding classes which may have been 'attracted' to the Gauḍīya Vaiṣṇava–brahmin equation.[25] Though the gosvāmīs were brahmins themselves and the *de facto* leaders of a tradition which purported to disregard caste, nevertheless they were 'as tenacious of [brahmanical] distinctions as the most rigid of the regular Hindoos: they [did] not eat with their own disciples, and [were] careful to marry amongst families professing the ancient religion.'[26] Yet, the caste equation which they encouraged for their followers lent social prestige to the *nouveau riche* who had secured land and wealth as a result of British control in Bengal. Most of the *nouveau riche* at the end of the eighteenth and the beginning of the nineteenth century were professed Vaiṣṇavas. Chakravarty speculates that this is to be attributed to the Permanent Settlement (1793) and the subsequent de-emphasis upon the role of violence among zamindars [*jamindāra*] who before British military consolidation had been accustomed to exercising martial power.[27] Particularly worthy of note in this regard were the Rājās of Cossimbājāra, Mahārājā Nandakumāra, Govindarāma Mitra, the 'Black Zamindar' of Calcutta, the Rājās of Shobhābājara, the Ṭhākuras of Pathuriaghata and Jorasanko, and countless others.[28] By becoming *jāt*-Vaiṣṇavas low-caste zamindars could improve their social status.

Yet, by far the largest segment of Gauḍīya Vaiṣṇava specialists were mendicants and they were associated with the least reputable elements of society. It is, of course, difficult to discern the perception of Vaiṣṇava mendicants in the pre-British period. But there is no doubt that from the late eighteenth century onward, itinerant Vaiṣṇavas came under attack: 'The majority of the followers of Choitunya subsist either wholly or in part as public mendicants; and amongst these, numbers of thieves are to be found. It has lately been ascertained, that persons of this description are very numerous: they assume the profession of Voiragee, or religious mendicant, and receive the reverence of the people as persons eminent for sanctity, but are in reality common robbers. They do not all appear to subsist by mendacity; many of them make necklaces, twine, etc. merely that they may appear to their neighbors as persons subsisting by a lawful profession.'[29]

Most Vaiṣṇavas did not proselytize but rather lived in seclusion in ākhḍās which were scattered throughout the countryside of Bengal. Notable ākhḍās existed in Calcutta, Bardhamāna, Nadia, Murshidabad,

Malda, and Birbhum.[30] But there was no central organizing body and the tradition was kept alive mainly through the spoken word. As Gautama Bhadra has pointed out Vaiṣṇavism was traditionally linked to orality and performance rather than texts and silent reading.[31] He makes the argument that the recitation tradition was well-established in India with the *Kāris*: reciters of the Qur'*an*; *Granthi*s: reciters of the *Granthasāheb*; and *Bhāgavati*s: reciters of the *Bhāgavata*—and that for many *Bhāgavata pāṭha* was a form of *sādhana*. There was for a long time in Bengal an intimate connection between manuscript copying and pāṭha. We know this from the post-colophon statements of many surviving manuscripts from the medieval and early modern periods.[32]

Before the nineteenth century, reading was not merely a matter of eyes darting across a page, lips remaining still. It was not a solitary act. It was rather a matter of speaking, listening, performance. In school students learned to read aloud. In the religious ceremonies and purāṇic recitation sessions that they attended, the functionary (*kathaka* or *pāṭhaka*)—whether in Sanskrit or Bengali—read aloud, verbalized; and the audience listened. Bhadra notes that the traditional Bengali dyad of *pāḍa-sonā* is not insignificant in this regard.[33] Until the mid-nineteenth century anyway, reading (pāḍa) axiomatically implied listening (śonā). The two were an inseparable couplet. And apropos of Vaiṣṇavism sacred texts, religious instruction and verbal performances all went hand in hand until the advent of the vernacular press. 'The *yugalavandi* [couplet] of reciting written matter and listening to it inspired every Bengali home to promote copying of manuscripts. Manuscripts were meant for pāṭha, to be audible for people.'[34] Manuscripts were ritually honoured with *pūjā*s. *Sad* brahmanas came to houses during hosted *āsara*s. 'Everyday, before and after pāṭha invoking the grace (*vandanā*) of the manuscript was compulsory.'[35]

This was the way things were in Bengal even before the coming of the press. But manuscript production was expensive and time consuming and thus—though socially and rhetorically valorized—rare. As William Ward wrote in 1811: 'Amongst the millions of Hindoos there is not to be found perhaps a single book-seller's shop.'[36] For, though manuscripts written on *tāla* leaves were used and valorized, copying them was a prohibitively expensive and potentially dubious enterprise:

> ... besides the paper, the natives pay, for copying, one roopee or twelve annas for every 32,000 letters: according to this, the price of the Mahabharutu will be sixty roopees; of the Ramayunu, twenty-four; of the shree-Bhaguvutu, eighteen, and of other books according to their size. The paper upon which books are written, called toolatu, is coloured with a preparation composed of yellow orpiment and the expressed

> juice of tamarind seeds, to preserve it from insects ... . The Hindoo books are generally in single leaves, with a flat board at the top, and another at the bottom, tied with cords, or covered with a cloth. They are about six inches broad and afoot and a half long. The copying of works is attended with the creation and perpetuation of endless mistakes; so that a copy can never be depended upon until it has been subjected to a rigid examination.[37]

In the mid-nineteenth century voluntary associations, through the effective utilization of the press, began to refashion loose Vaiṣṇava organizational ties. Some Vaiṣṇavas formed groups in the new mode and there were attempts at the use of the press. Particularly worthy of note was the foundation of the *Haribhaktipradāyini Sabhā* in 1852. This was the earliest lay Vaiṣṇava association. In 1856 it began publishing a journal called *Sāmvatsarikasamvādapatrikā*.[38] This was the fourth attempt to publish a Vaiṣṇava journal. Before there had been journaling attempts with the *Bhāgavata Samācāra* (1831), the *Bhaktisūcaka* (1835), and the *Nityadharmānurañjikā* (1846).[39]

From the 1850s onward various voluntary associations or *harisabhā*s developed with the intention of creating a public space where Vaiṣṇava ideas could be talked about. But these harisabhās were few and far between with the only truly successful one being the Haribhaktipradāyinī Sabhā in 1852. In fact, Vaiṣṇavism remained, until the 1870s, one of the most embarrassing religious modalities for the urban bhadraloka. Kṛṣṇa in particular caused problems for reformers who felt awkward about defending the relationship of Kṛṣṇa and Rādhā, or even the much less 'scandalous' stories of the child Govinda stealing butter and frolicking with the *gopī*s. The theological problems associated with reconciling a puritanical Victorian morality with the figure of Kṛṣṇa were compounded by the negative perception of Caitanya Vaiṣṇavas in particular.

BHAKTIVINODA ṬHĀKURA AND THE STATUS OF GAUḌĪYA VAIṢṆAVISM

It was into this complex environment that a Hindu College-educated Deputy Magistrate, Kedārnātha Datta Bhaktivinoda Ṭhākura, insinuated himself in 1869 with a mission of recovering or, more accurately, re-creating a Gauḍīya Vaiṣṇava tradition which could meet the social and intellectual demands of colonial petty-bourgeois life. Saddened by critiques and negative portrayals of Vaiṣṇavism after having come to adore its central text, the *Śrīmat Bhāgavata*, Bhaktivinoda determined to instruct his fellow countrymen in the doctrines and practices of the remarkable indigenous tradition which they had been uniformly overlooking in favour of positivistic atheism, popular imported cults, and inferior local varieties of ideology and practice. In a speech given in 1869 Bhaktivinoda chastized his fellow citizens: 'The Bhagavata has suffered alike from shallow critics both Indian and outlandish. That book has been accursed and denounced by a great number of our young countrymen, who have scarcely read its contents and pondered over the philosophy on which it is founded.'[40] Bhaktivinoda considered the bhadraloka rejection of Gauḍīya Vaiṣṇavism to be based upon spurious and ill-conceived notions of what the tradition *really* valorized.

Far from being a hindrance to progress and modernization Gauḍīya Vaiṣṇavism was, for Bhaktivinoda, the ideological formation most suitably positioned for the execution of bhadraloka modernizing projects. Addressing the reformer *par excellence* Bhaktivinoda asserted: '... he (Rammohan Roy] would have done more if he had commenced his work of reformation from the point where the last reformer in India [Caitanya] left it.'[41] By recovering and re-appropriating an 'imagined' Vaiṣṇava heritage as discerned through the Śrīmat Bhāgavata and its companion volume in the Gauḍīya tradition, the *Caitanya Caritāmṛta*, Bhaktivinoda sought to purge Vaiṣṇavism of its unseemly excrescence and present an 'original' Gauḍīya tradition in a manner tempered by modern developments. His project was to reintroduce *śuddha* (pure) Vaiṣṇavism to that class of Bengali society which had, for so long, ignored or despised the religion of Caitanya, considering it to be antithetical to its own projects.

To accomplish his goal of re-creating a tradition which he too felt had degenerated, Bhaktivinoda deployed his accumulation of cultural capital, bureaucratic expertise, and a zeal for institutionalization in an effort to consolidate the Gauḍīya tradition that he envisioned. His *modus operandi* was to take from the 'West' what was good and profitable while at the same time insisting upon a rigorous and thoroughgoing indigenism articulated through textual exegesis and the development of a centralized authority and canon. Bhaktivinoda, for the most part, eschewed the extant tradition that he found in Bengal in the mid-nineteenth century. He agreed with the critics of Gauḍīya Vaiṣṇavism that the religion, as popularly practised, was in a state of decay. However, his solution to the problem was not to dismiss Gauḍīya Vaiṣṇavism *tout court*—as was the case with Rāma Mohāna Rāya and Debendranātha Ṭhākura—but rather to retrieve the *fundamentals* of the religion as discerned through a strict reliance upon its most sacred literature *sans* perversion. For Bhaktivinoda, religious truth was located in texts and reading sacred texts was a form of sādhana.

Bhaktivinoda took for granted the truism that reading was a useful and worthwhile practice. He understood that public opinion was generated and manipulated through the press and reading. So with this in mind he embarked upon a campaign of writing and publishing the likes of which had never before been imagined among Vaiṣṇavas. Over the course of thirty years he wrote many books, edited several newspapers (including the *Śrī Viṣṇupriyā Patrikā* with Śiśira Kumāra Ghosa), and printed a definitive journal which attracted the readership of the literati of his day. Through his manipulation of the press and his emphasis upon reading, Bhaktivinoda was able to recreate the Gauḍīya tradition in the image of his bhadraloka *habitus*.[42] And the tradition that he sought to reclaim or recreate would no longer be located primarily in praxis and physical community, but rather in ideology and imagined community. Although the elements remained the same, the foregrounding and backgrounding of ideology and praxis respectively, were effected through the agency of the press.

Bhaktivinoda's position in the existing Gauḍīya hierarchy was complex. Owing to his partial acceptance of the bhadraloka critique of the extant tradition in addition to the fact that he was a *kāyastha* bureaucrat and not a traditionally sanctioned brahmin gosvāmī, Bhaktivinoda was forced to negotiate a unique position for himself within the contemporary Gauḍīya Vaiṣṇava power structure which would lend his reforms legitimacy in the eyes of his anti-establishment bhadraloka comrades while at the same time remaining consonant with selected sectors of the living community. He did this by skilfully keeping 'traditional' and 'modern' idioms in dialogue.[43] Through the juxtaposition and inversion of modern and traditional tropes, long existing elements of Vaiṣṇavism were repackaged in specifically contemporary ways while recently popularized ideas and innovations were clothed in the language of tradition and history.

Similarly, imported technologies were deployed for specifically indigenous purposes. In this way, the relatively novel 'Western' institution of the printing press was used to disseminate traditional sacred Vaiṣṇava literature and to promote the primary Vaiṣṇava value-orientation of *mādhurya rasa* on a scale which had never been achieved before and in a systematic manner which rendered certain texts and interpretations authoritative. Yet at the same time, ideas and discourses relating to quintessentially nineteenth-century social concerns such as caste equality, widow remarriage, temperance, and positivism were recast as age-old debates resolvable without reference to texts and thinkers outside of the tradition.[44]

Accordingly Bhaktivinoda was able to carve out anew discursive space within Gauḍīya Vaiṣṇavism relevant to bhadraloka concerns. Bhaktivinoda's activities both reflected and generated new understandings of religious power and authority within the tradition such that the rural centres of influence in Navadvīpa, Purī, and Vṛndāvana were challenged and rhetorically subordinated through the relocation of disciplinary and legitimizing power in the ascending urban metropolis of Calcutta. By effectively manipulating the new structures of authority and legitimization rendered operative by the colonial bureaucratic and educational system Bhaktivinoda was able to enter the Vaiṣṇava fray from a position of strength and power. Through the use of the press and his esteemed social position as a Deputy Magistrate in Bengal, his activities were designed to wrest the tradition from the rural brahmin gosvāmīs and choṭoloka '*sahajiyā*s' who had allowed the 'true' (*śuddha*) teachings of Kṛṣṇa and Caitanya to degenerate and become either irrelevant or the objects of ridicule. Bhaktivinoda sought to retrieve Gauḍīya Vaiṣṇavism from its perceived state of degradation and demonstrate its relevance to the modern bhadraloka.

THE PRESS AND THE 'RECOVERY' OF VAIṢṆAVISM

In the first six decades of the nineteenth century, publishing on Vaiṣṇava themes was minimal. The colonial documentarian James Long listed the publication of only one Vaiṣṇava book every eight years between 1801 and 1817, one book every year and a half between 1818 and 1843, and six Vaiṣṇava books per year from 1844 to 1852.[45] Of course, the modest increases in book production were indicative of both rising literacy rates and the expansion of the colonial education system for the first thirty odd years of the vernacular press; but the general lack of Vaiṣṇava publications vis-à-vis other types of literature is equally telling of a general disinterest in themes Vaiṣṇava before the 1850s. We know of a few stray copies of Vaiṣṇava religious texts and poems being published in the first half of the nineteenth century and we know too of a prolific output of poor quality Vaiṣṇava and scandalous quasi-Vaiṣṇava literature from the Baṭṭalā presses.[46] Yet by and large Vaiṣṇavism was uniformly ignored by the literati who found it more interesting and edifying to write books about education, social issues, poetry, and history rather than religion. To the Western-educated bhadraloka intellectuals before 1857 who sought to reform and indeed reshape Bengali society *en toto*, the religion of Caitanya Mahāprabhu was most emphatically *not* to be considered a religion worth writing or reading about.

However, by the middle of the nineteenth century something had changed. Vaiṣṇavism in Bengal by the 1860s had begun to capture the imagination of middle-class intellectuals and social reformers. As has often been pointed out, the post-rebellion (1857) period was one of great significance for the middle class. The period has been described by the social historian Sumit Sarkar as one of introspection.[47] Partha Chatterjee has deemed it a proto-nationalist period when middle-class bureaucrats began to realize the 'rule of colonial difference' which meant that there would always be an unbridgeable divide between ruler and ruled.[48] Whatever the appellation given to this crucial period of Bengali history and whatever the teleological insinuation of the name applied, with respect to Vaiṣṇavism there is no doubt that the last three decades of the nineteenth century saw an efflorescence of Vaiṣṇava literary production. From Baṅkimcāndra's *Kṛṣṇa Caritra* in 1884 to Keśava Cāndra Sena's pamphlets in the 1870s and 1880s; from Dineśa Cāndra Sena's *Bāṅgla Bhāsa o Sāhitya* (1896) to Śiśir Kumāra Ghoṣa's *Śrī Amiya Nimāi Carita* (1898), the reality of the Vaiṣṇava 'Renaissance' is unassailable.[49]

The most important event in the history of Vaiṣṇava publishing, however, may have been the appearance in 1881 of Bhaktivinoda Ṭhākura's *Sajjanaṭosanī*.[50] In the fifty odd years before *Sajjanaṭosanī* was published there had been a few Vaiṣṇava journals printed but none of these had lasted for more than two or three issues and their readerships were quite limited.[51] Yet, with the publication of *Sajjanaṭosanī* we see the first attempt to begin to structure a diverse or even nascent community through the medium of print. Its target audience consisted of influential and educated bhadraloka members of the Bengali intelligentsia who were turning to Vaiṣṇavism at this time. *Sajjanaṭosanī* ran for over thirty years with Bhaktivinoda as the editor and during that period Bhaktivinoda was able to create a vibrant structured community which would quickly become the largest and most powerful entity within the Gauḍīya Vaiṣṇava sampradāya of Bengal. In hindsight we can see that Bhaktivinoda's efforts to delimit and 'rationalize' the tradition for bhadraloka audience had a profound impact through the creation of the Gauḍīya Maṭha which in turn led to the later development of the global Gauḍīya Vaiṣṇava movement of ISKCON. Together these organizations make up the largest and most powerful Vaiṣṇava institutional blocks in West Bengal today. But they have their roots in the journal which Bhaktivinoda published.

In the remaining sections I will explore several key areas where Bhaktivinoda endeavoured to set the orthodox parameters of the community which was being forged. Due to the constraints of space I will highlight the most relevant material from my translations of three critical volumes of *Sajjanaṭosanī*: Vols 1, 4, and 6—which, taken together, provide a representative sample of the hopes, aspirations, and agendas of the early community from 1881 to 1893. In those early years it was published sporadically. The material in volume 1 sets the tone for all subsequent issues of the periodical and volume 6 marks the pinnacle of the early community's maturation when they established Māyāpura as an alternative pilgrimage site to the traditionally accepted *tirtha* of Navadvīpa and Bhaktivinoda retired from his job in the government so that he could devote himself full time to leading the new community.

SAJJANAṬOSANĪ AND THE DEFINITION OF A VAIṢṆAVA

Bhaktivinoda's *Sajjanaṭosanī* represents the first systematic attempt to structure and institutionalize Gauḍīya Vaiṣṇavism. In 1881 as the bhadraloka recovery of Vaiṣṇavism began in earnest Bhaktivinoda wrote: 'At present the *Bhaktiṣāstra*s have been more or less abandoned. Here and there some fragmentary discussions can be found. So too there are several books that have been published but these cannot be easily located. And even if they were available, these books are in terrible condition as they have not been in demand. It is therefore the duty of spiritual seekers to gather together all relevant books and by publishing them to facilitate the spiritual progress of the people.'[52] The interesting thing about what Bhaktivinoda writes, is that even as late as 1881 there was still no coherent or reliable means of access to the Gauḍīya Vaiṣṇava tradition through the medium of print. Bhaktivinoda indicates that Gauḍīya Vaiṣṇavism in 1881 was still considered to be a lost tradition, an ideological constellation, a praxeological imperative, a mode of being-in-the-world which had somehow been lost during the colonial and Muhammedan periods.

What has to be remembered is that before Bhaktivinoda, the Gauḍīya Vaiṣṇava sampradāya in Bengal was largely unstructured. There were really no truly operative hierarchies of authority and there was no institutional coherence as the vast majority of people who would call themselves Vaiṣṇavas were only loosely affiliated through *mahānta*s and ākhḍās. Vairagīs and gosvāmīs existed but, from what the historical records reveal, they were only connected through their *saṅkīrtana* sessions, melās, patronage ties, and maybe, ideological similitude. But if one wanted to know what defined a Vaiṣṇava or what Gauḍīya Vaiṣṇavism taught as a whole, or better still, how to defend it against attack, one had no reliable way of going about discovering this. Or rather, there was no way of discovering the tradition in print; prepackaged and available for consumption.

Vaiṣṇava Organization and Definition

In *Sajjanaṭosanī* Bhaktivinoda sought to begin the process of reclaiming the Gauḍīya tradition which he perceived to have all but disappeared. Throughout the thirty-odd years that he edited his journal he reprinted sacred Vaiṣṇava texts; he wrote book reviews of scores of books dealing with Vaiṣṇava themes; he solicited and published works of devotees and lay followers in his diasporic community of readers; he wrote Vaiṣṇava fiction; he wrote articles dealing with pilgrimage and initiation; and commented on the news of the day from a Vaiṣṇava perspective. What all of this served to do was to begin to define what it meant to be Vaiṣṇava. Probably the most important concern for Bhaktivinoda in his journal (as well as his books) was to define or delimit what a Vaiṣṇava was and, so too (maybe even more importantly), what a Vaiṣṇva was not. Bhaktivinoda popularized the negative adjectival form of Vaiṣṇava: *avaiṣṇava* (meaning un-Vaiṣṇava or non-Vaiṣṇava). His journal was a thirty-year meditation on one issue: What is a Vaiṣṇava? Articles from the fourth volume of *Sajjanaṭosanī* are exemplary of his concerns. They include articles on: 'Vaiṣṇava Sub-Sects', 'Performing Kīrtana', 'The Five Sacraments', 'A Critical Assessment of the *Bāuls*', 'Nature and Signs of a Vaiṣṇava', 'Vaiṣṇava Dharma', 'Call for Vaiṣṇava Competence', 'Instruction for Vaiṣṇavas', 'The Temperament of Vaiṣṇavas', 'Brāhmanas as Vaiṣṇavas', and so on.[53]

What we should remember with respect to the power relationships involved in this process of defining Vaiṣṇavism is that Bhaktivinoda sought to structure and delimit a coherent and defensible set of practices and beliefs that he could propagate as normatively Vaiṣṇava to a literate middle-class audience. He endeavoured to contest the missionaries' and colonial establishment's devalorization of reading 'superstitious' literature. Addressing this problem of rejecting books which had been anathematized *a priori*, Bhaktivinoda encouraged his countrymen to actually read the Vaiṣṇava texts without prejudice. Bhaktivinoda wanted to unearth a pristine Vaiṣṇavasim sans perversion.

To do this Bhaktivinoda distinguished between what he called 'pure' Vaiṣṇavism and that which he called 'phony' Vaiṣṇavism. And though Bhaktiviooda aligned his brand of Vaiṣṇavism rhetorically with the 'pure' (śuddha) gosvāmīs of Navadvīpa and Vṛndāvana, he nevertheless showed few signs of having had significant instructional contact with them and in fact often criticized mahantas and gosvāmīs who refused to adhere to his rigid code of Victorian morality. The fact that there is, even today, debate and confusion regarding Bhaktivinoda's *śikṣa-guru* is telling of his relative disconnection from any authoritative elements in the amorphous community which he sought to discipline. In other words, the fact that no one is quite sure whether Bhaktivinoda's śikṣa-guru was Bipina Bihāri Gosvāmī or Jagannātha Dāsa Bābājī is indicative of the fact that Bhaktivinoda never made this clear in his writings and thus showed himself to be less concerned with self-proclaimed Vaiṣṇavas on the ground and any existing hierarchies than with that 'imagined' Vaiṣṇavism which could be discerned textually through the recovery and printing of books.[54] Bhaktivinoda's pure Vaiṣṇavism was to be found in his instructional literature and the sacred texts which he interpreted through the lens of his colonial education and middle-class upbringing.

What is most significant in this regard is the severing of Bhaktivinoda's Vaiṣṇavism; again, a Vaiṣṇavism which has become all but normative in Bengal today; from the existing unstructured Gauḍīya Vaiṣṇava, sampradāyas at the end of the nineteenth century. The power move, I would argue, in Bhaktivinoda's use of the press, was not simply a contestation of colonial and missionary norms through the reclamation of Vaiṣṇavism (though it certainly was that), but also an attempt on the part of a powerful middle-class bhadraloka reformer to redefine a tradition or community which would conform to the dictates of his particular habitus. And this in turn served to rhetorically marginalize the vast majority of people who thought of themselves as Vaiṣṇavas—whether gosvāmī, vairāgī, or jāt-Vaiṣṇava.

The groups of self-proclaimed Vaiṣṇavas which came under the most strident attacks from Bhaktivinoda included those who were rumoured to practise certain varieties of sexual sādhana. Bhaktivinoda was wont to condemn these groups both on moralistic and ideological grounds. He had the mind of a reformer and considered deviance and improper understanding of theological precepts to go hand in hand. This procedure had the double effect of compounding the missionary critiques of Vaiṣṇavism while at the same time distancing the 'pure' (śuddha) Vaiṣṇava community, which Bhaktivinodā was trying to create, from the practices of those who misunderstood the 'true' import of the scriptures. 'There are certain sampradāya which are absolutely non-Vaiṣṇava, however followers of these sampradāya insist on harming pure Vaiṣṇavas by calling themselves Vaiṣṇava. Foremost among these sampradāya are the Bāulas, Neḍās, Saina, Sahajiyā, and Ativāḍī. All of them plead the name of Lord Gaurāṅga and show off doing *upāsanā* [worship/prayer] ... but what is regrettable is that the instructions that they preach and act as sādhana are all contradictory to true Vaiṣṇava *dharma*. The Bāulas and Darvesas [dervish] would argue that during his travels as a dervish, Sanātana Gosvami preached these views. Followers of Neḍā and Saina would point out Vīrabhadra, the loyal follower of Nityānanda as their founder; the Sahajiyās would proclaim their vulgar view addressing a union between Śrī Rūpa Gosvāmī and Mirabai. It is quite obvious that all of these views are contradictory to the holy Vaiṣṇava dharma.'[55]

But the question is: obvious to whom? The answer is not far to seek. For the fact that these self-proclaimed Vaiṣṇavas were not *really* Vaiṣṇavas must have been obvious to anyone who adhered to Bhaktivinoda's middle-class code of morality. Bhaktivinoda's critique of choṭaloka practices was based upon two principles: first, that sexual sādhana was morally offensive; and second that such practices were not really Vaiṣṇava. In fact, not only were they not Vaiṣṇava, but they were exactly that which is not Vaiṣṇava. They were avaiṣṇava. 'According to Vaiṣṇavism the practice of cavorting with women is quite harmful. There is no harm in seeking refuge in the *varnāśramadharma* and to have a married wife to take care of bodily needs. ... However, pseudo-Vaiṣṇavas such as the Baulas, Sainas, Darvesa, etc. will often abandon their wives and indulge in licentious association with other women, arguing that such repellent behavior is actually sādhana!'[56] Bhaktivinoda seemed to be especially concerned to point out that mystico-erotic varieties of Kṛṣṇa worship were not in fact 'Vaiṣṇava' if they went beyond the mental plains of *rāgānūgā bhakti* and descended into the corporeal or material realms of actual sexual sādhana. One of the most interesting things about Bhaktivinoda's critique of, what he perceived to be, morally repugnant practices, is the way in which he conflated ideology and praxis such that the age-old Indian philosophical debate between monism (*advaita-vāda*) and dualism (*dvaitavāda*) could be mobilized in the cause of condemning 'licentious' sects. Bhaktivinoda thought of them to be heterodox and philosophically aligned with the non-dualists; a position ideologically incompatible with the requisite servility to Kṛṣṇa. Again, he wrote:

The views of the [heterodox] sects are often advaitavāda. The reason being that Saina, Baula, Darvesa, all of them would proclaim the *nirviśeṣa* [without distinction] view of the formless and ultimate state. On attainment of liberation mortal beings won't have any servility to Kṛṣṇa, rather the *jīva*s themselves would grow as Kṛṣṇa. These lyrics are sung by them. They have written booklets in poor Bengali sprinkled with Sanskrit .... They keep these booklets hidden and they will not allow them to be circulated in public. But with great trouble I have been able to acquire and read some of them. There is no doubt that the Baula and Darvesa views are advaitavāda and therefore totally contradictory to pure Vaiṣṇavism.[57]

This ingenious strategy of acknowledging missionary critiques of Gauḍīya Vaiṣṇavism while at the same time distancing his vision of an 'orthodox' and 'orthopraxis' community from the very same critiques had the effect of rendering colonial dismissals of Vaiṣṇavism moot. Bhaktivinoda's Vaiṣṇavism was one that could stand the weight of critique because he deployed the very same criticisms as the colonial establishment. The community that he promoted was defined negatively vis-à-vis the vast majority of those who considered themselves to be Vaiṣṇavas. It is interesting to note that, in his efforts at definition and delimiting, Bhaktivinoda effectively excluded maybe three-quarters or more of the professed Vaiṣṇava population from the ranks of true 'Vaiṣṇavas'. What we see in Bhaktivinoda's journal is more than just an attempt to defend Vaiṣṇavism on the ground or to put into print the positions and teachings of a structured, pre-existing, indigenous tradition with which Bhaktivinoda is engaging. Bhaktivinoda is reflecting in his journal the exact beliefs and practices of self-proclaimed Vaiṣṇavas. Rather, what Bbaktivinoda does is to create a coherent and well-defined set of beliefs and practices (discernible through sacred texts and the dictates of a colonized conscience) which is defensible with respect to colonial and missionary critiques. At the same time, this 'Vaiṣṇavism' which Bhaktivinoda develops is exclusionary and indicative of an attempt by a middle-class religious reformer to utilize the press for the purposes of disciplining and ultimately constructing a coherent, orthodox, and orthoprax community—defensible and available for bhadraloka consumption.

Again, an article that Bhaktivinoda wrote in volume of *Sajjanatoṣanī* is indicative of his temperament and the importance of texts and reading to his project. In an article discussing controversies regarding Caitanya from within and without the sampradāya, he attempted to address problems and criticisms by purging negative elements. He sought the assistance of leaders who agreed with his reforms of Vaiṣṇavism in his attempts to discipline the community.

Listen oh devotees! During the last four hundred years innumerable problems have arisen within the Gauḍīya Vaiṣṇava sampradāya. It is the foremost duty of the successors to the *ācārya*s weed out all of the undesirable elements.[58]

There was of course always a tension for Bhaktivinoda. For there were already people in Bengal who either professed to be Vaiṣṇavas or were, at least, considered to be Vaiṣṇavas by the majority of the population and not all of them could be so easily dismissed as the morally offensive *advaitavādī*-Sahajiyās and Bāuls. Bhaktivinoda was forced to acknowledge this fact and he attempted to discipline and define the amorphous potential community under the auspices of his brand of reformed Vaiṣṇavism. In order to define the terrain that needed to be conquered Bhaktivinoda conceptualized a division of his Vaiṣṇava community into four subgroups:

1. *Mantrācārya*s (The moral leaders of the community).
2. Vaiṣṇavas embracing the vow of seeking alms (Vairāgīs).
3. Those men who have received *dīkṣā* yet remain within the *varnāsrama* system (*Gṛhastha*).
4. Persons who are known as belonging to the Vaiṣṇava caste [Jāt-Vaiṣṇava].[59]

Particularly problematic for Bhaktivinoda were the second and fourth groups. For they were the segments of Bhaktivinoda's 'imagined' community which, not only comprised the most visible sectors of the Vaiṣṇava sampradāya but also caused the most controversy and embarrassment. Jāt-Vaiṣṇavas had always attracted the lowest castes to their ranks and were also, fairly or unfairly, associated in the minds of many with prostitution, thievery, promiscuity, decadence, and general incivility. Bhaktivinoda's primary audience was clearly middle class. The annual lists of subscribers to *Sajjanatoṣanī* read like who's who accounts of *vaidya* and *kāyastha* bureaucrats in the colonial bureaucracy. These apparatchiks were *varnasrāmī bhadraloka* Vaiṣṇavas who were literate (likely conversant in Sanskrit, English, and Bengali), financially stable and in close contact with the British. They occupied the upper echelons of the emerging class system in and around Calcutta. Bhaktivinoda admitted that jāti- or caste-Vaiṣṇavas had to be acknowledged as Vaiṣṇavas *per se* but he was unambiguous about their position in his hierarchy and the need for them to be disciplined. So much so that he often seemed exasperated by their very existence. He felt them to be a threat to the 'pure' community that he envisioned and thus sought to distance his householder audience from them lest they might be contaminated by the excesses of choṭaloka avaiṣṇavism.

> Though jāt-Vaiṣṇavas are devoid of pure devotion nevertheless they insist that they be accorded the honor of being treated like real Vaiṣṇavas. And, unfortunately, that demand is now actually being honored by many uncritical varnāsramī Vaiṣṇavas.[60]

Bhaktivinoda saw this as a serious threat. For him pure (śuddha) Vaiṣṇavas were those who had chosen to follow Kṛṣṇa. His community would have to accommodate certain 'misguided' lineal descendants of pure Vaiṣṇavas from previous ages. But a true Vaiṣṇava was one who had voluntarily chosen to follow the injunctions of the Vaiṣṇava *śāstras*. The idea that existing social hierarchies and categories were fluid and permeable was a hallmark of Bhaktivinoda's thinking. He felt that the caste system itself should be based, not upon lineal descent, but rather upon personal inclination. Though he admitted that the fruit (*phala*) of one's actions in previous lives (one's *karma*) played a definitive role in one's current inclinations, nevertheless, one's status as a brāhmana, kṣatriya, vaiśya, or śudra was dependent upon disposition, not birth.[61] Thus, one who by temperament was inclined to read the *Bhāgavata Purāṇa* would be a brāhmana; one who preferred to be in the military or work in governmental offices would be a ksatriya, and so on. It is not therefore surprising that Bhaktivinoda put little importance on one's claimed status as a Vaiṣṇava by birth. To be a Vaiṣṇava meant to think and behave like a Vaiṣṇava.

For Bhaktivinoda one could not know whether or not one was thinking and behaving like a Vaiṣṇava without the guidance of a spiritual preceptor. Again, a common thread in Bhaktivinoda's thinking was his insistence that a 'competent' guru or preceptor be engaged for the determination of one's proclivities and potential.

> The doer of deeds being unable to ascertain his own abilities should, therefore, first question a competent guru for help. It is the duty of the guru to find out what should be the proper method of doing anything. It is for this reason that men should choose competent gurus.[62]

Though the question of what makes a competent guru is begged, nevertheless the point that a superior is needed in order to properly function as a Vaiṣṇava is clear. Bhaktivinoda saw this as one of the crucial reasons for the failure of Vaiṣṇavas to organize themselves into a coherent block which could stave off criticism. He felt that the failure of Vaiṣṇavism in the nineteenth century was a failure of effective leadership. What was needed to anchor the community on a firm mooring was the proper leadership of ācaryas had proven themselves worthy with their own preceptors and lived their lives in accordance with the Vaiṣṇava scriptures:

> The revered mantrācāryas should give *mantra* to deserving persons only after they have proven themselves worthy by remaining faithful to the dictates of the śāstras. Especially important in this regard is the *Haribhaktivilāsa* ... . As a result of not following the dictates of the sacred texts there has been a downfall of both *guru* and disciples with corresponding deviation in the sampradāya ... . In this way the Vaiṣṇava dharma of Lord Caitanya has been inexcusably blemished.[63]

The ambivalence between textual authority and lineal authority as indicated in the passage was typical of Bhaktivinoda's thinking. Though he valorized the category of gurus and mantrācaryas which should technically have overlapped with the category of traditional gosvāmīs in Navadvīpa and elsewhere, nevertheless it was the *text* that was most important (in this case the Haribhaktivilāsa) for Bhaktivinoda. Both traditional guru and disciple had proven themselves 'unworthy' in the past. The 'deviations' within the Gauḍīya sampradāya were clear signs of this. It was only through a reliance upon texts that the tradition could be recovered. Mantrācaryas and 'revered' gosvāmīs were to be sought out but they were to be disciplined and constrained by sacred texts.

Bhaktivinoda understood the failure of leadership to have permeated all ranks of the potential Vaiṣṇava community. Even the many problems with the mendicant vairāgīs (considered likely to be Sahajiyās, Bāulas, etc.) could be laid at the feet of ignorance and separation from true mantrācaryas who might have been able to give proper religious instruction. Bhaktivinoda considered the troubling vairāgīs to be unschooled in the scriptures and unchecked by qualified preceptors.

> Many kinds of problems have arisen among so-called Vaiṣṇavas who subsist on alms and begging because there has been no critical assessment made of their qualifications by a qualified guru. In truth the right to take on the vow of alms-seeking is a privilege.[64]

The hierarchy that Bhaktivinoda envisioned was clear. A mendicant was to answer to a mantrācarya (more likely to be a bhadraloka reformer than a traditional gosvāmī) and a mantrācarya was to adhere to the dictates of the sacred literature which in turn Bhaktivinoda was publishing, condensing, and commenting upon.

In order to bring the jāt-Vaiṣṇavas and vairāgīs into the fold of respectable Vaiṣṇavas who adhered to the precepts of the śāstras, Bhaktivinoda called in 1887 for a dialogue among those leaders (whether *brāhmaṇa gosvāmī* or newly converted bhadraloka bureaucrat) who agreed with his views regarding the future of his fledgling community.

> In order to correct these problems a *sampradāya doṣaśodhanī sabhā* needs to be hosted in order to bring together the four types of Vaiṣṇavas in order to eliminate the problems. I submit with folded hands that we, the honorable mantrācaryas, should convene such a sabhā and make every attempt to remove the problems in the community.[65]

As it happened Bhaktivinoda would meet with like-minded leaders again and again for the next twenty years in order to lend structure and coherence to the community that he sought to discipline.

Vaiṣṇava Seva

One of Bhaktivinoda's chief criticisms of the existing community was directed against the traditional institution of Vaiṣṇava *seva*. Bhaktivinoda did not have any quarrel with the idea of seva as such, but he did perceive its customary mode of execution as problematic and indicative of the overall degeneracy of Gauḍīya Vaiṣṇavism in the late nineteenth century. In the sixth volume of *Sajjanaṭosanī* Bhaktivinoda summed up his difficulties with traditional Vaiṣṇava seva:

> Serving a Vaiṣṇava is the main duty of a householder. But it is important to know how to serve a Vaiṣṇava. Nowadays [*ekala*] when someone wants to serve a Vaiṣṇava, then he brings some men who are called Vaiṣṇavas and makes a priest cook a lot of food to feed them. We cannot condone this kind of work ... .[66]

Note especially the distinction between the romanticized past (*sekala*) and the degenerate present (ekala). This nostalgia for a pristine history served as a powerful weapon against the unsatisfactory nature of the colonial present. Yet, ironically it was the reformist dispensation of the colonial present which both enabled the critique in the first place and provided the means for escaping the degenerate practices which had become the hallmarks of Gauḍīya Vaiṣṇavism in Bhaktivinoda's time.

Bhaktivinoda agreed with the colonial criticisms of Vaiṣṇavism which imputed all manner of greediness, moral turpitude, and lack of sincerity to the so-called Vaiṣṇava community. Of course, the practice of inviting Vaiṣṇavas to the house of a potentate or wealthy jamidāra had long been a tradition in Bengal. Such meetings served to establish connections of hierarchical dependence between the wealthy *baraloka* and the Vaiṣṇavas. A magnanimous patron would call a meeting of Vaiṣṇavas if he wanted to display his wealth while at the same time expressing his spiritual solidarity with the religious specialists by making a contribution in the form of food, money, and other gift offerings. Vaiṣṇavas, for their part, would utilize the opportunity to be fed good food, to commune with like-thinking practitioners, and to receive money and gifts while they dressed up in their most evocative Vaiṣṇava begging clothes. Bhaktivinoda saw this as a system steeped in false consciousness. He described it in the following way: 'One *charidara* goes and invites a hundred Vaiṣṇavas. Receiving the invitation the Vaiṣṇavas stop whatever they are doing and go and get dressed up. They effect a display of *bhakti* in the hopes of getting food and money.'[67]

Whether or not Bhaktivinoda was correct in his attribution of mundane concerns motivating Vaiṣṇavas who participated in the institution of Vaiṣṇava seva, what is undeniable is the fact that Bhaktivinoda perceived the system to be morally and spiritually bankrupt. The gatherings obviously provided the occasions for the reaffirmation of social hierarchies and patronage networks and Bhaktivinoda realized this with absolute clarity. He realized that the distribution and acceptance of gifts and money [*daksina*] was an integral part of Vaiṣṇava seva in Bengal but he perceived this to represent a threat to the purity and integrity of the religious enterprise. Bhaktivinoda considered the ostentatious displays of wealth to be vulgar and the acceptance of monetary gifts to be spiritually suspect:

So too these days [ekala] we see ākhḍās of *bhekdhari* Vaiṣṇavas. There are icons of God in these ākhḍās and people come to these places to offer pūjā to God and to give *prasādama* to the Vaiṣṇavas. This is not a bad thing but the householders invite Vaiṣṇavas from the akhdas to their houses and feed them and give them gifts of money. This is not the right way for a Vaiṣṇava to act .... One should take care of a Vaiṣṇava if he comes to his home but it is absolutely inappropriate to give money. A Vaiṣṇava should not take money [dikṣina] from a householder. This ritual has come from brāhmanas. It is necessary for us to stop this ritual.[68]

Clearly Bhaktivinoda saw the institution of Vaiṣṇava seva in the modern day to have been infected with the materiality that he deemed indicative of *brāhmaṇical* degeneracy. Like his British counterparts Bhaktivinoda worried about the affected mendacity of certain unscrupulous Vaiṣṇavas and the greed of brāhmanas.[69] However, he took great pains to lay the blame equally at the feet of householder Vaiṣṇavas who enabled and encouraged such practices.

Begging in general was a problem for Bhaktivinoda. Realizing its centrality to the practice of Vaiṣṇavism on the ground in Bengal he realized that it could not be completely done away with. Nevertheless, he was extremely suspicious of the people who went out begging in Bengal. Bhaktivinoda thought that many of them were not truly Vaiṣṇavas but rather imposters:

We now see what the situation of begging is in Bengal nowadays. Seeing Vaiṣṇavas refuse to beg, many unscrupulous men and women take advantage of the situation. Those women who refuse to work for their livelihood leave their beds in the morning, do their household chores and without changing clothes dress themselves up in order to go from door to door taking Gaurāṅga's name. Before lunch a woman can collect three or four *śera*s of rice. She cooks some of it and sells the rest .... As a result of all of this one cannot get servants [*sebaka*, *sebika*] easily.[70] If one can gain so much in two or three hours then why should one serve? Giving alms began as a way of helping pure Vaiṣṇavas. Now it has become a business.[71]

Bhaktivinoda was most distrustful of these unscrupulous women who he felt were ruining the good name of Vaiṣṇavas throughout Bengal. He felt that the name of Gaurāṅga was being taken in vain for material purposes by those who were not even legitimate Vaiṣṇava ascetics.

However, even among those who really were Vaiṣṇava mendicants, there were unsavoury elements. According to Bhaktivinoda Vaiṣṇava beggars had become a scourge in Bengal. Since many of them were lazy and unwilling to work, they had become aggressive and crude. 'Some Vaiṣṇavas have decided that they will not do any work in this world. They will only beg. So now householders cannot get rid of them. People come in groups and beg. Until they get something they use harsh words and harass the householders. If there is no one in front of them, they will steal a pot or pan or maybe some clothes—whatever they can get their hands on. They are dangerous to householders.'[72]

Bhaktivinoda thought that these beggars were really out for material profit and that they were not Vaiṣṇavas seeking to stay alive. He perceived mendicity to be a business and maybe even an unlawful business at that. Bhaktivinoda compared the unscrupulous Vaiṣṇava begging networks to a syndicate extorting money from innocent householders: 'Actually beggars get so much from begging that in a few days they have houses, animals, etc. Sometimes beggars threaten the householders so much that they have to take out loans in order to pay the beggars off.'[73] Whether or not Bhaktivinoda was exaggerating the power of beggars to extort money from householders, the distaste for mendacity among the bhadraloka Vaiṣṇavas like Bhaktivinoda was clear.

Still, Bhaktivinoda determined that the majority of difficulties involved with begging came from sectors of society which were not *really* Vaiṣṇavas. Though they may have professed and extolled the name of Caitanya, those who engaged in such avaiṣṇava practices were by definition not Vaiṣṇavas. Anyway, claimed Bhaktivinoda in a self-contradictory manner, Vaiṣṇavas could barely exist through mendacity in Bengal. They would have to do some work if they wanted to live:

In Vraja [Vṛndāvana] Vaiṣṇavas earn their living by begging. Householders in Śrī Vrajamaṇḍala do not eat rice and *dāl* like in Bengal. They eat *ruti* and fried chickpeas. If Vaiṣṇavas come to their doors they give one piece of ruti to each of them. If a Vaiṣṇava gets one piece of ruti from 10 to 15 houses then he can have his food for the day. For a long time Vaiṣṇavas in Sri Vrajamaṇḍala have subsisted on ruti ... . However, in Bengal, people do not eat ruti. Householders in Bengal eat rice and dāl. In Bengal Vaiṣṇavas may not be able to subsist through begging alone because not all people offer pūjā to God and therefore it is not always possible to get *prasāda*.[74]

The difficulty in Bengal was that there were not enough Vaiṣṇava householders to feed all the legitimate Vaiṣṇavas. And, in addition, even when householders would feed Vaiṣṇavas, they would often give uncooked rice and thus hamper the devotional efforts of the mendicants.

As people do not understand what they are allowed to give a Vaiṣṇava, they often give a handful of uncooked rice. I mention this to point out that Vrajamaṇḍala Vaiṣṇavas can have ruti without any problem but in *Gauramaṇḍala* they have to cook the rice. For this they need wood, pots, etc. And as they have to cook the food this all takes a lot of time so *bhajana* is hampered. So, even though Vaiṣṇavas beg in Gauramaṇḍala the issue is not so simple [as it is in Vraja] ... . For this reason [real] Vaiṣṇavas do not often beg [that is, do *madhukari*) in Bengal.[75]

In general Bhaktivinoda had difficulties with the entire system of begging (Vaiṣṇava seva) that he found in Bengal in the last three decades of the nineteenth century. Convinced that the wealthy exploited the system for the purposes of ostentation and domination, he expressed his distaste for large gatherings of Vaiṣṇavas partaking in the festivities of a patron. Irritated by the thuggery of bands of unscrupulous beggars, he lamented the burden placed upon ordinary householders. But most of all, Bhaktivinoda was concerned for the purity and integrity of the Vaiṣṇava community as a whole (that is, the one that he was imagining) as he saw the institution of begging to represent an obvious pitfall to legitimate Vaiṣṇava practice. Summing up his views on the matter, he wrote: 'It will not hurt a thing if this custom dies out. A householder will be better served if he gives just a little bit of food to a hungry man or some sweets to a Vaiṣṇava sādhu. But that must be the limit! Householders are committing a crime by giving alms to beggars who use begging as a business. Now, in the time of the reformation of society, this custom should be abolished.'[76]

Book Reviews

Another use to which Bhaktivinoda put his journal *Sajjanṭosanī* was that of literary criticism. Over the years Bhaktivinoda used *Sajjanṭosanī* to express his views, either vouchsafing or anathematizing texts which were being produced by affiliate and rival devotees in the burgeoning Vaiṣṇava publishing industry. In nearly every issue of *Sajjanṭosanī* Bhaktivinoda and his editorial staff offered book reviews of countless Vaiṣṇava or quasi-Vaiṣṇava books published between 1881 and 1914. In this way Bhaktivinoda began to discipline the literary production of the community that he envisioned through criticism. Though he was not defining a 'canon' *per se*, he nevertheless made clear to his followers which books were in alignment with his enterprise and which were counter-productive. Bhaktivinoda's journal served as a clearing house for Vaiṣṇava publications. Favoured texts would be advertised in

Sajjanṭosanī and praised in the editorial pages. By clarifying which books were acceptable and which were not, Bhaktivinoda hoped to establish an orthodox literary tradition which remained faithful to the dictates of his colonial reforms.

The reviews in Volume 6 (1893) of *Sajjanṭosanī* are indicative of Bhaktivinoda's project. That year Bhaktivinoda and his editors reviewed nearly a dozen Vaiṣṇava publications. In the May edition of *Sajjanṭosanī* they reviewed the *Jīvanacarita of Śrīmad Raghunātha Dāsa Gosvāmīn* by Aghoranātha Chattopadhyaya claiming that the book was 'very beautiful and written quite well'. Bhaktivinoda gave the author high critical marks for extensive research and critical method while he praised the general effort of collecting biographies of noteworthy historical figures: 'The author got the biography of Śrīla Dāsa Gosvāmī with great effort. The more it is possible to collect such biographies of [noteworthy] devotees the better it will be.'[77] In the same issue, Bhaktivinoda favourably reviewed a Sanskrit play by Kṛṣṇānanda Vidyabachaspati. One of Bhaktivinoda's primary goals in publishing generally was to provide the bhadraloka easy access to the sacred Vaiṣṇava literature that had been kept from them in the English schools and bookstores. In *Sajjanṭosanī* Bhaktivinoda sought to make readers aware of Vaiṣṇava materials that were being published and to encourage them to collect and read as many books as possible. In the second issue of the sixth volume of *Sajjanṭosanī*, Bhaktivinoda advertised a translated edition of the *Rāmacaritamānas* of Tulasīdāsa that was published by the Gauḍīya Maṭha and wrote a word of encouragement. The edition has an 'extremely easy Bengali translation of each verse with many added *ślokas* and poems from books like the *Śrī Caitanyacaritāmṛata*, etc.'[78] Other books were advertised including the *Bhagavad Gita*, *Caitanyasikṣāmṛta*, *Śrī Śrī Kṛṣṇavijāya*, *Viṣṇusahaśranāma*, *Navadvīpa Māhātmya*, etc. By advertising books and by writing critical/adulatory descriptions of them, Bhaktivinoda hoped to control what his followers and comrades were reading through persuasion and dissuasion.

One of the recurring themes in Bhaktivinoda's paternalistic assessment of books which he thought would be harmful for devotees to read was the notion that all of those who were literate were deeming themselves worthy of writing books. As a well-educated, high ranking bhadraloka official, Bhaktivinoda did not hide his aversion for what he perceived to be wrong-headed reformist critiques of Vaiṣṇavism. Bhaktivinoda found himself in the middle of a cultural debate and he was quite content to be there. With respect to the Vaiṣṇava establishment, Bhaktivinoda represented modernity and colonial reason, but contrasted with the rabid reformers of Young Bengal and its legatees, Bhaktivinoda was happy to defend the neo-tradition which he endeavoured to create. Against the defamatory generalizing remarks about Vaiṣṇavas that he found in Śrī Manmathanātha Mitra's *Premamāla*, Bhaktivinoda wrote: 'Pure Vaisnavas will be hurt by reading this. The stench of *māyāvada* is here in the book .... Manmathababu has written "We are surprised to see the favourable opinion regarding adultery and recklessness in the modern Vaiṣṇava *samāja*. Because of their sinful acts, the country has become a living hell." By saying this Manmathababu has expressed his ignorance of our modern Vaiṣṇava samāja. He does not know that in addition to the Sahajīya, Bāulas, Neraneris, and other self-willed samprdāyas, there is a group of pure Vaiṣṇavas ... . The faults that he mentioned do not exist in them.' Bhaktivinoda chastized Mitra by claiming (without a trace of irony!) that literacy alone did not give one the right to pronounce judgments or intervene in traditional religious matters. 'Nowadays, there is a big problem. Those who simply know how to read and write k, kh ... think that they can start to give advice like a guru!'[79]

Still, Bhaktivinoda was by and large supportive of reformist tendencies, as long as they bolstered his arguments for a pure brand of Vaiṣṇavism which straddled the traditional/modern divide. In his efforts to reclaim Vaiṣṇavism from the ashes in which colonial attacks and brāhmāṇa dominance had left it, Bhaktivinoda endorsed the use of modern methods and critical history by others. As he had made effective use of Western conceptions of history and historical method himself in his Śrī Kṛṣṇa Samhita, Bhaktivinoda set the tone for those who would follow in his footsteps. Bhaktivinoda had set the tone and did not shy away from embracing modernizing works which utilized a variety of methods and means to legitimize (*adhunika*) Gauḍīya Vaiṣṇavism. In a review of Candravinoda Pāla Choudhuri's *Śrī Śrī Caitanyadeva O Premadharma* he wrote: 'Candrabābu's sense of historical method is based on Western science and we can see that clearly in many places. Nowadays it is popular. Candrababu quoted from the Bible to make his argument strong. Old Vaiṣṇavas won't like this but if someone goes through all of the śāstras of all of the countries objectively, then this sort of deduction is acceptable. Besides, it is not good to be scornful of any book ... . Candrabābu is a Vaiṣṇava who is brave and ready to take the best things from other religions. He has done his duty as a Vaiṣṇava and we appreciate it.'[80]

Generally speaking, Bhaktivinoda was appreciative of books which supported his vision of Vaiṣṇavism and were condemnatory of those which either attacked his vision or were supportive of the problematic traditionalist practices which he sought to eradicate. Book reviews became one more method in an overall printing campaign designed to discipline the existing community by making it conform to an emerging religious bhadraloka habitus.

Over the course of his religious career, Bhaktivinoda would go on to establish an 'alternative' pilgrimage site to the gosvāmī-controlled Navadvīpa across the Bhāgīrathī river in Māyāpura, West Bengal. He would capitalize on his understanding of voluntary associations and 'modern' forms of organization through the establishment of the Gauḍīya Mission (later to become the Gauḍīya Maṭha). Publishing over a hundred books he would become the most prolific Bengali Vaiṣṇava writer in history (until the mid-twentieth century anyway) and his name would circulate across the globe. The Vaiṣṇavism which he imagined and the very real communities that it spawned were deeply embedded in his middle-class habitus. So too groups and peoples who were excluded from membership in his community were precisely those who could not be defended with respect to middle-class moods and motivations. For Bhaktivinoda, 'pure' Vaiṣṇavas were morally chaste, literate (or at least submissive to the dictates of the śāstras as interpreted by Bhaktivinoda), and voluntarily accepting of a certain type of dualist Vaiṣṇava theology. Bhaktivinoda's Vaiṣṇava community was hand-picked from the larger Gauḍīya Vaiṣṇava universe in nineteenth-century Bengal. It was exclusive but it was defensible.

CONCLUSION

Bhaktivinoda Ṭhākura's use of the printing press in the form of his monthly journal in the 1880s inaugurated a process of defining and delimiting Gauḍīya Vaiṣṇavism *per se* for a middle-class audience. Bhaktivinoda eschewed the colonial pressures to disregard Vaiṣṇavism and instead embraced a religion that he felt to be rationally defensible. His project of reclaiming and defining served the dual functions of packaging a normative brand of acceptable or 'pure' Vaiṣṇavism which could be produced and reproduced through the medium of print *ad infinitum*, while at the same time responding to colonial criticisms of the 'tradition'. Bhaktivinoda's definition of Vaiṣṇavism represented a creative indigenous response to the pressures of the colonial period; as a tool of colonial domination, the 'engine of improvement' was adapted for specifically indigenous purposes. Bhaktivinoda was able to use the printing press to contest the colonial project of 'development' and 'modernization' which explicitly disavowed any use of the press to further indigenous forms of religion.

In the process of generating a form of Vaiṣṇavism which could withstand critique and 'public' scrutiny, Bhaktivinoda began to consolidate and delimit a Vaiṣṇava orthodoxy and orthopraxis which would find its *telos* in the powerful twentieth-century institutions of ISKCON and the Gauḍīya Maṭha. The brand of Vaiṣṇavism which they now propagate as normative had its origins in Bhaktivinoda's attempts to purify Vaiṣṇavism and sweep it clean. This new brand of middle-class Vaiṣṇavism served to rhetorically marginalize many of those who considered themselves to be Vaiṣṇavas but did not adhere to the social mores and theological dualism which Bhaktivinoda demanded. This marginalization lent a distinct class angle to the project of revitalization. It was the result of colonial pressures and a creative indigenous response that led to Bhaktivinoda Ṭhākura's creation, through the medium of print, of a middle-class Vaiṣṇavism in the last three decades of the nineteenth century.

ENDNOTES

1. 'On the effect of the Native Press in India,' *Friend of India*, Quarterly 1 (1821): 121. Italics mine.

2. For the classic statement on the importance of metaphors as indicators of horizons of meaning, see George Lakoff and Mark Johnson, 1980, *Metaphors We Live By*, Chicago: The University of Chicago Press.

3. 'State of the Native Press', *Friend of India,* Quarterly 1(1825): 143. Italics mine.

4. In this essay I follow the example of the early Baptist missionaries by deploying the term 'press' to refer not only to periodicals nor to the technology of printing as such but also to the cluster of ideas, practices, and literary products which are attendant upon printing technology as a whole.

5. For useful discussions on the use of the press by 'Hindu' reformers, see Kenneth Jones, 1989, *Socio-Religious Reform Movements in British India*, Cambridge: Cambridge University Press; and Amiya P. Sen, 1993, *Hindu Revivalism in Bengal 1872–1905*: *Some Essays in Interpretation*, Delhi: Oxford University Press, pp. 81–284.

6. On the idea of the 'subject' I am indebted to Michel Foucault's understanding of the dual nature of the term. 'There are two meanings of the word "subject": subject to someone else by control and dependence, and tied to his own identity by a conscience or self-knowledge. Both meanings suggest a form of power that subjugates and makes subject to.' Michel Foucault, 'The Subject and Power,' in James D. Faubian (ed), 2000, *Michel Foucault: Power*, Volume 3 of the *Essential Works of Foucault 1954–1984*. Edited by Paul Rabinow, New York: The New Press, p. 331.

7. The Bengali term *bhadraloka* is the appellation most often used to describe the urban bourgeois or middle class of nineteenth- and twentieth-century Calcutta. The moniker was used self referentially by members of the class and was a marker of distinction and refinement. It is a compound noun stemming from the roots *bhadra* (refined, civilized, superior) and *loka* (man, men, person, people). Its most appropriate analogue in English is the term 'gentleman' or 'gentlemen'. It is at once an indicator of class belonging and class distinction. Its rhetorical other is the term *chotaloka*—tellingly, the small people: *chota* (small, little), *loka* (person, people). The literature on the *bhadraloka* is enormous and implicit in virtually all studies of nineteenth-century Bengal but the two classic works are B.B. Misra's, 1961, *The Indian Middle Classes: Their Growth in Modern Times*, London: Oxford University Press; and John McGuire's, 1983, *The Making of a Colonial Mind: A Quantitative Study of the Bhadralok in Calcutta, 1857–1885*, Canberra: Australian National University.

8. Foregoing traditional discussion of the 'public' and 'private' spheres in discussions on nationalism, Chatterjee deploys an alternative heuristic schema consisting of 'outside' and 'inner' domains. 'By my reading, anti-colonial nationalism creates its own domain of sovereignty within colonial society well before it begins its political battle with the imperial power. It does this by dividing the world of social institutions and practices into two domains—the material and the spiritual. The material is the domain of the "outside", of the economy and of statecraft, of science and technology, a domain where the West had proved its superiority and the East had succumbed. ... The spiritual, on the other hand, is an "inner" domain bearing the "essential" marks of cultural identity. The greater one's success in imitating Western skills in the material domain, therefore, the greater the need to preserve the distinctness of one's spiritual culture ... .' Partha Chatterjee, 1993, *The Nation and Its Fragments: Colonial and Postcolonial Histories*, Princeton: Princeton University Press, p. 6. Chatterjee's distinction enables and, in fact, encourages discussions of cultural hybridity and mediation apropos of colonialism which is a step in the right direction of retrieving social agency for the indigenous population—an agency which is often disguised in discussions of nationalism which pertain only to politics and economics.

9. On the role of the imagination and 'print capitalism' in the construction of communities see Benedict Anderson's classic statement in his, 1983, *Imagined Communities: Reflections on the Origin and Spread of Nationalism,* London: Verso.

10. Addressing this issue of fatigue and the need for religious revival, a Hindustani (Lal Behari Dey?) wrote in *The Bengal Magazine* '...what with files of dockets to write, statements to give and accounts to examine, what with the impatience and excitability of his superiors manifesting themselves in those somethings called "blowings up", is it any wonder that the Babu [*bhadraloka*] is tired of his existence, and curses the day of his birth? ... You will perhaps consider me a fool for saying this, but troth compels me to say in plain English that the Babu needs religion to expand his mind and soul, religion to sweeten the

trials of life, and religion to prove in him a well of water springing up into everlasting life. The great want of the Babu community is religion. Their community has, like all other communities, a variety or multiplicity of wants, but its greatest want, its crowning desideratum, is religion.' A. Hindustani, 'The Great Want of the Babu Community', in *The Bengal Magazine* 3 (1875): 326–32.

11. For a collection of the most cogent arguments along these lines, see Vasudha Dalmia and Heinrich von Stietencron (eds), 1995, *Representing Hinduism: The Construction of Religious Traditions and National Identity,* New Delhi: Sage Publications.

12. For more on the notion of 'hybridity' vis-à-vis colonial cultural encounter in nineteenth-century Bengal see Gyan Prakash 'Science between the Lines', in Shahid Amin and Dipesh Chakrabarty (eds), 1995, *Subaltern Studies IX*, Delhi: Oxford University Press, or more recently his (1999), *Another Reason: Science and the Imagination of Modern India*, Princeton: Princeton University Press. Cf. Homi Bhaba, 'Signs Taken for Wonders: Questions of Ambivalence and Authority under a Tree Outside Delhi, May 1817', *Critical Inquiry* 12 (Autumn 1985), pp. 144–65.

13. See Partha Chatterjee, 'The Disciplines in Colonial Bengal', in his (ed.), 1996, *Texts of Power: Emerging Disciplines in Colonial Bengal*, Calcutta: Samya, pp. 1–29; as well as his *The Nation and Its Fragments*, especially p. 36.

14. I realize that by concentrating upon the missionaries of Srirampura in the 1820s I am not exhausting the full range of missionary attitudes or strategies in the nineteenth century. Obviously, the category of 'Mission' is as complex and internally differentiated as concepts such as 'Empire' and 'Subaltern'. However, I believe that concentrating upon the earliest discussions of the press so soon after the lifting of governmental restrictions in 1818 provides the ideal counterpoint to the nationalist and revivalist movements of the 1870s, 1880s, and 1890s. The two periods bring into sharp focus the distinctions between what was hoped to be achieved on the ideological level by the missionaries and what eventually occurred in practice.

15. See Dipesh Chakrabarty, 'Radical Histories and the Question of Enlightenment Rationalism: Some Recent Critiques of Subaltern Studies', *Economic and Political Weekly*, XXX, 14 (8 April 1995): 752. Cf. Alexander Duff, 1839, *India and India Missions*, Edinburgh, pp. 629, 667.

16. There were actually two schools of thought regarding the role of education in the process of conversion for Christian missionaries. Antony Copley in his *Religions in Conflict* draws upon a useful distinction between 'itinerating' and 'education' as strategies of conversion. Regarding these strategies he writes: 'In the mid-century ... the great debate lay between itinerating, the dramatic, and direct confrontation with Indian religions, by word of mouth, in the bazaar, the mela, the village, and the slow, more indirect, but less erratic, reliance on education, above all of India's new anglicized elite in secondary education.' Antony Copley, 1999, *Religions in Conflict: Ideology, Cultural Contact and Conversion in Late Colonial India*, Delhi: Oxford University Press, p. 14.

17. *FOI*, Quarterly, 1 (1825): 155–6. It is interesting to note in this regard the marked shift in sentiment over the course of the twenty-odd years from the inauguration of press activities among the Sriramapura missionaries at the turn of the century to the 1820s. Under the influence of an orientalist mood, two of the first books to be published in Bengali by William Carey were the Mahābhārata and the Rāmāyaṇa in 1802. Though the *Purāṇa*s had always been the most controversial elements of the Hindu corpus, it nevertheless appears that by the 1820s, any Hindu religious literature being produced by the native presses was considered suspect.

18. Ibid., p. 154.

19. 'Gauḍīya Vaiṣṇavism' in this essay refers to the specific variety of Vaiṣṇavism which traces its lineage to the sixteenth-century Bengali spiritual leader/reformer Sri Krsna Caitanya. Although the adjectival label 'Gauḍīya' (Bengali) is problematic for descriptions of Vaiṣṇavism before the nineteenth century I will use it anyway favouring it over the most notable and equally appropriate rival 'Caitanya Vaiṣṇavism' owing to its Bengali specificity and the common use of the term today among scholars and members of the tradition. It is clear from the historical record that all manner of heterogeneous religious groups and factions were lumped together under the rubric of Caitanya Vaiṣṇavas or Gauḍīya Vaiṣṇavas in the nineteenth century. In this sense it was most often deployed to imply an undefined 'Other' worthy of critique and avoidance. While this usage threatened to render the category heuristically impotent, it nevertheless reflected the concerns of those who were involved in constructing the category negatively before the reforms of the 1880s and 1890s.

20. William Ward, 1811 [second edition 1818], *A View of the History, Literature, and Mythology of the Hindoos: Including a Minute Description of Their Manners and Customs and Traditions from Their Principal Works*, Vol. 2 Serampore: Mission Press, p. 175; cf. Bholanath Chunder, reprint 1969, *Travels of a Hindoo*, Vol. 1, London: Trubner and Company, pp. 35ff; and Walter Hamilton, reprint 1971[1920], *Description of Hindustan*, Vol. 1, Delhi: Oriental Publishers, p. 208. Also see Ramakanta Chakravarty, 1985, *Vaisnavism in Bengal 1486–1900*, Calcutta: Sanskrit Pustak Bhandar, pp. 385–401. The figure of one-fifth of the population of Bengal being followers of Caitanya first appears in Ward (1811) and then is taken up by Chunder and Hamilton. How Ward came to this figure is unknown. The number is probably on the low side. It is interesting to note that Ward contradicts himself in Vol. 2 of his *Account*. On page 175 he claims 20 per cent of the population of Bengal as Vaiṣṇavas, on page 447 he writes that 'out of sixteen Hindoos in Bengal, five will be found to be of this sect'—i.e., 31 per cent.

21. Ākhaḍā—a place where Vaiṣṇavas assemble for religious worship.

22. H.H. Wilson, 1862, *Essays and Lectures Chiefly on the Religion of the Hindus*. Edited by Reinhold Rost in two volumes. Vol. 1 'A Sketch of the Religious Sects of the Hindus', London: Trubner and Company, p. 169.

23. Ward, *View*, p. 174.

24. Chakravarty, *Vaiṣṇavism*, p. 391.

25. Ibid., p. 389.

26. Ward, *View*, p. 447.

27. See Chakravarty, *Vaiṣṇavism*, pp. 387–9.

28. Cf. Ibid.

29. Ward, *View*, p. 448.

30. Haridasa Dasa, 471 GA [1957], *Gauḍīya Vaiṣṇava Jīvana*, Vol. 2, Navadvīpa: Haribola Kuṭira, pp. 133, 205–6.

31. See Gautama Bhadra, Oct.–Dec. 1993, 'Kathakatāra Nānā Kathā', in *Saṃskṛti Viṣayaka Yogasūtra*. Special edition on *Uniś Śataka O Viś Śatakera Bāṅglā Kathakatā*. Eds Vinaya Ghoṣa and Gautama Bhadra.

32. Cf. Hara Prasad Sastri, edited and revised by Jogendra Nath Gupta, 1949, *A Descriptive Catalogue of the Vernacular Manuscripts in the Collections of the Royal Asiatic Society of Bengal*, Vol. IX (Bengali Manuscripts, Calcutta).

33. Bhadra, 'Kathakatā', p. 169.

34. Ibid.

35. Ibid., p. 173. Cf. Ward, *View*, p. 220.

36. Ward, *View*, p. 151.

37. Ibid., p. 599.

38. Brajendranātha Bandyopādhyaya, 1379 BS [1970], *Bāṅglā sāmayika patra*, Vol. 1, Calcutta: Baṅgīya Sāhitya Pariṣad, p. 141.

39. Cf. Ṭoni Ke. Sṭuyārṭa and Henā Basu, 'Bāṅglāya prakāśita vaiṣṇava sāmayika patrikā: ekṭi tathya nirdeśika suci', *Baṅgīya sāhitya pariṣad patrikā* 90:2 (1390 BS [1981]): 1–8. Stuyārta and Basu give the initial date of the *Nityadharmānurañjikā* as 1843 though I have been unable to confirm the earlier date.

40. Bhaktivinode Thakur, 1998, *The Bhagavata: Its Philosophy, Ethics and Theology*, Kovvur, Andhra Pradesh: Sri Ramananda Gauḍīya Math, p. 8.

41. Ibid.

42. About the notion of *habitus*, Pierre Bourdieu writes: 'The structures constitutive of a particular type of environment (e.g. the material conditions of existence characteristic of a class condition) produce *habitus*, systems of durable, transposable *dispositions*, structured structures predisposed to function as structuring structures, that is, as principles of the generation and structuring of practices and representations which can be objectively "regulated" and "regular" without in any way being the product of obedience to rules, objectively adapted to their goals without presupposing a conscious aiming at ends or an express mastery of the operations necessary to attain them and, being all this, collectively orchestrated without being the product of the orchestrating action of a conductor.' Pierre Bourdieu, *Outline of a Theory of Practice*, translated by Richard Nice (Cambridge: Cambridge University Press), p. 72.

43. I am using the terms 'traditional' and 'modern' here but recognize their limited utility. I use neither of them to make a normative judgment about grand historical changes but rather find them useful as a shorthand way of indicating pre-colonial and colonial developments.

44. It is interesting to note in this regard how in his *Śrī Śrī Caitanya Śikṣāmṛta.* (Śrī Caitanya Gauḍīya Maṭha: Śrī Dhāma Māyāpura, 488 Śrī Gaurābda [1974]), 'Bhaktivinoda discusses a wide array of contemporary social issues, without reference to the Western thinkers, with which, he indicates elsewhere, he is fully familiar. Instead all of the references in support of his arguments in favour of a modern Vaiṣṇavism come from the *Śrīmat Bhāgavata, Caitanya Caritāmṛta,* etc.

45. Data from Jatindramohana Bhaṭṭācārya (ed.), 1990, *Bāṅglā mudrita granthādira tālikā: Vol. 1, 1743–1852*, Calcutta: A. Mukherjee.

46. For an interesting history of the Baṭṭalā presses in Bengali, see Śrīpantha [Nikhila Sarkāra], 1997, *Baṭṭala* Calcutta: Ānanda Publishers Pvt. Limited.

47. Sumit Sarkar, 1998, *Writing Social History*, Delhi: Oxford University Press, pp. 196–7.

48. See Chatterjee, *Nation and Its Fragments*, pp. 35–75 passim.

49. Baṅkimcāndra Caṭṭopadhyaya, *Baṅkim racanābalī*, 2 Vols. Edited by Jogesa Cāndra Bagal (Calcutta: Sāhitya Saṁsad. 2nd Edition B.E. 1361–63 [1954–6]); Dineśa Cāndra Sena, *Bāṅglā Bhāsa O Sāhitya* (Comillah: Caitanya Press, 1896); Śiśira Kumāra Ghoṣa. *Amiyo Nimāi Carita*, 6 Vols (Calcutta: Āmṛta Bājār Patrikā Office, 1958–68).

50. Kedārnātha Datta (ed.), 1881–1904, *Sajjanaṭosanī*, Kalikātā: Vaiṣṇava Depository Press.

51. After extensive research I have been able to locate only seven short-lived Vaiṣṇava periodicals before *Sajjanaṭosanī*. They are: *Bhāgavata Samācāra* (1831), *Bhaktisūcaka* (1835), *Nityadharmānurañjikā* (1846), *Sāmvatsarikasamvādapatrikā* (1856), *Advaitatattvapradarśaka* (1856), *Śrī Caitanyakirtikaumudī Patrikā* (1861), and the *Nityānanda Dāyinī Patrikā* (1870).

52. Kedārnātha Datta, *Sajjanaṭosanī*, 1 (1881): 37.

53. Datta, *Sajjanaṭosanī* 4 (1887), passim.

54. The debate concerns the two chief lineal successors to Bhaktivinoda. Two of his sons, Lalitā Prasāda Datta (seventh son) and Bimala Prasāda Datta (Bhaktisiddhānta Sarasvaī—fifth son) claim descent through their father's *paramparā*. Lalitā Prasāda's *vaṃśa* maintains that Bhaktivinoda's *śikṣa* guru was the same as his *dīkṣā* guru: Bipina Bihārī Gosvāmī of the Bhagnapara *sampradāya*. However, the Gauḍīya Maṭha, consolidated by Bhaktisiddhānta Sarasvatī, claims a *Vairāgī śikṣa* guru for Bhaktivinoda in the person of one Jagannātha Dāsa Bābāji, a famous holy man of Navadvipa. The debate seems to revolve around two issues: first, Bipina Bihārī Gosvāmī came from the Nityānanda *Vaṃśa* of Bhagnapāra and was thus a supporter of *rāganugā bhakti* whereas Jagannātha Dāsa Bābājī did not appear to be so; and second that Bipina Bihārī Gosvāmī was a householder whereas Jagannātha Dāsa Bābājī was not and thus the latter lends legitimacy to the vow of *saṃnyāsa* taken by most members of the Gauḍīya Math, whereas Bipina Bihārī Gosvāmī's *gṛhastha* status would appear to lend credibility to the married status of Lalitā Prasāda and his followers at the *maṭha* in Birnagara. For an introduction to this still raging debate, see Brian

Marvin, *The Life and Thought of Kedarnath Dutta Bhaktivinoda: A Hindu Encounter with Modernity* (University of Toronto Ph.D. Dissertation, 1996), pp. 263–88.

55. Datta, *Sajjanaṭosanī* 1 (1881), pp. 67–8.

56. Ibid., p. 69.

57. Ibid., p. 68.

58. Datta, *Sajjanaṭosanī* 4 (1887), 1.

59. Ibid., p. 2.

60. Ibid.

61. For a detailed description of Bhaktivinoda's theory of caste and birth, see his *Śrī Caitanya Śikṣāmṛta* Chennai: Śrī Gauḍīya Maṭha, 4th edition, 512 Gaurābda (1998), pp. 84–91

62. Ibid., p. 85.

63. Datta, *Sajjanaṭosanī* 4 (1887): 4.

64. Ibid.

65. Ibid., p. 5.

66. Datta, *Sajjanaṭosanī*, Vol. 6, no. 1, p. 15.

67. Ibid.

68. Ibid.

69. Ward, *View*, pp. 447–8.

70. Presumably because the peasant-servant pool would rather beg than work.

71. *Sajjanaṭosanī*, Vol. 6, no. 3, p. 58. Cf. Ward, op. cit., p. 448.

72. *Sajjanaṭosanī*, Vol. 6, no. 3, p. 58.

73. Ibid.

74. Ibid., p. 57.

75. Ibid., pp. 57-8.

76. Ibid., p. 59.

77. *Sajjanaṭosanī*, Vol. 6, no. 2, p. 39.

78. Ibid., p. 40.

79. *Sajjanaṭosanī*, Vol. 6, no. 4, pp. 74–6.

80. *Sajjanaṭosanī*, Vol. 6, no. 8, pp. 177–8.

Mahima Dharma Ascetics
A Case Study on Popular Asceticism and its Patronage Structure in Rural Orissa

Lidia Julianna Guzy

This essay presents preliminary results of on-going research on Mahima Dharma, an indigenous religious reform-movement in rural Orissa. Partial results of recent fieldwork carried out in Dhenkanal among ascetics (*babas*) and devotees will be discussed. Through travels with two Mahima Dharma ascetics, rituals as well as local and regional networks were investigated. The research reveals some socio-structural features of the new ascetic religion and its local patronage structure upon which the essay will concentrate.[1]

MAHIMA DHARMA

Mahima Dharma, literally 'the glorious *dharma*', represents a contemporary ascetic tradition of Orissa. It recruits its followers mainly from the rural and, only recently, also from the tribal population of the region.[2] The main features of the new religion are asceticism, a caste-denying character, and a conception of God that lies between henotheism and monotheism.[3] Mahima Dharmis worship Mahima Alekh as the highest, unwritten (*a-lekh*),[4] indescribable, and only god. Mahima Alekh is conceived to be *sunya*—the void—all and nothing. This god can only be approached by meditation, an ascetic lifestyle, and ritual practices and is thus opposed to idol worship. The concepts and values go back to the founder of the religion, Mahima Gosvmi, who lived at the beginning of the nineteenth century. His origin is unknown, but for his devotees Mahima Gosvami is considered to be the incarnation of Mahima Alekh. According to legends Mahima Gosvami came from the Himalayas and appeared at Puri in 1826 where he began his religious mission throughout Orissa. For the next twenty-four years, Mahima Gosvami is said to have meditated in the Kapilas hills of Dhenkanal. There he lived for the first twelve years on fruits and roots of the forest delivered to him daily by a Savara[5] Chief. During the following twelve years Raja Bhagirati Mahindra Bahadur, the King of Dhenkanal, used to supply Mahima Gosvami with a daily portion of milk. After a long period of meditative preparation, Mahima Gosvami is said to have started preaching in the Feudatory States of Orissa.[6]

Earlier historical and Indological investigations by Eschmann (1978) emphasized that Mahima Dharma is 'an autochthonous Hindu reform movement' (ibid.: 375) which derives 'its criticism of the Hindu tradition directly from the tradition itself' (ibid.). Eschmann's main thesis concerns the dynamics of indigenous regional traditions in correspondence with pan-South Asian forms and ideas. Dube later investigates the historical development of Mahima Dharma as a sect contesting dominant structures in the nineteenth century (Dube, 2001: 149–78) and undergoing changes within the processes of institutionalization. Dube found that Mahima Dharma is to be seen as a 'transformation of a subaltern religiosity' into 'an institutionalized religious order' (Dube 1999: 98; 125). In this vein, my own research focuses on the socio-anthropological analysis of the living religious traditions of Mahima Dharma in the villages of Dhenkanal, which coincide with the region of its origin. Predominant in Dhenkanal is the monastic, polycentric[7] structure of the ascetic tradition. The monastic organization is always connected with local ruling elites who provide for the ascetics (babas). In Dhenkanal, the asceticism of Mahima Dharma reflects the patronage system between the local leaders and babas. The case study of Mahima Dharma asceticism in rural areas leads to the conclusion that the Hindu tradition of renouncing the outer-world is to be analysed in relation to local powers.[8] Politics on a rural level operate within the idiom of patrons in relation to ascetics. By sponsoring the holy men, rituals as well as the places of worship, worldly patrons gain religious benefits and the moral reconfirmation to be a good ruler.

This essay will focus on reconstructions of the local patronage system reflected in the recent popularity of Mahima Dharma asceticism in rural Orissa.

THE ETHNOGRAPHIC SETTING

The research presented here was conducted in a small village of Dhenkanal—Jaka[9]—where one of the mythical places of Mahima Goswami is situated. In this holy area *(tungi)* two semi-migrant ascetics—so-called babas—reside from time to time. Through travels with the babas the ethnographic encounter was gradually enlarged to several other religious centres in the district. During fieldwork three social categories could be determined:

1. Celibate ascetics (babas), the specialized elite of the movement;
2. lay householder devotees (*bhakta*s); and
3. devoted lay householder patrons of the ascetics who are simultaneously *bhakta*s as well as local headmen of villages or village-segments.

Mahima Dharma combines otherworldly renunciation of the ascetics with *bhakti* religiosity of the householders. This also includes traditional forms of local leadership. My hypothesis is that Mahima Dharma in Dhenkanal should be analysed within the framework of concepts of local leadership in terms of a patronage system rather than within the paradigm of a subltern discourse, although the popularity of Mahima Dharma amongst the rural and recently tribal population[10] represents a temptation to do so.

THE CONTEXT OF THE *BABAS*

The babas with whom I worked, Promot Das and Vira Das, had had twenty to twenty-five years of ascetic practice. At this time they represent the middle strata of the hierarchy within the monastic organization of Mahima Dharma. The stages of world renunciation begin with the role of a young wandering *tyagi* for about ten to fifteen years. This role then leads to a senior *das,* who, as a semi-migrant ascetic, maintains a sort of continuous sacred residence for a further fifteen to twenty-five years. Finally the role culminates in the position of authority assumed by the most senior *abadhuta samnyasin* who only on special ritual occasions would move barefoot from his permanent sacral abode.

The monastic hierarchy rests upon a remarkably strong principle of seniority (cf. Table 1).

Ideally, every Mahima Dharma ascetic is considered a wandering samnyasin. In reality, ascetics differ in terms of seniority and in relation to religious tasks performed, therefore making holy men more or less mobile. Mobility and social independence are grounded in the ideal of

TABLE 1

tyagi	10–15 years of a *wandering period.*
ß	
das	Further 15–25 years of *semi-migrant* existence combined with semi-permanent residence at one place.
ß	
abadhuta samnyasin	Stage of the most senior *samnyasin* who resides permanently in a sacral abode.

world renunciation that demands one to leave worldly relations tied to the family and the caste *(jati).*[11] An ascetic will never marry and never come back to the place of his birth. He is considered socially dead, a living phantom[12] who—while physically living—has reached the highest status of religious deliverance, *moksha.* As one who is not 'of this world', he still goes out into the world in order to become a specialist of several fire-rituals *(ghiopura, chatordosi, jagia).* He survives only by begging and by his devotion to God. The ascetic ideal of Mahima Dharma is therefore deeply embedded in the traditional Indian ideal of world renunciation.[13] Still, the fire-ritual as the crucial characteristic of Mahima Dharma ascetics represents a contradiction of the classical ideal where the ascetic is an '*anagni*', someone who has left the fire (of the house)![14] The focus on the fire ritual, instead, would lead to the conclusion that Mahima Dharma asceticism borrows from the dominant brahmanic culture and its Vedic heritage.[15] Nonetheless, one should not ignore the official affirmation of Mahima Dharma ascetics to be 'anti-brahmanical'. The locally specific configuration of Indian ascetic, Vedic (brahmanic) heritage, and its indigenous critique reveals a syncretistic feature of Mahima Dharma. Mahima Dharma can thus be seen as a popular tradition of asceticism which fits well into the heterogeneity and syncretisms of Indian local traditions.

CODE OF CONDUCT FOR THE ASCETICS

Ascetics of all stages, tyagi to abadhuta samnyasin, have to obey the rules of conduct *(guruagya)* which Mahima Gosvami gave to his followers. The religious duty of the ascetics prescribes the following thirty-two rules of conduct.[16] The main principle of ascetic life in Mahima Dharma is the severe discipline. Discipline of mind, body, and action provides a framework for ethical and ritual life conduct. The babas worship the highest and only god Mahima Alekh without interference. They live in simplicity, without property, and are devoted to a radical trust in God. The rules include strict celibacy, no idol-worship, vegetarian diet, daily prayers seven times before sunrise and five times before sunset, no meal after sunset, one meal *(vikhya)* from one devotee a day, a strong restriction on staying more than one night in one village (and that too always outside the house), and, finally, the ritual obligation to perform jagia (fire-ritual) for the well-being of the society.

The matrix of the rules of conduct presented above shows some of the ideal-typical features of South Asian religiosity; they consist of practices of ritual specialists whose ortho-practice is seen as a proof of their deep obeisance to the religious laws of *dharma.*

SHAKTI—THE MIRACULOUS POWER OF ASCETICS

Asceticism, as a strict discipline of body and mind for the babas, represents the main way to deification. For the laymen (bhaktas) it is the main religious technique for gaining salvation in terms of a better rebirth. Ascetics, in contrast to their worldly laymen, will never be reborn. Those who in Weber's words could be described as 'religious virtuoso'[17] gain through discipline and control of their body and mind, a divine power called *shakti.* Babas become acrobats of their spiritual powers. As such, they perform miraculous changes: they cause rain, transform barrenness into fertility, make marriage prophecies, ask oracles for reasons of bad luck or illness, and give auspicious blessings. In the eyes of their devotees, they have risen from human bodies to become living gods.[18] All divine capacities of the babas derive from one source—the discipline of their body and mind rooted in the radical chastity that creates shakti, the principle of divinity. Only the control of their body transforms their biological potentials into a metaphysical power. As metaphysical athletes they achieve the highest and most difficult aim: liberated from the phantom world, they will never be reborn. Like Mahima Gosvami, the incarnation of Mahima Alekh, they will exhale their existence and transform to the nothingness of sunya. Only gods are absolutely mortal in Mahima Dharma; the humans are caught in the phantom deaths and rebirths of the world.

CENTRE AND PERIPHERY OR THE POLYCENTRALITY OF MAHIMA DHARMA

The institutional and official centre of the monastic organization is Joranda, a holy city in Dhenkanal. It is here, where the most senior abadhuta samnyasins live, that the majority of young tyagis are instructed.

Joranda itself is polarized between ascetic groups called the *Balkaldhari* and the *Kaupindhari.* These groups occupy their own ritual spaces within the holy city. Originally 'Balkaldhari' and 'Kaupindhari' referred to a differentiation based on the seniority of the babas. The oldest babas (called Balkaldhari) are permitted to wear solely a cover made from the bark of the Khumbi tree only. The younger babas (called Kaupindhari) wear clothes made from cotton. The main reason for underlying conflicts within and between baba groups is found in the violation of the principle of seniority. Thus, the Kaupindhari do not consider the Balkaldhari samnyasins as their senior brothers and so do not respect them adequately. By contrast the Kaupindhari regard themselves as equal to the others and reject any ranking between different spiritual fraternities. Currently such conflicts have reached the level of court cases. In consequence, many babas and devotees prefer to focus on centres situated at the periphery of the Mahima Dharma movement, that hold greater attraction. According to the devotees, four peripheral centres exist besides Joranda:

1. Kamakhianagar
2. Barampur
3. Joka
4. Angarabanda

These five centres including Joranda are called '*tirtha*s' and represent mythical places where Mahima Goswami lit his first fire-ritual (jagia). Each one of the places is regarded as a hidden centre. All five centres were controlled by former Feudatory States. Joranda, Kamakhianagar and Jaka belonged to the Feudatory State of Dhenkanal; Angarabanda was under the administration of the Hindol king. Barampur had its own political autonomy, at least according to the oral history of the devotees.

Each tirtha contains holy relics of Mahima Gosvami, such as his firewood, his wandering stick, his fly-whisk, or his ritual instruments. In addition to these tirthas, other holy places exist in the vast rural landscape of Orissa. Among them, Bhima Bhoi's sanctuary—Khalliapalli near Sonepur—is of great importance. Bhima Bhoi, a Khond in origin, as the legends tell, was a mythical blind poet who is regarded as the first enthusiastic propagator and devotee of the religion. His devotion to Mahima Gosvami and to his religion has yielded impressive masterpieces of Oriya literature.[19] However, since the place where Bhima Bhoi lived and died does not contain traces or relics of the founder of the religion, it is not recognized as a tirtha by the monastic authorities of

Joranda. This point reveals the diversity within the Mahima Dharma movement and the special role of Bhima Bhoi and his followers. Bhima Bhoi's tradition in Mahima Dharma is especially widespread in the former Redhakhol (Rairakhol) State. Bhima Bhoi, the layman, was here surrounded by his householder followers in the nineteenth century. For the theology of Mahima Dharma, his poetic compositions gained the status of holy books with an obligatory character. They were assembled in collections called *Stuti Chintamoni* and *Bhajan Mala*. Moreover, Bhima Bhoi's tradition displays an ambivalent character. Since the followers do not respect the authority of Joranda and its ascetics but consider Bhima Bhoi as their main *guru*, the community of Bhima Bhoi represents a separate tradition within Mahima Dharma.[20]

This corresponds with a remarkable polycentrality structuring the sacred geography of Mahima Dharma. Even though Joranda represents the official centre where processes of systematization and institutionalization take place, peripheral centres still appear to be locally autonomous.

SOCIAL PATTERNS OF DEVOTION

Travelling with the babas revealed that Mahima Dharma is popular mainly amongst the *chasa*-population (peasants) and, on a smaller scale, amongst some craftmen's *jati*s—such as *bodhei* (carpenter) and *gudia* (sweet-maker). It thus displays a specifically rural character. Moreover, the *harijan* jatis are also attracted by the religion. The following social features of the practitioners of the new religion were most common:

1. The majority of the peasant devotees belong to rich landowner families.
2. Next to the landlords, most other practitioners own at least some land and are not considered as 'poor'.[21]
3. The practitioners generally have a background of Mahima Dharma tradition within their own male ancestry of the patrilineage.
4. Recent access to education and government services is often combined with an interest in Mahima Dharma.

The last characteristic was especially noteworthy within the harijan jatis. The roles of Mahima Dharmis can be differentiated into:

1. Ascetic babas providing priestly services;
2. ritually active lay-devotees (bhaktas); and
3. ritually passive 'believers' (vis-à-vis) who are deeply interested

and display respectful attitudes towards the new dharma and the ascetics.

BHAKTAS AND PATRONS

I have already introduced the role of ascetic babas. In contrast, a bhakta is a householder who undergoes *dikhya*—initiation—through which he is bound strictly to follow the rules and ritual duties of the code of conduct. A simple *gerua*-coloured piece of cloth, a vegetarian diet, refusal of alcohol, and the gradual adoption of chastity even in marital life are the householder's regulations. For householders, the religious duties consist of the regular performance of *darshana*[22] exercises, seven times before sunrise and five times before sunset. After darshana in the evening, no meal may be eaten. Moreover, the householder's duty includes service of the babas (*seva*) by donating food *(vikhya)* which simultaneously makes him a patron of the holy men. We may differentiate thus between:

1. Ordinary 'householder patron' (bhakta) of ascetic babas; and
2. 'institutionalised patrons' *(poriposaka)* who act as patrons of one of the holy mythical places where the babas reside temporarily and where the monthly fire-ritual (chatordosi) takes place. Such an 'institutionalized' patron is likely to be a wealthy landowner whose ritual duties consist in monetary and land donations. For the chatordosi ritual, which takes place the night before full moon, the 'institutionalised patron' is obliged to guarantee the amount of vegetarian nutritional ingredients needed for the ritual to be distributed amongst the village children on the following morning *(balelila)*. They can also arrange for a more 'private ritual'—the ghiopura—which consists of the same ritual ingredients but differs in the private (familial) motivation for the patrons.[23]

Patrons donate money for nutritional security of babas, for holy institutions, and for fire-rituals. All these donations are called *dan*. An ascetic should never directly take money-donations—*dan*—into his hands. Nevertheless there are several modes to receive it without breaking the rule. One mode is not to touch money directly but for instance some time after it is laid down on the ground or floor. The prayer performed by babas in holy institutions, the fire burning while fire-rituals, and the donated food consumed by ascetics, all these activities interconnect ritual and economic transactions revealing the strong interdependence between ascetics and their patrons.

POWER CONFIGURATIONS IN RITUALS

In theory, every villager could be a patron of the fire-ritual provided he could afford a minimum amount of 1000 rupees. This implies a certain amount of wealth, which is usually combined with a high social status. I found myself in an empirical situation in which the rituals were all patronized by the local ruling elite of wealthy peasant landowners.

Throughout the district of Dhenkanal I could locate only chasa landlords who patronized the five tirthas. Chasa is the general category for agricultural caste in Dhenkanal. *Chaso/chasi* meaning the cultivating of land, chasa is the common category for the peasant caste. Within the chasa *jati* different subcategories exist.[24] What is important for the present context is that the chasa category always had a ruling elite cooperating with local kings, the so-called *khodhayat* strata of the chasa. It is said that only one group of the chasa category, the *kolotua* chasa, had the privilege to carry out the local ruling activities. But since the category chasa is fluid and not precise enough, it has become a medium of contest and an instrument of constructing local ruling identities by claiming to be a *khondayat chasa.* The process of categorical construction has succeeded insofar that, in general, the claim of the *khondayat* category belonging to a higher status is 'legitimate' and applied to the chasa of the coastal regions.[25]

According to historical narratives, the chasa landlords came to Orissa through the settlement-policies of petty *raja*s. They administered the newly colonized forest areas. In contrast to the situation prevailing in coastal Orissa where brahmanic bureaucrats assumed administrative tasks (Pfeffer, 1978),[26] the hinterland of Orissa was administered by chasa landlords (local ruling elite). In return for their administrative work, they received land-donations to which rights the services of the village castes were attached. By owning large amounts of land, which could be rented—and by controlling human labour—which could be requested by the landlords, 'royal' authority was practically represented by them. From generation to generation chasa landlords acted as village headmen *(prodhano).* They were also the first firm disciples of Mahima Gosvami. In the hinterland of Orissa, one might speak of local rulers' dynasties of chasa landlords. The local ruling elite seems to be embedded in the traditional model of Indian kingship and its structure of 'little kingdoms' (Cohn, 1962; Dirks, 1979, Schnepel, 1995).[27] 'Religious policy' in Indian kingship relates kings to temples and creates political legitimacy by ritual activities (Kulke, 1978: 125).[28] The complexity of the 'multi-level totality' of the subject certainly cannot be approached in this essay (Galey, 1989: 185).[29] Nevertheless, the fact that Mahima Dharma is very much connected with the descendants of the former local ruling elite seems important. They continue till today the religious worship of their forefathers. The 'royal habitus' of the chasa landlord devotees can be described in the following manner:

1. From the beginnings of the Mahima Dharma movement, their sanctuaries (*akuisyatya mandiras*) served to demarcate and symbolize the territories of chasa landlords.
2. The funding of fire-rituals (jagia) for the village as well as the long-term mentorship of Mahima Dharma ascetics are religious tasks expected to be performed by chasa landlord: devotees. The funding of rituals demonstrates the generosity of the ritual patron and in this way legitimates him as a 'good/moral' local ruler.

The religious tradition, Mahima Dharma with its ascetic values is ideologically[30] apolitical, but the traditional structure of 'sacred patronage' exercised by worldly patrons with reference to holy ascetics reveals a strong interdependency between the political and the religious/ritual sphere. In this sense local politicians and even Members of Parliament are considered patrons of Joranda and of the other tirthas. The donator of the *tungi* (holy place) of Jaka, for instance, was the descendent of the former petty raja of Dhenkanal. As a Member of Parliament in the 1980s he donated a large sum from governmental funds in order to restore the former meditation place of the founder of the religion, Mahima Gosvami. After his dismissal from politics, his successor continued to be a patron of the small tungi in order to gain the voices of the rural population.

In the context of the regional calamity due to the effects of the super-cyclone in Orissa (end of October 1999), some local politicians (BJP) organized 'religious meetings' in schools and invited a lot of Mahima Dharma babas for this occasion. Politicians gave talks, babas gave their blessings, and those who suffered deplored their miserable situation. Such meetings were accompanied by collective meals for the whole village where the 'meeting' was held. Local politicians demonstrated their proximity to ascetics and performed social service by donating a collective meal. For electoral purposes local politicians reconstructed the traditional ideal of *dharmaraja* ('righteous king') through sacred patronage of holy men. By revitalizing the concept of the 'good/moral ruler' they hoped to convince the rural voters.

As Galey puts it, the continuity of the Indian kingship model can be seen today in Indian politics.[31] 'Holy men' (*sadhus*) consulting political leaders is very common, revealing a crucial alliance between ascetics and political contexts. In this sense the role of Hindu saints in the complex formation processes of religious identity and, finally, Hindu nationalism are extensively analysed (Van der Veer, 1996).

The local patronage of Mahima Dharma ascetics reveals a locally specific configuration in which a popular ascetic tradition interrelates with local politics.

This also demonstrates the present-day reality of the traditional ideal of the 'righteous king', implying the vivid interplay between local politicians and holy men.

Mahima Dharma asceticism in rural Orissa can thus be regarded as a modern re-actualization of the traditional kingship pattern at a local level.

SACRED ECONOMY

In recent times, social climbers through education and government services, for instance *harijan*s, made attempts to become ritual patrons. Since the value of ritual generosity is related to high social status, aspirants to social mobility try to imitate the habits of the ruling class. Patronizing a Mahima Dharma ritual is equivalent to acting symbolically as a local ruler. However, the harijans' rights to ritual patronage of Mahima Dharma are limited to monetary donations. Food prestations are excluded.[32] Since money is an inanimate matter, it cannot pollute[33] and for this reason can also be accepted in ritual transactions. Monetary capacity in rural India offers the lower castes a new possibility of entering the soteriological market. Religious salvation can be obtained with monetary donations. With sacrifices of money, the accumulation of good *karma* for the next (better) rebirth is possible, without any differentiation of caste.

Monetary donations in the context of Mahima Dharma are indispensable for the performance of jagia-ritual. They are thus to be seen in the framework of a sacred economy. Money does not possess a value in itself, but is a medium of exchange as part of the competitive process in which different social sections struggle for 'symbolic' and 'salvatory capital'. 'Symbolic capital' relies on the principle of reciprocity that governs transactions of gifts which will come back to the donor in the form of social respect or higher social status (Bourdieu, 1980: 205–21).[34] 'Salvatory capital' depends upon the idea that money will be transformed into 'religious funds' which will ultimately influence the fate of the subsequent existence of the self. Thus, money donations circulate in the form of ritually transformed and accumulated capital of salvation. By extending monetary patronage over rituals of ascetic babas, harijan-patrons gain the same kind of access to salvation as all the higher castes. In this, a reform of traditional Hinduism may be discerned. But in spite of this emancipatory aspect of the 'salvatory forms of capital' in the sacred economy of Mahima Dharma, social authority still remains largely with the old patrons. 'Symbolic capital' is confined to traditional social and ritual roles within the socio-religious hierarchy of the caste-system[35] and cannot be achieved in another context. Apart from the monetary patronage of the rituals of the ascetic babas, the aspirant of social mobility remains 'the old Untouchable' for the higher castes in his village.

Still, within the *own* community, *harijan bhakta*s could demonstrate their achieved higher social status and they especially expressed it through money donations.

CULTURE OF POETRY AND ORAL LITERACY OF MAHIMA DHARMA

Amongst the rural population Mahima Dharma presents a great attraction as an 'enlightened' reform movement. This popularity lies in its strong reference to a sophisticated corpus of oral literature produced by Bhima Bhoi. For all Mahima Dharmis, the singing and dancing of Bhima Bhoi's poetry is synonymous with education and, as such, permits even illiterate devotees to perform, and demonstrate literacy.

During the fire-rituals of Mahima Dharma, the babas as well as the male householders sing in alternating choral groups in a passionate, hymnic way. The sung recitations of religious devotion are accompanied by castanets *(gini),* tambourines *(kanjoni),* and moderate dancing moves. This type of oral literacy is used, moreover, as an argumentative and rhetorical aid in religious discussions and for teaching devotees from diverse backgrounds. Mahima Dharmis frequently take recourse to poetical verses while leading theological discussions. They argue by singing *bhajan*s and thus convince their audiences. Since all texts are sung in Oriya and bhajans are known since the days of childhood, educational differences pose no barrier for participating in and showing Mahima Dharma devotion. All those who show devotion by singing, dancing, and reciting the poetic verses by memory are equally welcome to the babas.

THE SOCIOLOGY OF PRAYER[36]

The prayer called *darshana*[37] plays a main role in the ritual practice of Mahima Dharma. The prayer itself is a ritual that consists of several exercises of the body. For babas as well as for bhaktas, religious devotion—bhakti—to Mahima Alekh is not only mediated on through mental concentration but is especially expressed by the language of the body. The sequence of the prayers includes invocations of the name of the God, as well as performances of a complex crossing of arms and legs. Before sunrise babas and bhaktas fall down seven times to the earth; before sunset they worship God five times. Falling to earth during prayer is always accompanied by complex bodily exercises. The performances of darshana-ritual represent for babas as well as laymen the public demonstration of religious orthodoxy and obeisance to the rules of religious life conduct. The right form of the bodily prayer is synonymous with the 'right' ideas of Mahima Dharma. An accurate practice—the ortho-practice—of the sequences of the prayer proves credibility and orthodoxy—the 'right' rule—within one's own life conduct. In this sense, asceticism in Mahima Dharma requires adherence to the rules of the founder of the religion. The prayer is considered a hygienic medicine for body and mind. As such, performance of the prayer demonstrates an internalized 'moral' purity within the individual steps towards salvation. Thus, practices of prayer reveal the antique Greek meaning and etymology of *áskesis* as 'exercise', crucial for the internalization processes of ascetic ethics in Mahima Dharma.

CONCLUSION

Mahima Dharma is a polycentric religious tradition in which organizational segments exist as locally autonomous units. Heterogeneity is thus a visible feature within the movement. Still, it appears predominantly as the religion of the local chasa ruling elite. Its recent rural spread and popularity could be appraised as a local *re*-forming of traditional patterns of local leadership being closely associated with Mahima Dharma ascetics. Mahima Dharma asceticism could thus be considered as a local re-actualization of the traditional pattern of Indian kingship operating within a local patronage system between local rulers and ascetics. The popular asceticism of Mahima Dharma combines tradition, its critique, and its affirmation in a syncretistic manner. On the one hand, and in spite of its dogmatic denial of caste, local values of status are *re*-constructed by the belief-system of Mahima Dharma. On the other hand, emancipatory aspects can be shown to exist in 'salvatory forms of capital' as part of the sacred economy, which is open for all castes. Within the sacred economy Mahima Dharma ascetics initiate a sacrificial '*do ut des*'[38]–model.[39] The monetary gift becomes a 'sacrifice of money'. The principle of soteriological reciprocity by which the sacred economy is structured is seen in the obligatory character of the gift.[40] All who have given, respectively sacrificed, gain the right of soteriological regeneration in the next life. Thus, the emancipatory moment lies in the gift/sacrifice of money. This is not tied down to the hierarchy of the caste system. The monetary gift guarantees all donors a soteriological 'surplus' in the next life and the demonstration of achieved higher social status through the generosity of money donation. In this life it facilitates climbing the social status ladder by imitating the habits of the ruling. A further emancipatory characteristic is embedded in the culture of poetry and in the bhakti tradition of rural Orissa. The poetry of Bhima Bhoi is considered to be an expression of oral literature and deep religious emotion. Knowledge of poetry or its declamation is taken as being synonymous with 'education'. Performances of oral literacy during Mahima Dharma rituals provide participants with an equal access to emotional worship and intellectual religious discourses. Emotion and poetry are demonstrated by rhetorical competitions and indicate intellectual investigations on the theology of Mahima Dharma. In this sense, the rhetoric of sung poetry breaks with the traditionally restricted intellectual hegemony of the brahmins and opens theological discussions to members of all castes.

Finally, the ethics of asceticism in Mahima Dharma are inscribed in the body of babas and bhaktas. By control and discipline of the body, a physical matrix of values of world renunciation is created. In an embodied—internalized—manner, the laymen are on the path to a better rebirth, whereas the bodies of the babas already incarnate the human temples of god.

ENDNOTES

1. I would like to thank the Deutsche Forschungsgemeinschaft (German Research Council) for the generous grant without which the research could not have been conducted. Due to the generous help of Prof. P.K. Nayak, University of Bhubanesvar, the research could be undertaken. The essay represents the primary results of my fieldwork from September 1999 to February 2000. Further investigations will be completed after the next period of fieldwork. Thus, the essay is to be seen as a presentation of work-in-progress results, not as the results of a finished research-project.

2. See Eschmann, A. 1986 (1978). 'Mahima Dharma: An Autochthonous Hindu Reform Movement', pp. 374–410, pp. 386–7; T.R.B. (1968–9). 'Impact of Satya Mahima Dharma on Scheduled Castes and Scheduled Tribes in Orissa' (pp. 44–76) in *ADIBASI*, vol. X, no. 1: 52.

Apart from my own observations during a fieldwork among tribal population in the Koraput district, conducted from September 2000 to March 2001 I can confirm this statement. The structure of the spread in tribal areas will not be discussed in this essay.

3. In reference to the neologism of Friedrich Max Müller, henotheism means the belief-system in one highest god to whom the devotee is mostly emotionally attached. It implies the existence of other inferior gods. Monotheism means the belief in one and only one god.

4. *a-lekha* being explained to me as 'not to write/unwritten' refers to the everday usage. The term itself means in Sanskrit 'without writing', 'illiterate' indicating a pejorative meaning.

5. Savara—also referred to as Soara/Saura or Sahara—is the name of a Scheduled Tribe in Orissa. See, Senapati, N. and P. Tripathy (eds), 1972, p. 104. In Dhenkanal the Savara people are especially living in the neighbourhood of the Malaygiri hill (ibid.: 48). Besides the Khonds and the Gonds, they represent the aboriginal societies of the district of Dhenkanal (ibid.: 422). Dhenkanal city, the capital of the district, is said to owe its name to the Savara Chief called Dhenkanal (ibid.: 427).

6. For further information on the places of Mahima Gosvami's travels in Orissa, see Senapati, N. 1972. 'Appendix Mahima Dharma', in Senapati, N. and Tripathy, P. (eds), pp. 443–8.

7. Concerning the feature of polycentrality in Mahima Dharma, see especially the work of Johannes Beltz, 2001, 'Disputed Centres, Rejected Norms, and Contested Authorities. Situating Mahima Dharma in its Regional Diversity', paper during the Annual DFG conference at Salzau, May 2001.

8. For a broad discussion on the topic of patronage and kinship in theories on South Asia, see Quigley, D. 1999 (1993).

9. I thank all my hosts in Jaka, where I profited from the great friendliness of the family of Jagan Mohan Sahu and of the whole village.

10. The first statistics about the spread of the new religion in tribal regions were compiled by the Tribal Research Bureau and undertaken by Shri A. Das, Shrimati Kiran Bala Devi, and Shri N. Das in the year. (See: T.R.B. 1968–9, 'Impact of Satya Mahima Dharma on Scheduled Castes and Scheduled Tribes in Orissa', *ADIVASI*, Vol. X, no. 1: 43–76). By way of comparison I conducted a research among converts to the new religion in the so-called tribal areas of the Koraput region in the year 2000–01. In the last decade, proselytizing ascetics from Dhenkanal spread the religion among the local population of Koraput where approximately 22 per cent of the total population are from tribal origin. The statistics compiled by the Tribal Research Bureau in 1968–9 indicate an existence of the religion in tribal areas of Orissa since around 1950. Through several interviews with babas of Mahima Dharma during my field research in Dhenkanal (1999–2000) proselytizing activities of the babas in Koraput could be confirmed during the wandering-period of every ascetic for this time. According to my recent observations in Koraput, similar activities by babas from Dhenkanal

could only be observed during the annual conversion time in February/March. (Temporal) proselytizing activities can thus be assumed for the last fifty years in this region.

According to my observations, two generations of converts to Mahima Dharma or Alekh Dharma could be found in Koraput. They mostly represent aged persons (50–60 years) whose adult (20–35 years) children recently underwent the initiation in the last ten years. Approximately 10 per cent of the local population can be assessed as belonging to Mahima Dharma and sharing the new religious identity. Issues of conversion, invention of tradition, and processes of acculturation combined with Mahima Dharma will not be discussed in this essay. See Guzy, L. 2002. 'Negative Ecstasy or the Singers of the Divine: Voices from the Periphery of Mahima Dharma', in G. Pfeffer (ed.), 2002, *Periphery and Centre: Groups, Categories, Values*, Delhi: Manohar.

11. See Dumont, L. 1966, 'Appendice B. Le renoncement dans les religions de I'Inde' (pp. 324–50).

12. For comparison of the *samnyasin* with the ghost of the dead *(preta)*, see Sprockhoff, J.F., 1980, 'Die feindlichen Toten und der befriedete Tote', pp. 263–84.

13. For further comparison, see Ghurye, G.S. (1953), Burghart, R. 1983, 'Renunciation in the Religious Traditions of South Asia', in *Man* (*N.S.*) 18: 635–53.

14. See Olivelle, P. 1992; Michaels, A. 1998.

15. Here I am referring to the work of Fritz Staal. See, Staal, F. 1983.

16. For detailed descriptions, see Eschmann 1986 (1978), pp. 394–5 and T.R.B. 1968–9, p. 50.

17. Weber, M. 1972 (1922). *Wirtschaft und Gesellschaft,* Tubingen: J.C.B. Mohr, p. 327; see also the complete Chapter V 'Religionssoziologie (Sociology of religion)', pp. 245–381.

18. The deification of humans to gods recalls to mind the classical studies of J.G. Frazer who speaks of similar phenomena as of 'god-humans'. See Frazer, J.G. 1989 (1922), pp. 131–5.

19. See Mohapatra, S. 1983.

20. See the essay by Johannes Beltz in this present volume, pp. 230–52.

21. In the rural context, land means wealth and social status.

22. In the context of Mahima Dharma, *darshana* does not refer to the common visual devotion (see Eck, D.L. 1881. *Darshan: Seeing the Divine Image in India.* Chamberburg, Anima) to the deity, but to the physical exercise performed by the devotees in order to praise God Alekh.

23. The issue of fire-rituals, their exact procedures, and conceptions of purification demands a separate discussion which cannot be approached in this essay.

24. For more details, see Senapati, N. (ed.) 1972, p. 96.

25. See Senapati, N. (ed.) 1972, p. 96; Nayak, P.K., 'Marriage Prestations among the Chosa of Orissa'. Unpublished manuscript held during the *European*

Conference of South Asian Studies, Toulouse, 31 August–3 September 1994. I would like to thank P.K. Nayak for permitting me to use his unpublished manuscript for discussion.

26. I refer to the *Sasana* villages studied by Pfeffer, G. 1986 (1978), 'Puri's Vedic Brahmins: Continuity and Change in their Traditional Institutions', in A. Eschmann, H. Kulke, and G.T. Tripathi (eds), 1986 (1978), pp. 421–37.

27. Term refers to the works of Cohn, B.S. 1990 (1962), 'Political Systems in Eighteenth-century India: The Benares Region', pp. 483–99; Dirks, N. 1979. 'The Structure and Meaning of Political Relations in a South Indian Little Kingdom', in *Contributions to Indian Sociology*, vol. 13, no. 2, pp. 169–206; Schnepel, B. 1995. Bhubanesvar: Utkal University.

28. The characteristic of ritual and politics in pre-colonial India is emphasized by Kulke, H. 1978, 'Royal Temple Policy and the Structure of Medieval Hindu Kingdoms' (pp. 125–38) and 'Early Royal Patronage of the Jagannatha Cult' (pp. 139–56) in A. Eschmann, H. Kulke, and G.T. Tripathi (eds) 1986 (1978).

29. Galey, J.C. 1989. 'Reconsidering Kingship in India: An Ethnological Perspective', in Galey, J.C. (ed.), pp. 123–87.

30. I use the term 'ideology', in the sense of value-ideas referring to Dumont (1966) .

31. Reference to lectures given by J.C. Galey, EHESS 1998–2001.

32. Food and its transactions represent in South Asian context a main metaphor for the 'pure–impure' idiom of the caste-hierarchy. On the relations of food, impurity, commensality, connubiality, and caste-hierarchy, see Dumont 1986 (1966) especially chapter VI (pp. 168–95); on food, substances, impurity, and caste, see Marriott 1968.

33. See: Douglas, M. 1966.

34. Bourdieu, P. 1980, 'Das symbolische Kapital (The Symbolic Capital)', pp. 205–21.

35. See Dumont, L. 1966, *Homo Hierarchicus. Le système des castes et ses implications.* Paris: Gallimard.

36. Using this term I refer to the work of M. Mauss: Mauss, M. 1968 (1909), 'La prière et les rites oraux', pp. 357–477.

37. See endnote 22.

38. Translation: 'I give and therefore you give'.

39. See Hubert, H. et Mauss, M. 1968 (1899), 'Essai sur la nature et la fonction du sacrifice', pp. 193–307.

40. Mauss, M. 1990 (1950).

REFERENCES

Bourdieu, P. 1980. 'Das symbolische Kapital (The Symbolic Capital' (pp. 205–21), in Bourdieu, P., *Sozialer Sinn.* Frankfurt: Suhrkamp.

Burghart, R. 1986. 'Renunciation in the Religious Traditions of South Asia', *Man (N.S.)* 18: 635–53.

Cohn, B.S. 1990 (1962). 'Poltical Systems in Eighteenth-Century India: The Benares Region' (pp. 483–99), in B.S. Cohn, *An Anthropologist among the Historians and Other Essays,* New York: Oxford University Press.

Dirks, N. 1979. 'The Structure and Meaning of Political Relations in a South Indian Little Kingdom' (pp. 169–206), *Contributions to Indian Sociology,* Vol. 13, no. 2.

Dube, I.B. 1999. 'Taming Traditions: Legalities and Histories in Twentieth-Century Orissa', in G. Bhadra, Parakash, and S. Tharu, *Subaltern Studies X: Writings on South Asian History and Society,* Delhi: Oxford University Press, pp. 98–125.

Dube, I.B. 2001. 'Issues of Faith, Enactments of Contest: The Founding of Mahima Dharma in Nineteenth-Century Orissa', in H. Kulke and B. Schnepel (eds), *Jagannath Revisited: Studying Society, Religion and the State in Orissa*, Delhi: Manohar, pp. 149–78.

Douglas, M. 1966. *Purity and Danger: An Analysis of Concepts of Pollution and Taboo.* London: Routledge and Kegan Paul.

Dumont, L. 1966. *Homo Hierarchicus. Le système des Castes et Ses Implications.* Paris: Gallimard.

——. 1966. 'Appendice B. Le renoncement dans les religions de l'Inde' (pp. 324–50), in ibid., *Homo Hierarchicus. Le Système des Castes et Ses Implications.* Paris: Gallimard.

Eck, D.L. 1981. *Darshan: Seeing the Divine Image in India.* Chambersburg: Anima.

Eschmann, A. 1986 (1978). 'Mahima Dharma: An Autochthonous Hindu Reform Movement' (pp. 374–410), in A. Eschmann, H. Kulke, and G.T. Tripathi (eds), *The Cult of Jagannath and the Regional Tradition of Orissa,* New Delhi: Manohar.

——, H. Kulke, and G.C. Tripathi (eds) 1986 (1978). *The Cult of Jagannath and the Regional Tradition of Orissa,* New Delhi: Manohar, pp. 421–37.

Frazer, J.G. 1989 (1922). *The Golden Bough* (German version). Reinbeck bei Hamburg: Rororo.

Galey, J.C. 1989. 'Reconsidering Kingship in India: An Ethnological Perspective', (pp. 123–87), in ibid. (ed.), *Kingship and the Kings: History and Anthropology, Vol. 4.* London–Paris–New York: Harwood Academic Publishers.

Ghurye, G.S. 1953. *Indian Sadhus,* Bombay: Popular Prakashan.

Guzy, L. 2002. 'Negative Ecstasy or the Singers of the Divine: Voices from the Periphery of Mahima Dharma', in G. Pfeffer (ed.), *Periphery and Centre: Groups, Categories, Values*, Delhi: Manohar.

Hubert, H. et Mauss, M. 1968 (1899). 'Essai sur la nature et la fonction du sacrifice', in Mauss, M., *Oeuvres 1.* Paris: Editions de Minuit, pp. 193–307.

Kulke, H. 1978. 'Royal Temple Policy and the Structure of Medieval Hindu Kingdoms', and 'Early Royal Patronage of the Jagannatha Cult', in A. Eschmann, H. Kulke, and G.C. Tripathi (eds), *The Cult of Jagannath and the Regional Tradition of Orissa,* New Delhi: Manohar, pp. 125–38, 139–56.

Mauss, M. 1968 (1909). 'La prière et les rites oraux', in M. Mauss, *Oeuvres 1. Les Fonctions Sociales du Sacré.* Paris: Les Editions de Minuit, pp. 357–477.

——. 1990 (1950). *Die Gabe* (The Gift). Frankfurt: Suhrkamp.

Marriott, M. 1968. 'Caste Ranking and Food Transactions. A Matrix Analysis', (pp. 133–72) in M. Singer and B. Cohn (eds), *Structure and Change in Indian Society*, Cambridge: Cambridge University Press.

Michaels, A. 1998. *Der Hinduismus: Geschichte und Gegenwart.* München: C.H. Beck.

Mohapatra, S. 1983. *Bhima Bhoi: Makers of Indian Literature,* Delhi: Sahitya Akademi.

Pfeffer, G. 1986 (1978). 'Puri's Vedic Brahmins: Continuity and Change in their Traditional Institutions', in A. Eschmann, H. Kulke, and G.C. Tripathi (eds), *The Cult of Jagannath and the Regional Tradition of Orissa,* New Delhi: Manohar, pp. 421–37.

Quigley, D. 1999 (1993). *The Interpretation of Caste,* New Delhi: Oxford University Press.

Schnepel, B. 1995. *Little Kingdoms in India Reconsidered.* Occasional Paper 5. Bhubanesvar: Utkal University.

Senapati, N .1972. 'Appendix Mahima Dharma' (pp. 443–8) in N. Senapati and P. Tripathy (eds), *Orissa District Gazetteers, Dhenkanal,* Cuttack: Orissa Government Press.

Senapati, N. and P. Tripathy (eds) 1972. *Orissa District Gazetteers. Dhenkanal,* Cuttack: Orissa Government Press.

Staal, F. 1983. *Agni: The Vedic Ritual of the Fire-altar, I–II*, University of Berkeley.

Sprockhoff, J.F. 1980. 'Die feindlichen Toten und der befriedete Tote' (pp. 263–84), in Stephenson, G. (ed.), *Leben und Tod in den Religionen. Symbol und Wirklichkeit.* Darmstadt: Wissenschaftliche Buchgesellschaft.

T.R.B. 1968–9. 'Impact of Satya Mahima Dharma on Scheduled Castes and Scheduled Tribes in Orissa', *ADIBASI*, Vol. X, 1: 44–76.

Veer, P. van der. 1996. *Religious Nationalism. Hindus, and Muslims in India,* Delhi: Oxford University Press.

Weber, M. 1972 (1922). *Wirtschaft und Gesellschaft,* Tubingen: J.C.B. Mohr.

Bhima Bhoi

The Making of a Modern Saint

Johannes Beltz

Bhima Bhoi is one of Orissa's most interesting literary and religious figures of the nineteenth century.[1] He was a disciple of Mahima Gosain, the legendary founder of the Mahima Dharma movement.[2] As the prominent historian Chittaranjan Das (1951: 160) rightly pointed out, 'Although Mahima Gosain was the founder of Mahima Dharma, it was really the works of Bhima Bhoi, the blind poet, that brought home to all people the essence and excellence of the new doctrine.' Indeed Bhima Bhoi's importance should not be underestimated. The major part of the popular devotional poetry that characterizes Mahima Dharma is attributed to him,[3] and as a matter of fact more than one critic has taken him not only to be the successor of Mahima Gosain but also to be the actual propagator of Mahima Dharma.[4] Furthermore Bhima Bhoi protested against almost everything that generally characterizes 'orthodox' Hinduism, that is, the reference to the Veda as a sacred scripture, idol worship, temple cult, pilgrimage, and brahmin priesthood.[5]

SOURCES AND FIELDWORK

Bhima Bhoi's significance is contrasted by the absence of reliable documents about him.[6] He did not expose any autobiographical details in his writings and the very few references about his life are difficult to understand, and allow contradictory interpretations. The secondary sources such as newspapers and administrative reports are also quite contradictory and confusing.[7] However, we do possess a large number of stories and legends which are orally transmitted and widely circulated. How to deal with this kind of texts? In some of the existing biographies about Bhima Bhoi, they are quoted without inquiring into their legendary character. In others they are objected to because they do not contain any 'true fact' and are as such without any historical value. I believe these conclusions are misguided when it comes to understanding the meaning and significance of Bhima Bhoi. In fact I decided to systematically collect all those legends and strange stories which are absent in 'scholarly' books. It goes without saying, however, that these stories tell us more about how Bhima Bhoi is imagined and less about him as an authentic historical person. These texts are hagiographic documents and should be valued as such.[8] Thus, this essay is not a historical study about the person who was Bhima Bhoi but rather discusses the impact which he had, and still has today. In other words, starting from the idea that saints are not born but made, I want to look into the complex process of constructing a religious biography. My interest lies in the challenge Bhima Bhoi presented, and still presents for the people who narrate his life story.[9]

Before exposing the many and contradictory ways in which Bhima Bhoi is represented, my fieldwork should be mentioned. From 2000 to 2001 I visited several places in western Orissa which have special links with Bhima Bhoi—Khaliapali, Jatesingha. Kankanpada, and Kandhara. Interviews were conducted among the ascetics of the *Balkaladhari* and the *Kaupinadhari* order, as well as among the lay people. It seems that in western Orissa Mahima Dharma is very popular among the so-called downtrodden communities, and especially among the 'Untouchable' Ganda-Panas. However, people from other communities and higher social strata are also equally attracted to it. I met devotees who are carpenters (*Khabala*), farmers (*Chasa*), oil makers (*Teli*), fisherman, milkman, and weavers (*Meher*). It is reported that even brahmins have accepted this religion; this was an information that I was not able to verify.

I did not interact exclusively with initiated members of the Mahima Dharma sect. The circulated stories of Bhima Bhoi break the boundaries and cross all frontiers of caste and creed in villages and towns. One has to keep in mind that his poems are very popular, not recited by professional artists only.[10] His *bhajanas* (devotional songs) are sung at many occasions, and his *malikas* (prophecies) are widely known.[11] There is something more remarkable about his *bhajanas*; it is said that they possess healing powers. People have been cured from diseases, snake-bites, and possession of evil spirits. It seems that by reciting them and by praying to Mahima Alekha, barren women can get pregnant. Bhima Bhoi has also become an object of intellectual discussion. During the last decades he has been politically appropriated as a great freedom fighter and a vehement critic of communalism. He is cast as the forerunner of women's emancipation and a great protagonist of Oriya language. He manifests Orissa's contribution to the Indian cultural heritage. For instance, when the Sahitya Akademi asked for a poetic passage from each of the fourteen Indian languages, a couplet of Bhima Bhoi's *Stuticintamani* was chosen.[12] The number of associations, schools, and colleges which are operating in Orissa in the name of Bhima Bhoi are numerous, and several research institutes are created in his name.

As mentioned above, my sources consist of printed books and booklets as well as interviews; therefore a continuity between literature and oral narration may be presupposed. I do consider both categories of texts as equally interesting and authentic. It should be recalled in our analysis that the texts about Bhima Bhoi's life are collected from a variety of people with different social and political backgrounds. The context of each of these texts is specific and requires proper understanding. But in their diversity, all texts are comparable. They imagine the life of Bhima Bhoi and give a coherent sense to it. Beyond their specific context, common topics can be extrapolated and cultural patterns analysed. In this sense my essay is open for further research on hagiography, biography, and autobiographies in an inter-cultural and comparative perspective.

BHIMA BHOI'S ORIGIN

Hagiographies usually answer the question of the origin of their hero. Let us accept that Bhima Bhoi was a historic person and that he was born in the middle of the nineteenth century. We cannot provide the exact year because the definite answer is not only outside our field of investigation, but also irrelevant to our research. Bhima Bhoi's origin is as mysterious as his life. Let us quote from his magnum opus *Stuticintamani*. Bhima Bhoi repeatedly claims here to originate from a poor Kandha family (that means he is a tribal). He further reports that his father died when he was born. He seems to have lost his mother also, since he calls himself an orphan. The little Bhima Bhoi had therefore to start working at a very young age:

> I have no friends nor brothers, no mother no father to save me from the troubles and sorrow. I have no well-wisher nor relations, I am a helpless orphan creature.[13]

Or:

My father left me from the time of my birth keeping me without support in a desperate condition. How could I get food and enjoyment easily if so desired, [...] From the age of twelve I had to spend days tending cattle in the forest.[14]

However, one should keep in mind that the context of these verses indicates an explicit religious meaning. Bhima Bhoi is not reciting biographical data but talks about his guru. He describes his painful existence and asks the guru to save him from that. Bhima Bhoi's major concern is his sorrow and his salvation. Again and again, he narrates how he suffered in his childhood and how he met his guru at the age of four.[15]

One could ask if Bhima Bhoi is not hiding his origins voluntarily. As a true mystic he would have no interest in revealing his family background. Indeed, there are hardly more biographical references in his other poetic creations. The absence of authentic biodata is contrasted by numerous miraculous 'birth stories'. In almost all villages in the region of Kandhara and Redhakhol, stories circulate. One of them reads:

There was a man called Danara Bhoi and he was Kandha. Once he went into the forest in search of some wood and found an abandoned male child on a lotus leaf. He gave the child to his wife who was unable to conceive, and they took care of him.

This is the simplest version of the event, and also very straight because no fantastic religious topics appear. It sounds as if the story could really have happened. Some variations affirm that Bhima Bhoi was an abandoned, illegitimate child. But in all varieties, a consensus exists on the fact that he was found in a palm grove and that his adoptive parents were Kandhas, that is, tribals. The names of his adoptive parents may differ, but it is always a barren woman who needs a child. In some stories a divine element clearly appears: Mahima Gosain comes to know about the pain of the childless Kandha couple and decides to help. The crucial issue remains that Bhima Bhoi has no 'real' parents. On certain occasions I was told that Bhima's birth happened in the same way as Krishna's did, that is, as a divine emanation. The fact that Bhima Bhoi has no biological parents reinforces his holy character.

The divine origin of Bhima Bhoi is reaffirmed and canonized by a current which places Bhima Bhoi in the *pancashakha* tradition.[16] According to this idea. Bhima Bhoi's appearance was predicted by Achyutananda Das, the famous Oriya poet of the fifteenth century. In his *Kalpa Samhita*, he is quoted to have said that Radha would take birth again in the world and will be called Bhima Bhoi. It was also said that she would be reborn in a Kandha family and that she would have poetic talent. Whilst this idea may be of recent origin, it is nonetheless interesting for our investigation. Through this prediction Bhima Bhoi is integrated into the dominant Vaishnava tradition. What is even more interesting is the fact that this reappropriation has worked very successfully. I was told many times during my interviews that Mahima Gosain and Bhima Bhoi form a couple, like Krishna and Radha. Bhima Bhoi was the Radha of divine eternity; he never came out of a woman's womb (*ayonisambhuta*). Certain *bhakta*s (devotees) declare that Bhima Bhoi was the *avatara* (incarnation) of Bhagavan. Others claim that his father was Alekha Swami. To repeat once again, this statement does not inform us about the real origin of Bhima Bhoi, but rather shows us the manner in which his followers revered him as a divine being.

In general, Bhima Bhoi's poor social background is positively recognized. It culminates in the statement that although born in a poor Kandha family, he still rose to a place of power and praise because of his intelligence. Bhima Bhoi becomes a spiritual guide, a model to follow. In fact, Bhima Bhoi is envisioned as a tribal poet. It is said that in Orissa prior to his coming, only brahmins were recognized as poets, and that Mahima Gosain changed that state of affairs by making Bhima Bhoi the first *Adivasi* poet. This statement ignores that Sarala Das, the author of the Oriya version of the Mahabharata. was a *shudra*. Whether a historical fact or not, Bhima Bhoi is seen as a challenge to the brahmin hegemony. However, one has to keep in mind that this claim is made by non-Adivasis.[17] Perhaps the literary elite promote Bhima Bhoi's tribal background to integrate the tribes into the mainstream? One could consider this discourse also as an attempt to reappropriate Bhima Bhoi as an agent for the ongoing Hinduization of autonomous tribal cultures. Being originally a tribal, he becomes the representative of a modern and reformed Hinduism.

It is interesting that Bhima Bhoi also appears as the voice of the subaltern and the underprivileged. An important part of the Ganda-Panas, a caste of so-called 'untouchables' from western Orissa converted to Mahima Dharma and took Bhima Bhoi as a symbol of their own.[18] Bhima Bhoi is seen as one of their own, a poor and a low-caste man. He is praised as the prophet of the dalits affirming their envy of social recognition. Through him, a universal brotherhood is formulated: the 'untouchables' are also Hindus. And they practise the 'true' Hinduism without idols because they know the sacred but hidden meaning of the Vedas.

But again this discourse is contested (whenever the caste factor enters the discussion, contradictory stories are bound to appear). Indeed, some intellectuals declare that Bhima Bhoi although raised as a tribal, was a brahmin by birth. This claim is based on the stereotype that only brahmins were able to write literature and talk about religious matters. How could a tribal compose such beautiful songs? In order to prove his noble birth, it is recalled that Bhima Bhoi had a fair complexion. Others are more modest in their claims by recognizing that he probably was not born a brahmin but that he was, at least, as educated as a brahmin. By saying this, the supremacy of brahmins is still safeguarded. The debate indicates clearly a social conflict among the so-called higher and lower castes.

It is not only the birth and the social background which are controversially discussed. There is a long-standing debate amongst Indian scholars about the question of where Bhima Bhoi was really born. Joranda, Gramadiha, Jatesingha, Kamrapali, and Kumarkeli are all places where the local people are able to show the lotus pond where the little Bhima Bhoi was found. This is not the place to list or discuss such theories. This question is, again, outside our area of investigation. But I would like to add that this problem does not represent a mere abstract debate. There exists a dynamic competition between different villages, local persons, and institutions; persons develop new stories about the *janmasthana* (birthplace) of Bhima Bhoi, and they are keen to defend their ideas against others. So-called 'scientific' proofs are constructed, schools are named after him, and his statues are erected in order to promote local interests. The person of Bhima Bhoi is imagined and appropriated in many contexts and with diverse intentions. It is interesting to observe how the different positions are negotiated.

THE BLIND POET

Though Bhima Bhoi never presented himself as a blind person, there exists a hagiographic tradition which declares him blind. Among scholars, contradictory opinions and stories circulate about Bhima Bhoi's blindness.[19] As I have argued already in the introduction of this essay, it is not my aim to discover the 'historic' Bhima Bhoi, that is the person he was in reality. I think that the question of whether he was really blind or not is beyond my field of investigation. However, one should keep in mind that in his compositions, no reference is made to a physical handicap. The few passages where he speaks about blindness could be understood as metaphors: Bhima Bhoi thinks of himself as blind without his guru. Furthermore, he often uses verbs of vision. But instead of arguing why he was not blind, let us adopt another perspective. I suggest taking the accounts of his blindness as interesting texts to look into. In other words, I suggest looking at his blindness in terms of a hagiographic topic.

His blindness, being without any doubt an important motif of his life story, is generally connected to his first meeting with Mahima Gosain. Keeping in mind the importance of the first encounter between the guru and his *shishya* (disciple) in Indian hagiographic writing, let me quote this story. According to Biswanath Baba (1991: 53), the story of how Mahima Swami (*Prabhu*), who was accompanied by Govinda Baba, came to meet Bhima Bhoi is as follows:

Both the preceptor and his disciple reached the village Gramadiha, which is situated near Redhakhol, in the middle of the night. In front of the door of Bhima Bhoi's house, Swami called: 'Bhima Bhoi!' Bhima Bhoi heard the voice and was surprised. He replied, 'Who are you? Why are you calling me in the middle of the night?' Hearing this answer from Bhima Bhoi, Prabhu replied, 'We have reached here because of your past virtues. Come quickly!' Hearing this, Bhima Bhoi replied, 'If you have reached here due to my past virtues, then give me the power of vision. I'm blind. If you do so, I'll be informed about my virtues'. Prabhu commanded, 'Receive the power of vision.' By the mercy of Prabhu, Bhima Bhoi suddenly received the power of seeing. Knowing about the miraculous deeds of Swami, he opened the door immediately and went outside. He found the preceptor and his disciple both waiting near the door just like the sun and the moon. Bhima Bhoi prostrated in front of the preceptor and his disciple. Prabhu blessed Bhima by laying his hand on Bhima's head. Then he ordered, 'O Bhima, get up!' According to his order he got up and offered prayers with folded hands. Then he asked: 'O Prabhu, for what reason have you appeared here so suddenly? Please, command kindly and mercifully to the wretched.' Prabhu replied, 'Prabhu has miraculously incarnated in a bodily form in order to preach the Satya Mahima Dharma in the present Kaliyuga. You will be initiated into this dharma.' [...] After that, Mahima Swami clapped his hands thrice on the head of Bhima Bhoi and transferred on him the gift of poetry. This gift would automatically develop from his inner heart in order to spread the glory of the Satya Mahima Dharma. Bhima Bhoi was overwhelmed with joy and offered *saran* at the feet of Swami. He asked him, 'Prabhu, I have seen your feet because you have given me the power of vision. I do not want to see the worldly objects with that outer eye. Prabhu bless me to become unable to see these outer objects.' Swami replied, 'You will get back to your previous stage.'

Bhima Bhoi is presented in this story as a mere disciple of Mahima Gosain. He is not a genuine poet but a servant who has to write what his guru will tell him. Bhima Bhoi resists and states his inability to do this. But Mahima Gosain does not accept his excuses and orders him to fulfil his mission. This is, again. a common topic which can be found in other comparable hagiographies: the saint is always overwhelmed by the presence of his guru, often he refuses to serve him because he finds it too difficult. In fact, in Biswanath Baba's story, Bhima Bhoi's blindness is used to underline the ultimate authority of Mahima Gosain. Bhima Bhoi's poetic creativity and autonomy are annihilated. He personally has nothing to say. He is just the pen in the hand of his guru.

Interestingly, Biswanath Baba (1991: 56) tells another story about Bhima Bhoi composing his first poetry. It was at the time when Bhima Bhoi was keeping cattle near Redhakhol. One day, he fell into an old and broken well in Kandhara. Though people tried to help him, he refused to come out. He stayed in the well and told the people that the one who would save him would be the same as the one who had brought him there. So it happened. In the night, he saw a big foot, took it and was drawn out of the well. It is said that from this moment on Bhima Bhoi composed poetry. To my knowledge it is only Biswanath Baba who combined the well story with Bhima Bhoi's first poems. Usually the story is that Bhima Bhoi fell into the well and was saved by Mahima Swami. The fall is seen as a proof of Bhima Bhoi's faith in his guru.

In addition to Biswanath Baba's narrative, I would like to refer to the story of Sur Das, the blind Braj poet. The comparison with Bhima Bhoi is doubly interesting because Sur Das also falls into a well and voluntarily renounces the return of his vision. The choice of blindness strikes a parallel with the story of Bhima Bhoi. Both stories seem to be so similar because we are in the midst of hagiographies where blindness is a religious issue. But if it seems likely that Sur Das was not blind at all—as John Stratton Hawley suggests—what does that mean? If blindness is such an important religious topic, what is the inherent significance of it? Let us quote Hawley (1984: 15) who considers that the account of Sur's blindness 'not only preserves the purity of vision upon which so much hinges in the Varta, but strengthens it: even when Sur sees, he sees nothing but Krishna.'

Let us mention the concept of *darshan* and its significance in Hinduism. The 'look' is the core in the relationship between the deity and the devotee. The eye is a testimony of truth but is, after all, also negligible. The saint who, like God, knows everything does not need to look. Axel Michaels (1998: 257) writes: 'Blindness can be higher knowledge. The visible things can be illusion ...'. This is an important step towards the understanding of the problem. The poets of the *nirguna-bhakti* tradition think that God is in its essence without form and quality (*nirguna, nirakara*). Accordingly then, the visible world is only illusion! In the words of Michaels (1998: 257): 'The true understanding does not need eyes but knowledge and inner vision.'

Given such an insight we may now have gained a better understanding of the significance of Bhima Bhoi's blindness. I am proposing that it may be considered to be normative within the sphere that is traditionally assigned to rare spiritual humility. In this sense, the blind Bhima Bhoi fits well into the Indian canon of hagiography. His blindness is less an attribute which refers to his physical outlook, or to his physical abilities, than the consequence of his religious attitude. He is preaching the void, the empty. God has no form, and there is no idol to worship. How can this be better illustrated than by the image of Bhima Bhoi as a blind poet? It could also be argued that his blindness permits him to concentrate on god. Sight would allow him to witness other things which may spoil him. The blindness is the culminating point in the narrative about the holy Bhima Bhoi, conveying the intensity of his love for god.

However, we have to understand that the people who imagine Bhima Bhoi as blind do not adhere to the 'rationalistic' discourse on Bhima Bhoi that is typical for the intellectual elite who promote him as a social revolutionary. In the latter case, he is depicted as watching the world with open and attentive eyes. His blindness is read as a metaphor of spirituality. Bhima sees what happens around him as being part and parcel of this world. He saw the nature, the human injustice, the social inequalities, the poverty, and all the problems which humans faced in their lifetime. His altruism, his social engagement are imagined as a reaction to what he saw. It could be that this discourse is quite recent and the result of a more rationalistic appropriation of Bhima Bhoi. This indicates that there is a changing emphasis in the perception of this person.

THE CONSTRUCTION OF A SOCIAL REFORMER

It is said that Bhima Bhoi revolted against all kinds of social evils. He questioned local hierarchies, kings, brahmins, and the traditional role of women. Bhima Bhoi is depicted as the first social revolutionary of modern Orissa. He fought against the British and tried his best to reform Indian society. Bhima Bhoi is further imagined as a saint who sacrificed his personal life for the well-being of other people. He did not renounce his noble mission when people burned down his house, or threw stones at him, or spat at him and threatened him with death. He was driven out of his village and imprisoned several times.[20]

Bhima Bhoi is believed to have questioned the authority of local kings. One old man of the Kankanpada village told me that the Raja Niladri Singh Deo of Sonepur wanted Bhima Bhoi to pass an ordeal through fire in order to test his holiness. But the Raja died of a snakebite the night before the ordeal was to take place. Bhima Bhoi's integrity as a holy man could not be questioned. It is also said that the attempt of the king to test the holiness of Bhima Bhoi has caused an everlasting malediction of the royal family of Sonepur. Due to this evil king, the family had to abdicate and the royal palace, being abandoned by his owners, was destroyed.

It is also said that Bhima Bhoi opposed caste distinctions *(jatigata vibheda)* and accepted disciples from all communities, even untouchables. According to him there is only one caste, that is, humanity (*manava jati*).[21] In other words, there are only men and women. It is often said that his criticism of caste provoked people to place sanctions on him. They could not bear that he accepted people from all communities and that he treated them equally. There is a related story in which Bhima Bhoi was beaten up and thrown into the well in Kandhara because he was acting against the *jatikuladharma.* Let us recall that Biswanath Baba (1991: 56) gave a rather different interpretation of the event. According to him, the well story narrates how Bhima Bhoi came to write his first poetry. Again we can see that events and narrative elements can vary and can be used on more occasions than one. In other words, literary topics and motifs can be combined and used in many ways, according to the communicational context in which the narrative is situated. Be it an accident or a royal punishment, there exists today a well in Kandhara which is remembered as the place were Bhima Bhoi was saved by his guru. The old structure has recently been replaced by an enormous concrete construction. With the help of public money, a huge memorial has been erected in order to commemorate the incident. The villagers proudly take the visitors to the well; regular festivals are organized where the obligatory procession path incorporates a trip around the well. Thus, the place of Kandhara has been integrated into the sacred geography of Mahima Dharma.

Bhima Bhoi is further known for being radically opposed to superstition and idol worship.[22] The Census Report of 1911 even stated that he wanted to destroy Lord Jagannath's image in Puri.[23] It is said that he believed that if the image was destroyed, it would convince the Hindus of the futility of their religion, and they would embrace the new faith. In obedience to his command, a body of his followers marched to Puri and tried to break into the shrine of Jagannath. Riots broke out; people entered the temple, and one person died mysteriously. The details of the story are not at issue here but rather the commonly accepted statement that Bhima Bhoi participated in or at least encouraged the attack of the Jagannath temple. According to Anncharlott Eschmann (1975: 10), it seems very unlikely that Bhima Bhoi directed that incident although it was connected with him. Bhagirathi Nepak (1997: 72) goes a step further and doubts that the attack on Jagannath was sanctioned by Bhima Bhoi. Biswamoy Pati even questions the participation of any Mahima Dharmee in the attack. He rightly observes that 'this event is virtually forgotten by the followers of the cult today, who are almost embarrassed about it' and concludes that the colonial powers invented a conspiracy in order to stop the growing Mahima Dharma movement (Pati, 1997: 132). Again, this conclusion seems exaggerated, as Ishita Banerjee's recent article (2001) has shown.

The question remains as to why the event has been forgotten or why it is voluntarily ignored by the Mahima Dharmees of today. Nepak (1997: 71) has drawn the attention to the fact that Bhima Bhoi was an admirer of Jagannath. He did not question the existence of the god, but the worship of a piece of wood in Puri. One has to keep in mind that the Mahima Dharmees appropriated Jagannath as the first disciple of Mahima Gosain.[24] In other words, Orissa's *rashtra devata* was peacefully incorporated into the Mahima Dharma religion. That seems to be the reason why the so-called 'fanatic' attack on the Jagannath temple of Puri did not enter the collective memory of the Mahima Dharmees. The new Mahima Dharma has replaced the Jagannath cult and the Mahima *gaddi*s at Khaliapali and Joranda are holier and more important than the Jagannath's *tirtha* in Puri.

WOMEN EMANCIPATOR OR RENUNCIANT?

It is widely accepted that Bhima Bhoi lived with four women, two 'worldly' and two 'spiritual' consorts: Sumedha, Rohini, Saraswati, and Annapurna. According to different stories, Sumedha, Rohini, and Saraswati were offered to Bhima Bhoi as servants. Their parents were staunch followers of Mahima Dharma with a deep admiration for Bhima Bhoi.

Regarding Annapurna, things are different since she joined her own will. It is said that she followed only the order of Mahima Gosain. But as a matter of fact she stayed with Bhima Bhoi having the strong desire to offer him her *seva* (service). After Bhima Bhoi's death, the management of the ashram came into her hands. Concerning Bhima Bhoi's relationship with her, one piquant question remains. Did he adopt a life of chastity? Interestingly most Mahima followers pretend that he was never married and that his relations with women were only 'spiritual'. It is said that Annapurna was living a life of austerity and moral purity. It is even claimed that she was a goddess. As his principal spiritual consort, her shoes *(paduka)* are till today kept together with Bhima Bhoi's in Khaliapali and are worshipped on special occasions. Concerning the nature of their relationship it is generally stated that it was purely spiritual. In an interview I was told this:

Annapurna, a brahmin girl, devoted her life to Bhima Bhoi and came with him to Khaliapali. Annapurna's relatives were not happy with that. They spread the rumour that Bhima Bhoi had abducted the brahmin girl. Furious as they were, they went to see Bhima Bhoi. They disrobed him. But what did they discover? They saw that he had no penis. After that they understood that his relationship with Annapurna was only spiritual.

But what about the other women? Surprisingly they got pregnant. Did Bhima Bhoi beget children although he was not supposed to procreate? How can one justify this? A story reads:

Narayan Das and Mohan Das, the fathers of Sumedha and Rohini, came once to Bhima Bhoi and complained that they had not gained anything from delivering their daughters to him. Then Bhima Bhoi pasted vermilion on the forehead of Sumedha and Rohini. As a result, Kapilesvar, a son and Labanyabati, a daughter, were born.

In another story it is said that Sumedha's mother came once from Ragapali to Khaliapali to pray to Bhima Bhoi. She wanted to take *darshana* in Khaliapali. She prayed to him that her daughter should always be happy. For her, it was clear that being a woman she should also become a mother. Bhima Bhoi smiled and promised to fulfil her desire smearing some *bibhuti* (holy ashes) on Sumedha's forehead. And, of course, the result came immediately. After three days she gave birth to a son.

However, some texts suggest that his followers, or at least a section of them, disapprove of this development. Let us quote an interesting passage from a letter written by the Assistant Secretary to the Chief Commissioner of the Central Provinces (no. 3069–161), dated 17 August 1881. In the sixth paragraph, the author writes about Bhima Bhoi:

(Bhima Bhoi) exercised great influence over his followers. The relations existing between him and a female companion, however, excited suspicion among his adherents, who, however, did not venture to question the purity of his conduct until the woman became pregnant. Bhima endeavoured to deceive his followers by telling them that the woman would give birth to Arjun, who would root out all unbelievers. The(y) believed this story, and waited until the child was born, when to their great surprise, they found that the woman gave birth to a girl. Bhima accounted for this by saying that it had recently been revealed to him that the woman would give birth to a female, who would destroy all the unbelievers by means of her charms. The child, however, died a few days later, and Bhima then tried to mislead his followers still further by saying that the fairy had quitted [sic] this world because she had found it filled with vices of mankind. He was now deserted by most of his followers, who formed a separate faction but he is still highly adored and honoured by the remainder.[25]

Interestingly this is the story about a child who died shortly after his birth. In other words, the mentioned child is neither Kapilesvar nor Labanyavati. Further, the rather negative characterization of Bhima Bhoi needs our attention. He is described as misguiding and cheating his followers. The same radical criticism is expressed by the authors of the Census of India from 1911 who repeated the same story. In the same year, in 1911, B.C. Mazumdar wrote his famous article entitled 'Alekhism' as a part of his book *Sonpur in the Sambalpur Tract.* In this article we find the same statement that Bhima Bhoi begot children and that this fact created much dissent among his followers. However, his judgement is less harsh. Let us quote the passage (Mazumdar, 1911: 34):

> Bhima Bhoi as a matter of fact did beget two children—one a son and another a daughter—on two women, who became nuns and lived at Khaliapali in Bhima Bhoi's math. Both these women are still living at Khaliapali with the children begotten upon them. It was nineteen years ago that first a daughter and then after two months a son were born having Bhima Bhoi for their father. The disciples were no doubt very much shocked at it, but Bhima Bhoi explained it to them that he brought one male and one female child into existence with a view to give to the world one ideal woman and one ideal man. How these two ideal beings are behaving now could not be ascertained by me.

It is certain that the existence of women within the ashram was the major reason for the twist between Joranda and Khaliapali. It is told that some ascetics came from Joranda to burn down Bhima Bhoi's ashram in Gulunda because he had transgressed the rules regarding procreation. In fact, an important section of the Joranda ascetics regard him as a heretic. It seems very clear that in their mind the propensity to procreate is the root of all evil. According to their ascetic ideal, the perfect man is one who gains full control over sexual desires. The ascetics are expected to contemplate every morning on the organs of generation without becoming stimulated so that ultimately complete detachment from sexual proclivity might be obtained. That is, their minds are able to dominate their bodily functions. According to that ideal, a holy man has no sexual feelings. But one should keep in mind that though Joranda represents the most powerful and influential Mahima Dharma monastery today, other 'heretic' currents do exist apart from Khaliapali where till today women are living as *sannyasinis* in the ashram. The Satya Svadhin Mahima Dharmis of Kardula went even a step further. Having founded their independent 'sect' they demand that all members get married. It is said that because Bhima Bhoi was a *grhastha* (householder), all members of their group should be grhasthas also.[26]

One should, indeed, interpret this conflict in a positive way. I was told that Bhima Bhoi went to Joranda after the death of Mahima Gosain and that he was terrified by the local form of worship. He left the place swearing that he would never return and founded in 1877, under the patronage of Raja Bahadur Niladhar Singh Deo, his own ashram in Khaliapali where he could accept women as disciples. In this sense, Bhima Bhoi can be seen as advocating the emancipation of women. He said that there is no difference between men and women in his ashram at Khaliapali. It is reported that he chose Annapurna, a brahmin woman, as a companion which was an affront to the traditionalists who do not approve of any relationship between a low-caste man and a high-caste woman. In fact, Bhima Bhoi's ashram can be seen as a counterpart to the ashram of Joranda.

But there are other stories. Bhima Bhoi's chastity is contested by his own writings. Indeed, in his *Cautisha Granthamala*, he admits to having several wives (!) and made explicit erotic references.[27] But again, this fact is voluntarily ignored by some Mahima Dharmees. Others disqualify these poems as being composed *before* he became a saint. And again others read them as allegories of his love towards his guru. There are again apocrypha about Bhima Bhoi which regard him as a 'womanizer' in his youth. He is imagined as being fair and muscled, having a strong and hairless body. It is also reported that he enjoyed wearing women's clothing. It appears that this is an interesting field of investigation. However, people are reluctant to talk about this rather unusual aspect of Bhima Bhoi. In fact, if one looks into his poetic composition, one finds a lot of references to sex and physical enjoyment. He never claimed to be an ascetic or to have renounced his status of a householder.[28] On the contrary, there exist a certain number of passages where he openly refuses to adopt a chaste lifestyle.

We see that Bhima Bhoi does not fit into the canonical picture of a saint who lives his life in devotion to god and austerity. This leads to diverse reactions among his followers which can be illustrated by the narratives mentioned above. The first option is to adversely criticize Bhima Bhoi and to reject his immoral attitudes. The Balkaladharis of Joranda clearly express this opinion. The second option is to ignore all accusations and to see Bhima Bhoi as well as his children as a kind of divine incarnations, being above the physical world of sex and gender. Being divine, Bhima Bhoi can emanate children, staying with women yet refraining from touching them.

CONTESTED HAGIOGRAPHY

It has become clear that most of the stories about Bhima Bhoi have to be understood in the context of Indian hagiographies. His biography makes a lot of references to 'classic' mythological sequences as well as contemporary political discourses. Hagiographic topics such as his divine origin and his devotional lifestyle are mixed with discourses about social emancipation and reform. The controversies mentioned above concerning the life of Bhima Bhoi result from the different perspectives from which he is examined. These controversies culminate in the following question: if and to what extent, Bhima Bhoi was against orthodoxy, tradition, brahmanic hegemony, Vedas, and ritualistic Hinduism?

Further we must examine the people who create and the institutions that promote these stories. Discourses are not created in an empty space but embedded in social interactions. The first institutionalized group to examine is the ascetic order. The documents concerning the juridical debate between the Balkaladharis and Kaupinadharis of Joranda are especially revealing for our investigation.[29] It is not the question of who is superior, nor the struggle concerning the temple management, property, money, influence, nor domination which attracts me, neither do the arguments, the enquiries, replies, and court decisions. What makes this controversy interesting is the fact that Bhima Bhoi is a reference in the ongoing fight of influence among these two groups. There seems to be a different reception of Bhima Bhoi: while the Kaupinadharis claim to follow Bhima Bhoi's books as the main source, as their holy book, the Balkaladharis seem to take Bhima Bhoi as one amongst others. They do not seem to accord him a special position. In an open letter Biswanath Baba, who was one of the main actors in this debate, presents his point of view. Speaking for the Balkaladhari community, he says that the books of Bhima Bhoi are not taken as books laying down regulations or roles of conduct but they are accepted as religious books, and they are read along with others.[30] Bhima Bhoi, having accepted two brahmin ladies, deviated from the principles of Mahima Dharma. According to Satrughna Nath, spokesman of Biswanath Baba, sannyasins from Joranda should not stay in Khaliapali and should not take any food.[31]

On the other hand, the Kaupinadharis accept Bhima Bhoi's writings as a code and authority.[32] Bhima Bhoi is either considered as the absolute authority, the mouthpiece of Mahima Swami, or as just one writer among others. In the final judgement of the court it is stated that the Balkaladharis are the legitimate owners of the Mahima Gadi in Joranda and that their authority should be respected. They are now officially recognized as the legitimate representatives of the Mahima Dharma religion. The Kaupinadharis have lost. The argument of Biswanath Baba has been accepted, and the predominant role of Bhima Bhoi as it was projected by the Kaupinadharis is nullified. Biswanath Baba's group not only recognizes other Hindu scriptures such as the *Manusmriti* as equally—or even more—important but also argues that the philosophy of Mahima Dharma is in full accordance with the Vedas, the Puranas, and the Bhagavadgita. According to them Mahima Dharma is nothing else but true Vedanta. Bhima Bhoi's revolutionary and challenging positions are neutralized and annihilated. The particularity of Mahima Dharma due to Bhima Bhoi's extraordinary criticism becomes less visible. In other words, the challenging appeal of the Mahima Dharma movement which led some people to conclude that the Mahima Dharmees are a separate, that is, a non-Hindu sect, is disappearing. Biswanath Baba functions here as a motor of an ongoing saffronization.[33] According to him, it is impossible to consider Mahima Dharma as different from Vedanta and sanatana dharma. Mahima Dharma has become part of the dominant Hindu mainstream.

In this ongoing process of interpretation, adaptation, and reappropriation of Bhima Bhoi, the Mahima Dharmees of the Kardula village represent another contrasting agent. Their *matha* was founded by a certain Satya Narayan Baba. Whilst all members—as well as the founder himself—belong to the Ganda caste, they claim that people from other castes such as brahmins, chasa, and dumal also take *diksha* and join them. One has to notice that in Orissa the Gandas are treated as untouchable. The converts seem to question everything in Mahima Dharma. For example, they worship an image arguing that no one ever condemned idol worship. Interestingly they legitimate their difference by insisting that they alone are the true followers of Bhima Bhoi. According to Satya Narayan's wife, who is still very much alive, her husband was an incarnation of god. She claimed that he continued the mission of Bhima Bhoi when he had left this world. He completed the unfinished work attracting a large number of followers and disciples. In fact, this section of the Mahima Dharmees illuminates clearly the subaltern aspect of the Mahima Dharma. The so-called down trodden communities have adopted the Mahima cult as their specific religion in order to protest against their social and religious exclusion. But the explicit anti-brahmanism represents only one current of the totality of the Mahima Dharma movement, for we have to recall that Joranda is not a subaltern institution but a powerful monastery supported by rich farmers and upper castes.

Bhima Bhoi is not only appropriated and contested within the Mahimite community. He has become a vehicle of affirming a specific cultural Oriya identity. Bhima Bhoi is promoted as one of the founding fathers of Oriya literature. He is considered to be a national integrator. Through him tribal and Vedic culture became united and harmonized. He was preaching universal love, a universal message among the rich and the poor, among the kings and the Adivasis of the jungle. Many institutions in the name of Bhima Bhoi exist. Let us take only the Bhima Bhoi Samadhi Pitha Trust of Khaliapali (Sonepur) as a significant example.

As a saint Bhima Bhoi is believed to offer solutions to contemporary problems. The hagiographic narratives are orientated to representing an example to follow; the educational aspect is very expressive. Let us quote Sudhakar Das (2000: 6), a Reader in Oriya from Sonepur College who says:

> In the present context, age-old problems like casteism, ignorance, and poverty are still persisting, newer and more vicious challenges like communalism, violence against women, especially rape and dowry torture, corruption and degradation of moral values are confronting the people, almost paralyzing the growth of the nation. At such time, the thinking of Bhima Bhoi, the revolutionary, the visionary, philosopher, and poet might provide a solution.

Equally Gorekanath Sahu (1999), lawyer and journalist from Sonepur states:

> The application of the great thinker's philosophy can find the elusive solution to the myriad of problems by which the society has been plagued.

Bhima Bhoi is a hero above all creeds and religions; he is no longer a preacher of Mahima Dharma. He becomes a universal saviour, an example of universal humanity. In fact, Bhima Bhoi has become more and more an object of diverse political and religious discourses. Congress politicians have appropriated Bhima Bhoi as the direct precursor of Gandhi and prophet of Indian Independence. Ancharlott Eschmann (1978: 407) quotes a booklet which culminates in identifying Bhima Bhoi as fighter for the unification of India under the banner of sanatana dharma. I have to add that Bhima Bhoi also represents the significance of western Oriya culture in a pan-Indian context. He is currently easily integrated in the separatist discourse demanding an independent Koshal Pradesh. More and more intellectuals reclaim Bhima Bhoi as man of the soil demanding that his writings be published in their original language, Sambalpuri. Bhima Bhoi is used as a critic of the coastal hegemony and a forerunner of western Orissa's fight for recognition.

Let me mention another interesting phenomenon. From the scientific point of view it has always been highlighted that the Mahima Dharma is an autochthonous reform movement which developed independently from Christian influences. This would be the principal characteristic which distinguishes it from other so-called neo-Hindu reform movements such as the Arya Samaj or the Ramakrishna Mission. This statement is partially correct. Bhima Bhoi was not in the position to become influenced by Western missionaries. He did not travel to Western countries; his cultural background was very different from that of Vivekananda. However, we have to be very careful with arguments based on this assumption. Firstly, we should remember that Bhima Bhoi did establish some contact with Christianity. We know that he was accused of being a secret Christian though he refused this vehemently. Secondly, it should be reminded that the discourse of Bhima Bhoi's Indianness is much used by nationalist Hindus. They always argue that the Mahima Dharmees are 'real' Hindus and that they were not influenced by any Christians. They emphasize, on the contrary, that Bhima Bhoi *resisted* the Christians. Being a tribal, he did not convert to Christianity but reformed Hinduism. Doing so, he saved the masses from becoming Christians. In that way Bhima Bhoi is a true nationalist, defending the Hindus against the foreign missionaries. Significant is the anti-Western and anti-Christian tone of this discourse.

Thus far we have seen the nationalistic interpretation of Bhima Bhoi. But there are other voices to be heard. As I have already argued, Bhima Bhoi is a matter of ongoing negotiations between different socio-religious groups. In Sonepur I had an interview with a Christian pastor which culminated in the question of whether Bhima was Christian or not. He, of course, argued that Bhima was Christian, having converted due to some divine visions. But he was a secret Christian. He could not declare it openly because people would torture him. He had already suffered so much when people had tried to kill him. While not particularly esteeming this argumentation, it does reveal some interesting facts. The pastor belonged to the Ganda-Pana caste and heard that I was interested in Bhima Bhoi. By telling me that Bhima Bhoi was Christian he tried to stoke my curiosity. He tried to impress me. It is the dynamics of this communicational situation which I want to stress. In a competition, in a fight for recognition, influence, prestige, and superiority, Bhima Bhoi's reference becomes a valuable argument.

CONCLUSION

It has become clear that Bhima Bhoi is imagined in many ways: a poet, a freedom fighter, a prophet, a *bhakta*, a *santha*, and even as an incarnation of god. The question is then how one can analyse the diversity of interpretations. First of all, it has to be admitted that he was without any doubt an extraordinary person and that he must have had a charismatic personality. Bhima Bhoi further seems to defy all attempts at characterization. From the reading of his poetry, one easily imagines his complex and contradictory personality. He definitely was above any kind of sectarian affiliation or dogmatism. He was a poet, a householder, a mystic, and a devotee.

With a rich hagiographic tradition in mind, people started narrating Bhima Bhoi's life. Certain narrators might have been inspired by his complex personality. Most of the stories circulate independently from the historicity of the depicted events or persons. They follow a culturally determined canon of religious topics such as miraculous birth, conversion, healing powers, and sagacity. Supreme human qualities such as altruism or secular virtues such as a sense of social equality, national integration, and patriotism, are the other recurrent topics which can be extracted. Bhima Bhoi is even commemorated as a semi-divine person within an explicit mythological framework. Attempts are made to Hinduize Bhima Bhoi, but they remain ineffective since contesting narratives continue to circulate. In fact, the extraordinary regional and cultural diversity which characterizes Mahima Dharma in Orissa opposes this kind of appropriation.

In other words, Bhima Bhoi is re-actualized in different contexts and is part of diverse religious discourses and political projections. His life is permanently reinvented and canonized by particular persons and institutions. The multiple and contradicting biographies reveal social conflicts as well as different models of sainthood. Ascetic ideals compete with ideas on social reform, religious authorities are contested. I do stress the contradicting dynamics involved in the process of creating Bhima Bhoi's life story since there is no such thing as a normative hagiography, canonized by a certain institution. In the case of Bhima Bhoi we have seen that there are many texts competing with one another, each claiming to be an authority. It is only through a synchronic perspective that variations and contradictions can be seriously taken into account. A diachronic perspective will show which topics dominate and which stories disappear. This is an ongoing process, and no definite account of the life of Bhima Bhoi can be given. New discourses about him will either erase (such as the scientific one which I circulate) or contribute to his sainthood.

ENDNOTES

1. The present research was funded by the German Research Council (DFG). However, it could not have been done without the help of my many Indian friends and colleagues. I am especially grateful to Kedar Mishra from Sonepur for his assistance and Dr Gourang Charan Dash from Anugul for providing me with numerous documents. The passages of Bhima Bhoi's *Stuticintamani* have been translated into English by Sanjeeb Kumar Nayak.

2. For more detailed information on the theology, history, and organization of Mahima Dharma in Orissa, see the works of Eschmann (1978), Deo (1999), Banerjee (1999 and 2001), Mishra (1998), and Lidia Guzy's contribution in the present volume.

3. See for example the widely circulated edition of Bhima Bhoi's collected works published in 1991 by Karunakara Sahu: *Bhaktakavi Bhima Bhoi Granthavali* (Oriya), Cuttack: Dharmagrantha Store.

4. See for example Basu (1911: 161), Mazumdar (1911: 139) or Sharma (1942: 35).

5. The notion of 'orthodox Hinduism' is problematic since the term Hinduism is itself a construction and a descriptive abstraction designing a very complex and contradictory ensemble of theological concepts, cultural norms, and ritual practices. In the absence of any centralized religious authority, the term of orthodoxy has therefore a quite distinct meaning. It designates generally brahmanic Hinduism.

6. Cf. S. Mahapatra (1983); B. Nepak (1997); S. Nath (1990).

7. Cf. Debendra Dash's (1997) re-edition of articles on Bhima Bhoi published in Oriya newspapers of the time.

8. Hagiography refers to the body of literature describing the lives and veneration of the Christian saints. The literature of hagiography embraces acts of the martyrs (that is, accounts of their trials and deaths); biographies of saintly monks, bishops, princes, or virgins; and accounts of miracles connected with saints' tombs, relics, icons, or statues. As Hawley (1987), Callewaert, Snell (1994), and Mallison (2001) have shown, this concept can be used to study stories of Muslim saints, Buddhist Bodhisattvas, or Hindu poets in a comparative perspective.

9. The New Testament is a famous example of the misreading of religious 'biographies'. For a long time, theologians tried to find out the historical facts about the life of Jesus by eliminating systematically all legendary elements in the Gospels. Contemporary research has abandoned the idea of getting any objective information about Jesus himself and analyses the New Testament as a collection of stories *about* Jesus written in specific communicational contexts. Cf. Wilhelm Egger, *Methodenlehre zum Neuen Testament*, Breisgau, Herder, 1987.

10. Some *bhajans* of Bhima Bhoi are available on audio-cassettes: *Mahima Alekh (Bhimabhoi Bhajan),* presented by Arabinda Mudul, recorded at J.E. Studios, Cuttack, produced and distributed by Jagannath Electronics, Cuttack;

Bhimabhoi Bhajan, presented by Mana Mahapatra, recorded at J.E. Studios Cuttack, produced and distributed by Jagannath Electronics, Cuttack.

11. Bhima Bhoi is believed to have predicted the 'Super Cyclone'. From his *Padmakalpa* he is quoted: 'All of a sudden a cyclone will come and swallow all villages, towns, and countries', cf. *Ghora Kali Yuganta 1999–2010* (Oriya) edited by A.K. Sahu, 1999, Cuttack: Dharmagrantha Store.

12. The couplet reads: '*Prāṇīṅka ārata duhkha aprameta, dekhu dekhu kebā sahu, mo jīvana pache narke praḍithāu, jagata uddhāra heu*'. B. Nepak (1998: 42) translates: 'Boundless is the anguish and misery of the living. Who can see it and tolerate? Let my soul be condemned to hell, but let the universe be redeemed.'

13. *Stuticintamani*, 2.15.

14. Op. cit., 21.16–17.

15. Op. cit., 21.7–11.

16. The term *pancashakha* means 'the five friends' and denotes a mystic movement in medieval Orissa of which Achyutananda Das is one of the most important representatives. See C. Das 1951.

17. Interestingly the Mahima Dharmees who originate from the Desi tribe of Koraput, do not have any knowledge about Bhima Bhoi. See the fascinating research undertaken by Lidia Guzy (2001).

18. On behalf of the Ganda-Panas, see the monograph of Nityananda Patnaik and Sarat Chandra Mohanty 1988.

19. According to N.N. Basu (1911: 161), Satrughna Nath (1990: 11), Chittaranjan Das (1951: 160), and Ancharlott Eschmann (1978: 382), Bhima Bhoi was blind from his birth. However, according to Bibhuti Mishra (1998: 64–8), Sitakant Mahapatra (1983: 10–ll), and Bhagirathi Nepak (1997: 96), Bhima Bhoi was not blind at all.

20. See *Stuticintamani,* 20.6–7 and 20.13.

21. Op. cit., 92.1.

22. In his *Stuticintamani* 1.12, he says for example: 'Abandoning the worship of gods and goddesses made of clay and stones, I have been meditating on you only with deep sincerity and steadfastness with the hope of getting salvation.'

23. *Census of India*, 1911, Religion, Chapter iv, p. 212.

24. It is told that Lord Jagannath incarnated as Jagannath Das who later became Govinda Das, the founder of the ashram in Balasingha, cf. Biswanath Baba (1991: 41); Sahoo (2001: 73); Eschmann (1978: 382).

25. The transcript of the letter is kept in the Orissa Archive of the South Asia Institute in Heidelberg.

26. In a personal communication Martin Fuchs confirmed parallel observations. According to him, most of the dalits with whom he interacted in Dharavi, the largest slum settlement in Mumbai, seem to disregard unmarried men. Could one conclude that this represents a common characteristic or a cultural pattern among so-called lower or non-brahmin castes?

27. He uses for example the word of *amrita* (mythic nectar of eternal life) to designate the male semen; the female vagina is termed *padma* (lotus).

28. In *Stuticintamani* 63.10 he admits to enjoying the pleasures of this world. Moreover he does not see any harm in it.

29. The *Balkaladhari*s put on the bark of the Kumbhi-tree, claiming that their vestment signifies spiritual superiority. According to them, every novice *(tyagi)* first gets a *kaupina* cloth from his guru, and if he is approved, the *balkala*. The *Kaupinadhari*s wear loin-cloth of red ochre dyed cloth because according to them Mahima Gosain gave the *balkala* only to a limited number of disciples, that is the sixty-four *siddhas*. In other words, the Balkaladharis claim to be on the top of the sacred hierarchy, but the Kaupinadharis do not recognize this claim and fight for an equal recognition.

30. Deposition by Abadhut Biswanath Baba before the Commissioner of Endowments, Orissa, Cuttack, 28 March 1961, South Asia Institute, Orissa Archive, MSS 175.

31. See an interview with Anncharlon Eschmann on 30 July 1971. The transcript of the interview is kept in the Orissa Archive of the South Asia Institute in Heidelberg.

32. Cf. 'Shri Mahima Gadi, Joranda', signed C. Mohapatra, Commissioner of Endowments, 4 October 1967, South Asia Institute, Orissa Archive, MSS 175.

33. Satrughna Nath (1990: 99) wrongly translates the term *geru* designing the earthen colour of the ascetic robe, as saffron.

REFERENCES

Bannerjee-Dube, Ishita. (unpublished) 1993. 'Of Poets and Texts: Bhima Bhoi and Mahima Dharma', *Religion and Society in Orissa: Mahima Dharma in the Nineteenth and Twentieth Centuries*, Calcutta: Ph.D. Dissertation, Calcutta University. pp. 57–110.

——. 1999. 'Taming Traditions: Legalities and Histories in Twentieth-Century Orissa', in G. Bhadra, G. Prakash, and S. Tharu (eds), *Subaltern Studies X, Writings on South Asian History and Society*, New Delhi: Oxford University Press, pp. 98–125.

——. 2001. 'Issues of Faith, Enactment of Contest: The Founding of Mahima Dharma in Nineteenth-Century Orissa', in H. Kulke and B. Schnepel (eds), *Jagannath Revisited*, New Delhi: Manohar, pp. 149–77.

Bhoi, Bhima. 1991. *Stuticintamani* (Oriya), Cuttack: Dharma Grantha Store.

Biswanath Baba, Abadhuta. 1954. *An Exposition of Satya Mahima Religion*, Cuttack: L.N. Press.

——. 1974. *Philosophy of Mahima Dharma: Mahima Dharma Darsan*, Cuttack: Mahimagadi Dhenkanal: Mahima Dharma Granthakosa Bhavan, R.B. Coop, Press.

——. 1991 [1935]. *Mahima Dharma Itihasa* (Oriya), Mahimagadi Dhenkanal: Mahima Dharma Granthakosa Samiti.

Callewaert, Winand M. Rupert Snell (eds). 1994. *According to Tradition: Hagiographical Writing in India*, Wiesbaden: Harassowitz.

Das, Chittaranjan. 1951. 'Studies in Medieval Religion and Literature of Orissa', *Vishva Bharati Annals*, 3, pp. 107–94.

Das, Sudhakar. 2000. 'Communalism versus Bhima Bhoi', *Bhima and National Integration, Smaranika 1999–2000*, Sonepur College: Sonepur.

Dash, Debendra. 1997. 'Bhima Bhoi o Mahima Dharma' (Oriya), *Eshana*, 34, June, pp. 120–52.

Deo, Fanindam. 1999. 'Institutional and Organizational Aspects of Mahima Dharma', Joseph T. O'Connell (ed.), *Organizational and Institutional Aspects of Indian Religious Movements*, New Delhi: Manohar; Shimla, Indian Institute of Advanced Studies, pp. 137–51.

Eschmann, Anncharlott. 1975. 'Spread: Organization, and Cult of Mahima Dharma', Nilamani Senapati (ed.), *Mahima Dharma*, Cuttack: Dharma Grantha Store, pp. 9–22.

——. 1978. 'Mahima Dharma: An Autochthonous Hindu Reform Movement', Eschmann, Kulke, and Tripathi (eds), *The Cult of Jagannath and the Regional Tradition of Orissa*, New Delhi: Manohar, pp. 375–410.

Guzy, Lidia. 2000. '"On the Road with the Babas", Some Insights into Local Features of Mahima Dharma', *Journal of Social Sciences*, 4 (4), pp. 323–30.

——. 2001 (unpublished). 'Voices of Gods. Ecstatic Alekhs and Local Configurations of Mahima Dharma', paper presented at the ORP-Conference at Salzau, May.

Hawley, John Stratton. 1984. *Sur Das, Poet, Saint*, Delhi: Oxford University Press.

—— (ed.). 1987. *Saints and Virtues*, Berkeley: University of California Press.

Mahapatra, Sitakant. 1983. *Bhima Bhoi*, New Delhi: Sahitya Akademi (Makers of Indian Literature).

Mallison, Françoise (ed.). 2001. *Constructions Hagiographiques dan le Monde Indien, entre Mythe et Histoire*, Paris: Librairie Honoré Champion (Bibliothèque de l'Ecole des Hautes Etudes, 338).

Mazumdar, B.C. 1911. *Sonepur in Sambalpur Tract*, Calcutta: Brahmo Mission Press.

Michaels, Axel. 1998. *Der Hinduismus: Geschichte und Gegenwart*, München: C.H. Beck.

Mishra, Bibhuti Bhusan. 1998. *Religious Reform Movements in Orissa (in Nineteenth Century)*, Jaipur: Publication Scheme.

Nath, Satrughna. 1977. *Biswanath Baba, a Saint, Self-realized in the Mahima Faith*, Cuttack: Dharma Grantha Store.

——. 1990. *Mahima Dharmadhara*, Bhubaneswar: Hemalata Nath.

Nayak, Prabitra Mohan. 2001. *The Voice of Silence, Sonepur Durbar, and Indian Cultural Traditions*, Bhubaneswar: Orissa Sahitya Akademi.

Nepak, Bhagirathi. 1997. *Bhima Bhoi: The Adivasi Poet Philosopher*, Bhubaneswar: Bhagiratha Prakashan.

Nepak, Bhagirathi. 1999. *Bhima Bhoi*, Bhubaneswar: Bhagiratha Prakashan.

—— (ed.). 2001. *Bhima Bhoi: The Greatest Adivasi Poet Prophet*, Bhubaneswar: Bhagiratha Prakashan.

Pati, Biswamoy. 2001. *Situating Social History, Orissa (1800–1997)*, New Delhi: Orient Longman.

Patnaik, Nityananda and Sarat Chandra Mohanty. 1998. *The Ganda, a Scheduled Caste Weaver Community of Western Orissa*, Bhubaneswar: Tribal and Harijan Research-cum-Training Institute.

Sahu, Gorek Nath. 1999. 'Bhima Bhoi Ideals Prescribed for Social Problems', *Asian Age*, 11 February.

Sharma, S.P. 1942. *Three Years in Orissa*, Calcutta: Thacker Spink and Co.

Vasu, Nagendra Nath. 1911. *The Modern Buddhism and Its Followers in Orissa*, Calcutta: Hare Press.

The *Seva* Ethic and the Spirit of Institution Building in the Mata Amritanandamayi Mission

Maya Warrier

At the heart of much of the discussion and debate surrounding renunciation in Hindu traditions lies the apparent contradiction between the otherworldly quest of renouncers and their involvement in the affairs of the world.[1] The trend of renouncers being active in this-worldly engagement goes back to the eighteenth century and even earlier, when north India witnessed the mobilization of ascetic orders into militant and trading groups, which bore arms and controlled property.[2] A significant development in Hindu renouncer traditions took place when the Swaminarayan order in the late nineteenth century, and later the Ramakrishna Mission in the early twentieth century,[3] redefined the notion of the ascetic renouncer as one who serves society and works towards its welfare and reform (Williams, 1984; Gupta, 1974; Beckerlegge, 1998, 2000). In more recent times, and particularly since the 1980s, the resurgence of Hindu nationalist or 'Hindutva' forces in contemporary India has led to a renewed interest in the study of renouncers, this time as 'Hinduizing' agents popularizing the nationalist ideology of Hindutva proponents.[4]

What has not received the attention it deserves in recent literature on Hindu renouncers in India is the phenomenon of the 'avatar-guru', and its implications for our understanding of renouncers and renunciation in the contemporary Hindu world. The phenomenon of the 'avatar-guru' is perhaps best exemplified by the figure of Sathya Sai Baba,[5] undoubtedly the most popular such guru in present-day India. His meteoric rise to prominence in the 1940s as a spiritual leader from Andhra Pradesh in south India rests on his claims to be an earthly incarnation of Shiva and Shakti. The purpose of his life on earth, he claims, is to fulfil a particular divinely-ordained mission—that of restoring to the modern world and its people the four principles of *satya* (truth), *dharma* (duty or righteousness), *shanti* (peace), and *prema* (divine love).[6] A more recent star in the Hindu religious firmament, again an avatar-guru believed by her devotees to be an incarnation of the goddess Devi, is Mata Amritanandamayi from Kerala. The Mata (mother) is believed to have 'descended' to the earth with the specific intent of alleviating humanity's sorrows.

Both Sathya Sai Baba and Mata Amritanandamayi appear to conform to the ideal of a renouncer in several respects. They are both believed to be single, celibate, and to lead austere and ascetic lives, apparently transcending caste and other social distinctions. Neither belongs to any of the existing guru-disciple lineages in India's renunciatory traditions; instead they derive legitimacy as gurus from their personal charisma and miracle-working abilities. Both belong to the *bhakti* tradition of Hindu faith, where individuals seek spiritual salvation by means of intense and personalized devotion to particular gods in the Hindu pantheon under the guidance of a guru or preceptor. In both cases, the object of devotion is the charismatic figure of the guru him/herself, whom devotees perceive as a divine entity. Of singular importance to the self-representations of these gurus is their claim to have been incarnated on earth as avatars in order to fulfil particular divine missions.[7] This claim serves to eliminate the tension between the renouncer's otherworldly orientation and his/her engagement with the affairs of this world. As avatars incarnated in this world to fulfil particular missions, these gurus are not only justified in their engagement in worldly matters, they in fact derive their legitimacy from this engagement. In other words, in order to justify their claims to be avatars, they must back these claims by actually appearing to fulfil their self-declared mission through active engagement with the world. This constitutes one of the most significant features of these avatar-gurus, marking them out as a modern force driving contemporary change in global Hinduism. The phenomenon of the avatar with a mission to accomplish is clearly a culmination of earlier trends, evident in the Swaminarayan order and the Ramakrishna Mission, towards redefining the ascetic as one who serves society and works towards its welfare and reform.

An important element in the avatar-gurus' endeavours to 'fulfil' their earthly missions is the setting up of institutional organizations towards that end. The institutional establishment headed by Sathya Sai Baba, the Sathya Sai Mission, with its network of schools, colleges, and hospitals bears testimony, in the eyes of devotees, to the leader's authenticity as an avatar. The Mata Amritanandamayi Mission, likewise, owns and manages schools, orphanages, management and engineering colleges, and computer training institutes. All these are seen as important indicators of the success of the Mata's divine enterprise. The institutional empires headed by these modern avatar-gurus serve several ends at once. Besides conferring a stamp of legitimacy and authenticity on the guru, they are also important means of garnering high-profile publicity for the leader and his/her mission. They are prominently advertised in the popular media and attract potential clients in large numbers. They secure far-reaching networks of influence for the guru, often spreading to the highest echelons of power through connections established with big businessmen, bureaucrats, and politicians.

In this essay, I examine the mechanics of institution building within the Mata Amritanandamayi Mission. Devotees of the Mata tend to attribute the phenomenal growth and spread of this organization in the course of the last two decades to the miraculous powers of their guru. In fact, however, it is the perseverance of the devotees and disciples themselves that has made this institution building possible in the first place. What is it that motivates the Mata's followers to contribute to her Mission's institution building activities? How does the Mata secure the enthusiastic participation of her devotees and disciples in her Mission's programmes of institutional growth and expansion? In answering these questions, I explore here the ethic of *seva,* or selfless service, propagated by the Mata. This ethic of seva, a vital component of spiritual striving among the Mata's devotees, is crucial to the spirit of institution building in the Mata Amritanandamayi Mission, and indispensable to its success as a fast-growing and increasingly popular guru-organization in contemporary India. In this essay I therefore explore the rationale for *seva* in the Mata Amritanandamayi Mission, the forms of seva rendered by devotees and disciples, and the means by which their seva effectively contributes towards the organization's institutional expansion and growth.

THE MATA AND HER 'MISSION'

Mata Amritanandamayi bases her claims to spiritual attainment on the strength of spontaneous ecstatic visions and mystical states. According to her biography,[8] the Mata was born on 27 September 1953, to a poor and low-caste family in a fishing village in Parayakadavu in south

Kerala's Kollam district.[9] Her only formal education was up to the fourth standard of the local primary school. The biography describes her childhood as one of great hardship and suffering, with her parents discriminating against her and ill-treating her on account of her dark complexion which marked her out from the rest of the family.[10] It also describes her as having exhibited extraordinary characteristics right from her infancy. From a very early age, the biography tells us, she displayed an unaccountable longing for Krishna, and spent most of her time in meditation, ecstasies, trances, and prayer. Her family and neighbours mistook the young girl's strange mystical behaviour for signs of insanity.[11] The high point in her life came at the age of twenty-one when first she realized her identity with Krishna, and subsequently with the goddess Devi. Central to her self-representations today are her 'Devi *bhavas*', regular public appearances when she dresses up in the regalia of the goddess and thus 'reveals' her goddess aspect *(bhava)* to her devotees (see endnote 7).

The Mata's teachings convey in essence the message of universal love. Due to the eclectic nature of her professed divinity, it is impossible to place the Mata within any one stream of Hindu devotionalism—Shaiva, Vaishnava or Shakta. She encourages devotees to worship God in whatever form they can best relate to.[12] For most devotees, as I noted earlier, the object of worship is the Mata herself, whom they regard not just as a guru but also, and more importantly, as a manifestation of *shakti* or female divine energy—a divine goddess 'descended' on earth in order to fulfil her divine mission of serving humanity.

The Mata Amritanandamayi Mission (henceforth MAM) was established in 1981 and has its headquarters in the leader's native village of Parayakadavu in Kerala's Kollam district. In the course of the late 1980s and 1990s, the MAM shot to prominence as a fast growing and highly successful enterprise, drawing hundreds of thousands of new devotees into its fold every year both in India and abroad, and commanding vast material resources, obtained mostly through generous donations from devotees across the world. The Mission's network today spreads out from Parayakadavu to branches and centres in more than twenty metropolitan cities and towns across the length and breadth of India, as well as to MAM bases abroad in the USA, Britain, France, Australia, Japan, Mauritius, Reunion Island, and Singapore. In the case of the Mata's Mission, as with that of Sathya Sai Baba, the bulk of the following in India comprises educated middle-class urbanites—a point that I will take up in greater detail in the next section.

The Mata Amritanandamayi Mission, according to its promotional literature, was founded 'in order to disseminate the message of spirituality, Universal Love, and selfless service to humanity, which shines through the life and teachings of the Divine Mother, Her Holiness Mata Amritanandamayi Devi'. The purpose of the Mata's life is described as 'serving suffering humanity'. 'Just as an incense stick spreads its fragrance as it burns itself out,' one of the MAM's many promotional pamphlets explains, 'Amma [Mata or mother in Malayalam, the leader's native language] wants to give Herself to others. Amma's only wish is that Her hand should always be on someone's shoulder, caressing and consoling them, and wiping their tears. Amma's whole life is an offering to the world.'

The Mata attributes humanity's 'suffering' to the absence of love in modern society. This absence of love, she argues, stems from an overwhelming obsession with the self, with material acquisitiveness, and an excessive preoccupation with consumerism. Her mission, as she defines it, is to restore selflessness, love, and compassion to their rightful place in the modern world. The most important means by which she seeks to communicate her message of love is by drawing individuals into her 'divine' embrace. Indeed it is her embrace that is the most unique aspect of the Mata, and for her devotees the most compelling. At public *darshans* (literally 'viewings', or more specifically occasions when devotees get to see their guru or god and visually feast on the latter's form—an important element in Hindu devotionalism)—devotees queue up in order to receive her embrace. The Mata takes each waiting devotee into her arms, and lavishes her love on them individually. She comforts those troubled by pressing personal problems in much the same way that a loving mother comforts a troubled child, and offers solutions to their problems. For most devotees the embrace is an intensely emotional experience, and many cry openly in her arms, even as they relish the comforting intimacy of her motherly touch. Devotees believe she also intervenes in their personal lives, resolving conflicts, and solving problems in miraculous ways, thus assuring them of her constant love and protection. They see her as an all-knowing, all-powerful presence on earth, whose love can see them through the worst crises once they surrender to her divine will.

In reaching out to her 'children' across the world in order to comfort them and offer solutions to their problems, the Mata travels widely, moving from city to city within India visiting her ashram branches and offering local devotees a chance to meet her and receive her embrace. She also travels abroad every year, covering most MAM centres outside India. These annual 'world tours' and 'India tours', and the public programmes she conducts in the course of these tours where she embraces devotees individually, are the most visible feature of the Mata's mission to serve humanity and alleviate its suffering.

The Mata strives to fulfil her 'divine' mission of alleviating humanity's suffering not just by comforting the individuals who come to receive her embrace and offering miraculous solutions to their problems, but also by effecting a 'spiritual awakening' in them. The Mata's embrace is believed to serve as a springboard that launches devotees on a spiritual journey. Having sampled her love and compassion, they find themselves drawn into her larger scheme of cultivating their spiritual selves. The Mata trains several hundreds of spiritual aspirants at her ashram or spiritual retreat (the MAM's headquarters) in Kerala. These disciples, both male and female, lead a life of extreme austerity and discipline in the ashram, and strive towards spiritual growth under the tutelage and guidance of the Mata. When the Mata deems them spiritually 'mature', they are initiated into *brahmacharya,* the life of a celibate ascetic. Later in their spiritual journey, they are initiated into *sannyasa* or renouncerhood.[13] Not all her followers are committed to a life of renunciation, asceticism, and austerity. For her lay devotees the Mata recommends simple spiritual practices intended to awaken their inner spirituality and gradually work towards effecting their detachment from the material world. She assures them that the spiritual observances she prescribes will not only lessen their engagement with the material world in imperceptible ways, but also ease their worldly suffering.

Another vital aspect of her mission to 'serve society' is the setting up of charitable institutions to serve the poor and needy. Among the Mata's charitable ventures are free housing schemes for the poor, pension schemes for poor widows, orphanages, a school and hostel for 'tribal' children in Paripally (Kerala), a hospice in Bombay for the terminally ill, an old age home at Sivakasi (Tamil Nadu), and an industrial training centre at Puthiyakavu in Kerala's Kollam district. Besides this, and as mentioned earlier, the Mata has also instituted several high-profile establishments catering to the more affluent sections of India's population. They include high-cost educational institutions where students are charged substantial amounts of money as fees. The MAM runs a chain of twenty-two schools spread through various cities in the country, and operates institutes of computer technology in Chennai (Tamil Nadu), and Karunagapally and Kochi (Kerala). It also runs an institute of management, an engineering institute, and an institute of advanced computing, all located in a sprawling campus in Ettimadai near Coimbatore in Tamil Nadu. In May 1998 the MAM inaugurated the high-profile Amrita Institute of Medical Science and Research in Kochi, Kerala. This institute is described in the MAM's promotional literature as a 'multi-super-speciality hospital', intended to provide specialized services in health care at nominal costs to the poor even as it charges its rich patients for the high quality services offered.

All these institutions are seen as means by which the Mata furthers her mission of reaching out to ever larger numbers of people and serving humanity in diverse ways. By displacing other deities and living in the world as self-proclaimed gods and goddesses, avatar-gurus like Mata Amritanandamayi and Sathya Sai Baba make devotion or bhakti a highly intimate and personal experience for devotees, thus making their goals of proximity to the divine and of god-realization that much more immediate and accessible (Fuller 1992: 178).

THE MATA'S URBAN 'MIDDLE-CLASS' DEVOTEES

The Mata's devotees comprise a heterogeneous lot. They include foreigners, mostly from the rich countries of the West, and Indians, both those residing in India and those living abroad. This study focuses on the Mata's Indian devotees, most of whom are educated affluent Hindus living in India and abroad.[14] They include government officials, lawyers, doctors, teachers, college lecturers, journalists, managers in multinational corporations or in smaller private concerns, computer software personnel, engineers, and scientists. They share some broad similarities as English-speaking, educated, well-to-do urbanites in white-collar employment (many in the newer and more prestigious occupations involving high-tech skills, with comparatively high earnings).

These individuals, by their own reckoning, belong to the much-talked-of, yet somewhat nebulous and indistinct category that has come to be known as India's 'middle classes'. There are no clear markers to indicate the precise occupational ranks, income levels or educational achievements that define the middle classes as a separate and distinct category. Yet India's 'middle classes' are the subject of much discussion and debate in the popular Indian press, as well as in academic writings on India. These 'middle classes', though small in size in relation to the rest of the population, are widely said to comprise, in absolute terms, a sizeable constituency of more than two hundred million, that is, over 20 per cent of the country's total population of just over a billion.[15]

The category that is today recognizable as India's 'middle classes' has swelled in size considerably since the days of colonial rule. In the early–to–mid-twentieth century, the main constituents of the 'middle classes' were primarily cosmopolitan anglophone intelligentsia in the liberal professions, as well as business and commercial groups.[16] After Independence, and particularly in the closing decades of the twentieth century, there have been many new recruits to the 'middle classes' owing mainly to the growth of Indian industry, and the liberalization of the Indian economy in the 1980s. Industrialization and liberalization opened up new opportunities in India's business and service sectors, leading to rising incomes, and increasing the purchasing power of upwardly mobile persons in urban India who benefited from these new developments. Significant numbers of wealthy farmers too spread their networks of interest into the commercial and service sectors, and joined the ranks of the middle classes.[17]

Among the devotees of the Mata I met in the course of my fieldwork, most of whom readily identified themselves as members of India's 'middle classes'. There were persons descended from the older middle-class intelligentsia of early and mid-twentieth century India, as well as newer recruits to this category, mainly first or second generation migrants to India's metropolitan cities. Most had a formal education up to graduate level, and many were highly qualified in specialized areas such as medicine, information technology, business management, and engineering.[18] These persons see a good education as vital to ensure their upward (social and economic) mobility and access to global opportunities. Many of these persons also command transnational connections and operate in a world of accelerated flows of capital, technology, and information across countries. Among the devotees of the Mata, whom I met, many had travelled abroad, to study or work or to visit close relatives residing in foreign countries.

The consumption patterns of my informants, which conformed largely to certain 'global' standards, reflected their exposure to the larger world beyond India's frontiers. Commodity consumption was central to the construction of social identity and status among my informants. Most of them revealed a keen awareness of consumer items available in the market.[19] As Pinches (1999) rightly points out, consumer items operate for most individuals as principal signifiers of social status and achievement. There are thus certain 'positional goods' (ibid.: 32) that separate the urban 'elites' from the less advantaged—these include cars, often in the latest models, expensive dwellings, clothes with designer labels, meals bought at expensive restaurants and modern fast-food centres, expensive holiday package tours, recreational facilities, and mobile phones.

These features of the urban middle classes are reflected in their religious lives and in the kind of religious organizations in which they choose to participate. The Mata Amritanandamayi Mission addresses a specifically modern middle-class following, offering its spiritual teachings and prescriptions as a means to counter the 'excessive' materialism of its adherents. It also taps the resources that these middle-class devotees have to offer, making use of their skills, educational qualifications, their spheres of local influence, and their transnational connections, in diversifying its activities and ensuring the Mission's steady growth and institutional expansion.

Scholars exploring the appeal of modern gurus to India's urban middle classes have tended to perceive the latter as suffering some kind of 'lack' in their lives which they supposedly seek to compensate by attaching themselves to a guru.[20] The lives of India's middle-class urbanites, these scholars argue, are characterized by rootlessness, alienation, and anomie. These persons lack an anchoring in traditional Indian social units such as joint families, village communities, and caste networks, and are therefore on the lookout for alternative communities which they often hope to find within a guru's following. They are out of touch with traditional values, belief systems, and ritual complexes and they seek to revive these elements in their lives by submitting to a guru who may then appear as a repository of ultimate truths. They are also traumatized by the fast pace of change in India's urban environment and seek security and stability in the guru's fold.

While it is tempting to explain the appeal of modern gurus in terms of this need-based approach, my findings regarding the Mata's devotees do not bear out these propositions. None of the devotees of the Mata with whom I interacted in the course of my study appeared to experience the modern world of urban India as alienating or destabilizing in any way. They did not seem to suffer from an acute sense of 'lack' in terms of social, moral or religious anchoring. Most of the devotees of the Mata I encountered were individuals who had benefited vastly from the changing conditions in India's political economy and who had done well for themselves by seizing the opportunities that came their way. For these individuals, their experience of modern India's fast-paced urban environment has resulted not so much in a sense of instability and despair as in the hope of increased possibilities and multiplying opportunities in every sphere of life, including that of religion. What appears to attract these individuals to modern gurus like Sathya Sai Baba and Mata Amritanandamayi then is not the hope of securing anchorage in a religious community or regaining touch with 'traditional' modes of religious faith and practice, but quite the opposite. It is (as I have argued elsewhere)[21] the choice, freedom, and flexibility these gurus allow their devotees in negotiating their faith in highly personalized and individual ways that makes them appealing in the eyes of their followers.

It is important to note here that India's 'middle classes' have been an important focus of recent commentaries on the resurgence of Hindu nationalism in India since the 1980s.[22] Many such commentaries posit a direct correlation between the expansion of the middle classes since the 1980s, and the rise of Hindu nationalist forces in the same period, arguing that present-day Hindus suffer from a sense of alienation and defeat as a result of the legacy of India's colonial experience and their own exposure to post-colonial modernity.[23] According to this argument, organizing themselves as a militant Hindu force and directing their hatred towards the 'enemy', the Muslim, has enabled these Hindus to recover their self-confidence, recuperate their 'masculinity', and assert their selfhood as Hindus and Indians.

While supporting the militant campaign for a Hindu nation may be one of the ways in which some sections of India's Hindus ('middle classes' and others) have, in recent times, responded to their encounter with modernity, it is certainly not the only way in which modern Indians have sought to cope with forces of social change. During my fieldwork, I discovered that devotees of the Mata were not centrally concerned with questions of nationhood and Hindu nationalism. Hindutva was certainly not a favourite topic of conversation among my informants, and even when pressed to comment on aspects of politicized religion in the country, their answers were mostly vague and disinterested. Some claimed they did not know enough about the Hindutva phenomenon to comment on it, others denounced the Hindutva campaigners as 'fanatics' and self-seeking political manipulators. Most devotees were keen to draw a distinction between 'spirituality' (which is how they preferred to describe their faith in the Mata) and the 'politicized religion' of Hindutva campaigners. The latter, in their view, is divisive and seeks to define a 'community' of adherents by constructing boundaries between 'insiders' and 'outsiders', whereas the former is a private quest concerned with individual self-enhancement rather than community or nation building.[24]

These points are certainly borne out if one compares and contrasts notions of the ideal self, as it is conceived by devotees of Mata Amritanandamayi, with those attributed to supporters of the Hindutva cause (van der Veer, 1994a, b; Tonnesson and Antlov [eds],1996; Ludden [ed.], 1996; Jaffrelot, 1996, 1998; Hansen and Jaffrelot [eds], 1998; Basu and Subrahmanyam [eds], 1996; Sarkar, 1993; Hellman, 1994). Some important areas of contrast pertain to the key motifs around which selfhood is constructed in each case. In the case of the Hindutva proponents and supporters, this motif is Ram, the epic hero of the Ramayana, believed to be an avatar of Vishnu, who is widely depicted in the propaganda of the 'Sangh Parivar' Hindu supremacists in his aspect as a warrior king, wielding bow and arrow, representing martial valour, and suggesting a state of readiness for confrontation and battle (Davis, 1996; van der Veer, 1987b). This representation provides a striking contrast to the central MAM motif, the Mata herself, again an avatar, but one representing compassion and maternal love, and promising to enfold the devotee in her loving and all-encompassing embrace. Related to this is a second point of contrast, this time in the way the 'enemy' is defined. For Hindutva ideologues, the enemy is the Muslim, who, as the demonized other, is the object of their intense communal hatred (Davis, 1996: 49–51; Sarkar, 1993: 165–66; Jaffrelot, 1996, 1998; van der Veer, 1987b). In the case of the Mata's devotees, there is no external enemy. Instead the enemy is located within oneself, in the form of accumulated *prarabdhas* (negative karmic burden) which must be eliminated if the individual is to progress towards his or her spiritual goal. Third and most important, the construction of selfhood in the Hindutva scheme of things is envisaged as a process of recuperating masculinity, the overcoming of a perceived emasculation of the Hindu self—a common, deep-running theme in Hindu nationalist discourses and organizations (Hansen, 1996; van der Veer, 1996; Alter, 1994 a, b). In sharp contrast to this, the devotees of the Mata envisage the construction of their own selfhood in very different terms. Theirs is certainly not a quest for re-masculinization. If anything, it is an effort at 'feminization' (though none of my informants perceive their selfhood thus in polarized gender terms) whereby they seek to revive their emotional selves, and enhance their receptivity to the Mata's love and compassion.

THE RATIONALE FOR *SEVA*

One of the most important components in this private and individual 'spiritual' quest of Mata Amritanandamayi's devotees is seva. Seva in its broadest sense simply means service. It could be service directed towards society, towards an individual, towards one's parents, towards God, or towards one's guru. The word has Sanskrit roots and appears in several Sanskrit-derived Indian languages. In specific social and historical contexts, the notion of seva assumes particular meanings and orientations. The notion of guru seva, or service to one's guru, for instance, is much elaborated and refined in several Hindu devotionalist traditions and determines the precise nature of guru-*shishya* (disciple) links in each (Babb, 1987; Juergensmeyer, 1991). The same is true of seva to particular deities as part of their worship in temples (Bennett, 1990; van der Veer, 1988). Seva as humanitarian service was practised as early as the late nineteenth century by ascetics in the Swaminarayan tradition (Williams, 1984). This ideal of seva was later popularized by Swami Vivekananda in the early part of the twentieth century, and informs the spiritual striving of the renouncers of the Ramakrishna Mission (Beckerlegge, 1998, 2000; Gupta, 1974). Seva as voluntary service to the nation is central to the activities of the Rashtriya Swayamsevak Sangh, a militant Hindu supremacist organization which fiercely champions the cause of Hindutva or Hindu nationalism in contemporary India (Beckerlegge: this volume). These are but a few examples of the different meanings attached to the word seva in different contexts and traditions.

Common to all these different meanings, however, is one key idea which distinguishes seva from other kinds of action. The ethic of seva hinges centrally on the notion of 'selflessness'. Seva as an ideal-type is service rendered impersonally and selflessly, not with the expectation of reciprocity, reward, protection or patronage. Ideally it is rendered anonymously, as a service intended for the good of the beneficiary and not for enhancing the reputation of the benefactor. Seva thus rendered counts as meritorious action for the one who renders it. This understanding of seva as an ideal-type, though clearly distinct from actual patterns of behaviour, does however serve as a yardstick against which those rendering different kinds of seva come to be evaluated (Mayer, 1981).

Mata Amritanandamayi prescribes selfless seva as an indispensable component in the spiritual practice of her devotees and disciples. Seva in the MAM is not understood specifically as seva to the guru, to God or to humanity. What comes to count most commonly as seva in the MAM are services directed towards the upkeep, promotion or expansion of the MAM. The upkeep of the MAM entails the everyday running of its several institutions and involves devotees in seva directed towards their smooth day-to-day operation and management. The promotion of the MAM requires actively striving towards garnering publicity for the Mata, and organizing campaigns to raise awareness about her and her teachings and to win her ever more devotees. The expansion of the MAM entails planning for the establishment of new institutions, raising funds for these new ventures, and working towards their successful completion.

All such service, provided it is rendered without expectation of reward, is seen as meritorious activity. Seva in the MAM's scheme of things helps 'burn up' the cumulative ill effects of 'negative karmas' in previous births, and hastens the individual's progress towards ultimate release from the endless cycle of birth, death, and rebirth.[25] Seva is considered particularly relevant in the modern age as an effective counter to the selfishness, egotism, and mindless acquisitiveness seen as characteristic of modern consumerist societies. This idea is particularly appealing to the Mata's more affluent devotees who, by rendering small acts of seva to the Mata and her Mission, derive the satisfaction of enhancing the spiritual element in their lives and accumulating spiritual merit, thus counterbalancing the negative karmic effects supposedly accruing from material acquisition.

Seva in the MAM is thus defined not in terms of any particular kind of service, but in terms of the spirit of selflessness that should ideally inform the act of service. Any service—to the Mata, to the Mission or even to one's fellow-devotee—is an act of seva provided it is imbued with a spirit of selflessness. Devotees see the Mata as an exemplar in this respect, and her self-proclaimed mission of serving humanity as the ultimate expression of selfless service and compassion. In extolling the Mata's boundless love, they often emphasize that she herself stands to gain absolutely nothing from her humanitarian mission. They point to the vast material resources which the MAM commands and which it puts to use in its various institutions, contrasting this with the Mata's own humble lifestyle, her meagre requirements, and the austere way of life of her disciples in the ashram. All her love, they assert, is channelled towards society, and there is nothing she retains for herself. Her love, therefore, is unalloyed in its selflessness and compassion. The Mata herself makes this point. She says:

> Children, this ashram is not Amma's. This place exists for the world. It belongs to you, to all the people who come here. Mother, in fact, has no interest in establishing ashrams or other institutions. She would not have done any of these things if it were not for the world. Amma does these things to help the world. The world should not be filled with selfish people. There should be a few places where at least a handful of people can work and serve selflessly. The beauty and charm of selfless love and service should not die away from the face of this earth. The world should know that a life of dedication is possible, that a life inspired by love and service to humanity is possible.[26]

In the devotees' eyes, the Mata leads exactly the kind of life of tireless service that she preaches. Disciples in the ashram describe her as constantly engaged in social work. A frequently expressed concern about the Mata is that she never rests but carries on serving others unceasingly, without a thought for her own welfare. Her busy tours of ashram centres in India and abroad, her long hours of darshan, her supervision of administrative tasks in the MAM, the time she spends instructing and guiding her disciples in the ashram, and attending to huge volumes of correspondence from devotees worldwide—all these and more are seen to take up every minute of the Mata's life so that there is never a moment when she is not serving the needs of humanity in one way or another. This is seva as an ideal-type which devotees strive to emulate, but which, in their own reckoning, they seldom achieve.

RENDERING *SEVA* WITHIN THE MAM

Following the Mata's example, the ascetics undergoing spiritual training in the ashram too are expected to lead a life not of seclusion and meditation, but one of active seva. Defining her conception of an ideal renouncer, the Mata explains:

A sannyasin is one who has dedicated his entire life, both external and internal, for others, for the good of the world. ... In order to set an example, a sannyasin should also performs actions while living in this world. He should not sit idle saying, 'I have attained the state of actionlessness, therefore I don't have to do any work.' This will set the wrong example that others will follow. Even after attaining the state of perfection, a true sannyasin who lives in this world of pluralities will be very dynamic, active, and creative on the outside. But he will be totally silent within.

Elsewhere she says, 'If a *sadhak* [spiritual aspirant] does not work, he is cheating the world and cheating God in the name of spirituality.'[28] Asked by a devotee whether a monk, having renounced the world, should engage in material affairs at all, the Mata answers: 'Sannyasa ... is not renouncing the world and action. [It is] renunciation of the fruits of action. It is the dharma of the sannayasis to lead the world.'[29] 'Spirituality', she says, 'is not sitting in a corner with closed eyes. We should be read to become everyone's servant and also to see all equally. Going out into the world tomorrow, all of you should serve everyone without selfishness ...'.[30]

For the Mata's ascetic disciples, seva is a compulsory part of their spiritual training, and they are put through a rigorous service regimen. Most of their seva comes to be rendered within the institutional set-up of the MAM itself. According to her renunciate disciples, the Mata's charitable and other institutions serve a dual purpose. They are beneficial not only for the recipients of her charity but also for those of her disciples who are assigned responsibilities in these institutions, because the institutions afford them an opportunity to render seva, and to hasten their own spiritual progress.

One of the key sites where the ascetic disciples of the Mata come to render their seva is in the ashram headquarters in Kerala. The ashram runs on the principle of communal service. All the residents are required to perform some form of voluntary work (seva) benefiting the ashram as a whole. Each of the Mata's ascetic disciples is assigned specific duties by the authorities—either the Mata herself or the senior sannyasis who manage the affairs of the ashram. Thus some are assigned to the ashram's computer wing where they are expected to feed data into the MAM's rapidly growing computer network.[31] Others are assigned duties in the ashram's accounts section where they keep track of the MAM's income (mostly donations from devotees—an important mode of seva for those who have the means) and expenses (the cost of maintaining the establishment, supporting the seven-hundred-odd ascetics, travel expenses of the Mata and her entourage, and so on). Yet others are responsible for cleaning the ashram, managing its stores, clearing out garbage, cooking for the entire ashram community in its dark and damp kitchens, organizing accommodation for the permanent residents and for visitors, sorting the in-coming mail, managing the ashram's fax, telephone and e-mail facilities, making arrangements for the Mata's yearly tours, and keeping in touch with MAM centres in India and abroad. One area of activity that engages scores of disciples is the ashram's press and publications division, which requires services as diverse as editing and proof-reading the articles that are to appear in the MAM's journals and books, providing art design and illustrations, and finally, printing, binding, and despatching the publications to the MAM's branches and centres in India and abroad.

All these varied activities are performed within the ashram without any hired help. The ashram relies almost entirely on the seva or service efforts of its residents. New entrants to the ashram who wish to renounce their worldly lives and embark on a spiritual programme under the Mata's tutelage are expected to prove their dedication and commitment to their spiritual practice by performing satisfactorily whatever task they are assigned. In the case of very young entrants, the ashram authorities usually encourage them to complete their studies, and often finance their school or college education up to whatever level the aspirant wishes. Most complete at least their first degree—in subjects ranging from English literature, Sanskrit and philosophy, to commerce, computer science, and engineering. Some go on to study further and obtain degrees at the Master's level. The ashram invariably has a use for whatever knowledge and skills the disciples acquire, and encourages them to utilize these skills in their service efforts. Many such disciples go on to render specialized services at the MAM's various educational and charitable institutions, working in such diverse capacities as teachers, managers, accountants, and software experts at different levels in the MAM's vast organizational structure.

The Mata actively encourages not just her renouncer disciples but also her householder devotees to render seva as part of their spiritual endeavour. Indeed their contributions have been indispensable to the growth and expansion of the MAM. Lay devotees usually render their services at the local ashram branch in their town or city. These branches are usually set up at the initiative of the Mata's local following. For them, the setting up of a branch of the MAM in their city or town is an act of adoration and worship of the Mata. Devotees come together, form a seva committee, and, with the permission of the MAM headquarters, take on the onerous task of collecting funds to finance the purchase of land and the construction of the ashram building. This project often takes several months, if not years, to complete.

Once the local branch has been set up, the Mata appoints her ascetic disciples to head it and oversee its activities. They organize weekly pujas, collective rituals, discourses and *bhajan* sessions at the ashram branch which the local devotees attend. They also preside over such projects as building a local Brahmasthanam temple (a temple unique to the MAM),[32] an Amrita Vidyalaya (school), or an orphanage, using the resources (money, influence, time, and effort) that devotees place at their disposal. The local following comes together periodically to organize blood donation camps, or mobilize food and clothes distribution schemes for the poor, all under the initiative and supervision of the resident ascetic disciples.[33] Besides this, they attend to numerous administrative and organizational tasks at the branch office, all of which count as seva. Each such act is a means of glorifying the Mata, and contributes towards her promotion and publicity.

Every year the local branch steps up the pace of its activities in time for the Mata's annual visit. Individual devotees volunteer to take on specific responsibilities in preparation for the event. Some take charge of publicity, or book venues and prepare programme schedules for each day of the Mata's stay in the city, while others busy themselves making arrangements for the accommodation not just of the Mata but of her entire entourage of more than a hundred disciples from the MAM headquarters who usually accompany her on her tours. The local devotees thus come together under the supervision of the resident ascetic disciple to make a collective and concerted effort towards making the Mata's visit a grand success. This too counts as seva.

The seva rendered by the devotees and disciples constitutes the building blocks of the Mata Amritanandamayi Mission. The MAM (and other spiritual organizations like it) may in fact be seen to serve as a giant redistribution mechanism which harnesses the diverse resources of its followers and channelizes these towards its own growth and expansion. There are three important factors in the way seva is organized within the MAM that makes the system particularly effective. These are discussed below.

FREEDOM AND FLEXIBILITY IN CHOOSING ONE'S PREFERRED MODE OF *SEVA*

The Mata allows devotees complete flexibility, freedom, and choice in rendering seva. Seva, in the Mission, is not any one type of activity and does not follow a standardized format for all devotees. Instead, it assumes diverse forms depending on individual skills, capabilities, inclinations, and constraints. No one form of seva is considered more meritorious than another, and no seva is evaluated in terms of the kind of work done. My fieldwork at the ashram branch in Delhi revealed how modes of seva for the local devotees differ widely according to the individual's age, personal commitments, hours of employ in the workplace, family composition, personal energy and drive, health, and income level. Thus, younger people engaged in full-time employment and with young children to tend at home, do not often spend more than a few hours every weekend on seva. Older people, with fewer family commitments, retired from active service, and leading otherwise unhurried lives, often volunteer longer hours of service according to their personal inclinations and aptitudes.

A journalist in his mid-forties whom I interviewed in Delhi said that his seva consisted of a few hours spent every week with the young children at the orphanage attached to the local ashram branch. This journalist lived with his family in a housing complex an hour's drive from the branch. He explained how geographical distance and the pressures of work prevented him from devoting more hours to service at the orphanage. Every Sunday, however, he made it a point to drive to the orphanage where he helped the children with their schoolwork, introduced them to new sport and leisure activities, and often treated them to sweets and other savouries that his wife prepared at home. He often came with his family, and encouraged his two young sons to participate in this seva activity.

Another devotee, a middle-aged housewife, spent far more time in the local ashram branch than the journalist. At the ashram, she spent long hours in the reception room, attending to phone calls, and receiving visitors. For her this seva was a welcome means of filling up long empty hours each day. This devotee often resided at the ashram branch for several days at a time in order to avoid the trouble of commuting daily.

A third devotee, an elderly woman retired from service as a translator at a language centre in the city, was actively engaged in the affairs of the local Amrita Vidyalaya, one in a chain of MAM schools now operating in more than twenty centres across India. When I interviewed her, the Delhi school had classes only at the primary level, and she along with one or two other women, was serving as a kindergarten teacher for the school's handful of students. Her husband, also a devotee of the Mata, helped with the publication of the Hindi edition of the *Matruvani*, a monthly spiritual journal published by the Mission.

All these varied activities constitute seva in the Mata Amritanandamayi Mission. Much of this seva is sporadic and negotiated on a day-to-day basis by devotees according to changing work schedules and personal commitments. The options cover a wide range, and include, most importantly, monetary donations to the MAM's various institution building efforts. Most devotees succeed in finding some form of seva suited to their individual disposition and preference. While devotees cherish the sense of involvement and participation which comes with the smallest piece of work performed with sincerity and dedication, the MAM is assured of a steady flow of dedicated seva from them to meet the bulk of its human resource requirements.

TAPPING INDIVIDUAL CAPABILITIES

Self-effacement and humility are the hallmark of seva as defined by the MAM. Exemplary seva entails performing even the humblest task with extreme sincerity and with no thought of personal gain. Devotees believe that the Mata treats all kinds of service equally, the only consideration being that the service should be rendered with utter devotion, humility, dedication, and commitment. Seva rendered with the expectation of tangible rewards, or with a sense of pride and achievement in the tasks performed, is no seva. As such, seva in its ideal form must eventually lead to the elimination of the devotee's egoism and individuality, and to a levelling of personalities. This, however, does not always appear to be the case.

Rather, seva in the MAM often seems to be patterned after the very things it ideally seeks to negate—the individual self-worth and egotism of followers. To be recognized individually by the Mata, and to be assigned tasks by her, is a rare privilege for devotees and disciples. The Mata often singles out individual devotees and requests them to perform particular services for the Mission. To devotees, it is a rare honour to be thus 'chosen' by the Mata for a particular task. The honour is even greater when there are other individuals hoping to be assigned the same task, a feature hardly conducive to self-effacement.

Devotees agree that the Mata's discernment of individual capabilities and inclinations is invariably accurate. They often express wonder at her ability to size up her devotees and entrust them with tasks according to the strengths and resources she sees in each one. They describe her as a 'shrewd personnel manager' with an uncanny ability to appraise individual worth. One devotee in Delhi, retired from a high-ranking government position in the Indian Administrative Service, commented thus on what he saw as the Mata's excellent administrative and managerial skills.

> Apart from her spiritual personality, she has an administrative personality as well. For instance, things like management .... The way she manages the big organization ... the decisions taken at the top level ... delegation, control ... that is one side .... Then, who is capable of doing what, what to expect of particular individuals, assessing capabilities ... there again I consider her a remarkable genius.

This devotee's services were solicited in the early stages of the MAM's growth in Delhi, when the local ashram branch was only just being set up. He described himself as a 'leading citizen of Delhi', who was approached by the Mata to oversee the initial MAM operations in Delhi.

> The committee [comprising devotees seeking to organize an ashram branch in Delhi] had been formed, and many people wanted me to be the Seva Samiti [service committee] president. There were lots of others fit for the role, politicians, MPs ... but they wanted me to be president for two reasons, one that I was an active organizer, known in different circles here, and secondly that I was above politics and acceptable to rival political groups .... I was hesitating because of my various commitments .... One day ... while she was on a visit here ... Amma called me to one side and told me: Child, you must do my work for me here .... I said, how can I possibly do that, but with your blessings I will try .... She said, you will be able to do it. You have to take care of the education of young children, provide a home for orphans, care for the old, those afflicted with disease .... She was all the time referring to humanitarian purposes ....

It was important for this devotee that the Mata wanted him to serve her 'humanitarian' purposes in Delhi rather than manage the activities related to spiritual or ritual matters. He saw himself inclined towards the former and disinterested in the latter.

She never asked me to do anything spiritual or religious. She possibly thought there are persons much more enlightened than me in those respects ... and I am not a person who has that kind of capability or even inclination ... .

This, for him, was a sign of the Mata's discernment and expert assessment of his skills and inclinations. He was thus one of the chosen few directly assigned responsibilities by the Mata and given an opportunity to serve her. He considered it a rare privilege that the Mata had singled *him* out as the individual to be assigned responsibility for the MAM's initial operations in Delhi, when there were so many others hoping to be entrusted with the same responsibility. This work, even while it qualified as 'selfless' service in the devotee's narrative, not only gave him a sense of personal worth and self importance, but also deepened his devotion to the Mata. In return for the rare honour of having been thus 'chosen' by her for the coveted task, he then tried his best to ensure that the work was performed entirely to the Mata's satisfaction.

Tapping individual capabilities and resources is the most important means by which the Mata expands her institutional base and sets up new ventures in diverse areas. In planning and executing her vision for the 'multi-super-speciality hospital' in Kochi (Kerala), for instance, the Mata utilized the skills and know-how of an Indian doctor previously practising in the USA, who gave up his professional life in order to be able to participate more fully in the Mata's ashram. He, his wife, and their two children renounced their affluent and secure lifestyle in the USA to enter the ashram as spiritual aspirants. This doctor was then given charge of the proposed hospital in Kochi, and through several years' painstaking effort, he used his knowledge of medicine and medical institutions to realize the Mata's vision of this hospital. Today it is one of the leading medical establishments in Kerala, equipped with the latest facilities for the diagnosis and treatment of a wide range of diseases, and employing a team of highly qualified and well-paid doctors from India and abroad.

Similarly, the management and engineering institutes at Ettimadai (Tamil Nadu) are the result of the efforts of a young engineer, now an ascetic disciple of the Mata, and the head of this modern educational establishment. With single-minded devotion, he worked to realize the Mata's vision of a 'model engineering college' that would excel in what the Mission refers to as 'value-based' education. The computer institutes, likewise, are the result of the hard work of another renouncer disciple of the Mata, a highly qualified individual with a doctorate in computer studies from Bombay's prestigious Indian Institute of Technology, who decided to devote his life to spiritual pursuits under the guidance of the Mata. He too was encouraged to put his intellectual capabilities to use for setting up computer training institutes in Kerala and Tamil Nadu. In all three cases, these individuals' investments of time and effort in the respective MAM enterprises have earned them a special local standing in the Mata's devotee circles, and greater proximity to the Mata. Their example has in turn inspired other devotees and disciples of the Mata, trained in medicine, computer technology, engineering or management to serve in these institutes, and has thus given them an opportunity to put their knowledge and skills to use in the service of the Mata.

REWARDING *SEVA*

Just as her devotees and disciples cherish any opportunity to serve the Mata, they also look to her for approval when rendering their individual seva. Personal recognition by the Mata is seen as proof of divine grace, an important factor in devotees' commitment. It also serves as an impetus for continued and intensified devotion on the part of devotees. This recognition can take different forms. For her ascetic disciples, the most important form of recognition comes when, after several years of 'probation' as a spiritual aspirant, the Mata finally deems an individual fit to be initiated into *brahmacharya* or, for those who have already entered brahmacharya, into the state of *sannyasa*. For her lay devotees, recognition mostly has to do with the Mata singling them out and acknowledging their individual commitment. Sometimes this recognition is of a formal, institutionalized nature. For instance, in the early 1990s, the MAM organized a campaign to boost the sales of its monthly spiritual journal, the *Matruvani*, published at the MAM headquarters. This was the *Matruvani* Pracharana Yajna (*pracharana* = publicity/popularization, *yajna* = mass effort). This drive to boost the *Matruvani*'s sales and subscription figures was intended as a campaign to publicize the Mata and her Mission more widely and win more individuals to the Mata's fold. At the end of the campaign, individual devotees who had secured the largest number of new subscribers were formally recognized, and their names and photographs published in the *Matruvani*.

Recognition by the Mata not only convinces devotees of their own state of blessedness and gives them the much-needed assurance that the Mata is aware of their every little act of service, but also enhances their position in the group, since the Mata's acts of recognition are public, and witnessed by other devotees as well. In the absence of personal recognition from the Mata, devotees experience phases of despondence and uncertainty. They struggle to find explanations as to why the Mata takes no notice of them. The experience of one north Indian devotee, a manager in a private firm in Delhi, is a case in point. His narrative pertains to the time when he was still new to the local devotee circle. He attended a spiritual discourse by one of the chief renunciate disciples of the Mata who was on a visit to Delhi, where the speaker happened to mention the MAM's plans to build a temple in the city.

He said somebody had donated land and they planned to construct a temple here. It was for the Delhi devotees to organize the money ... . I, like crazy, started running around for donations ... . I went to my contacts and said, please give me the money ... . I collected quite a huge sum ... . I was still an outsider, not part of the team [of active Mata devotees in the city], and nobody paid any attention to me. Finally as the work progressed they came to accept me because I was bringing in more and more money. And then it so happened that Amma said she wanted a hall to be built in the premises. They were having enough problems with the temple itself; how was this to be done. At that point I got two or three more people to help out. Swamiji [the resident ascetic disciple overseeing the affairs of the Delhi branch] was very happy with me. Everybody here thought, indeed this man [referring to himself] has done so much. I too thought I had done a lot. I had a sense of achievement. I was like the ant—an ant carries a single particle of dust on his back and thinks he is carrying the whole world. I thought Amma would acknowledge my efforts, give me special treatment ... .

She was here for four or five days. But she wouldn't even look at me. I was miserable—like a child whose mother refuses to look at him when he feels he has done so much for her. On the last day [of the Mata's visit] there was a committee meeting of twenty or thirty people, and they said, why don't you attend too, you have done so much. At the meeting Amma looked at everybody in turn but she would not look at me. She ignored me completely. This was a game she was playing for us—so that whenever ego comes, she must tell us ... . I started realizing only later ... . On that last day, when she spoke to everybody, gave instructions, she refused to look at me. I had that feeling of pride in my achievement, which should not have been there. I felt I had done so much. Then I realized the reason also [for the Mata's apparent indifference]. That is the difference between other gurus and her. Other gurus will tell stories and convey the message verbally. She will not tell you anything. Just her presence—her presence is more than sufficient to shatter anybody's ego ... .

This devotee thus did not receive the signs of recognition that he anxiously awaited. However, he saw this lack of recognition from the Mata not as an indication that his services had been futile, but as a reminder from her not to lay too much store by his efforts. He saw her neglect of him not as indifference but as a rap on the knuckles from a loving mother whose message to her son was not to take pride in small seva achievements but to learn the lesson of humility and selflessness while serving her. Some years later, the recognition did come, but in a different way. This time, on her trip to Delhi, the Mata paid a visit to his house.

The Mata's visit to devotees' homes is, in their eyes, among the most highly coveted signs of recognition from her. It not only acknowledges the devotee's love for, and seva to, the guru, but also provides the devotee an opportunity to serve the Mata once more, and in a most sublime way—as a host extending his hospitality to an esteemed guest. Providing hospitality to a goddess is for most devotees a cherished, and at the same time daunting, task. Devotees usually make all out efforts to ensure that the Mata is comfortable during her short stay (lasting about a couple of hours) in the house. They seldom know till the very last minute whether it is their house the Mata will grace by her presence, and several devotees wait in readiness in the hope that she will bless them with a visit. Her choice of one particular home rather than another is mostly governed by considerations of expediency, but for devotees, it indicates the chosen household's state of grace, and therefore bestows upon it a unique position of privilege.

The devotee whose efforts to serve the Mata went unrecognized at first, narrated as follows the sequence of events leading up to the Mata's visit to his newly purchased home in Noida, an industrial township on the outskirts of Delhi. Throughout the narrative he uses the collective pronoun, we, to include his immediate family—his wife and three children.

> When Amma came in March '97, I asked Amma if she would come to our house. She merely laughed. We were not sure she would come. We prepared ourselves ... . We said, if Amma comes here, we should do everything we can. That was the feeling before—though afterwards we felt we had failed miserably. But we felt we should do everything that we can, and I think that is the point. God comes to that house where we are desperately longing for her to come.

The Mata was to go to Noida on the appointed day for a public programme at 3:30 p.m. Prior to the programme she was to visit any one of her devotee households in the area. There were about eight or ten houses for her to choose from. This devotee was not sure even on the morning of the visit whether his would be the chosen house. He asked the ascetic disciple in charge of the local ashram branch whether he might be the lucky one:

> I asked swamiji this question. The swami said, look, in the case of Amma, who can tell? You can never predict Amma's actions. Even the swamis can't tell ... . He said, keep your house ready. Amma might come. We deliberated. We said, if Amma doesn't come, fine. She goes to somebody else's house, doesn't matter. But we will be ready for her ... .
>
> Two or three hours before Amma came, some ashramites came and readied the

room we had set aside for Amma. So that was an indication that she would come ... . We had prepared lunch for her ... . As soon as she came, she went inside her room ... She rested there, then got up and went for her bath ... . She then called the family members to her side—spoke lovingly to us for five minutes. Then she did the puja.

We had kept her photograph and her puja *samagri* [paraphernalia] ready in the living room. She sat down there and she chanted, you know. The way she did the puja, loudly, it was truly divine. She was chanting mantras and it was absolutely powerful. I couldn't understand anything, but I could feel the energy, and the vibrations. They were absolutely divine ... . There were a few people here before she came, but after she arrived, more came. She sang bhajans [devotional songs], distributed the *prasad* [consecrated food offering] that we had prepared ... . Still, I tell you, I wept afterwards. She came to our house and we could not give her that welcome that we should have given to the Divine Mother, the Almighty. We failed miserably, that was my feeling later on.

For this devotee, the Mata's visit to his home was the high point of his relationship with her. The 'Divine Mother', the 'Almighty' had actually visited his home and blessed it with her divine grace.[34] He had done everything he could to make the visit comfortable for the Mata, but in hindsight he regretted not having done more. For no amount of hospitality and seva, to his mind, was 'enough' when the guest concerned was the guru herself. Most significant, however, was this devotee's evident pride that it was *his* house that had been singled out for this singular honour. This was the individual recognition that he had craved, and having received it, he felt enriched.

In the preceding discussion I have described three factors that contribute greatly towards making the MAM's institution-building effort a grand success. These are firstly, the freedom and flexibility allowed to devotees to render whatever kind of seva is best suited to their dispositions; secondly, the tapping of devotees' individual capabilities in securing their contributions (seva) towards this effort; and thirdly, the individual recognition that the Mata and her Mission invariably confer on persons rendering seva that is noteworthy for its volume and intensity. Each of these aspects of seva serves to secure the mass participation of the Mata's devotees in the MAM's efforts towards building, maintaining and managing its vast and expanding institutional network. This institutional network, in its turn, forms the main support base for the Mata in furthering her 'divine' mission to alleviate suffering and infuse love into the modern world.

CONCLUSION

Institution building and expansion, I have argued in this essay, is an important means by which modern avatar-gurus seek to further their professed 'mission' in the world. Their active engagement with the affairs of this world, mediated through their elaborate institutional establishments and networks, serves not only to secure for them wide-ranging publicity but also, and more importantly, to legitimize their claims to being 'avatars' incarnated upon the earth in order to serve a specific worldly end.

The contributions of devotees and disciples in terms of financial and other resources are, in turn, indispensable in furthering the institution-building efforts of these avatar-gurus. In this essay I have examined the case of one such popular avatar-guru in contemporary India, Mata Amritanandamayi. The main motivating factor that induces devotees to contribute towards this spiritual leader's institution-building efforts, I have argued, is the ethic of seva as popularized by the guru. This ethic of seva, as it is conceptualized and practised within the MAM, is particularly appealing to the Mata's urban middle-class devotees. The Mata defines excessive consumerism—an inescapable part of the everyday lives of her (lay) urban middle-class devotees—as the main cause for the accumulation of their 'negative karmic burden', the source of all their worldly sorrows. Seva, in this scheme of things, is an effective means of countering this karmic accumulation. Rendering service to the MAM, as these devotees come to see it, is a spiritually cleansing activity that paves the way for a happier life in this world and for further spiritual enhancement and growth. Likewise, in the perception of the Mata's renouncer disciples, seva is indispensable to their spiritual striving and hastens their progress towards ultimate salvation.

Not only are these middle-class devotees keenly motivated to engage in seva activities within the MAM, their privileged place in Indian society also gives them a unique advantage in rendering the kind of services that the MAM requires. Their educational qualifications, their occupational skills, their social connections, the influence many command in important political and business networks, and indeed their material wealth which the more well-off often donate generously to the Mata, all go a long way in providing the MAM with exactly the kind of resources it needs to facilitate its institutional expansion and growth.

It is worth noting here that though the Mata's devotees invariably extol her professed humanitarian concerns, they do not themselves appear to share a sense of personal responsibility for society's welfare or feel personally committed to its betterment. It is important for most devotees that the Mata's is a modern, this-worldly enterprise which aims at social welfare, and actively engages her renouncer disciples as well as lay devotees in activities directed at serving society. Their own participation in her social service activities, however, is seldom motivated by philanthropic concerns.[35] Theirs is not so much seva as altruism but is, far more importantly, seva as panegyric. It constitutes an expression of the Hindu topography of the self (Appadurai, 1990) where the prototypical act of worship is the glorification of the divine, in this case the Mata. This in turn is meritorious activity, believed to place devotees in a state of blessedness and grace, and to hasten their progress towards individual salvation.

The Mata in her turn, by fostering an ethic of selfless service among her devotees and disciples, and by tapping individual capabilities and resources in building up her institutional network, utilizes effectively her own skill at resource and personnel management, in expanding her institutional empire. Rather than put her devotees and disciples through a common and forced regimen of service activity, she relies on their individual potential, their resources, inclinations, aptitudes, and talents, allowing for flexibility and choice in devotees' participation in seva activities. No resource or talent is unwanted or out of place within the MAM. Each one is put to good use, and it is these resources that comprise the key building blocks of the MAM's vast and expanding institutional network. The MAM also has in place an effective system of rewards for services rendered by individual devotees, which ensures their enthusiastic participation in the MAM's activities. Devotees are rewarded for their seva in small but, for them, highly significant ways. The most significant reward is personal recognition from the Mata, and it is in anticipation of such reward that devotees find renewed motivation for their seva efforts.

Seva, as practised within the MAM, diverges significantly from its ideal of rendering service selflessly, anonymously and without the expectation of reward. Even so it serves a very important practical function within the MAM—it secures the enthusiastic participation of its followers in its institution-building activities. Seva thus works as a self-propelling force within the MAM, ensuring its continued growth and spread, and winning the Mata ever more publicity and an ever larger following, now and in the foreseeable future.

ENDNOTES

1. See Dumont 1970; Burghart 1978, 1983a, 1983b; van der Veer 1987a, 1988; Heesterman 1985; Parry 1994.

2. See Cohn 1964; Kolff 1971; Lorenzen 1978; van der Veer 1988: 130–7; C.A. Bayly 1983: 143; Pinch 1996. Khare's (1984) study of ascetic leaders among Lucknow's 'Untouchable' *chamars* shows how these ascetics, even

while they uphold the ideal of world renunciation, simultaneously symbolize the pragmatics of 'world management' and actively engage in social reform and protest.

3. My thanks are due to Gwilym Beckerlegge for his comments and suggestions on earlier versions of this essay, and for discussions on points of comparison/contrast between the Ramakrishna Mission and the MAM.

4. Studies of the 'saffron wave' (saffron being the colour representing renunciatory values in Hinduism) have focused on the links between Hindu right-wing politics and the role of modern-day renouncers in propagating a nationalist discourse based on Hindutva (Jaffrelot 1996; McKean 1995; van der Veer 1994a, 1987).

5. On Sathya Sai Baba, see Exon 1997; Swallow 1982; Taylor 1987; Babb 1987, 1991; Chryssides 1999: 179–93; and White 1972. Gombrich and Obeyesekere (1988: 53–5) discuss Sai Baba's urban middle-class following in Sri Lanka, where he is incorporated into Buddhist faith as an incarnation of Buddha. Howe (2002) likewise discusses the emergence of a Sathya Sai Baba following in the complex and fast changing religious landscape of contemporary Bali in Indonesia.

6. Chryssides (op. cit.).

7. While it is not unusual to find devotees make claims on behalf of their guru regarding the latter's presumed avatar status, the phenomenon of a guru making this claim on his or her own initiative is a relatively new and noteworthy development in the Hindu world. According to some devotees of Mata Amritanandamayi, it is they, rather than the Mata herself, who make the claim that she is an avatar. This assertion is important, given the value placed on self-effacement in Hindu renunciatory traditions. The ideal-typical renouncer does not flaunt his or her own abilities or assert his/her enlightened status; it is for others to discern the extent of the renouncer's spiritual achievements. In the case of the Mata, it is true that she often makes self-denigrating statements about herself, denying that she is an avatar or a goddess. She does, however, claim to 'reveal' her divine status to devotees during her Devi *bhavas*, episodes when she dresses up as a goddess. It is important to note that during these episodes, which the Mata describes as an 'unveiling' of her true divine self, devotees perform a ritual of worship (puja) before the Mata, a ritual otherwise addressed only to the idols of gods and goddesses in Hindu temples and household shrines. The *bhavas*, the Mata's interpretation of their meaning, and the ritual performed during the bhavas, all appear to confirm the Mata's 'avatar' status and her ready acknowledgement of the same.

8. The biography, which is the single 'official' version of the Mata's life story published by the MAM, was originally published in Malayalam in 1986 but has since appeared in translation in several other languages, including English, French, and Hindi. The version of the text I referred to was an English rendition by Swami Amritaswarupananda, the Mata's chief disciple and the Vice President of the Mission. [Swami Amritaswarupananda (1996), *Mata Amritanandamayi: A Biography*, Kollam, Kerala: Mata Amritanandamayi Mission Trust].

The biography covers a span of twenty-seven years, from the time of the Mata's birth to the establishment of her Mission.

9. The biography identifies her as belonging to the Araya (fishing) caste, a group classed in both pre- and post-Independence ethnographies (including census reports and other official accounts) as 'economically backward'. The state of Kerala classes this group as one of the 'Other Backward Classes' for purposes of 'reservation' benefits in educational institutions and certain categories of employment. My enquiries in the village revealed that the Mata's father marketed fish for a living. The family was very poor (like other members of the fishing community) and the parents lived, along with their eight children, in a small two-room hut by the coast. They had themselves had no formal education but sent most of their children to school.

10. As Harlan and Coutright (1995: 9) rightly point out, dark complexions are negatively valued in India and are generally considered less desirable than light ones, especially in the context of marriage negotiations which take into account the fairness of the bride.

11. Descriptions in the Mata's biography echo themes common to hagiographies of *bhakti* saints (and also Muslim *pirs*: cf. S. Bayly 1989) many of which read like eulogistic accounts of the extraordinary, often mad-like characteristics displayed by these 'divine' figures. See for instance McDaniel's (1989) accounts of the hagiographies of bhakti saints in Bengal, Swallow's (1982) account of Sathya Sai Baba's biographical narrative, and Babb's (1987) reference to the biographies of three gurus, including Sathya Sai Baba.

12. There is a striking similarity between the religious styles of Mata Amritanandamayi and Sathya Sai Baba in this regard. The latter too reveals a marked eclecticism that allows devotees considerable freedom in choosing their particular spritual method or approach. Sarkar 1992 notes this same catholicity in the teachings of the popular nineteenth-century Bengali mystic, Ramakrishna. 'Catholicity for Ramakrishna', Sarkar (ibid.: 1553) notes, 'was inseparable from bhakti: all forms and paths were valid, provided they were followed with genuine devotion'. This catholicity (which as Sarkar points out, has now come to be represented as a timeless essence of Hinduism), informed Ramakrishna's attitude towards non-Hindus. In Ramakrishna's words (as quoted by Sarkar): 'There is a pond with three or four *ghats* [banks]. Hindus call what they drink *jal*, Muslims *pani*, the English water. He is called Allah by one, some say Brahma, others Kali, still others Ram, Hari, Jesus or Durga ...' (ibid., 1533). The same attitude is exemplified in the Mata's teachings as well, and this similarity in the the two gurus, separated by nearly a century in time, is a significant factor enhancing the Mata's appeal and establishing her authenticity in the eyes of devotees.

13. Since Mata Amritanandamayi has herself not been formally initiated into an ascetic lineage, the first of her disciples to be given *diksha* was initiated not by her but by a monk belonging to the Ramakrishna Math. This disciple then initiated others in the MAM. The initiation rituals, the system of probation, and the two levels of ascetic life—first as *brahmachari*, and then as *sannyasi*—all

follow the pattern in the Ramakrishna Order. See Sean Carey (1987) for a detailed ethnographic description of initiation into monkhood in the Ramakrishna Math.

14. The Mata does have a small non-Hindu (Christian and Muslim) following within India as also a small number of low-income devotees from urban and rural backgrounds, mostly the beneficiaries of her charitable ventures. Both in terms of numbers, as well as the extent of their involvement in the Mission's activities, these individuals constitute only a tiny fraction of her total Indian following, the bulk of which comprises hundreds of thousands of urban affluent middle-class persons.

15. There are no clear estimates of the size of India's middle classes. Varma (1998) describes several attempts in the 1990s (the early years of India's post-liberalization era) to define them in terms of income levels and consumption patterns. Those making these attempts (government-sponsored research organizations, as well as private industrial concerns) are not agreed on the yardsticks for delineating the middle classes. 'Several figures were bandied about,' writes Varma (1998: 170), 'ranging from two hundred million to five hundred million.' From Varma's discussion, it appears that two hundred million would serve as a modest but not unrealistic estimate of the size of India's middle-class population.

16. See Gordon 1978; Ray 1979; Markovits 1985; C.A. Bayly 1983; Varma 1998. The extensive historical literature on India's colonial intelligentsia (an important constituent of the 'middle classes' of the late nineteenth and early twentieth centuries), treats this category as disproportionately important in contributing to the rise of 'modern' nationalist ideologies and political organizations in the colonial period.

17. In the 1980s and 1990s, media and business attention came to focus on India's expanding middle classes and their 'insatiable propensity to consume'. At international forums they emerged as a key selling point for India, bearing testimony to India's economic progress, and promising a vast potential market for foreign investors (Misra 1961; Frankel 1988; Khanna 1987; Lakha 1999; Ninan 1990; Appadurai and Breckenridge 1995; Varma 1998).

18. It is true for most of these individuals, as Beteille (1991) argues, that the ideology of meritocracy has, to some extent, displaced that of ascription. Thus their social and economic status derives not from their place in a given caste hierarchy, but from their capital, credentials, and expertise. (See S. Bayly 1999, especially Chapters 8 and 9, on the complex issue of caste identities in modern India).

19. See Appadurai and Breckenridge 1995; Ninan 1990; Robison and Goodman 1996; Varma 1998.

20. See, for instance, Swallow 1982; Babb 1987, 1991; Kakar 1984; Varma 1998; and Fuller 1992.

21. Warrier 2000 and 2003.

22. Freitag 1996: 26; Shah 1991: 2921; Chibber and Mishra 1993: 665–72; Parikh 1993: 684.

23. See Nandy 1985, 1990, 1995; Madan 1987a, 1997; Chatterjee 1986, 1993, 1997; Baxi and Parekh 1995. The oversimplified and essentializing assertions of these writers have been challenged by Khilnani 1997; Baber 1996; Vanaik 1997; C.A. Bayly 1985, 1998; Upadhyaya 1992; Basu and Subrahmanyam (eds) 1996.

24. Many of Heelas' (1996) observations regarding the New Age movement, especially with regard to its language of self-spirituality, its emphasis on self-actualization, self-enhancement and adherents' assumption of self-responsibility in realizing the spiritual goal, are true of the Mata's devotees as well. These devotees are concerned primarily with self-growth and inner experience, and do not appear greatly concerned about issues pertaining to communal or group identity.

25. The Mata's explanation of human suffering in terms of the Hindu doctrine of karma and rebirth is by no means unique to the MAM. It is merely one more variant of a larger body of belief in karma, afterlife and *moksha* (salvation) which, in its myriad forms, informs Hindu religious life in diverse contexts (Keyes and Daniel [eds] 1983; Sharma 1973; O'Flaherty [ed.] 1980).

26. *Awaken Children* V (1993: 122), San Ramon, California: Mata Amritanandamayi Center.

27. *Awaken Children* IV (1992: 174), San Ramon, California: Mata Amritanandamayi Center.

28. Ibid., 219.

29. *Awaken Children* I (1989: 35), Kollam, Kerala: Mata AmritanandamaJi Mission Trust.

30. Ibid., 116.

31. The Mission has a web site at www.ammachi.org and maintains links to other sites which provide information on various aspects of the MAM. Interestingly, these websites often solicit *seva* through the cyber network for specific purposes, electronically seeking volunteers for specialized services required in the Mission.

32. This temple, both in architecture and in thematic representation, appears as a simplified and abbreviated version of the more complex temple structures characteristic of the southern part of Kerala (Pillai 1985; Stein 1978; Bernier 1982). Within each Brahmasthanam (abode of Brahman—the supreme consciousness or divine essence) the idol or *pratishtha* comprises a single block of stone bearing the images of four different deities—those of Devi, Siva and Ganapati, and a serpent god. According to the Mission's literature on the Brahmasthanam, the four images symbolize the principle of unity in diversity, as also of the various stages of an aspirant's spiritual progress. There are Brahmasthanam temples in several MAM centres across India. The idol in each such temple is consecrated by the Mata. Through the ritual of consecration, the Mata is believed to transfer her own divinity to the image and thereby 'energize' it. Daily pujas conducted by her disciples serve to maintain the energy within the image. During the Mata's yearly visits to the temple she conducts special pujas which are believed to re-energize the idol and infuse it anew with divine power.

33. Some of these seva activities belong to a common repertoire of social service engagements undertaken by a wide range of organizations in India including religious reform movements like the Arya Samaj (Gold 1991), newer right-wing groups like the Rashtriya Swayamsevak Sangh (ibid.), Beckerlegge (this Volume) as well as devotionalist orders like the Swaminarayans (Williams 1984), the Ramakrishna Mission (Gupta 1974; Beckerlegge 1998, 2000), the Radhasoamis (Juergensmeyer 1991), and the Sathya Sai organization (Babb 1987, 1991). Most religious organizations in India now engage in some charitable and social service activity, mainly because the Indian government requires non-profit religious institutions to divest themselves of their income periodically if they are to retain their tax-exempt status. Spending on medical, educationa,l and other charitable projects is a convenient means of achieving this, and has the added benefit of garnering favourable publicity for the religious organization.

34. Compare Laidlaw's 1995 descriptions of Jain renouncers on their alms rounds visiting the homes of lay devotees. Though the context in which devotees honour their guests is different in either case, there are certain points of similarity in terms of the unpredictability of the visit which lends an aura of expectancy and mystery to the event, and the sense in which the household concerned feels honoured by virtue of the fact that it was the chosen one. Laidlaw's comment (ibid.: 320) that for the householders, the act of giving 'is at the same time an expression of devotion and an act of homage, comparable to the offerings they make in temple worship', holds equally true for the devotees of the Mata.

35. Cf. Varma 1998; Haynes 1987.

REFERENCES

Alter, J. 1994a. 'Celibacy, Sexuality, and Transformation of Gender into Nationalism in North India', *Journal of Asian Studies* 53 (1): 45–66.

——. 1994b. 'Somatic Nationalism: Indian Wrestling and Militant Hinduism', *Modern Asian Studies* 28 (3): 557–88.

Appadurai, Arjun. 1990. 'Topographies of the Self: Praise and Emotion in Hindu India' in Catherine A. Lutz and Lila Abu-Lughod (eds), *Language and the Politics of Emotion*, Cambridge: Cambridge University Press.

Appadurai, Arjun and Carol A. Breckenridge. 1995. 'Public Modernity in India', in Carol A. Breckenridge (ed.), *Consuming Modernity: Public Culture in a South Asian World*, Minneapolis and London: University of Minnesota Press.

Babe, Lawrence A. 1987. *Redemptive Encounters: Three Modern Styles in the Hindu Tradition*, Delhi: Oxford University Press.

——. 1991 'Sathya Sai Baba's Miracles', in T.N. Madan (ed.), *Religion in India*, Delhi: Oxford University Press.

Baber, Zaheer. 1996. 'After Ayodhya', *Dialectical Anthropology* 21 (3/4): 317–43.

Basu, Kaushik and Sanjay Subrahmanyam (eds). 1996. *Unravelling the Nation: Sectarian Conflict and India's Secular Identity*, Delhi: Penguin.

Baxi, Upendra and Bhikhu Parekh. 1995. *Crisis and Change in Contemporary India*, New Delhi and London: Sage.

Bayly, C.A. 1983. *Rulers, Townsmen and Bazaars: North Indian Society in the Age of British Expansion 1770–1870*, Cambridge: Cambridge University Press.

——. 1985. 'The Pre-History of "Communalism": Religious Conflict in India 1700–1860', *Modern Asian Studies* 19 (2): 177–203.

——. 1998. *Origins of Nationality in South Asia: Patriotism and Ethical Government in the Making of Modern India*, Delhi and Oxford: Oxford University Press.

Bayly, Susan. 1989. *Saints, Goddesses and Kings: Muslims and Christians in South Indian Society 1700-1900*, Cambridge: Cambridge University Press.

——. 1999. 'Caste, Society, and Politics in India from the Eighteenth Century to the Modern Age', *The New Cambridge History of India Series* IV (3), Cambridge: Cambridge University Press.

Beckerlegge, Gwilym. 1998. 'Swami Vivekananda and *Seva*: Taking "Social Service" Seriously', in William Radice (ed.), *Swami Vivekananda and the Modernization of Hinduism*, Delhi: Oxford University Press.

——. 2000. 'Swami Akhandananda's *Sevavrata* (Vow of Service) and the Earliest Expressions of Service to Humanity in the Ramakrishna Math and Mission', in Antony Copley (ed.), *Gurus and Their Followers: New Religious Reform Movements in Colonial India*, Oxford: Oxford University Press.

Bennett, Peter. 1990. 'In Nanda Baba's House: The Devotional Experience in Pushtimarg Temples', in Owen M. Lynch (ed.), *Divine Passions: The Social Construction of Emotion in India*, Berkeley: University of California Press.

Bernier, Ronald M. 1982. *Temple Arts of Kerala: A South Indian Tradition*, Delhi: S. Chand.

Beteille, André. 1991. 'The Reproduction of Inequality: Occupation, Caste, and Family', *Contributions to Indian Sociology* (n.s.) 25 (1): 3–28.

Burghart, Richard. 1978. 'The Founding of the Ramanandi Sect', *Ethnohistory* 25: 121–39.

—— 1983a. 'Renunciation in the Religious Traditions of South Asia', *Man* (n.s.) 18: 635–53.

——. 1983b. 'Wandering Ascetics of the Ramanandi Sect', *History of Religions* 22: 361–80.

Carey, Sean. 1987. 'Initiation into Monkhood in the Ramakrishna Mission', in Richard Burghart (ed.), *Hinduism in Great Britain: The Perpetuation of Religion in an Alien Cultural Milieu*, London: Tavistock.

Chatterjee, Partha. 1986. *Nationalist Thought and the Colonial World: A Derivative Discourse?*, London: Zed.

——. 1993. *The Nation and its Fragments: Colonial and Postcolonial Histories*, Princeton, New Jersey: Princeton University Press.

Chatterjee, Partha. 1997. *A Possible India: Essay's in Political Criticism*, Delhi: Oxford University Press.

Chibber, Pradeep and Subhash Mishra. 1993. 'Hindus and the Babri Masjid: The Sectional Basis of Communal Attitudes', *Asian Survey* 33 (July): 665–72.

Chryssides, George D. 1999. *Exploring New Religions*, London: Cassell.

Cohn, B.S. 1964. 'The Role of Gosains in the Economy of 18th and 19th Century Upper India', *Indian Economic and Social History Review* 1: 175–82.

Das, Richard H. 1996. 'The Iconography of Rama's Chariot', in David Ludden (ed.), *Making India Hindu: Religion, Community, and the Politics of Democracy in India*, Delhi: Oxford University Press.

Dumont, Louis. 1970. 'World Renunciation in Indian Religions', in L. Dumont (ed.), *Religion, Society, and Politics in India: Collected Papers in Indian Sociology*, Paris: Mouton.

Exon, Bob. 1997. 'Autonomous Agents and Divine Stage Managers: Models of (Self) Determination amongst Western Devotees of Two Modern Hindu Religious Movements', *Scottish Journal of Religious Studies* 18 (2): 163–79.

Frankel, Francine R. 1988. 'Middle Classes and Castes', in Atul Kohli (ed.), *India's Democracy: An Analysis of Changing State-Society Relations*, Princeton, New Jersey: Princeton University Press.

Freitag, Sandria B. 1989. *Collective Action and Community: Public Arenas and the Emergence of Communalism in North India*, Berkeley and Oxford: University of California Press.

——. 1996. 'Contesting in Public', in David Ludden (ed.), *Making India Hindu: Religion, Community, and the Politics of Democracy in India*, Delhi: Oxford University Press.

Fuller, C.J. 1992. *The Camphor Flame: Popular Hinduism and Society in India*, Princeton, New Jersey: Princeton University Press.

Gold, Daniel. 1991. 'Organized Hinduisms: From Vedic Truth to Hindu Nation', in M.E. Marty and R.S. Appleby (eds), *Fundamentalisms Observed*, Chicago: University of Chicago Press.

Gomrich, Richard and Gananath Obeyesekere. 1988. *Buddhism Transformed: Religious Change in Sri Lanka*, Princeton, New Jersey: Princeton University Press.

Gordon, A.D.D. 1978. *Businessmen and Politics: Rising Nationalism and a Modernizing Economy in Bombay 1918–33*, New Delhi: Manohar.

Gupta, K.P. 1974. 'Religious Evolution and Social Change in India: A Study of the Ramakrishna Mission Movement', *Contributions to Indian Sociology* (n.s.) 8: 25–50.

Hansen, Thomas Blom. 1996. 'Recuperating Masculinity: Hindu Nationalism, Violence, and the Exorcism of the Muslim "Other"', *Critique of Anthropology* 16 (2): 137–72.

Hansen, T.B. and C. Jaffrelot. 1998. *The BJP and the Compulsions of Politics in India*, Delhi and Oxford: Oxford University Press.

Harlan, L. and P.B. Courtright. 1995. *From the Margins of Hindu Marriage:*

Essays on Gender, Religion, and Culture, New York and Oxford: Oxford University Press.

Haynes, Douglas. 1987. 'From Tribute to Philanthropy—The Politics of Gift-Giving in a Western Indian City', *The Journal of Asian Studies* 46 (2): 339–60.

Heelas, Paul. 1996. *The New Age Movement: The Celebration of Self and the Sacralization of Modernity*, Oxford: Blackwell.

Hellman, Eva. 1994. 'Dynamic Hinduism', *Seminar* 417: 49–58.

Heesterman, J.C. 1985. *The Inner Conflict of Tradition: Essays in Indian Ritual, Kingship, and Society*, Chicago and London: University of Chicago Press.

Howe, Leo. 2002. *Hinduism and Hierarchy in Bali*, Oxford: James Currey.

Jafrelot, Christophe. 1996. *The Hindu Nationalist Movement in India*, Delhi: Viking.

——. 1998. 'The Politics of Processions and Hindu-Muslim Riots', in A. Basu and A. Kohli (eds), *Community Conflicts and the State in India*, Delhi: Oxford University Press.

Juergensmeyer, Mark. 1991. *Radhasoami Reality: The Logic of a Modern Faith*, Princeton, New Jersey: Princeton University Press.

Kakar, Sudhir. 1984. *Shamans, Mystics, and Doctors: A Psychological Inquiry into India and its Healing Traditions*, London: Allen Unwin and Company.

Keyes, Charles F. and Valentine Daniel (eds). 1983. *Karma: An Anthropological Inquiry*, Berkeley: University of California Press.

Khanna, Sushil. 1987. 'The New Business Class, Ideology, and the State: The Making of a New Consensus', *South Asia* (n.s.) 10(2): 47–60.

Khare, R.S. 1984. *The Untouchable as Himself: Ideology, Identity, and Pragmatism among the Lucknow Chamars*, Cambridge: Cambridge University Press.

Khilnani, Sunil. 1997. *The Idea of India*, London: Hamish Hamilton.

Kolff, D.H.A. 1971. 'Sannyasi Trader-Soldiers', *Indian Economic and Social History Review* 8: 213–20.

Lakha, Salim. 1999. 'The State, Globalization, and Middle-Class Identity', in Michael Pinches (ed.), *Culture and Privilege in Capitalist Asia*, London and New York: Routledge and Kegan Paul.

Lorenzen, David N. 1978. 'Warrior Ascetics in Indian History', *Journal of the American Oriental Society* 98 (1): 61–75.

Ludden, David. 1996. *Making India Hindu: Religion, Community, and the Politics of Democracy in India*, Delhi: Oxford University Press.

Madan, T.N. 1987. 'Secularism in its Place', *Journal of Asian Studies* 46(4): 747–59.

——. 1997. *Modern Myths, Locked Minds: Secularism and Fundamentalism in India*, Delhi: Oxford University Press.

Markovits, Claude. 1985. *Indian Business and Nationalist Politics 1931–39: The Indigenous Capitalist Class and the Rise of the Congress Party*, Cambridge: Cambridge University Press.

Mayer, Adrian C. 1981. 'Public Service and Individual Merit in a Town of Central India', in A.C. Mayer (ed.), *Culture and Morality: Essays in Honour of Christoph von Furer-Haimendorf*, Delhi: Oxford University Press.

McDaniel, June. 1989. *Madness of the Saints: Ecstatic Religion in Bengal*, Chicago: University of Chicago Press.

Mckean, Lise. 1995. *Divine Enterprise: Gurus and the Hindu Nationalist Movement*, Chicago and London: University of Chicago Press.

Misra, B.B. 1961. *The Indian Middle Classes: Their Growth in Modern Times*, Oxford: Oxford University Press.

Nandy, Ashis. 1985. 'An Anti-Secularist Manifesto', *Seminar* 314: 14–24.

——. 1990. 'The Politics of Secularism and the Recovery of Religious Tolerance', in Veena Das (ed.), *Mirrors of Violence: Communities, Riots, and Survivors in South Asia,* Delhi and Oxford: Oxford University Press.

——. 1995. *Creating a Nationality: The Ramjanmabhumi Movement and Fear of the Self*, Delhi and Oxford: Oxford University Press.

Ninan, T.N. 1990. 'Rise of the Middle Class', in Robin Jeffrey et al. (eds), *India. Rebellion to Republic: Selected Writings 1857–1990*, Delhi: Sterling.

O'Flaherty, Wendy D. (ed.). 1980. *Karma and Rebirth in Classical Indian Traditions*, Berkeley: University of California Press.

Parikh, Manju. 1993. 'The Debacle at Ayodhya: Why Militant Hinduism met with a Weak Response', *Asian Survey* 33: 673–84.

Parry, Jonathan. 1994. *Death in Banaras*, Cambridge: Cambridge University Press.

Pillai, V.R. Parameswaran. 1985. *Temple Culture of South India*, Delhi: Inter India.

Pinch, William. 1996. *Peasants and Monks in British India*, Berkeley: University of Chicago Press.

Pinches, Michael (ed.). 1999. *Culture and Privilege in Capitalist Asia,* London and New York: Routledge.

Ray, Rajat. 1979. *Industrialization in India: Growth and Conflict in the Private Corporate Sector 1914–47*, Delhi and Oxford: Oxford University Press.

Robison, Richard and David S.G. Goodman. 1996. 'The New Rich in Asia: Economic Development, Social Status, and Political Consciousness', in Robison and Goodman (eds), *The New Rich in Asia: Mobile Phones, McDonald's, and Middle-Class Revolution*, London and New York: Routledge and Kegan Paul.

Sarkar, Sumit. 1992. '"Kaliyuga", "Chakri", and "Bhakti": Ramakrishna and His Times', *Economic and Political Weekly* 18 July: 1543–66.

——. 1993. 'The Fascism of the Sangh Parivar', *Economic and Political Weekly* 30 January: 163–67.

Shah, Ghanshyam. 1991. 'Tenth Lok Sabha Elections: BJP's Victory in Gujarat', *Economic and Political Weekly* 21 December: 2921–4.

Sharma, Ursula M. 1973. 'Theodicy and the Doctrine of Karma', *Man* (n.s.) 8: 347–64.

Stein, Burton (ed.). 1978. *South Indian Temples: An Analytical Reconsideration*, New Delhi: Vikas.

Swallow, Deborah A. 1982. 'Ashes and Power: Myth, Rite, and Miracle in an Indian God-Man's Cult', *Modern Asian Studies* 16: 123–58.

Taylor, Donald. 1987. 'Charismatic Authority in the Sathya Sai Baba Movement', in Richard Burghart (ed.), *Hinduism in Great Britain: The Perpetuation of Religion in an Alien Cultural Milieu*, London and New York: Tavistock.

Tonnesson, S. and H. Antlov (eds). 1996. *Asian Forms of the Nation*, Richmond, Surrey: Curzon.

Upadhyaya, Prakash Chandra. 1992. 'The Politics of Indian Secularism', *Modern Asian Studies* 26 (4): 815–53.

Van der Veer, Peter. 1987a. 'Taming the Ascetic: Devotionalism in a Hindu Monastic Order', *Man* (n.s.) 22: 680–95.

——. 1987b. 'God Must be Liberated: A Hindu Liberation Movement in Ayodhya', *Modern Asian Studies* 21 (2): 284–301.

——. 1988. *Gods on Earth: The Management of Religious Experience and Identity in a North Indian Pilgrimage Centre*, London: Athlone.

——. 1989. 'The Power of Detachment: Disciplines of Body and Mind in the Ramanandi Order', *American Ethnologist* 16: 458–70.

——. 1994a. 'Hindu Nationalism and the Discourse of Modernity: The Vishva Hindu Parishad', in M.E. Marty and R.S. Appleby (eds), *Accounting for Fundamentalisms*, Chicago and London: University of Chicago Press.

——. 1994b. *Religious Nationalism: Hindus and Muslims in India*, London and Berkeley: University of California Press.

——. 1996. 'Gender and Nation in Hindu Nationalism', in S. Tonnesson and H. Antlov (eds), *Asian Forms of the Nation*, Richmond, Surrey: Curzon.

Vanaik, Achin. 1997. *The Furies of Indian Communalism: Religion, Modernity, and Secularization*, London and New York: Verso.

Varma, Pavan K. 1998. *The Great Indian Middle Class*, Delhi: Penguin.

Warrier, Maya. 2000. *The Appeal of a Modern Godperson in Contemporary India: The Case of Mata Amritanandamayi and Her Mission* (Unpublished Ph.D. dissertation), University of Cambridge.

——. 2003. 'Processes of Secularization in Contemporary India: Guru Faith in the Mata Amritanandamayi Mission', *Modern Asian Studies* 37(1): 213–53.

White, Charles J. 1972. 'The Sai Baba Movement: Approaches to the Study of Indian Saints', *The Journal of Asian Studies* 31: 863–78.

Williams, R.B. 1984. *A New Face of Hinduism: The Swaminarayan Religion*, Cambridge: Cambridge University Press.

Index

Contributors

ANTONY COPLEY has retired as Reader in Modern History at the University of Kent. Currently he is Honorary Senior Research Fellow. Recent publications include *Religions in Conflict* (1997) and ed., *Gurus and Their Followers* (2000). He is currently completing a book on English writers and Indian spirituality.

GWILYM BECKERLEGGE is Senior Lecturer in Religious Studies at the Open University, UK. Recent publications include *The Ramakrishna Math and Mission: The Making of a Modern Hindu Movement* (2000) and ed., *The World Religious Reader* (2nd edn, 2000). He is the editor and contributor to a forthcoming volume of essays *From Sacred Text to Internet* and is currently completing a study of *seva* in the Ramakrishna Math and Mission.

PETER HEEHS is Archivist in the Aurobindo Archives. Recent publications include *Nationalism, Terrorism, Communalism* (1998) and *The Essential Writings of Sri Aurobindo* (1997). He is presently at work on an anthology of Indian spiritual writing and on a biography of Sri Aurobindo.

THERESE O'TOOLE is Research Fellow in the Department of Political Science and International Studies at the University of Birmingham where she is currently conducting qualitative research into political participation. She was awarded her doctorate from the University of Hull in 1999. Its subject was a critique of theories of nationalism, with a focus on India and with the cow protection movement as a case study. It was entitled *The Politics of Nationalism: Secularising the Sacred Cow.*

HARALD FISCHER-TINÉ taught for several years in the South Asia Institute, Heidelberg and is presently Assistant Professor in the Department of

South Asian History, Humboldt University, Berlin. His doctorate from Heidelberg was on National Education in colonial India. He has published several chapters on the Arya Samaj. He is currently working on a post-doctoral project on white 'subalterns' in colonial India.

HILTRUD RÜSTAU has now retired from the Institute for Asian and African Studies, Humboldt University. She is one of the editors of *Indian Culture: Continuities and Discontinuities (In Memoriam Walter Ruben, 1899–1982)*. She has published widely on the new religious movements and is currently writing on female wisdom in Hinduism.

JASON FULLER is doing a Ph.D. in Religious Studies and is Briton Martin Fellow in South Asia Regional Studies at the University of Pennsylvania. The title of his dissertation is 'The Sweeper of the Market: Bhaktivinode Thakur and the Creation of Bourgeois Vaisnavism in Colonial Bengal'.

LIDIA JULIANNA GUZY is Lecturer in the Department of Social Anthropology and the Department of Religious Studies, the Free University, Berlin. She has a Master's degree in Social anthropology from the Ecole des Hautes Etudes en Sciences Sociales, Paris. She is employed in the Orissa Research Programme, funded by the German Research Council. Her doctoral research project is on the Mahima Dharma. Publications include, 'On the Road with the Babas: Some Insight into Local Features of the Mahima Dharma' in Hardenberg (ed.), Special Edition, *Journal of Social Sciences*, Vol. 4, No. 4.

JOHANNES BELTZ is Research Fellow in the South Asian Institute of the University of Heidelberg. He studied protestant theology in Halle and Strasbourg and Indian studies and religion in the Universities of Lausanne and Paris. He received his Ph.D. in 1999. He has worked and published on the Untouchable castes in Maharashtra and their conversion to Buddhism. His *Mahar, Bouddhiste et Dalit, Conversion religieuse et emancipation sociopolitique dans l'Inde des castes* was published in 2001. Currently he is Assistant Curator in Indian art at the Rieberg Museum, Zurich.

MAYA WARRIER is Lecturer in the Department of Theology and Religious Studies at Lampeter, the University of Wales, where she teaches Hinduism and the anthropology of religion. She was awarded a Ph.D. from the University of Cambridge in 2000, with the title, 'The Appeal of a Modern Godperson in Contemporary India: The Case of Mata Amritanandamayi and Her Mission'. This will shortly be published.

